★ ★ ★

SORE WINNERS

★ ★ ★

★ ★ ★

SORE
WINNERS

(And the Rest of Us) in George Bush's America

★ ★ ★

JOHN POWERS

D O U B L E D A Y

NEW YORK LONDON TORONTO SYDNEY AUCKLAND

PUBLISHED BY DOUBLEDAY
a division of Random House, Inc.

DOUBLEDAY and the portrayal of an anchor with a dolphin are
registered trademarks of Random House, Inc.

Book design by Fearn Cutler de Vicq

Library of Congress Cataloging-in-Publication Data
Powers, John, 1951–
Sore winners : (and the rest of us) in George Bush's America /
John Powers.—1st ed.
p. cm.
ISBN 0-385-51187-6
1. Political culture—United States—History—20th century. 2. Popular
culture—United States—History—20th century. 3. United States—Politics
and government—1989– 4. United States—Social conditions—1980–
5. Bush, George W. (George Walker), 1946– I. Title.
JK271.P65 2004
973.931—dc22 2004045482

PRINTED IN THE UNITED STATES OF AMERICA

July 2004
First Edition
10 9 8 7 6 5 4 3 2 1

For my father, who proudly shook the hand of
Senator John F. Kennedy.

And for my mother, who once said, "You're supposed to treat
people decently no matter who they are. If you don't know
that, you don't know a goddamn *thing."*

Keep cool but care.

—McClintic Sphere, in *V.*

Contents

SORE
WINNERS

The Digital Presidency

> When I was coming up, it was a dangerous world and
> we knew exactly who they were. It was us versus them.
> And it was clear who them was. Today, we're not so sure
> who they are, but we know they're there.
>
> —GEORGE W. BUSH

The book you are holding had its beginnings in the worst political
mistake of my life.

In early November of 2000, I made the eighteen-hour flight to Los
Angeles from Singapore, where I was spending a year, to vote in the first
election of the new millennium. I wasn't returning for the presidential
race, which had pulled off the feat of being neck-and-neck without
once becoming interesting. Like most people on the left, I had no
fondness for Al Gore, who combined Richard Nixon's clammy ambition with the know-it-all smugness of Hermione Granger. Nor did I
find any allure in the fastidiously dreary Ralph Nader ("I'll bet he still
lives with his mother," said my own seventy-five-year-old mom, cackling with disdain). That choice deserved, at best, an absentee ballot. I
was coming back to help oust my Republican congressman, James
Rogan, who not only spearheaded the attempt to impeach Bill Clinton
but once earned a 100 percent favorable voting record from the
Christian Coalition while getting 0 percent from the ACLU. That was a
record worth flying across the Pacific to vote against in person.

And George W. Bush? He was a faintly comical blip on my personal
sonar—not to be voted for, of course, but also not to be taken seriously.
When I thought of him at all, he came across as a manufactured nonen-
tity who would surely lose. What a prediction! Looking back on it now,

I'm embarrassed at how carelessly I'd read the pop culture tea leaves. 2000 was a year in which *Gladiator* was the touchstone summer smash and went on to be named Best Picture, *Who Wants to Be a Millionaire?* became the top-rated TV show, and *The O'Reilly Factor* dominated the bestseller list—not exactly a trifecta to make one think, "The zeitgeist is begging for Al Gore." Still, at the time, Bush seemed little more than a nepotismal cipher, a blandly "electable" consensus candidate for a Republican Party desperate to reclaim power by seizing the middle ground. Even if he won the election, how much harm could he really do?

I was far from alone in thinking this way. On election night, after glumly voting for Nader, I went to a party in Topanga Canyon, a one-time hippie paradise that is now a mecca for prosperous bohemians. Not a soul had voted for Bush. As the results came in and it appeared he was winning, the crowd was let down but not overly concerned. The country was prosperous and faced no credible foreign threats, so it hardly mattered that Bush couldn't name the general (what was his name again?) who'd seized power in Pakistan. People laughed about his verbal pratfalls and mocked his sense of entitlement, which was obviously the size of an aircraft carrier (Gore's was merely the size of a cruise liner). He was, in Philip Roth's fine phrase, a mere mist of a man. I remember a writer drunkenly saying that Shrub, as he called Bush, was little more than an historical hiccup, the kind of dispensable space-saver who nearly always succeeds a powerhouse president—"the way his old man follows Reagan for one term, and then—bam!—he's history."

Later that night at LAX, awaiting my return flight to Asia, I watched the returns in a skybar, surrounded by businessmen who clearly approved Bush's apparent victory. Yet even they couldn't muster any excitement. Nor did their mood dampen when the numbers suddenly got murky and it became possible that Gore might yet pull it out. They, too, sensed that the 2000 election was no big deal. After all, the country was so perfectly divided that neither man, once elected, would dare veer far from the middle of the road. Boarding the plane, I felt confident about two things. The winner would be known by the time I reached Singapore, and Nader had spoken the one great truth of the election: It didn't matter whether Gore or Bush won.

(Trust me, this didn't seem quite so dumb at the time.) Had a fellow passenger told me then that only three years later President George W. Bush would be reckoned an international juggernaut, I would have nodded politely and moved to another seat where I could watch *Erin Brockovich* without having to sit next to a loony.

Which only shows how wrong you can be.

By the time I settled back in L.A. next July, I was startled by how different America felt. The candidate who lost the popular vote—and was handed Florida's electoral votes under circumstances fishier than anything you'd find at the Miami Seaquarium—was governing as if he'd been given a mandate to bulldoze America to the right. He passed a $1.35 trillion tax cut for the well-off that turned a budget surplus into a deficit, horrified most of the civilized world by cavalierly scuttling long-standing treaties, and turned energy policy over to Dick Cheney, whose top-secret task force was a skybox for Republican donors and lobbyists. Thwarting me at every turn, Bush even named my vanquished congressman, Jim Rogan, the Under Secretary of Commerce for Intellectual Property and Director of the United States Patent and Trademark Office.

Perhaps because he'd scraped into office, Bush was the sorest of winners, treating those who opposed him with a dismissive disdain, and enjoying thoughtless treatment from the media, which tended to portray him as a lazy, malaprop-spouting goofball. Back during the Clinton years, I used to cackle each time the right's manatee-shaped morality czar, Bill Bennett, galumphed onto a talk show and brayed, "Where's the outrage?" Six months into the Bush presidency, I was bawling the same thing. And so were millions like me who didn't merely oppose the president's policies but his whole vision of America.

Had it not been for September 11, 2001, Bush's early performance might well have ruined him. We'll never know what he would have done without the terror attacks. What's certain is that Bush has proved to be more overpowering than anyone imagined. In less than one term, he has left a far bigger footprint on American life than Bill Clinton did in two. Perhaps because he was so long considered a lightweight, he's drawn to grand initiatives and bold strokes. He doesn't just take big risks, he *likes* taking them: massive tax cuts, a huge expansion of Medicare, a reconstructed Middle East, the Bush Doctrine of preemptive war. And he's been unnervingly, unswervingly effective at putting this agenda across.

To his opponents' great horror, being president is the only thing George W. Bush has ever been any good at. Far from being a middle-of-the-road clock-puncher, he's a genuine force—a radical conservative, a canny political operator, and, contrary to his endlessly repeated campaign pledge, a divider not a uniter. Has any previous leader been so often compared to both Winston Churchill *and* Adolph Hitler? Rather than being just a one-term wonder, Bush has become a resonant figure whose true significance remains enigmatic. Is he simply the last gasp of the old ruling order, run by paternalistic white businessmen who think they know what's best for America, or the first step of a new kind of corporate oligarchy that uses "homeland security" to follow bullying policies abroad and roll back civil liberties at home?

Ever since the assassination of John F. Kennedy, it has become routine to take the measure of a president after a thousand days. At that point in Bush's presidency (which he cockily began calling "my first term"), one thing had grown clear. If Bill Clinton was the classical analog president—eager to hug the whole world and make everyone love him—Bush is our first fully digital model. He sees the world in ones and zeroes, blacks and whites, eithers and ors, Usses and Thems. And the world has come to return the favor. Every day I receive scads of e-mails that don't simply detail Bush's every transgression, real and imagined, but impute to him a kind of wicked omnipotence. He's the *real* evildoer, to be blamed for everything from infant deaths in Iraq to the North Korean nuclear crisis to the supposed McCarthyism endured by Sean Penn on his way to his Oscar.

Such feelings aren't limited to die-hard liberal bloggers with too much time on their hands. Near the end of Operation Iraqi Freedom, which was not the same as an end to the war in Iraq, I attended a wedding banquet in Los Angeles. The restaurant was filled with middle-class guests who, like most Americans, don't normally spend all that much time thinking about politics. These weren't activists who took to the streets against the Iraq War, though they probably opposed it; their idea of being progressive is to vote Democrat and recycle Diet Coke cans. Yet these people were even more vituperative about Bush than your average Parisian. They were part of the majority who voted against him in 2000, and most of them dislike him far more today than they did back then. No, "dislike" is too mild. Although conventional wisdom once had it that the right hated Clinton personally while liberals hated Bush for his policies, this quickly stopped being true. Both the hard and soft left despise Bush with a dank, bitter loathing they never felt for his father, Ronald Reagan, or even Richard Nixon, whose Shakespearean monstrosity most liberals secretly held in a kind of reverential awe. Even with five o'clock shadow, grandeur is grandeur.

As we sipped champagne, we had the kind of pleasurably overwrought conversations that have become routine all over the country. We talked about Bush being the worst president ever. We quoted Paul Krugman's latest screed about how he's destroying the economy. We abhorred his smug smile, sneered at the way he says "terrist" and "newkiller" (Bush hatred is not without its snobberies), and mocked his habit of using the word "evil" to describe people who are, well, evil. A few minutes after a writer friend once again brought up the "coup" (meaning, of course, the Supreme Court decision that put the President in power), a total stranger admitted that he'd caught himself wishing the assault on Baghdad would turn into another Stalingrad— simply because such a calamity would ruin Bush.

"I read these polls saying he's popular," said a magazine editor, shaking her head, "and I ask myself, who *likes* this guy?"

The answer, at that point, was more than half of the country. His approval ratings were well over 60 percent, and among Republicans, they were an eerie 97 percent (the sort of numbers you got at plebiscites in Saddam's Iraq). His supporters have continued to be every bit as strident as his detractors. If Bush-haters believe that they embody enlightened values—why, we're almost European—his champions are convinced that they are the real Americans, who believe in morality, private property, and limited government (even if the President keeps expanding it). The left often caricatures such people, portraying them as either corporate thieves or red-state dupes who have Rush Limbaugh on their radio, the Good News Bible on their nightstand, and rifles on their gunrack in case they happen to meet any gays, racial minorities, or government agents in black helicopters. While some of the cliché is true—that old pill-popper Rush does have 14 million listeners—most Bush supporters, including evangelicals, are not ideologues. They are ordinary people who want a safe, orderly life for themselves and their kids and fear that American culture has lost its moral bearings.

Even though the Republicans currently control the White House, Congress, and the Supreme Court, many Bush-backers still feel beleaguered, if not downright enraged. Caught in the habit of underdog snappishness, they believe America is constantly being threatened by liberal elites, slippery foreign allies, and loco evildoers such as Osama bin Laden and Kim Jong-Il. That's why they watch Fox News in increasing numbers, boycott the Dixie Chicks, support school prayer, and still hate Bill and Hillary with an incandescent passion. When George Bush talks the language of Us vs. Them, these folks understand what he means in their bones. And they're drawn by his air of conviction, eager to believe that he really believes in what he's doing. More than anything, this is what most Americans want from a leader.

Much of the anger inspired by Bush's presidency is a predictable liberal reaction to the earlier relentless assaults on Bill Clinton, which, if not exactly a "vast right-wing conspiracy" (its workings were largely out there in plain sight), did mark an attempt to deny the legitimacy of a twice-elected president.* The right's fanatical hatred of Clinton

---

*Although I don't think the Lewinsky affair an impeachable offense, I thought (and still think) Clinton should have resigned. If you get caught being fellated by an intern in the Oval Office, you have dishonored your office and should leave. But even if you don't do the honorable thing, you should at least have the courage to tell the truth. Clinton wasted a year of the nation's time, frittered away his power, inspired crippling "wag the dog" scenarios, urged his cabinet to tell lies, and helped get his vice president defeated by Bush—all because he wouldn't admit a dingy little adultery that the country would have forgiven had he simply fessed up.

ushered in a new era in contemporary politics remarkable for its absurd lack of proportion. (Remember when scores of Republican congressmen wanted to replace FDR's head on the dime with Ronald Reagan's, simply because they were furious about a TV movie that CBS didn't even have the backbone to show?) Each time someone starts talking about Bush as a new Hitler, I remember the hour I once spent at my parents' retirement home in West Des Moines listening to one of their neighbors declaim that Clinton was "the most evil man in the history of the country." (I was tempted to sue on behalf of Charles Manson and Henry Kissinger.) In a broader sense, the feverish passions surrounding both Clinton and Bush are simply one expression of a culture increasingly goaded to extremes by the media's bottomless need for something exciting to talk about—be it Michael Jackson's weirdness, the Terminator's run for governor, Ann Coulter's self-aggrandizing rants, the trial of Martha Stewart, the *American Idol* voting, the D.C. sniper, Michael Jackson's arrest, the murder of five-year-old Samantha Runnion, the saga of *New York Times* faker Jayson Blair, Michael Jackson's plea of innocence, the midnight release of *Harry Potter and the Order of the Phoenix*, or the endlessly replayed footage, graciously put to music by Fox News, of bombs pounding Baghdad. And, by the way, did I mention Michael Jackson's preliminary hearing? Americans may no longer join political parties or turn up at the polls, but they do go see *Bowling for Columbine* or click on *The O'Reilly Factor* and through this act of spectatorship feel that they're actually doing something—or at least have the satisfaction of hearing someone articulate their feelings of frustration, impotence, and rage. We live at a time in which hysteria has replaced politics and consumption passes for social action. Fueled by the media's taste for extreme positions, we spend our lives being confronted with specious either-ors, of which "for us or against us" is only the tip of the iceberg: You either support invading Iraq or you are "objectively pro-Saddam." You either oppose invading Iraq or you don't know that Kissinger helped murder Salvador Allende. You either dislike frivolous pop culture or you lack "values." You either oppose gay marriage or you are antiwedlock, antireligion, anticivilization. Such bogus oppositionalism is our modern American key signature. It's used to wind us up, get our attention, and open our wallets. Manichaeism sells.

One could find no more fitting president for such a culture than George W. Bush, who, after winning a disputed election, governed as if he'd won in a landslide; who, in the era of great corporate scandals, runs an administration as secretive as Enron; who, in the aftermath of the worst terrorist attack ever committed on American soil, called on his fellow citizens not to sacrifice but to keep shopping. Love him or loathe him, he is the political figure who defines our time, and like John Kennedy or Ronald Reagan before him, he casts a long shadow over our culture. This doesn't always happen with presidents. No one talks of a Ford Era; when John Updike wrote *Memories of the Ford Administration*, he was being sly. Nor did the first President Bush loom large in the national consciousness. Although presiding over the fall of the Berlin Wall, the collapse of Soviet communism, and the first Gulf War, George H. W. Bush had, and continues to have, no resonance—his most memorable contribution to American culture was inspiring Dana Carvey's impersonation on *Saturday Night Live*. George W. Bush has also been the target of *SNL* send-ups, nearly all of them inept, yet his cultural reach extends far beyond that. We see his fractured image reflected all around us—in the rise of Fox News, the popularity of Darwinian game shows, the ubiquity of the neocon pundits, the left's crippling nostalgia, the reemergence of Cold War braggadocio, the $400 million box-office of *The Passion of the Christ,* the celebration of consumerism as self-expression, and the color-coded algebra of fear that has become part of every American's psyche. If you put together the President's policies, the artificiality of our political discourse, the shrieking of our pop culture, and the babble of information that bombards us every day, you have the unreal reality I think of as Bush World.

This book is a portrait of Bush's presidency—a critical portrait, although I would like to think not an hysterical one. Unlike so many other recent books, it is not primarily about lies, lying liars, and the great unraveling of our bushwhacked America, although such things do appear in these pages. Nor is it a behind-the-scenes look at the battles between the Departments of Defense and State (suave Colin and quick-draw Rummy going one-on-one) or the backroom whisperings of Dick Cheney, the President's cloven-hoofed Richelieu. In fact, this is not a political book in the customary sense of the term. Rather, it is a piece of pop mythology that explores the polarized culture of unreality over which Bush rules. Although I will be writing about his official actions (how could one ignore tax cuts for the rich or the open-ended War on Terror?), I'm more concerned here with the ideas, values, images, pop milestones—the unforgettable characters and shared moments—that have defined the presidency of George W. Bush and the politics of our everyday lives.

In Salman Rushdie's novel *Midnight's Children*, the narrator, Saleem Sinai, tells us, "To understand me you must swallow a world." The same is true, perhaps even truer, of understanding a president. While I wouldn't dream of claiming that I'm able to swallow anyone's world, George W. Bush's or the reader's, this book does seek to understand what our forty-third president represents by looking at the culture that he's helping to create and, equally important, the culture that created him and gave him power. To that end, the following pages offer a guided tour of the Bush World in all its funny, scary, contradictory absurdity: the swaggering brio of our two great white rappers, Eminem and Donald Rumsfeld; the blue-collar shtick of those populist millionaires Michael Moore and Bill O'Reilly; the promise of mass-market fame that is *American Idol* and the calculated sincerity of literary star Dave Eggers; the anti-gay passion that wants the Constitution to ban same-sex marriage and the huge popularity of *Queer Eye for the Straight Guy*; the metaphysical horror of Osama bin Laden and the forward-looking symbolism of Condi Rice and Hillary Clinton; the right-wing surge that got Rush Limbaugh hired as an ESPN football commentator (before he blew it) and the left-wing resistance that found literary lions Norman Mailer, Kurt Vonnegut, and Gore Vidal all loudly opposing the Iraq War, an act of conscience so impressive that this trio received that highest of contemporary accolades. Just like Bush's war team, they were photographed together by *Vanity Fair*.

Welcome, friends, to Bush World.

CHAPTER 1

The Six Faces of George W. Bush

Will the Real Slim Shady please stand up
Please stand up, Please stand up

—Eminem

On June 4, 2003, President George W. Bush held a diplomatic summit with Israeli Prime Minister Ariel Sharon and Palestinean Prime Minister Mahmoud Abbas at a palace in Aqaba, a small coastal city best known for the Hollywood-fed myth that it had once been captured by Lawrence of Arabia. After the day's discussions, the leaders strolled together toward the world's cameras, crossing a bridge built over a swimming pool. It was the kind of culminating image, fat with metaphor—the bridging of divided peoples, the President acting as a uniter—that the Bush White House likes to call "the money shot," perhaps oblivious of its porn-world associations. The President's advance team hadn't just mapped out the leaders' path, as earlier White House staffs might have done. They had asked the Jordanians to build a bridge over the pool so that Bush and the others could walk over water on their way to the banks of cameras. When the first bridge proved too narrow to accommodate the men side by side, the Bush people had it torn down and a new one built that *was* wide enough. They were well aware that this visual iconography would matter far more to American TV viewers than anything the President would actually say.

Ever since Parson Weems cooked up the story of George Washington and the cherry tree, our presidents have come robed in mythology, much of it consciously crafted. In the 1920s, the founding father of American advertising, Edward L. Bernays, was asked to help Calvin Coolidge fight the perception that he was icy and remote. Bernays brought Al Jolson and a cohort of his fellow vaudevilleans to breakfast at the White House, an event that prompted the humanizing headline "President Nearly Laughs"—and opened the gate for events staged by media advisors (or pseudo-events, as Daniel Boorstin termed them). Just as advertising has grown more sophisticated in the last eighty years, so has presidential image-making. If it was by serendipity that the musical *Camelot* opened less than one month after John F. Kennedy was elected president, it was his widow Jackie who, in her sole interview after his assassination, planted the idea of America happy-ever-aftering in that fantasy of JFK's White House.

Spooked by the power of Kennedy's dashing image, Richard Nixon put himself in the hands of media advisors in 1968, and, as Joe McGinnis famously chronicled in *The Selling of the President*, they pulled off an extraordinary feat. Tricky Dick was repackaged as The New Nixon, a changed man whose painfully forced smile was something a divided nation could believe in. Small wonder that the Nixon team's techniques were studied and refined by Ronald Reagan, who invested every manipulated scenario with enormous charisma, and Bill Clinton, who knew all the tricks in The Gipper's playbook—it wasn't for nothing that the boy from racy Hot Springs, Arkansas, sold himself as The Man from Hope.

The current White House has scrutinized these precedents and more. No president has controlled his PR more tightly than Bush, who watched aghast as his father lost control of his persona—going from sturdy Cold Warrior to vomiting babbler—and plummeted from 89 percent approval ratings in the summer of 1991 to 37.7 percent of the vote in the 1992 election. Conscious that presidents, like all consumer products, rise and fall on their image, his staff treats each event with the lavish precision of a Michael Mann movie. They'd never let *him* go on TV wearing a cardigan, as Jimmy Carter did in what's remembered as his ruinous Malaise Speech. He didn't actually use the word "malaise," but such is the power of myth. Bush's handlers know that they're courting trouble whenever they put him out there on his own. That's why he held only eleven solo press conferences in the first three years of his presidency (in the same period, his dad held more than sixty). Like Ben Affleck, who can't hold the screen all by himself, their man needs to be propped up with crack production design. When he spoke about the scandals at Enron, WorldCom, Arthur Andersen, Merrill Lynch, Adelphia, Dynegy, Rite Aid, and Global Crossing, he stood before a backdrop with the words "Corporate Responsibility" printed again and again as a kind of corroborative wallpaper; when he addressed the nation from Ellis Island on September 11, 2002, an advance team brought in special banks of lights so that the Statue of Liberty would be suitably commanding against the night sky, its pale radiance neatly echoing the blue of the President's necktie; when he served up a major speech on national security, he was carefully situated before Mount Rushmore, as if auditioning for his spot on the squad. And the White House does this sort of thing almost every day. No less a figure than Michael Deaver, who designed Reagan's PR blitzes, told *The News Hour with Jim Lehrer* that the Bush team has taken packaging a president to a startling new level. He called their work "absolutely brilliant," while conceding that including Bush's head with the Mount Rushmore quartet may have been going a bit "too far."*

Predictably, such transparent but skillful shaping of the President's image horrifies those who think that Bush is a latter-day Wizard of Oz (conveniently forgetting that Clinton did the same thing, albeit less blatantly). They point with glee to ex–Treasury Secretary Paul O'Neill's remark that, in cabinet meetings, the President was like a blind man in a room full of deaf people. They wonder if Bush really

---

*The image-building work extends to fiddling with documents that might reflect badly on the president. After Bush's May 1, 2003, "Mission Accomplished" speech aboard the U.S.S. *Abraham Lincoln*, the White House website ran a headline, "President Bush Announces Combat Operations in Iraq Have Ended." But as TheMemoryHole.com revealed, once the insurrection proved stronger than expected, somebody went back and added the word "Major" before "Combat."

calls the shots or whether he's a hologram created by Dick Cheney and Karl Rove. They decry the abyss dividing the way the President is presented and what his administration is actually up to behind closed doors: Did he and Cheney privately joke about that big Halliburton contract in Iraq? Critics want to probe behind the myth and learn exactly who did what and when and why. They want to get "inside" the "real" George Bush.

Why? Much of any presidency's meaning lies precisely in its constantly changing overlay of imagery, propaganda, rumor, and journalistic blather. To strip them away in search of the "real" president is like trying to find the real onion by peeling away the layers. This is especially true of George W. Bush, who, like John Kennedy four decades before him, has spawned an astonishing number of personas in a remarkably short time, many of them contradictory. Over the last four years we've had Bush as Regular Guy, Village Idiot, No-Nonsense CEO, Compassionate Conservative, latter-day Prince Hal, and, of course, Moby Dubya devouring any Democrat foolish enough to stray into his path. None of these myths is without its truth, and each has, at times, served the President's purposes. What matters here is not so much George Bush the real man as the idea of "George Bush"—the images of the man that America has been peddled over the last four years.

#1: A Regular Guy

During the run-up to the 2002 congressional elections, Bush broke all records for the number of days a president spent campaigning for his party's candidates. He seemed to be everywhere. Late one night on cable, supporters at a Republican rally explained why they liked him. Their reasons varied, to be sure ("He's strong," "He's a real leader," etc.), but were united by a common thread: The President was genuine, straightforward, *a regular guy*. Or as his advisor Karl Rove likes to put it, "He is who he is."

There's no denying that this is a potent tautology, identical to the one favored by no less a mensch than Popeye the Sailorman, but it does beg the larger question: Who *is* he? At first glance, one thing seems clear. He's not a regular guy. In fact, Bush could almost be the archetype of the *un*-regular guy, the spoiled rich kid perpetually mocked by our culture from *The Magnificent Ambersons'* unbearable Georgie to the high school snots in those 1980s John Hughes comedies. It's worth recalling that "Junior" Bush comes not merely from privilege but long-standing privilege. On his mother's side, he's related both to the British royal family (he's a distant cousin of Queen Elizabeth II) and to President Franklin Pierce; on the Bush side, he's the grandson of U.S. Senator Prescott Bush, an old-school WASP of the Eastern Establishment, and, of course, the son of George H. W. Bush—Congressman, CIA boss, Nixon frontman at the Republican National Committee, Vice President, and Commander in Chief. Like his father, he attended Andover and Yale and then, for good measure, went to Harvard Business School. But his youth, which lasted until he was almost forty, was not exactly impressive. He was a lazy student (specializing in the Gentleman's C), a tireless party animal with a DWI arrest in Maine, a lousy businessman, and a superb mama's boy. Countless Americans of his generation followed a similar youthful path and wound up working for John Deere or standing in the unemployment line. *They* actually completed their military service, though; Dubya couldn't be bothered. He ducked the Vietnam War by joining the Texas Air National Guard, jumping the queue to get in, and then, as we all now know, shortchanged his service with impunity: His dad was a congressman. Somehow, he wound up a rich man (estimated worth $9–$26 million) and President of the United States.

One might think such a background would have ordinary people fuming. Yet as Paul Fussell and others have so patiently noted, Americans don't view class in the strict European way. Individuals are defined less by birth, which they can't choose, than by personal style, which they can. In many ways, Bush does have the manner of a regular guy—his prodigal youth gives him an aura of rebellion against the hoity-toity ways of the elite. He enjoys sports and remains faithful, we're told, to his wife. He likes folksy plain talk and dislikes people who put on airs. He doesn't want to know all that much about current events. Even his onetime drinking troubles help establish his ordinary-guy bona fides: Everyone knows someone who's had alcohol or drug problems, and Americans admire those who fall and pick themselves up. A square during the sixties, when he was an Andover cheerleader and the chief Deke at Yale, he bristles at anything that smacks of bohemia or the counterculture. He is overt about his Christian faith, and in a country that's ever more openly religious (39 percent of Americans claim to be born again), this does make him far more "regular" than most Democratic politicians, or even his own family.

Where his father always came off as a faux Texan—"deep doo-doo" is not what littered the trail to the Alamo—Junior feels happiest in Texas, preferring the provincialism of its white oligarchy to the big-city ways back east, where people are uppity about his home state. Doubt his credentials, though, and he'll instantly remind you that he went to Harvard and Yale. While Bush's love for Texas is genuine—being "home" matters deeply to him—he's politician enough to milk its symbolism as a political asset; hence his 1999 purchase of a ranch eight miles from the white-flight suburb of Crawford. Located amid one of the most reactionary enclaves in the nation, this sprawling homestead not only lets him escape the media's prying eye but affords him chances to be photographed wearing cowboy boots and a belt buckle the size of a hubcap, manfully (and Reaganfully) cutting back brush. How many times in his life do you think he's done this *off*-camera?*

It would be wrong to belabor the image of Bush as a weekend rancher, for that's only a symptom of his real appeal. In a larger iconic sense, his public persona harks back to a vanishing yet still hardy ideal of white American masculinity, one embodied in today's movies by Harrison Ford, who, rather like the President, is good at making wisecracks that don't quite mask the surliness lying beneath. Like a less glamorous Jack Ryan or Indiana Jones, Bush comes across as a terse man of action whose pride is that he says what he means, means

*A lot of people work the Texas shtick. Although Molly Ivins went to Smith, got an M.A. from Columbia Journalism School, and was once a bureau chief for *The New York Times*, her own folksiness makes George W. Bush sound like George Plimpton.

what he says, and if you don't like it, too damn bad. The last president to court such an image was Harry Truman, who spent his final decades puffing up his reputation for straight shooting. Most regular guys can't afford to adopt such attitude—unlike Dubya, they don't have the connections to escape its consequences—but the fantasy appeals to them. That's precisely why Bush has been sold as a self-confident straight-shooter by both his handlers and the conservative journalists who have crafted his myth. "George W. Bush doesn't give a damn what you think of him," wrote Tucker Carlson in a much-vaunted *Talk* profile back in 2000, ignoring all the ways this attitude might be insidious (and dishonest) in a man prepared to soft-pedal his right-wing ideology to momentarily woo swing voters. "That may be why you'll vote for him for president."

The Bush team tries to reinforce his virile image by stressing his physicality; perhaps he was a macho cheerleader. We're told that he runs the mile in less than seven minutes (or did until he injured himself), ending the long national nightmare of Clinton's jiggly pale thighs. We're treated to displays like the tail-hook landing on the U.S.S. *Abraham Lincoln*—his abbreviated time in the Air National Guard came in handy, after all—which demonstrated how dashing the President could be in a flight suit. Norman Mailer has suggested that Bush could have made "a world-class male model," and though this wasn't meant kindly, the old brawler was onto a truth: The President never seems looser than when he's doing something purely physical. Bush was far more relaxed in that flight suit than he'd ever been in a business suit, let alone during any of his rare press conferences. In fact, the more you see him doing official business, the more you sense his tension at having to be presidential. It's there in his peculiar stride across the White House Lawn, elbows out like a clichéd French pedestrian, palms facing apishly backward (an echo of those ears?). It's there in the slightly clumsy way he whispers to his foreign guests as they stand before the media. It's there in the narrowed eyes inherited from his father that greet any question he fears might contain a hidden fish hook.

It's especially there in the strange workings of his lips. Back in the 2000 campaign, much was made of the Bush "smirk," and though he trained himself to stop doing it (except during thank-you speeches at fundraisers, where smirking reassures the investors), the constipated little frown that replaced it feels like the dark echo of the expression he's suppressed. His tight, downturned mouth gives him a slightly sour mien and reminds us that, for all the help he got from his affable dad, he truly is his mother's son. (Although Barbara Bush has a reputation as a gracious lady, those who know say she's actually about as kindly as a pedigreed pit bull.) Bush's ex-speechwriter David Frum describes the President in private as "tart not sweet," and we feel this. The Bush family hothead—he's their Sonny Corleone—he often seems to be fighting back a retort he knows he doesn't dare make. Not surprisingly, he's at his most compelling and least self-conscious when firing off zingers at the White House Correspondents Dinner or speaking the Wild West lingo of "Wanted Dead or Alive," whose clichés obviously stir something deep in him. Has there ever been a president who takes such obvious pleasure in announcing violence? Even when it gets him in trouble—like that all-too-succesful "Bring 'em on" to the guerrillas in Iraq—doing so puts him at ease.

Bush's often uncomfortable body language embodies a profound inner tension, one possibly linked to the alcohol abuse of his younger years.* Like many recovering addicts, he's possessed of a need for order that borders on rage; chaos is forever flapping its buzzard wings outside his front door. He insists on daily exercise, sets aside time each day for religious study (often waking to it), and, barring World War III, goes to bed each night by 10 P.M. No *Nightline* for Dubya. The man is hooked on routine. Campaigning for his father in 1992, he required

---

*Although Bush admits to having had a drinking problem, he stonewalled about his DWI arrest and refused to answer questions about using illegal drugs, implausibly claiming that to do so might somehow let others feel they were entitled to use them. (Try that defense out in court.) His tight-lipped approach couldn't be further from the openness of Ann Richards, his predecessor as Texas governor, who not only announced publicly that, in her younger days, she "smoked like a chimney and drank like a fish," but twenty-odd years later was still willing to discuss her alcoholism on *Larry King*. Liberals confess, conservatives repress. At least until they're caught, like Rush Limbaugh and William Bennett.

special trips back to his house in Texas; campaigning for himself eight years later, he disliked being away from his own bed, startling the reporters on his press plane by asking if they, too, traveled with their own feather pillow. (Talk about homeland security.) On his first visit to Europe as president, Bush became the only Chief Executive to grumble publicly about jet lag, which must have had his globe-trotting father cringing. There is, after all, only a five-hour time difference between Washington, D.C., and London, and one imagines that Air Force One is considerably more comfortable than the economy seats purchased by regular Americans. Then again, unlike most working people, he's been softened up by those month-long vacations in Crawford.

His uncommon need for order is shared by his wife, Laura Welch Bush, a onetime librarian who is his most appealing asset: After he said his famous words about wanting Osama bin Laden "dead or alive," she teased him, "Bushie, you gonna git 'im?" In fact, the sole truly charming moment of the 2000 Republican convention in Philadelphia came during the official biographical video: "When we met, I thought you were an intellectual," the candidate said to his wife. "And I *was*," she replied with the easy rapport of Myrna Loy bantering with William Powell in an old Thin Man movie. When reporters asked what he gave Laura for their twenty-fifth anniversary, he replied with a lewd wink.

By lots of standards, she does qualify as an intellectual. "Laura has a Texas-size passion for books," her husband says, and asked her favorite piece of literature, she named "The Legend of the Grand Inquisitor" from *The Brothers Karamazov*. (She must have been bitterly disappointed the first time she met John Ashcroft.) Still, despite Laura's warmth and intelligence, she always seems a bit shell-shocked, rarely saying anything that isn't dull—can you think of a more translucent First Lady? She seems to have never fully gotten over the great trauma in her past. At age seventeen, she ran a stop sign and killed a fellow student at her high school. One can only imagine what demons this would unleash in the mind of a smart, decent girl and what ruses it would take to hold them at bay. All these years later, Laura's known as a neat freak, continually straightening things up; in one of their houses, she even arranged their books according to the

Dewey decimal system. Small wonder that the Bushes' twin daughters, Jenna and Barbara, should turn out to be girls gone wild who (as James Wolcott noted with wicked accuracy in *Vanity Fair*) look like they should be jumping out of the cake at a bachelor party.

Bush's desire for order in his daily life extends to his habits of mind, which are largely exclusionary. If Clinton wanted to know everything— every name, every policy, every nuance of the Op-Ed pages—Bush prefers *not* to know. He told Fox News that he doesn't read the daily papers or feel the need to do so, although he may have said this just to wave a red flag before the easily riled bull of the liberal punditry. Intellectually and spiritually, this devout Christian is most comfortable lunging toward absolutes. Never is this clearer than in his black-and-white opinions of the War on Terror, its rhetoric ranging from vast moral abstraction (Good vs. Evil) to the paranoiac ultimatum "You are either with us or against us," which became a mantra in his administration. Although modern life's hardest challenge may be learning to function in the face of tension and uncertainty, Bush reveals a distinctively American impatience with ambiguity. It makes him antsy. He wants to *do* something about annoying countries like Iraq. As president, Dwight Eisenhower grumbled about how small countries were a pain in the ass with their vanities, internal squabbles, and desire to tweak the powerful, but he knew better than to be sucked in. "We must," he concluded, "put up with it." Bush's instincts run in the opposite direction. Each time the French insisted that the situation in Saddam's Iraq was more "complex" than the White House thought, this only made Bush want to simplify things by starting the invasion sooner.

This willingness to cut Gordian knots bespeaks one quality of good leadership—the willingness to take decisive action—yet one would feel better about it had Bush ever demonstrated an equal commitment to learning how to untie them. He's far less curious than his father, who, despite his trouble with "the vision thing," spent decades learning how things worked. In contrast, George W. has never troubled his head much about ideological principle, administrative functions, or the nuances of policy issues. Like a Hollywood producer, he has "people" to do that.

Possessed of a Crawfordite's instinctive anti-intellectualism—his cabinet's deep-dish thinker is, scarily enough, Donald Rumsfeld—he displays a lack of interest in ideas that unnerves even his admirers: Frum describes him as "often uncurious and as a result ill-informed," and, in an *Atlantic Monthly* essay favorably assaying "The Mind of George W. Bush," conservative historian Richard Brookhiser homes in on his lack of imagination. Still, his partisans suggest that such liabilities are outstripped by other intellectual virtues. "Bush has thought systematically about leaders his whole life," claimed Newt Gingrich, evidently unaware that he's describing his own hobbyhorse, not the President's, "and has a very wide repertoire of experiences. . . . He cues off things he probably doesn't even remember."

If Bush pays little attention to ideas—"I'm a gut player," he told Bob Woodward—he's a stickler when it comes to demanding fealty and ferreting out betrayal: He worked as "loyalty enforcer" for his father's 1988 campaign. No one in his administration is allowed to upstage him. When Frum's wife tactlessly credited her husband with coining the term "the Axis of Evil" (what a thing to boast about!), this once-favored speechwriter was soon out the door. Even doubting the President's intentions comes to be seen as a kind of disloyalty. He finds the very idea of a press conference profoundly insulting—Who are you to question *me*?—and treats challenges to his policies as if they were questions about his character. Asked about those sixteen fishy words in his 2003 State of the Union address about Saddam's supposed search for yellowcake uranium in Niger, he behaved as if the charges leveled against the speech somehow concerned the depth of his own convictions. "There's no doubt in my mind," he kept saying. "There's no doubt in my mind. . . . I'm confident in the decision I've made."

Then again, rigidity of mind need not be a crippling flaw in a leader and may well be preferable to the paralyzing excess of imagination that can show you the pitfalls awaiting any form of action. Few modern politicians talk more vividly than Mario Cuomo, yet he lacked the guts even to run for president. To the horror of his detractors, Bush is completely confident in who he is, even in his limitations, which allows him to transform his vices into virtues—his rigidity makes possible his enormous self-discipline. No president has been better at staying relentlessly "on message"; his lack of intellectual suppleness has proved to be a gift in a TV-centered culture whose citizenry has been suckled on saturation advertising. Where John McCain could hang himself with a thoughtless crack and Bill Clinton often didn't know when to shut up, Bush has no qualms about repeating the same words over and over.

This is a far cry from the classic stories of ordinary Joes who get political power—from Jimmy Stewart being appointed senator in *Mr. Smith Goes to Washington* to Chris Rock becoming the Democratic presidential contender in *Head of State*. In those tales, the regular guy proves his common-man heroism by abandoning protocol and talking from the heart. Not so George Bush. Well aware that he gets into trouble when forced to ad-lib, he sticks to the script as rigorously as Bob Hope. In the process, he has achieved a level of redundancy previously reached by only a handful of monks who spend their lives chanting the same few syllables into the Himalayan void. Although such robotic behavior has proved quite effective, it also has led millions of people to wonder if the president just isn't very bright.

#2: Dumb

All presidential elections are about fantasies—the dream of a Great Society, a president who will never lie to you, Morning in America. In 2000, the dominant fantasy was that the election did not matter. With its flourishing economy and unchallenged military, the United States apparently faced no critical issues, and neither Al Gore nor George W. Bush did anything to change the perception that politics was essentially meaningless. Both promised to govern from the center. Their contest was not about big ideas or first principles but the mere alignment of power, which party would control the White House.

While the Democrats were always going to nominate Gore, heir apparent to the Clinton legacy, the Republicans desperately needed an electable candidate with high name recognition, able to satisfy the party's conservative base yet woo swing voters scared by the GOP's right-wing extremism in the House of Representatives. Bush fit the bill perfectly. He'd been a popular governor in an era when that office kept producing presidents (Carter, Reagan, Clinton); even better, he'd governed a state in which the job is largely ceremonial, so he had no far-reaching ideological track record he would be forced to defend. It was easy to pass him off as the Republican version of a New Democrat. Unfettered by public awareness of what he actually stood for, Bush was free to play the Clintonian game of "triangulation," stealing key Democratic issues to take the edge off Gore's campaign. Based on money and calculation by party big shots, his nomination was the modern version of being anointed in a smoke-filled room.

Of course, Bush was not without liabilities—his nepotistic rise, a gubernatorial career best known for its short hours and long list of executed prisoners. Yet these turned out not to be defining issues. Instead, he became famous for being dumb. The problem really started during a Boston interview, when WHDH-TV's Andy Hiller ambushed Bush by seeing if he could name the heads of state in some of the world's hot spots. Asked about Pakistan, which had been recently taken over in a coup by Pervez Musharraf, Bush replied, "General . . . General. I can't name the general. General." Not exactly a reply to inspire confidence, especially as he seemed eerily unabashed by his ignorance—you didn't really expect him to *prepare* for an interview, did you? Although some reporters thought Hiller's questions a setup, Bush's stumbling non-answers were broadcast over and over, trans-forming his geo-quiz ignorance into the stuff of one-liners on late-night TV: The guy may be good at raising campaign contributions, but folks, he's as thick as a two-by-four. In his own day, Bush Senior had been mocked for his mastery of telegraphic gibbering—"Message: I care"—but Dubya pushed such inherited inarticulateness to new levels: "Is our children learning?" he once asked, in what remains his masterpiece of illiterate concision. And because he said such things all the time, you couldn't escape hearing about his latest mangled sentence and malaprop. Bushisms were swapped around water coolers, passed along in e-mails, and eventually collected by *Slate*'s Jacob Weisberg—who had published three volumes of them by mid-2003.

Although Bush's linguistic follies are funny—"I know how hard it is for you to put food on your family"—they aren't prattle. As Mark Crispin Miller has documented in *The Bush Dyslexicon*, the Rosetta Stone of Bush Speak, the President's bizarre statements are actually a mother lode of unspoken meaning. Sometimes, his words are a Freudian eruption in which he inadvertently blurts out what he really thinks: "Unfairly but truthfully, our party has been tagged as being against things"; "Higher education is not my top priority." At others, his failed jokes hint at hidden aggression, as when he weirdly told David Letterman, "I'm a uniter, not a divider. That means when it comes time to sew up your chest cavity, we use stitches as opposed to opening it up." The studio audience booed.

Most of the time, though, his garbled sentences serve as protective coloration, hiding his ignorance about policies or helping him evade tricky issues, as during one of the 2000 presidential debates: "Gas is a clean fuel that we can burn to—we need to make sure that if we decontrol our plants, that there's mandatory—that the plants are—must conform to clean air standards. The grandfather plants, that's what we did in Texas, no excuses. . . ." Such verbal indirection recalls Dwight Eisenhower, whose own legendarily incoherent sentences had method to their madness: Heading off to a press conference about trouble on the islands of Quemoy and Matsu, he told his press secretary, "Don't worry, Jim, I'll just go out there and confuse 'em." One imagines Bush employing a similar strategy himself, although as one might expect from one who suffered from dyslexia, he often appears simply to get stuck in the briar patch of his words, whether he's referring to "tacular" weapons or waxing philosophical: "There's an old saying in Tennessee—I know it's in Texas, it's probably in Tennessee—that says, fool me once, shame on . . . shame on you. Fool me . . . You can't get fooled again."*

*Any comparison between Bush and Eisenhower begins and ends with their bizarre language. If any president in American history entered the White House with nothing to prove, it was Ike. He'd already accomplished a bigger and more important job; he could toy with the office. His manhood and competence were never in question. The same, alas, cannot be said for Dubya, the only president in more than half a century who felt the need to show up in military garb.

Under normal circumstances, the perception of a presidential candidate as a blockhead would be enough to sink him. Think of poor Gerald Ford, who, in Lyndon Johnson's memorable phrase, couldn't fart and chew gum at the same time. But like a prizefight, an election often comes down to a battle of clashing styles, and Bush could not have been luckier in his opponent. Himself the scion of a dynastic political family, Gore inoculated the governor against charges of nepotism, especially as he, far more than Bush, fairly reeked of insider privilege—he had the calibrated smile of one raised inside the Beltway. Although Bush was better born, he was also folksier. Thanks to that, their contest sometimes recalled the famous "Log Cabin and Hard Cider" presidential campaign of 1840, when Virginia aristocrat William Henry Harrison narrowly defeated the humbly born Martin Van Buren in a contest that partly turned on food: While Harrison's backers claimed that he would be content with hard cider in a log cabin just like regular Americans, Van Buren was portrayed as snooty for enjoying such wicked European indulgences as raspberries. More important, Gore's preening intelligence changed the way people felt about Bush's supposed dumbness, which suddenly took on some of the crazy-lingo charm one associates with, say, Casey Stengel. Where it was Clinton's forte to soften his Rhodes Scholar braininess with unruly appetites that humanized him—he liked a Big Mac and an intern as much as the next guy—Gore reminded people of what they loathed about the homeroom monitor. He even married a girl who wanted to censor icky rock lyrics. Worse, he fell into the classic liberal trap of thinking (a) that it's enough to be smarter than your opponent and (b) that verbal prowess is the great measure of smarts. Sighing and rolling his eyes during the first presidential debate, he not only made Bush seem like a regular guy but led ordinary viewers to suspect Gore looked down on them: If the guy is this snooty toward the Republican presidential candidate, I can only imagine how he'd feel about *me.**

*Fifties liberals, especially intellectuals, worshiped Adlai Stevenson, thinking him more intelligent than Eisenhower, a military and political wizard who'd only managed to win World War II. In fact, the only way that the urbane Stevenson was smarter than Ike was in his ability to speak elegantly—nobody was ever better at crafting concession speeches.

Even the Vice President's strengths turned into liabilities. Hailed as a star debater, he was expected to trounce Bush in their head-to-head encounters. When that didn't happen, the pundits forgave Dubya his evasive, redundant, and dishonest answers; they began suggesting that he had been, to use his splendid term, "misunderestimated." Unlike Gore, who always wanted to seem a genius, he knew how to be genial. Americans nearly always vote for the happier-seeming candidate, and in 2000, that was Bush. On the campaign trail, he showed off his knack for self-deprecation, making light of his bad grades and delirious grammar. When Gore tried to do the same, his jokes made him seem even more of an android: "I. Am. Mocking. My. Self. To. Show. That. I. Am. Not. Self. Serious." Although Bush had proved himself more than willing to play political hardball—wooing racist voters in the South Carolina primary by smearing John McCain—he didn't seem desperate to win. Gore did. Positively Nixonian in his naked longing, he wanted the job so badly that he tapped into something cruel in the national psyche. Even many Democrats knew there would be no small shiver of pleasure in thwarting him.

The comparison to Nixon is fitting, for the 2000 election bore striking parallels to 1960, when JFK beat Tricky Dick in another questionable squeaker. In both elections, the shallow, unaccomplished son of a well-connected family ran against a sitting Veep whose president could have easily won a third term; in both, an evenly matched election turned not on big issues but on the public's distaste for the Vice President's personality; finally, in both, the results were so close they allowed for shenanigans. Although both Nixon and Gore were sweaty to win, it was actually their aristocratic opponents who played fast and dirty with the balloting—Kennedy helped by Mayor Daley's machine in Chicago, Bush by his brother Jeb (and the Supreme Court) in Florida. Never afraid to delegate, Bush simply handed things over to the family's Mr. Fix-it, James Baker III (from the Houston law firm of Abraxas, Voldemort, Beelzebub, and Baker), whose fate it is to keep saving the Republicans' bacon yet never win their trust. Even before the election, Bush's brother Jeb allegedly helped rig the results by knocking tens of thousands of blacks from the voter rolls, and what they did afterward was no less ruthless. Their endgame strategy was brilliant, be it Katherine Harris certifying the election, the so-called "Brooks Brothers Riot" (when Republican operatives stopped the last manual recount of votes in Miami-Dade), or Dubya's own insistence that the Florida votes had already been counted and *re*-counted—which was simply false.

This final lie was, in fact, only one of several big ones that Bush told during the campaign. Why didn't they get more play? The answer is simple. In the culture of television, every election quickly gels into a simple, self-reinforcing, high-concept story line, and in 2000, the official narrative was that Al Gore was a liar and George Bush was dumb. When America wasn't being told how vainglorious Al claimed to have invented the Internet or been the model for the hero of *Love Story* (in fact, he made no such claims), it was hearing all about Dubya's ignorance or hallucinatory syntax. Ironically, this official narrative had things precisely backward. In this election, Gore was clearly the dummy and Bush the liar. For starters, Gore was so busy trying to win *by himself* that he arrogantly distanced himself from the White House, letting Bush run against Bill Clinton without having to run against Clintonism. As a member of the Bush family [!] told Joe Klein, "I never understood why he didn't just turn to George in those debates and ask, 'Could you remind me, just what is it about peace and prosperity you don't like?'" Then, after disowning his own president and his administration's success, Gore duplicated one of Clinton's most disastrous blunders: He was cold, even hostile to the media. They responded in kind, dwelling on his fibs, scoffing at his last-minute stabs at populism, and sneering at his attempts to be with-it: *New York Times* reporter Frank Bruni could hardly have been more withering about Gore's decision to have his campaign video directed by *Being John Malkovich*'s Spike Jonze. Of course, if Bruni had personally liked Gore, the choice of Jonze would have been a feather in his cap. Journalists have been shamelessly honest about how much they enjoyed needling Gore; besides, the food on his plane didn't measure up. Where the Vice President offered stale sandwiches and PC treats like Fruit Roll-Ups, recalls *Time*'s Margaret Carlson, Bush offered "Dove bars and designer water on demand, and a bathroom stocked like Martha Stewart's guest suite. Dinner at seven featured lobster ravioli."

While Gore was being dumb, Bush was busy being dishonest. About whether he'd ever been arrested for driving while intoxicated. About his time in the Texas Air National Guard. About his support for a patient's bill of rights. About his desire for more energy legislation to limit pollution. About being *moderate*. But his lies and evasions were barely mentioned; indeed, Bush's whole political vision went virtually unnoticed by a press corps that may have been even less interested in the issues than the public. He helped this process along by brilliantly working reporters, a task that didn't come to him naturally. He had despised the media since the 1988 presidential campaign, when he felt the press treated his father unfairly: There's a well-known story of Dubya confronting *The Wall Street Journal*'s house liberal Al Hunt, who was dining at a restaurant with his wife and four-year-old child. "You fucking son of a bitch," Bush said, "I'm not going to forget what you wrote." Twelve years later, he had the self-disciplined professionalism to hide his feelings and do what was necessary. After he lost the New Hampshire primary to John McCain, he and his advisors decided to make him more available to the media, especially those traveling on his plane. This allowed him to use his one-on-one charm, bantering, pinching cheeks, and giving people nicknames (Bruni was "Panchito"), a habit more proprietary than folksy.

And boy, did it work. The media folks ate it up, guffawing at his jokes like corporate yes-men in a clumsy satire. If you've wondered how someone as supposedly dumb as Bush got elected president, you would do well to read Bruni's book *Ambling into History: The Unlikely Odyssey of George Bush* and watch *Journeys with George*, Alexandra Pelosi's vacuous behind-the-scenes HBO documentary about traveling on the press plane. What a depressing portrait of modern journalism. Forget about reporters doing legwork to tell you things you don't know about the candidates. Now they're content just to describe the campaign, to tell you about their lives as "the prisoners in a gilded cell" (to use Bruni's phrase for the people on the plane). For all his revealing anecdotes, Bruni can barely be bothered to talk about the candidate's record, his ideas about the economy and Social Security and international affairs, or the sources of his enormous financial war chest. He does, however, find time to slag *voters* for their lack of interest in the issues. And Bruni was covering Bush for *The New York Times*, which fancies itself the paper of record. Although *Journeys with George* is even shallower, it does have one signal virtue: It preserves on videotape just how willing reporters are to kiss the ring of power. If you think North Korea's parliament is invertebrate . . .

Even as George W. demonstrates his prowess at joking with media folk he actually disdains (he'd obviously honed his gibes in countless frat houses and locker rooms), the press corps reveals itself as a pack of self-described "lemmings" who weren't about to risk their access by asking him any tough questions. (When they make him unhappy, he cuts them off.) They do what they are told, ask Bush for his autograph (as if they are hacks interviewing Ashton Kutcher at a junket), and fawn like those desperate chicks on *The Bachelor* each time he strolls to their area of the plane. Watching such scenes is excruciating, not least because Bush's attempt to woo the media so obviously pays off. Where the reporters on the Democratic plane actively dislike Gore— dipping their coverage in carbolic acid—the opposite happens with Bush. As *The Financial Times*'s Richard Wolffe puts it to Pelosi, "He charmed our pants off."

Just so. The guy everyone thought was Jim Varney turned out to be J. R. Ewing. Still, presidential myths die hard. In the April after Bush assumed office, Comedy Central began airing the mirthless sitcom *That's My Bush*, created by *South Park*'s Matt Stone and Trey Parker, who may well have produced the whole show for the title's rude double entendre. The whole show was one gag about stupidity—"A Brilliant Man Deserves a Brilliant Sitcom," went its slogan. In the opening episode, George Bush took a cake in the face and Laura exposed herself at an abortion summit. *That's My Bush* was quickly canceled. Not so the pop-culture clichés about Bush's supposed dimness. Even after the big tax cut, war in Afghanistan, and Bush's triumphant campaigning in the 2002 elections, *Saturday Night Live* still opened with a skit in which the President kept getting confused about the number of U.S. Senators. Which only goes to prove, in Bush World, dumb is as dumb does.

#3: The CEO

Back in 1985, Ronald Reagan threatened to veto a congressional tax increase with a line from Clint Eastwood's *Dirty Harry:* "Make my day." But Reagan had a good-humored cockiness that called for big-screen bravado. Bush does not, and he knows it. His own approach to the presidency can be better summarized in a tagline from the second Dirty Harry movie, *Magnum Force:* "A man's got to know his limitations."

In the months after assuming the presidency, Bush maintained a comparatively subdued profile. He realized two things: Over half the electorate thought him a Great Pretender smuggled into power by a crooked Supreme Court, and he was taking over from a president whose charisma, like Reagan's, tended to dwarf everyone around him. It was somehow typical of Bill Clinton that, at age seventeen, he would have been filmed shaking hands with John Kennedy, the sort of mythic image that could be painted on the Oval Office ceiling by a modern Michelangelo. His actual achievements aside, Clinton was a big president, big in size, big in appetites, big in his love of the limelight—he was harder to get off stage than James Brown. Months after leaving office, he still excited newscasters more than his successor, being reviled for his disgraceful pardon of fugitive financier Marc Rich, mobbed by admirers in Harlem, accused of "trashing" the White House and Air Force One on his way out the door. The charge was false, but to steal a line from *The Lady Eve*, the right needs Clinton as the hatchet needs the turkey. The Bush White House planted bogus stories about looting and vandalism—which were reported with dutiful outrage by the stars at Fox News—then boasted that the new administration wouldn't speak ill of the former president.

It had always been Bush's tactic to position himself as the Anti-Clinton. He would replace his predecessor's sloppy psychological presidency with one attuned to outward respectability (this was termed "restoring honor and dignity to the White House"). Where Clinton was garrulous, Bush would be plainspoken; where Clinton spent his life in that moral gray zone where one ponders "what the meaning of 'is' is," he would see things in biblical black-and-white; where Clinton had a powerful feminist wife who helped shape policy, he would have meek Laura, an admirable adornment who was seen but not heard. In short, his presidency would mark the restoration of an earlier, better America. For if Clinton was the very emblem of the self-indulgent, sexually loose, pluralism-inhaling sixties-fed Baby Boomer—the Establishment version, to be sure—then Bush embodied the return of the paternalistic authority figure of the fifties, back before civil rights, Vietnam, birth control, and women's lib (all those things tend to merge in the conservative mind) drove the culture to relativistic ruin. With Dubya's election, the suits were back in charge. No longer would the president be Entertainer in Chief (as Kurt Andersen dubbed Clinton), plunging into crowds to rub up against their love. He'd be that great Republican archetype, the strong CEO who managed the country like a fine-tuned corporation, enjoyed the civilized pleasures of the country club, and knew that the business of America is business. After all, he had an M.B.A. from Harvard, didn't he?

Now, it was always slightly odd that the President and his people were so eager to promote the myth of Bush as the CEO president. For most of our history, the big boss has not been a beloved figure. People may admire the financial success of John D. Rockfeller, Henry Ford, or Bill Gates, but they know, often firsthand, that such tycoons made their fortunes by being ruthless toward the little guy. And if they didn't know, there were once muckrakers to tell them—Lincoln Steffens, Ida Tarbell, Upton Sinclair. But in the twenty years after Reagan came to office, American culture drifted into CEO chic. Barking chihuahua Ross Perot was taken seriously as a presidential candidate. The dotcom boom made running a company seem downright bohemian. While business magazines made demigods of bosses like General Electric's Jack Welch, who fired people first and asked questions later, *The New Yorker* ran Ken Auletta's endless profiles of media magnates whose lives were more fascinating than the lousy movies and TV shows their companies produced. Flushed with pride, the CEOs themselves churned out high-profile memoirs chronicling their heroic jaunts across the corporate Rubicon. The muckraker had been replaced by the ghostwriter.

When Bush took office, the fantasy of the conquering CEO was still going strong, so it stood to reason that his marketing team would make a point of telling us how his management style differed from his predecessor's: The new White House would be run in a businesslike fashion. Staffers wore dark suits and ties, not jeans and sneakers. You heard none of the casual profanity of the Clinton years (let alone LBJ's soaring cadenzas of obscenity); according to Frum, it didn't get much racier than "damn." Bush put a premium on loyalty, which meant that he would tolerate no leaks to the press. (Unless, of course, leaking served his political needs, like outing CIA operative Valerie Plame to discredit her husband, Ambassador Joseph Wilson, who'd blown the whistle on the State of the Union untruths about "yellowcake uranium.") Above all, the new president was punctilious about punctuality, zapping stragglers with a glare or a rebuke if they turned up only a minute or two late. Where Clinton's schedule was mercurial—he had the fluid time sense of a drug lord—Bush saw the clock as a metaphor. "When I come on time," an aide quotes him as saying, "that shows people I respect them, and that shows discipline." As you might guess, he flips if a cell phone rings during a meeting.

But while Bush proved good at setting a corporate tone, his earlier work as a CEO told a different tale. Had the media covered his financial past with half the care they devoted to Clinton's dinky investments, everyone in America would now know that our CEO president had been no great shakes as a businessman—a fact he himself seems to realize, judging from how little space he gives the topic in his autobiography, *A Charge to Keep*. You can't really blame him for playing it down, for his business history reads like a Brechtian satire. He started two unsuccessful oil companies, both of them bailed out by men with connections to a dad who, in this period, was first Vice President, then President. He became a board member of two other disaster-bound energy companies, the latter of which (after swallowing the former) was saved by an almost miraculous infusion of Middle Eastern money. Along the way, Bush's businesses were linked to Saudi oil millionaires and the notorious financial institution BCCI, nicknamed the "Bank of Crooks and Criminals." Even Bush's prize gig as front man for thirty-nine investors who bought the Texas Rangers—Dubya personally named the team's stadium The Ballpark at Arlington—came about through his father's connections. By all accounts, Bush worked hard building the Rangers, helping the team score a sweetheart deal for a publicly funded stadium. (He didn't worry about spending taxpayers' money here.) For an initial stake of $500,000, he walked off with $14.9 million when the team was sold.

Bush's skills as a businessman didn't exactly dazzle the real ones around him. David Rubinstein, the cofounder and managing director of the Carlyle Group (also known in some quarters as the second coming of the Illuminati) helped get Bush on the Carlyle Board as a favor, and thinking he was off the record, offered his judgment:

"Came to all the meetings. Told a lot of jokes. Not that many clean ones. And after a while I kind of said to him, after about three years, 'You know, I'm not sure this is really for you. Maybe you should do something else. Because I don't think you're adding that much value to the board. You don't know that much about the company.'

"He said, 'Well, I think I'm getting out of this business anyway. And I don't really like it that much. So I'm probably going to resign from the board.'

"And I said, 'Thanks.' Didn't think I'd ever see him again. He became President of the United States."

Kept afloat by such family ties, Bush's wheeling and dealing was miles from the old-fashioned ideal of the CEO as a reliable steward who helps a business prosper—creating wealth, looking out for the interest of employees as well as the shareholders, thinking about the company's success in the long term. Then again, he'd learned business during the greed-is-good, Gordon Gekko period when CEOs began arranging their companies' finances for their own maximum profit and relished a reputation for taking no prisoners. And it was precisely this ethos that Bush brought with him to the White House. His administration is filled with men and women who have also been CEOs or sat on corporate boards. The President and Vice President had been in oil, a business best known for making a handful of people rich but creating few middle-class jobs; Colin Powell was on the board at Gulfstream Aerospace; Donald Rumsfeld had been CEO at G.D. Searle pharmaceuticals and General Instrument; Condoleezza Rice had been on the board at Chevron; and even the Secretary of Labor, Elaine Chao, had been on the boards of Northwest Airlines, Dole Food Company, and the Hospital Corporation of America. Not surprisingly, when it came time to set policy, this group thought like members of the entrenched corporate elite—just like the President. Bush appointed as the Labor Department's chief lawyer Eugene Scalia, who made his name attacking worker's comp cases involving ergonomics; as head of the FCC, he named Colin Powell's son, Michael, whose values are revealed by his remark, "The free market is my religion."

This team championed divided tax cuts and railed against the Alternative Minimum Tax, a capital-gains levy most Americans couldn't explain at gunpoint. Using the kind of log-rolling, back-scratching, and legalistic pussyfooting associated with Mobutu's Zaire or Suharto's Indonesia, they invited energy execs and lobbyists—but not environmentalists—to attend secret meetings on federal energy policy. They pushed a $15 billion bailout for struggling airlines but did nothing to help the 100,000 workers who lost their jobs. And why should they? These days, layoffs and firings are reckoned sound business practice. If the world's headlines shriek about all the Bush campaign contributors who landed big contracts to rebuild Iraq, it doesn't matter.

Bush knows that a wise CEO plays to the board, not the stockholders. This is one source of his strength. Although he entered office as a minority president, he didn't listen to such pundits as *The New York Times*'s R. W. Apple, who urged him to govern cautiously from the center. Winning is its own mandate. Anyway, when you take over a company, you do what you want—even if you only outbid the competition by a single penny. And if other people don't like it, too damn bad. You do what it takes to make a profit. It's not like you're going to be there forever. Where a weakling like Clinton spent more money on polling than all previous presidents combined—he even polled to see whether he should tell the truth about Monica, and if so, which apology played best—a sore winner like Bush takes pride in playing hardball. He pushes for every single thing he can get on every issue ("We aren't going to negotiate with ourselves," he says), then uses sophisticated advertising to sell it to the public. Talking to *The New York Times* in September of 2002, Bush's chief of staff, Andrew Card, explained why the Bush team had waited until autumn to start promoting one of its key initiatives. "From a marketing point of view, you don't introduce new products in August." The product he was referring to here was war in Iraq.

Despite all this, the one thing you might expect from an Oval Office CEO is fiscal responsibility. But today's business leaders have learned not to measure success in the long run—everything is riding on the quarterly earnings statement. Nobody cares if your decisions will make the company stronger in three years. They want the profits right now; otherwise, you're a goner. Bush has obviously internalized this short-term mentality and applied it to politics as no president before him. While the supposedly undisciplined Clinton balanced the budget, Bush took a surplus and in less than three years ran up the biggest deficit in human history—nearly half a trillion dollars for 2003—with massive deficits predicted to continue until long after he's left office. He did this by pushing through those long-term tax cuts, fighting a $150 billion (for the first year) war in Iraq, and refusing to veto a single spending bill. Like a CEO who'll wreck a company's prospects to drive up the stock price so he can cash out at the max, Bush is prepared to hamstring future presidents and soak future taxpayers so that he himself doesn't have to make budget cuts that might cost him votes. And with a clumsiness that would have Keynes clutching his head in disbelief, he's managed to run up these deficits and still have the worst record of job creation—well over two million jobs lost—since Herbert Hoover ushered in the Great Depression.

A cynic might say that all this makes him a quintessential modern CEO. But while this is one Bush myth that's deadly accurate, his official image makers dropped it the moment the economy went sour and corporate scandals began sprouting like so many toxic mushrooms. Suddenly, CEOs weren't cool. They were the bastards who cashed in $50 million in stock options when the price was dishonestly high, then left employees with gutted pension plans and shares so worthless they could be carted around in wheelbarrows like Weimar Deutsche marks. They were guys like Enron's Ken Lay, once a great pal of Bush (who affectionately Dubya'ed him "Kenny Boy"), but whose name now inspires presidential amnesia.

Of course, Bush's backers will tell you that George W. Bush has more to offer than just the valuable life lessons he learned attending Harvard Business School and signing buyout checks from his father's cronies. He's also a man of deep faith who cares about ordinary people:

#4: A Compassionate Conservative

At a moment when George Bush is president and Republican leaders boast about becoming the "natural" ruling party for decades to come (so pony up now, boys, if you don't want us to forget you), it's easy to forget that, during Clinton's second term, the right looked to be on the wane—whole books were written on the subject of the emerging Democratic majority. Loosely bound by a belief in small government, the Republicans needed a message that could attract centrist voters spooked by the Gingrich Revolution while weaving together the sometimes contradictory strands of contemporary conservatism— Christian Fundamentalists obsessed with immoral behavior, libertarians who think government shouldn't legislate personal lifestyles, isolationist Paleocons who hate free trade, free-trade-loving Neocons hawkish on foreign adventures, corporate bigwigs who want lower taxes and less regulation, CPA types devoted to honest budgets, and barking dog pundits who roiled the electoral base with their daily outrage. To stitch this crazy quilt together—and make it electable—the Republicans needed a watchword at once alluring and amorphous. Enter "compassionate conservatism."

One instantly saw why Bush would wrap himself in the term. It contained a catchy, confidently alliterative *c*. It directly countered perceptions that the right is bigoted and heartless. And it carried a heady whiff of religiosity, at least for those in the know. Although Utah Senator Orrin Hatch had described himself as a compassionate conservative as early as 1981, the phrase first got traction after discussions between congressional Republicans and one of their intellectual heroes, Marvin Olasky, a University of Texas journalism professor who is one of Bush's friends and social policy gurus. Olasky's 1992 book *The Tragedy of American Compassion* argued that big government programs designed to help the underclass had actually done more harm than good by getting the poor addicted to welfare and sapping them of their inner resources. These inner resources, Olasky believes, are largely inseparable from the moral certainties of religious belief, specifically Christianity. Social problems are better solved through the private sector—churches, "faith-based" institutions, civic-minded corporations, and volunteers. Such is the underlying idea of compassionate conservatism, a theory that reinforced the agenda of those who wanted America to have less government and more Christianity, yet also managed to sound unthreatening, even benevolent. As the phrase could include or exclude almost anything—Anagramgenius.com rearranged its letters to produce "Conspire to save a vast income"—it made an ideal slogan. It provided the Republican candidate with what Brookhiser calls "a phantom framework." That is, the words sounded great while committing Bush to nothing, a commitment he's thoroughly honored.

The Christian underpinnings of Olasky's ideas appealed to Bush, who, having been raised in his parents' lazy aristocratic protestantism (they swapped the Episcopal church for the Presbyterian one when they moved to Texas), had turned around his messy life at forty after being born again. Although opponents are unnerved by his public professions of faith, unprecedented in a modern president, it must be said that Bush is not any sort of religious nut. He hasn't tried to Christianize American education, though he did appoint an Education Secretary, Rod Paige, who now and then sounds as if he might like to; he hasn't supported Ariel Sharon because he secretly believes in weird biblical prophecies; he has never joined Army Lt. Gen. William Boykin in declaring America "a Christian nation . . . and the enemy is a guy named Satan." On the contrary, his religious beliefs are less theological than personal. In classic American fashion, his faith embodies the therapeutic "mind cure" approach that William James famously termed "healthy mindedness." Religion helped straighten out Bush's troubled life and gave him the inner resources to become not only president, but a president confident in his own decisions. Rather than being obsessed with the fallen nature of Man (a conservative doctrine that clearly affected President Jimmy Carter), Bush has a vision of life in which evil largely exists in things *outside* the self. Such an outlook explains both his willingness to label others "evildoers" and his unwillingness ever to admit errors in public. This is not a man who sees himself as a sinner, original or otherwise.

Of course, the notion of Dubya as a compassionate conservative was bound to raise eyebrows. For starters, he has never been notably compassionate, and his fondness for cowboy rhetoric has done nothing to soften his image. True, he is known for being friendly to "little people" like hot-dog vendors and store clerks, but that's more *noblesse oblige* than concern for their living conditions. True, he told the nation that his favorite philosopher is Jesus Christ, but different people believe in many different Christs, and Bush is attracted to the notoriously self-righteous Pauline version. It has given him the certainty of a theocrat. He doesn't come off as one who would turn the other cheek or drive moneychangers from the temple (that's where he'd hold his fundraisers). He's not about to die for other people's sins. Although he famously tears up when meeting the victims of suffering—"I'm a loving guy," he likes to say—politicians' tears are cheap. George Bernard Shaw once observed that "anybody can be kind in emotional moments." The trick, he said, is "to be kind in cold blood." Bush's blood is often cold. Who can forget Tucker Carlson's description of him mimicking the appeals of death-row inmate Karla Faye Tucker, twisting his face and saying with a high-pitched whimper, "Please don't kill me"? Perhaps she didn't know that Bush was notorious for executing prisoners—152 in all, including her—and just as notorious for barely glancing at their appeals for clemency. Bush may sympathize with working Americans forced to live on very low incomes, but he still forgot to include 6 million of them (including many U.S. soldiers fighting in Iraq) in his $400 billion tax-cut proposal and, once reminded of his oversight, said he'd correct it—then didn't. He may feel genuine pity for those with disease, but he still made a cynical, incoherent decision on stem cell research (crucial to medical break-throughs) because he was pandering to religious groups who insist a microscopic embryo should have the rights of a living human being. Compassion isn't just awareness of another's suffering but the desire to help alleviate its causes.

The basic problem with "faith-based" social programs is that, although well-meaning, they often become a pretext for gutting gov-ernment programs while putting nothing in their place. Since taking office Bush has cut back federal spending for such success stories as AmeriCorps, which he proudly hailed before slashing its budget, and the venerable Head Start: He's shifting the program to the individual states, a defunding process disingenuously termed "opting in" (remi-niscent of those Internet boxes that you have to check if you *don't* want spam). Despite all his lip service to the faith-based programs that would supposedly work better than their government counterparts, he has done almost nothing to get them started. In early 2003, *Esquire* ran excerpts of a letter from John DiIulio, a high-level domestic policy advisor, who had recently resigned his post, distressed over how the administration was being run by "Mayberry Machiavellis" whose ideas about programs and policies never went beyond the politically expe-dient. That DiIulio specifically exempted the President from his criti-cisms is one measure of Bush's interpersonal skills.

Far from pushing for the compassionate conservative agenda, DiIulio wrote, the White House "winked at the most far-right House Republicans, who, in turn, drafted a so-called faith bill that (or so they thought) satisfied certain fundamentalist leaders and Beltway liber-tarians but bore few marks of compassionate conservatism and was, as anybody could tell, an absolute political non-starter. It could pass the House only on a virtual party-line vote, and it could never pass the Senate. . . . Not only that, but it reflected neither the president's own previous rhetoric on the idea nor any of the actual empirical evi-dence." Put simply, faith-based initiatives were a bust. Although Bush may have talked the talk of the good Evangelical—employing the "wonder working power" of religious code-phrases (to quote a line from a hymn he trotted out in the 2003 State of the Union address)— the Christian compassion in "compassionate conservatism" had gone badly missing.

Nor is Bush's conservatism what it once seemed. Back in the 1960s, Democratic Party liberalism was so dominant that Nixon not only accepted the Great Society programs but proposed universal health care—a proposal quashed by, of all people, Ted Kennedy, who felt sure he could hold out for a better plan. Now the frame of reference has shifted so far to the right that Clinton, who instituted welfare reform and grumbled that he was passing an Eisenhower budget, can be labeled a dangerous liberal. By such a standard, Bush has been able to govern as a centrist who fends off the loonier excesses of his party— opposing gay marriage but not squawking when the Supreme Court overturns Texas sodomy laws. But as Bill Keller pointed out in a much-quoted 2003 piece in *The New York Times Magazine*, he's a far more radical conservative than even Ronald Reagan. He has chosen a vice president from the hard right ("Cheney's voting record was slightly more conservative than mine," said Gingrich), promised the Christian right an antiabortion Supreme Court justice, run up a record-breaking national debt, and dived headlong into the most wide-sweeping foreign policy initiative in the last fifty years—remaking the world map. Listening to Bush's speeches during the 2000 election, the centrist swing voter would never have dreamed that he would govern as he has. The abyss separating Bush's moderate campaign rhetoric and his action has left liberals thinking him not the anti-Clinton but the Antichrist, a president who will systematically bankrupt the federal government in order to eventually roll back Social Security, Medicare, and other federal programs.

But liberals aren't the only ones feeling discombobulated. Even as he pushes the government ever farther right, Bush must occupy the center to get reelected in a country far less conservative than he is. This makes his presidency, like Clinton's, a tossed salad of mixed signals: He joined with Ted Kennedy on the No Child Left Behind Act, a much-vaunted education bill that, characteristically, he promptly proceeded to underfund; he pushed through a massive "prescription drugs for seniors" plan (fulfilling a campaign pledge made to counter Gore's own similar pledge) that favors drug and insurance companies; even as his own Justice Department went after the University of Michigan's affirmative-action program, he was far from unhappy when the Supreme Court didn't completely outlaw it. All this gives his presidency an air of ideological incoherence, even cynicism. Predictably, the mainstream American media were disgracefully slow to notice this—preferring to dwell on Bush's love of vacations, the behind-the-scenes influence of Cheney and Rove, and risible White House claims that Dubya had been pondering Aristotle's *Nichomachean Ethics.*

Bush's erratic, extremist policy making did not go unnoticed by his supposed allies. Free-traders groused about his raising steel tariffs, but he's gotta get those votes in West Virginia and Pennsylvania. Pat Buchanan blistered the President for violating the true conservative faith with his runamok budget and interventionist foreign policy. While *The Financial Times* drubbed his financial recklessness, *The Economist* dubbed him "Red George," concluding: "Mr. Bush seems to have no real problems with big government; it is just big Democratic government he can't take. One-party rule, which was supposed to make structural reform easier, also looks ever less savoury. Without a Congress that will check their excesses, the Republicans even under the saintly [Senate Majority Leader] Dr. [Bill] Frist, have reverted to type: rewarding their business clients, doling out tax cuts and ignoring the fiscal consequences." Echoing Paul Krugman's *New York Times* warnings that the United States was becoming a third world country, in early 2004 the International Monetary Fund released a report saying that the nation's foreign debt had grown so large that it threatens the world economy.

All this led Brookhiser to conclude, "Perhaps by the end of Bush's Administration we will know what 'compassionate conservatism' means; perhaps not." It's hard to imagine Bush caring. He is, after all, a supremely practical politician. He knows that this mythic catchphrase has already done its work. It's far too vague to come back to haunt him, as his father was by "Read my lips: no new taxes." He knows, too, that few Americans care about ideological purity, especially now. After that dark morning in September, they care less about having a president who feels their pain than one who isn't afraid to inflict it on others.

#5: Prince Hal

At 3:45 P.M., on September 10, 2001, George W. Bush made an appearance at the Justina Road Elementary School in Jacksonville, Florida, in order to promote his education package. He kidded around with his brother Jeb, the governor of Florida, talked about the importance of reading skills, and served up a minor Bushism: "There's too many of our kids in America who can't read today." It was a routine presidential PR event, and had history somehow decided to play leapfrog over the next day, landing on September 12, 2001, Bush might well be remembered most fondly for all the trappings of a minor presidency—the joshing, the photo ops, the bloopers. But eighteen hours later, on September 11, Bush was at the Emma E. Booker Elementary School in Sarasota. By now everyone has seen the photo of him learning about the second plane hitting the World Trade Center, features frozen, eyes gazing to infinity. Paranoiacs who insist that the President knew about the attack all along must reckon him not just a master conspirator but an actor able to quietly convey shock, fear, and bewilderment. By the time Bush left that school several minutes later—a teasingly mysterious delay that has yet to be properly explained—he and his presidency had been transformed.

In his *Diaries*, Robert Musil asked, "Who among us does not spend the greatest part of his life in the shadow of an event that has not yet taken place?" He was referring, one assumes, to our own mortality. But on September 11, the death of three thousand others allowed Bush to step into a limelight that neither he nor anyone else had anticipated. This process didn't go smoothly, and during the first few hours, Bush acted with singular ineptitude. When the first plane hit the World Trade Center, he remarked, "That's one bad pilot"—not exactly what you'd expect about an event that was bound to cause more than a few casualties. He fatuously called the suicide terrorists "folks," then let himself be flown to Louisiana and Nebraska when Harrison Ford would have been parachuting into the District of Columbia. (Later, he allowed his staff to float bogus stories that there had been threats against the White House that had kept him from flying back earlier.) Although the media were filled with endless comparisons to Pearl Harbor, Bush delivered no Roosevelt-style "Day that will live in infamy" speech. Watching Bush address the nation from the Oval Office Tuesday night, you knew that he himself hadn't found the proper language with which to lead the country. Even when wounded by an assassin's bullet—far more seriously than people realized at the time—Ronald Reagan managed to be reassuring. Bush did not. Yet everyone rallied around him anyway. Nobody wanted to criticize a president during wartime.

At least for a while, the 2000 election finally ended on September 11, 2001. The terror attacks instantly made his presidency legitimate—the country *needed* him to be Commander in Chief—and momentarily made him appear a centrist. What could possibly be partisan about defending the United States? If any one moment marked the sea change, it was Dan Rather's tearful appearance on *The Late Show with David Letterman* the first night it returned to the air after the attacks. For years, Rather had been a favorite piñata of the right, which reckoned him the exemplar of the media's liberal bias. But Gunga Dan has actually had a long history of going soft in the crunch. The night Nixon gave his resignation speech, he was easy on the old crook, and now, in the wake of September 11, Rather lost all detachment. Suggesting just how much respect he previously had for the President, he praised Bush for being "Giuliani-esque," then told Letterman, "I couldn't feel stronger, David, that this is a time for us—and I'm not preaching about it—George Bush is the President. He makes the decisions, and, you know, it's just one American, wherever he wants me to line up, just tell me where. And he'll make the call." Although this was carte-blanche patriotism at its most wounded and thoughtless, on that September night, millions of Americans agreed.

Talking to the country on September 20, Bush said, "Great harm has been done to us. And in our grief and in our anger, we have found our mission and our moment." These are among the most sincere words he has spoken as president. You could feel not only his anger—always one of his strongest driving forces—but also his belief that God had given him a higher destiny. After all, for any man whose mind runs to divine absolutes, there is something petty and inglorious about being known for zapping the estate tax or oil drilling in Alaska, however happy such things make your campaign contributors. But fighting a war against evil—and winning!—*that* has grandeur. And once he settled down, Bush at first acquitted himself surprisingly well. Although he made the inflammatory blunder of talking about a "crusade" against terror (which actually seemed to inflame Europe more than the endlessly evoked "Arab street"), he went out of his way to visit a mosque, the Islamic Center of Washington, urging citizens not to attack Muslim-Americans, a display of public decency far removed from FDR interning Japanese-Americans during World War II. More impressive was his restraint in not lashing out wildly against some imaginary target (he'd save that for later) but slowly marshaling his forces against Afghanistan. Had Al Gore been president, one doubts that he would have shown such restraint, not only because he gets rabbity under pressure but because any Democrat who delayed acting as long as Bush did would have the Republicans crying treason. Not altogether happily, the Bush team took its time, and, to the President's credit, he did firmly grasp the long-term danger posed by Islamo-fascist extremism. Even on the big things, he isn't always wrong.

As the events of September 11 redefined Bush's own sense of his presidency, the media were selling America the notion that it had a new, improved George W. Bush who was growing into his job. The turning point came when he visited Ground Zero and talked to the rescue workers with a bullhorn. If you witnessed his performance that day on TV, you know that he was better than he had been in his prepared addresses, but still uninspired and uninspiring. He did, at best, okay. But with no little goading from Bush's communications team, the occasion was treated as a legendary turning point, the moment it all clicked into place; actually, what had clicked into place was the media's decision to treat it as a turning point. And it wasn't enough that Bush was doing better than many of us feared—again, he enjoyed the benefits of being "misunderestimated"—his change had to take on a mythic dimension. Soon, everyone from CNN's Jeff Greenfield to *Hardball*'s Chris Matthews to *The National Review*'s Rich Lowry was comparing Bush's story to Shakespeare's Prince Hal, who starts off *Henry IV, Part I* as the wastrel son of King Henry IV—thieving, drinking sack, whoring around with that amoral old life force Falstaff—then throws off his youth in the final scene of *Henry IV, Part II* with his blistering rejection of Falstaff and assertion of his regal nature as King Henry V:

> *Presume not that I am the thing I was;*
> *For God doth know, so shall the world perceive,*
> *That I have turn'd away my former self;*

By the end of *Henry V*, the onetime layabout has led his troops to triumph in the Battle of Agincourt.

On the face of it, Prince Hal's ascent does make a seductive analogy to what happened to Bush, the erstwhile fratboy son of a president, who was compelled by destiny to spearhead a great battle of his own. If you look at Bush's demeanor before and after September 11, 2001, you see a man who has aged and grown more sober. When running for president, he had often startled the press by waving inappropriately or mouthing jokey words ("I love you, man") when he should have been attending to what was happening on the dais. Rather like the actor Bill Murray, who made a career of playing outside the frame of his screen comedies, Bush often acted out the classic Boomer desire to protect one's inner essence from the implications of one's actions—"I may be doing this, but it's not really *me*." Much of that loosey-goosey Bush vanished from public sight after the terror attacks—along with some of his previous attitudes. Shortly before the bombing of Baghdad, *The Daily Show* spliced together old footage so that candidate Bush, who opposed nation building, was debating President Bush, who supported it. It was an extremely clever piece of work, but unfair. Bush didn't go from being a foreign-policy "realist" to a Wilsonian advocate of democracy out of sheer willfulness or dishonesty. Like most Americans, the President's sense of foreign affairs had been transformed by the harsh realities of anti-American jihad: The United States had become the target of violent religious extremists, and something had to be done about it.

If such modest signs of growth are what people meant when they declared Bush the second coming of Henry V—"He's a boomer product of the Sixties," wrote *Newsweek*'s Howard Fineman, "but doesn't mind ermine robes"—the comparison is plausible if thin. (Unlike Prince Hal banishing his old friend Falstaff, Bush did not disavow his former cronies, unless pretending not to know Enron's Ken Lay counts as his version of "I know thee not, old man.") But things did not stop with commentators noting that Bush had become more serious. Clearly believing that Americans needed a president they could respect, the White House and the media set about elevating him into a major world leader. Articles appeared saying he was actually much smarter than everyone had thought, which was a bit like giving the Scarecrow a diploma. His lack of curiosity was reconceived as laser-beam focus on first principles. Pundits compared him to Ronald Reagan, FDR, and (with no little prodding from history enthusiast Karl Rove) Teddy Roosevelt, whose portrait the senior Bush had specially hung in the White House. When Dubya was terse, he was compared to plainspoken Harry Truman; after his writers began cribbing from famous speeches ("we will not waver, we will not tire"), he was promoted to Winston Churchill.

His handlers did all they could to insulate him. When it came time to declare war on Afghanistan, they put him in the Treaty Room, a symbol of peace, and sat him before a window, the Free World all sunny, manicured, and green behind him. Knowing that he's uneasy with his hands, they quickly moved the camera in on his face. To let him remain aloof from individual victories and losses, they left much of the day-to-day talk about fighting terrorism to his cabinet: stolid Colin Powell, scary John Ashcroft, gleeful Donald Rumsfeld (poor Tom Ridge). When Bush did speak, he was best remembered for the Wild West bluster—"dead or alive," "hunt 'em down," and "smoke 'em out"—that confirmed much of the world's worst suspicions: In foreign capitals, demonstrators paraded papier-mâché effigies of a Stetson-wearing president brandishing six-shooters; at a demonstration near Trafalgar Square, the Bush float looked just like Woody in *Toy Story*.

Perhaps no one thing did more to burnish Bush's image as a wartime leader than the bestselling *Bush at War* by Bob Woodward, who is himself one of America's great mythological creatures. If it has become a truism that journalism is the first draft of history, Woodward's books go that one better: They're the first draft of journalism. The guy gets unparalleled access to big Washington players because they know he'll let them spin their story yet rarely do what a hard-nosed reporter would—dig into the truth of their words, especially if it might make them look bad. He's far less generous to those who *don't* talk to him. This lack of intellectual complexity is what makes Woodward's books go down so easily. Pandering to their sources as well as the reader (Joan Didion has termed his work "political pornography"), they give the illusion we're seeing behind the scenes with unrivaled clarity. Never was this truer than in *Bush at War*, which instantly became a defining piece of pop iconography. Here Woodward created a myth that we're still living with, the saga of an untested president who rose from early mistakes to become a wartime leader in full control of his government. This is an "authentic" Bush who tears up with compassion, runs meetings with an iron hand, and makes a point of insisting that he doesn't want any photo-op wars. (One wonders exactly who forced him to do that *Top Gun* meets Leni Riefenstahl landing on the *Abraham Lincoln*.) *Bush at War* happily printed the legend. Small wonder that, almost alone among reporters, Woodward praises this White House for being so "responsive."

American culture was primed to accept such an idealized vision. Just as Ronald Reagan's vision of a bright, bold, anti-communist America found reinforcement in such iconic movies as the *Star Wars* series (which gave him the term "evil empire"), *Raiders of the Lost Ark*, and *Rambo*, so the planets were aligned to cast Bush as the leader in a great struggle. For the last few years, our culture has been enthralled by grand master-narratives—the *Harry Potter* tales, the *Matrix* trilogy,

Spider-Man, The Lord of the Rings, and the Left Behind series beloved of Evangelicals (which, in a genuinely witty touch, offers us an Antichrist who has been named *People*'s "Sexiest Man Alive"). All these yarns have the same underlying mythic structure: Through destiny or accident (that spider-bite!), an unlikely young man turns out to be a great hero (The One, as *The Matrix* has it) in the fight against evil. The parallels to Bush (and Prince Hal) are especially apt in the case of Harry Potter and *Lord of the Rings*'s resolutely unmagical Frodo Baggins, both the offspring of distinguished lineage, suddenly called on to battle satanic figures (Voldemort, Sauron) who have destroyed their families or communities. Of course, no president's popularity can be manufactured through hit movies and books— Jimmy Carter didn't ride the crest of *Rocky*-mania to a second term— but when pundits began talking about Bush's new seriousness or the President himself talked about good battling evil, they were addressing a country that, after September 11, 2001, had proved itself extraordinarily receptive to such storylines.

No matter that, in most ways, Bush remained precisely the same inarticulate CEO president who had entered office. If the War on Terror led most Americans to unite behind him, he didn't use this support to create a government of national unity. Before Agincourt, Henry V promised his men glory for their sacrifice: "He today that sheds blood with me / Shall be my brother." Before Afghanistan or Iraq, Bush called for no shared sacrifice—in fact, no sacrifice at all—but used his new power to promote his partisan agenda. Even his supposed new gravitas was more a matter of public relations than anything else. Given half a chance, he'd still blow it. Shortly before September 11, 2001, TV cameras had found Bush discussing the Middle East while slouching in a golf cart and picking sod from the cleats of his shoes. (His father looked on, as if eager to rebuke the kid for his bad posture.) One year later, back on the golf course, Bush stood at the tee and spoke about a bombing in Israel: "I call upon all nations to do everything they can to stop these terrorist killers. Thank you. Now watch this drive."

So much for growing into the job. Yet such moments did very little to alter the perception, constantly reinforced in the American media, that the President had become a major wartime leader. Showtime even began cranking out *D.C. 9/11: Time of Crisis* by professional jackass Lionel Chetwynd, an unabashedly pro-Bush docudrama that portrayed the President's behavior on that dreadful day in a far rosier light than any serious historian would accept. In this TV movie, the President *did* live up to Harrison Ford, becoming a two-fisted hero worthy of *Air Force One* (if not of Air Force One). He demanded that his plane be taken back to the nations's capital and mouthed tough-guy lines that were the purest Hollywood: "If some tinhorn terrorist wants me, tell him to come and get me! I'll be at home, waiting for the bastard!" Revealing just how much the President's reputation had changed, this commanding new Bush was played by Timothy Bottoms, the same actor who, in *That's My Bush!*, played him as a stumblebum.

But in another irony, by the time *D.C. 9/11* hit TV screens, the whole perception of George W. Bush had begun to change, and the show was greeted as something of a bad joke—if not actual camp, at least a laughable attempt to rehabilitate the President during what had not been Prince Hal's finest hour. But that would be later, in September 2003, when Bush's popularity had slipped and he had become an even more divisive president than Bill Clinton.

#6: Moby Dubya

"Power-worship," Orwell wrote, "blurs political judgment because it leads, almost unavoidably, to the belief that present trends will continue. Whoever is winning at the moment will always seem to be invincible." Few presidents have appeared more invincible than George W. Bush during the twenty months from September 11 to the official end of the "major combat operations" in Iraq. If you believed the media coverage, the War on Terror had transformed him into an historical giant, the Caesar of our modern-day Rome, bestriding the narrow world like a Colossus.

On the night of November 5, 2002, when Republicans grabbed a few additional congressional seats, the country was repeatedly told that Bush's "historic" success in these midterm elections proved his enormous popularity. Supposedly, America just loved the guy. Now, one could hardly blame the White House for gloating about how much they *weren't* gloating; after all, their side had come out ahead. But during hours of coverage memorable only for James Carville putting a wastebasket over his head—a good look for him, by the way— one waited in vain for the endlessly chattering TV pundits to inject some skepticism into the night's triumphalist story line. Anomalous-seeming midterm results are by no means unprecedented: At the peak of the Clinton impeachment fever in 1998, the Democrats gained House seats. Nor had Bush's tireless campaigning turned one-sided Senate races into landslides in the other direction. His personal appearances upped the Republican vote by only scant percentage points, often in states where the Democrats were fielding weak candidates, including Minnesota's Walter Mondale and Missouri's Jean Carnahan, surrogates for men who died in plane crashes. Against this electoral success, one had to weigh the appropriateness of a commander in chief who, on the brink of leading his country into war with Iraq, would set new presidential records for fundraising and barnstorming on behalf of a single party.

At the time, Bush appeared too powerful for such unseemliness to matter. Andrew Sullivan compared him to JFK, a *New York Times* article declared, "A Bush Dynasty Begins to Look Real," and on PBS, David Brooks offered doubters a warning that one imagines he would not repeat so strongly today: "Never, ever, ever, underestimate George W. Bush. It took me two years of being wrong about Bush before I finally got sick of it. The rest of the pundit class had better catch on. He is a leader of the first order." (Behold the wisdom of the power worshipers.) In its own way, the left felt the same thing, especially the Democratic Party, which was little more than a defeated ooze, an aging mollusk that misplaced its shell thirty years earlier. In 2002, it didn't even pretend to present an alternative. Facing a hard-line Republican president—whose conservative values the majority of Americans did not share—the party was nonetheless terrified of Bush's personal popularity.

Standing up to him fell to left-of-center pundits who spent their time wondering why a press corps that had obsessively nailed Clinton and Gore for small, private fibs failed to point out Dubya's habitual dishonesty on huge public issues of taxes and war. The President's ongoing success clearly tormented the proto-Bush-haters, and their rhetoric grew progressively more assaultive and frantic; suddenly everybody started sounding like the Gore-loving shrillers at Media Whores Online, a website that never stops baying about the administration's duplicity and the media's complicity with it. *Salon*'s Brendan Nyhan wrote an article called "Making Bush Tell the Truth About Iraq" (bring out the thumbscrews!), and from his catbird seat at PBS, the Lone Star Tiresias, Bill Moyers, saw nothing but doom. "If you liked the Supreme Court that put George W. Bush in the White House, you will swoon over what's coming. And if you like God in government, get ready for the Rapture." The hysteria grew so infectious that each time you turned on *The Capital Gang*, you half expected the pawky Democratic commentator Mark Shields to sprout fangs and snarl out a chorus of "Bad Moon Rising."

The White House took the liberal pundits' frothing as proof they had their opponents on the ropes. To be fair, the President and his people had every reason to be full of themselves. They had passed huge tax cuts that instantly wiped out the balanced budget that was Clinton's greatest achievement. They had won a war in Afghanistan and gotten the Congress to back their resolution permitting war in Iraq. They had the overawed Democrats thinking that blocking a few judicial appointments was some kind of legislative achievement, when the Republicans had actually blocked far more of Clinton's. Bush appeared to be moving from victory to victory, and when Baghdad fell without the feared bloodbath, his presidency looked unassailable. His handlers obviously thought so, arranging that "Mission Accomplished" photo op aboard the *Abraham Lincoln*. Although this stunt required far less virility than advertised—a few years earlier, the same landing had been made by Madeleine Albright—we all knew we'd be seeing it over and over in the President's reelection ads. Bush channeling Great Emancipator mojo!

In fact, this transcendent moment of glory was an illusion, and not only because it had been stage-managed by the White House communications team. Even before the Iraq war, Bush had begun his downward slide. While the right still backed him with the fervent loyalty his policies were designed to induce, Bush had thrown away the goodwill of voters who had cast their ballots against him but afforded him a second chance in the early days of the War on Terror. This remains his single most startling failure as president. September 11 hadn't merely legitimized his controversial ascension to office, it had offered him the chance to govern as a figure of national unity, defending the nation from malignant outsiders. Yet given a political gift that any other politician would kill for, he managed to turn the country even more bitterly divided than he'd found it. By Thanksgiving 2003, *Time* was running a "Love Him! Hate Him!" cover, showing Bush boasting the lipstick traces of his admirers but also a black eye from his enemies. He hadn't merely polarized the country, but he'd done it in the most alienating of ways—by steadfastly ignoring the point of view of anyone who disagreed with him. Naturally, liberal leftists disliked his tax policies and war plans; naturally, they couldn't stand his "bring 'em on" pronunciamentos, ill-tempered news conferences, and genius for rubbing an entire planet the wrong way. But what they *loathed* about him was his arrogance. Nobody expected Dubya to apologize for winning office through judicial fiat, but the losing side did expect him to display the sense of human fallibility that lies at the very heart of democracy—the humility, the capacity for doubt, the awareness that the other guy may actually be right. Bush not only lacks such feelings, he has enjoyed flaunting their absence: If you don't like what he's doing, well, Fuck you. ("The Bush people aren't big on constructive criticism," says *The Weekly Standard*'s editor, William Kristol.) Nobody was surprised when Bush said that he didn't care in the least what all those millions of peace marchers thought. "I do not need to explain why I say things," he told Bob Woodward. "That's the interesting thing about being the president. Maybe somebody needs to explain to me why they say something, but I don't feel like I owe anybody an explanation." Too bad Bush refused Saddam's offer of a debate. It would have been a real doozy.

In both style and substance, Bush drove the liberal left to distraction—he had become their Moby Dubya—and by the summer of 2003, they had their harpoons ready. *The Nation* put a pointy-eared Bush on the cover toppling the Statue of Liberty, *The American Prospect* called him "The Most Dangerous President Ever," and even *The New Yorker* couldn't resist taking a genteel swipe: Its cover showed Dubya riding a horse across the American desert, only the President was the one wearing blinkers. He was especially blistered on the Internet, where numerous must-read blogs—including Atrios, Daily Kos, and TalkingPointsMemo—sped up the news-cycle of fury: You could click on several times a day and be greeted by the outrage of the hour. Cyberspace was inundated with copies of Jonathan Chait's *New Republic* rant that began:

> I hate President George W. Bush. There, I said it. I think his policies rank him among the worst presidents in U.S. history. And, while I'm tempted to leave it at that, the truth is that I hate him for less substantive reasons, too. I hate the inequitable way he has come to his economic and political achievements and his utter lack of humility (disguised behind transparently false modesty) at having done so. . . . And, while most people who meet Bush claim to like him, I suspect that, if I got to know him personally, I would hate him even more.

It's not only the right that can get turned on by its rage. God, he was having fun.

These magazine attacks were just the appetizer for an autumn main course of Bush-bashing books that dominated bookstore display tables: Michael Moore's *Dude, Where's My Country?*, Paul Krugman's *The Great Unraveling*, Molly Ivins and Lou Dubose's *Bushwhacked*, Joe Conason's *Big Lies*, David Corn's *The Lies of George W. Bush*, Jim Hightower's *Thieves in High Places*, and, of course, Al Franken's funny *Lies and the Lying Liars Who Tell Them*, whose jeering eventually made one yearn for the soothing shriek of a peacock. Caught up in the polemical fray, most of these works were thin; the deluge of such titles made each individual volume seem smaller and less impressive, a recycling of the same anecdotes and the same undeniable evidence that Bush is a liar. "Okay, I *get* it," one thought after a while. "The guy doesn't tell the truth."

Problem was, neither did Clinton. By now, you can't outrage the public with the news that presidents lie; it's like saying that spiders spin webs. Still, the fact that these anti-Bush books topped the bestseller lists (often snuggling up next to liberal-bashing volumes by Bill O'Reilly, Sean Hannity, and Ann Coulter) suggested that hating the President wasn't just a duty but a pleasure. Smacking Bush became so obligatory on the left that, following Howard Dean's lead, other Democratic presidential hopefuls began trying to outdo one another in their histrionic fury at his behavior—even if they'd voted to sanction much of it. Dean's candidacy became popular not simply because liberal-left voters despised Bush, but because they also scorned the Democratic leadership for being outwitted in the 2000 Florida battle and proving themselves cowardly ever since. When ordinary people told you how much they hated Bush, they were often venting the rage unexpressed by the likes of John Kerry, John Edwards, Dick Gephardt, Joe Lieberman, Tom Daschle, and Hillary Clinton. Given the chance to oppose Bush on the Iraq war, the party's big shots had surrendered without even shooting back. You actually heard tougher attacks from old Nixon hands like Pat Buchanan and Kevin Philips, whose book *American Dynasty* would take a carpet beater to the whole Bush clan.

The venom of the attacks surprised everyone, even many on the left. The desire to be fair and balanced (so to speak) has long been liberalism's intellectual lighthouse and political reef. Over the last three decades, the right has largely cornered the market on political savagery, from R. Emmett Tyrrel's sub-Menckenisms in *The American Spectator* through *The Wall Street Journal*'s hatchet jobs on Bill Clinton to the dazzling riffs of Rush Limbaugh, who has no peer at turning free-floating anger into entertainment. Confronted with such expert hectoring, the left almost always stayed on the high road, appealing to the better angels of our nature; naturally, this only made liberals seem wimpy, effete, ineffectual. It was misery watching CNN's original *Crossfire* back when that bull-elephant Buchanan was paired with sly, bespectacled Michael

Kinsley, a good political columnist and hopeless TV personality. Buchanan would trumpet some conservative battle cry aimed straight at the listener's gut, and Kinsley would make a twinkly debating-society response that may have had some imaginary Oxford audience shouting "Hear! Hear!" but got him flattened in the rough-and-tumble of a TV talk show. You always wound up knowing what Buchanan thought about every subject, while wondering what exactly Kinsley believed in—other than his own ability to make deft arguments. Caught behind his frozen grin, he seemed perfectly aware that, when an elephant's charging you, it does no good to tell it to stop being unreasonable. And yet, paralyzed by his own ironic awareness of *Crossfire*'s absurdity, he couldn't stop himself from doing just that every single time.

It's one of Bush's perverse achievements that all this has changed. He's spawned an opposition in the conservatives' mirror image. Like Peter Parker after that radioactive spider-bite, the liberal left has muscled up. Although it still can't match the right's relentlessness and lack of proportion, it has finally begun to fight back. Sometimes a tad childishly. In their frenzy, the Bush pummelers often overdid it, like kids, just learning to swear, who use "shit" and "fuck" in every sentence to show they're cool. Hilariously, the left's embrace of the right's tactics got the conservative media into a lather. *The National Review* ran an article decrying the outbreak of "Bush Hatred," as if the President's actions had nothing at all to do with it; shortly before his death, *The Wall Street Journal*'s Robert Bartley upped the ante, suggesting that dislike of Bush was actually caused by the liberals' unconscious projection of their own shame at Clinton's immorality. Right-wingers began calling for the civility they had so gleefully disdained for decades. Not so much civility, mind you, that they would fault the RNC for running an ad that linked triple-amputee Viet vet Senator Max Cleland to Osama bin Laden. No, just enough civility so that the Bush-bashers would be condemned for writing all those bestsellers. The smartest version of this argument came from columnist Brooks, who had just begun his stint at *The New York Times*. Although his piece was tinged with bad faith—one doesn't recall him bemoaning *The Wall Street Journal* and *The Weekly Standard*'s scurrilous attacks on Clinton when he worked for those publications—it grasped an important political reality. As Brooks put it, the Culture Wars have been replaced by the Presidency Wars. That is, today's political fights have less to do with ideas or ideologies than with the moral and political legitimacy of whichever president happens to be in office. Such fights are amped up by rabid headlines, manipulative fundraising pitches, and media rabble-rousers whose careers depend upon keeping things at a fever pitch. And so, the right must insist that Bill Clinton was a sixties-style crypto-socialist, though he balanced the budget and pushed through welfare reform, and the left must insist that Bush's America is one inch from being Orwell's Oceania.

Although some liberals are unnerved by their side's newfound stridency, it was healthy for leftists to display some of the hearty animal spirits you find by the bucketful on the right. Besides, page by page, the anti-Bush bestsellers were vastly better documented and less delusional than those still-coming screeds that paint Clinton as a raping, drug-dealing, Osama-coddling traitor who murdered his friend (and Hillary's putative lover) Vincent Foster. At the same time, the Bush-bashing fiesta took us all one step deeper into a Good vs. Evil political universe in which the left, like the fundamentalist right, feels obliged to believe in demons. It's not enough to reject Bush's Medicare plan as a $400 billion, er, $550 billion botch that allows Bush to woo the electorate, appease the insurance and drug companies, co-opt the AARP, and still slide through a right-wing Congress. One must view the proposal as part of a brilliantly insidious master-plan to destroy the system altogether. It's not enough to note that Bush has been unpardonably lackadaisical about corporate malfeasance. One must act as if the problem began with him—no matter that companies like Enron did most of their dirty work on Clinton's watch. It's not enough to argue that the invasion of Iraq was a serious mistake made for a multitude of reasons, some of them honorable (and endorsed by most Democratic congressmen). One must believe that Bush is a power-mad cowboy angling for votes and oil-money contributions by killing innocent civilians in a helpless country. Bush doesn't have to be the worst president ever to be a really bad one.

The problem with turning George W. Bush into the white whale is not that it's uncivil, but that it's sloppy, encouraging the same intellectual and rhetorical laziness that marks the President's own us-and-them thinking. That happened to Gore Vidal, whose contempt for Bush has turned this sophisticate into a sneering Ahab. In a disdainful 7,000-word piece for *The Observer* of London widely distributed on the Internet, Vidal described the Bush-Cheney "junta" as "Hitlerian" and claimed the President deliberately didn't stop the 9/11 terror attack so he'd have an excuse to conquer Afghanistan, partly in the service of Unocal's oil plans. (To think Gore once slammed Oliver Stone for distorting history!) One sees why such a theory would appeal to Vidal's aristocratic vanity. His interpretation of American history has always focused on the elite that he himself was born into, thereby putting him (unlike the rest of us slobs) at the center of our national journey; that's *his* version of power worship. Trouble is, Vidal's explanation of 9/11 was bats—a grab bag of anti-American gibes, self-contradictions, and bogus pieces of "evidence" that look worse each day. If Afghanistan was invaded for the oil companies, why has the president let that country go to pot? Even worse, Vidal's analysis was embarrassingly naive coming from one who has always taken pride in his worldliness: He knows better than to think that foreign policy is made so simplistically. Although it's possible that Vidal believed he was being amusingly provocative—always one of his vices—such rubbish from a famous writer actually helped Bush by making his critics seem not merely unserious but unhinged. In fact, like all conspiracy theories, Vidal's account of Bush's machinations actually distracted him from exploring the reprehensible policies that the White House was enacting in plain sight.*

The irony of the Bush-bashing frenzy was that, like the claims that Dubya was dumb or a regular guy, a compassionate conservative or a

---

*Nation Books did the same by releasing *Forbidden Truth*, a discredited French conspiracy book that claimed 9/11 was provoked by U.S. threats against the Taliban on behalf of oil interests. *The Nation*'s publisher, Victor Navasky, justified publishing the book by telling *The Village Voice*'s Cynthia Cotts, "I think it's important to raise questions." Uh-huh.

modern Prince Hal, the attacks tended to shroud his presidency in still more myth. The bestsellers that treated him as a larger-than-life villain may have reassured Bush-haters that they weren't losing their minds in being appalled, but they didn't win many converts. Then again, neither did George W. Bush, whose approval ratings rose and dipped with the latest news—up with the capture of Saddam, down with the maimed corpses in Falluja—but never matched his popularity in the eighteen months leading up to war with Iraq. Through all these ups and downs, Bush continued to govern as he had from the beginning: like a man who didn't worry about bringing the country together. Like a man so certain he's right that opposing opinions aren't just wrong but contemptible. Like a man who appeared content to win reelection by 50.1 percent to 49.9 percent and not care if he had the lower figure so long as the electoral votes put him on top. This hardly seemed the smartest way to gain a second term. But as Garry Wills remarked in his book on Ronald Reagan, presidents are usually judged for what they're known to be good at—Nixon at foreign policy, Reagan at communicating, Clinton at managing the economy. Bush is not particularly good at any of these things. But polls show again and again that he does have one great asset that makes him a formidable incumbent. Like him or loathe him, the majority of Americans believe he shows *leadership*, especially in the battle against terrorism—even when they're not sure where he's leading them.

It's a belief he is happy to turn to his own use. "Every day, I'm reminded what 9/11 means to America," he declared in the summer of 2003. He should have added, "and what it means to my presidency." The dominating George W. Bush we now know was born on that day. It let millions overlook the rest of what's happened on his watch— corporate scandals, tax cuts for the rich, foreign policy gaffes (remember when he accidentally pledged to protect Taiwan against China?), astonishing budget deficits, environmental rollbacks, and millions of lost jobs. Without the terror attacks, he would surely have become a minor, failed president like his father.

CHAPTER 2

From September 11 to 9/11:
Birth of a Legend

September 11, 2001—that date will inject our brains.
>   —LARRY KING

L ooking back, it seems inevitable that September 11, 2001, would
become known as 9/11. Dates are unwieldy things—a headline
writer's nightmare—and mere hours after the planes hit the World
Trade Center, people instantly began seeking shorthand for an event
that didn't reduce itself to a few easy words. In that sense, September
11 proved to be a marketer's dream. Not only did 9/11 duplicate the dig-
its of the phone number for dialing Emergency, the "11" even offered a
visual echo of the two towers. Had the attacks come, say, two weeks
earlier, I wager we would not be talking of 8/28 any more than we refer
to the Kennedy assassination as 11/22 or the Pearl Harbor attack as
12/7. But you didn't need to be a whacked-out numerologist to grasp
that "9/11" was the sheerest magic—it packed the pop-culture snap of
a great movie title. And it still carries an incantatory power. Merely to
say "nine-eleven" (not nine-one-one) today calls up memories of terror and heroism, even if the collective form of such memories often
domesticates or obfuscates the meaning of what happened that day.
The *American Heritage College Dictionary* has already included "9/11"
among its entries, the only date in the whole book.

That morning's attacks were the most horrific thing to happen on
our native soil during any of our lifetimes, including Pearl Harbor
you could feel the tectonic plates of American life turn to liquid
beneath the floorboards—and I experienced them in the same way

that nearly the whole world did. I watched them on TV, transfixed by pictures that, in their spectacular ghastliness, beggared the fever-dreams of any Surrealist. At the best of times, human beings are drawn to grandiloquent images of destruction (the absence of good footage explains why the Pentagon attack left so little imprint), and here one's voyeurism came tempered with disbelief and dread. Like billions of others, I stared at each shot of the airplanes hitting the skyscrapers and watched them crumble over and over, like burning sticks of incense. We were given a harrowing reminder of something that those privileged to be Americans have often found it easy to forget: History hurts, and we are not immune.

Shortly after the second American Airlines jet crashed into the South Tower, CBS broadcast footage of hundreds of people rushing away from the building. A few looked terrified, many more stunned, and one, a beefy New York City policeman, sauntered by with a strange frozen smile. If this had been a movie—and in describing that day's events, flying-glass action pictures became the inevitable reference point—such a smile would tell us that the cop was a villain beaming in triumph. But here it could only have meant that he was at a complete loss. His world was literally collapsing around him, and he hadn't found the emotional vocabulary to know how to react. He wasn't the only one. In the hours that followed, everything felt unmoored. I got calls from sobbing friends, avoided zombie maniacs along the Ventura Freeway (I'd never seen so many accidents), and took stock of humanity's diverse ways of coping with disaster: While collectors flocked to Manhattan gift shops to invest in postcards of the downed towers, morons were sending death threats to Islamic schools in Los Angeles. Driving home from my newspaper at one the next morning, I accidentally cut off a guy doing about ninety. Under normal circumstances, I'm sure he would have just cursed me. But that night he tailed me for a creepy half hour through quiet streets and empty freeways, shrieking curses and threats, his face twisted with hatred. I was spooked, of course—this was L.A., after all, where road rage often comes armed—but obviously so was he. After a day of being bombarded by images provoking terror, he wanted to escape his passivity and lash out.

At the best of times, our media form a gigantic Ministry of Fear, daily winding us up with "special reports" about carjacking epidemics, constantly arriving killer bees, and the deadly bacteria lurking in those deli cases. On the day of the attacks, when fear was reasonable, it was ratcheted up even higher by confusion and impotent rage. While Gingrich talked to Bill O'Reilly about "Islama" bin Laden, the left-wing *Village Voice*'s Web page ran a headline that read simply, "The Bastards!" CNN indulged in the stunt of interviewing flight-phobic novelist Tom Clancy merely because he'd written a thriller about a similar attack. I braced for the worst—Clancy is, after all, an Oliver North manqué. But he launched into a monologue about how Islam is a religion of love, like Christianity and Judaism, and we shouldn't believe that the actions of a few madmen actually represent the whole Islamic faith. "My God," I remember thinking, "*Tom Clancy* has become the voice of reason." Even as it's scaring us to death, TV inevitably seeks to make everything feel familiar, and the networks quickly posted normalizing slogans up on the screen: "America Attacked," "Terrorism Hits America." Yet on this day they looked pathetic, tattered umbrellas held up to stop an avalanche. After all, it was one thing to declare that America was at war, as Dan Rather did, immediately dubbing the events "apocalypse, now." It was another to say this when you weren't sure who, if anyone, you were at war with. Then again, events had spiraled so far beyond anyone's expectations that the networks fell into numbing repetition—those towers just kept collapsing, those slogans kept reappearing—punctuated by bursts of rare honesty. At one point, Peter Jennings interviewed an intrepid freelance photographer, Kevin Sutavee, who had managed to take far grittier footage of the toppling towers than any network news crew. Sutavee said that the attacks embodied "the power of ignorance" but added that he understood why the disenfranchised might well hate capitalism. You knew that ABC News had to be utterly discombobulated or else it wouldn't have shown somebody saying *that* on the air so soon after a national tragedy. For one day, anyway, the American media felt as wide open as the world they so routinely neglect; the coverage was all over the map.

Over the next forty-eight hours, this changed. The chaos of September 11 congealed into the Legend of 9/11, a far deeper transformation than that suggested by the intellectual shorthand by which it became known. A set of mythic story lines were laid that became the foundation for what would become Bush World. The President became "Bush at War," a far more impressive-seeming fellow than he'd been on September 10. America decided to wield its might and remake the Middle East. The right got stronger, the left weaker, and ordinary citizens worried that their country was no longer safe. The White House used 9/11 as a reason for everything—tax cuts, environmental rollbacks, wars, and, of course, contributions to its 2004 war chest. We'd entered the age of Horrorism. After Apocalypse Tuesday, America knew that very bad things could happen—an atomic blast at the Orange Bowl, a suicide attack at McDonald's, the declaration of martial law, or a pogrom against American Muslims. Would our nukes turn Mecca to glass? In this climate of dread, one imagined sleeper cells in clean, well-lit apartments wiring together the dirtiest of suitcase bombs. And the media began telling us about the evil genius who pulled their puppet strings, a figure who seemed less a flesh-and-blood man than an emanation.

The Napoleon of Terror

An epic struggle demands a nemesis, and when most Americans first heard about Osama bin Laden in the hours following the attacks, they found one startling in his grandiosity. With that beard and those robes and the soulful eyes, he grabbed your attention, which is one reason why TV instantly treated him as a malevolent new star. His presence could "open" a Sunday news show the way Tom Cruise could *Mission: Impossible.* For Osama (as he was known in the Muslim world) wasn't merely the source of the terror visited on America, he was its mythic personification—Charles Manson to the nth power, a divinely inspired madman preaching a helter-skelter sermon of mass death and virgin-stocked paradise. And his diabolism was obviously infectious: The networks never tired of replaying those al-Qaeda training films, which had the same lousy production values as *The Blair Witch Project* but felt much, much scarier. Osama could show you fear in a handful of videotape.

Although bin Laden burst into our consciousness like some pulp-fiction supervillain, he was simply a man whose visionary ambitions made him the latest manifestation of a long tradition: Islamic history is lined with messianic leaders bent on restoring the true faith. Bin Laden wasn't even the first such figure in modern history. Back in the 1880s, when the Sudan was crushed by poverty and the cruelty of its Egyptian occupiers (backed by the British), the holy man Muhammad Ahmad ibn as Sayyid Abd Allah built a huge army bent on expelling all infidels from the holy lands and restoring the purity of Islam. Given his modest resources, he did uncommonly well. Calling himself the Mahdi (often translated "Messiah" but probably better rendered "the Guided One"), he imposed Islamic law over vast stretches of the Sudan, threatened the stability of Egypt, and eventually seized Khartoum, killing the fabled British general Charles "Chinese" Gordon before himself succumbing to typhus six months later.* It's an amazing tale, and by comparison with the Mahdi, who was a boatman's son, bin Laden's story smacks of the dilettante. The seventh son among fifty brothers and sisters, he was born into a mega-rich Saudi family whose values he rejected even as he took his cut of their dough. His Islamic faith carried him to Afghanistan, where he helped fight the Soviet occupiers, an activity that clearly gave him a taste for jihad. A delicate line separates the terrorist who fights for practicable changes from those who fall into the kind of right and left wing utopianism that made twentieth-century Europe such an abattoir; bin Laden crossed that line at some point, perhaps during the early 1990s. He moved from wanting to chase U.S. troops off sacred soil and topple

*The Mahdi lived on in popular culture, inspiring the messianic Islamic leader in John Buchan's 1916 spy novel *Greenmantle*. His battle with Gordon is depicted in the watchable 1966 Hollywood epic *Khartoum*, starring Charlton Heston as the general and Laurence Olivier as the Mahdi, another of those blackface roles that brought out his taste for ham. Olivier's Mahdi is more Peter Sellers than Osama bin Laden.

the sullied Saudi government ("Arab leaders worship the God of the White House" was his verdict) to declaring holy war against the West, singling out America, and vowing to prepare the world for the true faith of Islam. And he backed up this dream with his money. He wasn't just a high priest of holy war, he was a princely financier.

As Osama's story became known, I half-expected to see a network banner, "Battle of the Trust Fund Leaders." In so many ways, bin Laden was the Arabian alter ego of George W. Bush. Both came from rich, powerful families—which did business together—in communities built on oil. Both put in time as party boys (Bush topped bin Laden) yet eventually discovered deep religious devotion (here, Osama was the winner). Most important, perhaps, both thought in terms of theological absolutes, the glossy black-and-white of the faithful and the damned. Yet for all these disconcerting similarities, bin Laden clearly felt far more comfortable in his historical role than did Bush, especially in the weeks after September 11. Where the President seemed physically uncomfortable, bin Laden's fey smile was the perfect riposte to Bush's cowboy scowl. While he's nearly six and a half feet tall and profusely bearded, his affect is feminine, refined, with "delicate Yemeni features" (as Fouad Ajami once described them) and a creepy air of preternatural calm. Unlike Bush, bin Laden *did* know what to do with his hands when speaking—holding up his long index finger like an ancient prophet—but his manner was unnervingly droopy, fraught with a rich kid's spoiled languor. He possessed an ominous Black Hole charisma that recalled the sociopath in the recent Japanese thriller *Cure* whose mere presence induces those he meets to commit murder and then kill themselves.

Yet if his aura was otherworldly, he was grounded enough to recognize that his war against the West would be partly a battle of images, which is why his dispatches were constantly being handed to Al-Jazeera. Never was this clearer than on the day that President Bush announced the beginning of war against the Taliban. Shortly after that speech, a bin Laden basement tape made it to the world's TV screens. Gaunt and ethereal in his camouflage jacket, he gazed downward as if saddened by the barbarity of American air attacks on Afghanistan, although the cave tape was made *before* one American bomb fell. No matter. Bin Laden acted the martyr, playing on decades-old Islamic grievances (some of them very real), specifically linked his "holy" mission to Iraq and the Palestinians, and finished by reaffirming his ultimate goal—a doomsday showdown between "the camp of the faithful" and "the camp of the infidels." In a final fillip, he calmly took a sip of water, to assure the world that he faced the prospect of mass death with divine equanimity.

Perhaps sensing bin Laden's power to inspire terror, the Bush administration did everything it could to chop him verbally down to size. The President spoke of him in dehumanized terms: Osama was the vermin we had to "smoke out of his hole," the annoying mosquito that forced us to "drain the swamp." For his part, Secretary of Defense Donald Rumsfeld blithely mispronounced Osama's surname as *bin Layden*, and continues to do so to this day. (Had Bush done that, we'd have thought he didn't know the correct way to say it; with Rumsfeld, it just sounded like exuberant contempt.) Still, none of this official deflation could compete with the media's way of treating bin Laden as a demonic celebrity, constantly checking in with such Osama-watchers as John Miller and Hugh Grant–haired Peter Bergen (who lucked out by having his book *Holy Terror, Inc.* in the oven) and portraying bin Laden with the hokiest rhetoric. While an *Economist* headline declared him "The Spider in the Web," *Newsweek* was busy sculpting his bust for the Bad Guys Hall of Fame: "In history's long list of villains, bin Laden will find a special place. He has no throne, nor armies, not even any real territory, aside from the rocky wastes of Afghanistan. But he has the power to make men willingly go to their deaths. . . . He is an unusual combination in the annals of hate, at once mystical and fanatical—and deliberate and efficient. . . ."

Or consider the following encomium: "He is the organizer of half that is evil and nearly all that is undetected. . . . He is a genius, a philosopher, an abstract thinker. He has a brain of the first order. He sits motionless, like a spider in the centre of its web, but that web has a thousand radiations, and he knows well every quiver of each of them. He does little himself. He only plans. But his agents are numerous and splendidly organized." Except that's not actually a description of bin Laden. It's Sherlock Holmes telling Dr. Watson about Professor Moriarty, the master criminal who thrilled late-Victorian audiences. Sir Arthur Conan Doyle knew how to paint a villain, and so does our media. In their hands, Osama was becoming the stuff of fiction, an archvillain whose resonance far surpassed Conan Doyle's humble Napoleon of Crime.

Nor was he a mere despot like Saddam Hussein, the Middle East's reigning exemplar of conventional wickedness. Saddam's was the crude, greedy evil that's easy to grasp. Any child can understand why a man might want to be so powerful that he could grab all the treasure, bed any woman he fancies, and build monuments to himself. Such lavish selfishness is comprehensible because it's an extension of our everyday desires. In contrast, bin Laden's curdled fundamentalism (not so far from the extremist Christian, Jewish, and Hindu variants) was America's worst nightmare—the enraged, murderous underbelly of Enlightenment ideas of progress and rationality. Where the West was materialistic, he devoted himself to the spiritual; where the West sought creature comforts, he proudly chose to be ascetic; where the West embraced sweet reason, he followed the lodestar of faith; where the West tolerated pluralistic points of view, he saw only one Islamic truth; where the West rejected death, he embraced it as a higher calling. Even his language rebuked ours: President Bush took pride in his homespun Texas vernacular, but bin Laden spoke a literary Arabic whose florid eloquence offered his followers proof that he'd been touched by the divine. You cannot buy off such a man, one who wants an Islamic paradise on earth; nor, it turned out, can you easily capture him. He proved so elusive, in fact, that the Bush administration began to find it embarrassing. The President went months at a time without mentioning his name.

Just as bin Laden was the antithesis of Western values, so his terrorist network was the decentered shadow of Western social organizations. Al-Qaeda knew that you could fight great nations or huge corporations only by shattering their self-confidence with the tools of asymmeterical warfare—suicide bombings, hijacked jetliners, and the fear of such things that proves more crippling than the deeds themselves. While both globalizing capitalists and anti-WTO demonstrators believed you could create a just, modern, secular society, bin Laden and al-Qaeda wanted to tear down modernity itself. They would destroy both the globalizers *and* the antiglobalizers. Now, *that* was being radical.

Redolent of death and destruction, Osama bin Laden came to symbolize uncontrollable madnesses, Third World contagions, and incomprehensible cruelties done in the name of the divine. That's why, in the first days of the October 2001 anthrax attack on the U.S. mail, most people figured al-Qaeda must be behind it. For Osama's brand of symbolic fear was also engendered by the deadly bacteria *Bacillus anthracis*, which could enter your body and lay you low without your ever knowing it happened. Who among us didn't open letters more warily in those days? In a society based on luminous ideas of rationality and control, the notion of an unseen disease striking the body may be even more terrifying than the sight of planes striking skyscrapers. You can refuse to fly, but you can't stop breathing. Anthrax was the incarnation of our unconscious fears, and the ensuing runamok paranoia about biochemical weapons (gas masks, Cipro, unopened mail in the dustbin) erupted into people's lives just as unbearable sexual fantasies once invaded the bottled-up psyches of Freud's patients. In Osama's demonic fundamentalism, so much of what we have repressed—chaos, madness, the drive toward death— returned with a literal vengeance. So one should not have been surprised that the American response to his violent handiwork should itself carry overtones of religion.

Media Fundamentalism

In the early aftermath of the terror attacks, when the networks weren't broadcasting newly purchased footage of those jets crashing into the towers, they struggled to find a way of making sense of what had happened. For a brief, unplanned moment, American television became educational, giving information about bin Laden, summarizing the violently bleak modern history of Afghanistan, even mentioning the anti-Western ideas of Wahhabism, the dominant strand of Islam in Saudi Arabia. Much of the American public found this riveting stuff, sitting themselves before the media altar hour after hour in hopes of finding meaning in the events of September 11. And rightly. If anything in recent history should have given cause for reflection, it was that terrible morning. Yet the eeriest feature of the media blitzkrieg was how quickly it morphed from honest shock to the higher brainwashing, the media fundamentalism that discourages real thinking.

Within forty-eight hours, Americans were being told how to mourn and how to fight back. CNN shifted its slogan from "America Attacked" to "America's New War" (even before there was one), and CBS changed its tagline to the supposedly inspirational "America Rising." ABC's website offered downloadable American flags, Kmart printed a full-page version of Old Glory in the Sunday *New York Times*; naturally, anchormen sported flag-pins on their lapels as digitalized stars-and-stripes waved in the corner of the screen. While we were ceaselessly bombarded with poll numbers announcing nearly 90 percent approval of a war effort, you heard no serious discussions of what exactly it might mean to fight a "war" against "terror." Not a soul commented on the tin ear displayed by the moniker "Operation Noble Eagle" (remember it?), a much-vaunted domestic antiterrorism initiative that sounded less like a call to arms than the title of a lesser Jackie Chan flick. And the pathos was as bullying as the flag-waving. Stories about New York firemen or cops who risked and lost their lives came accompanied by captions ("American Heroes"), as if we wouldn't realize their bravery unless we were told; whenever a volunteer did something to help a victim, the accompanying TV story would put up an explanatory tagline such as "Quiet Acts of Heroism." One afternoon I was listening to a radio interview with English journalist Robert Fisk, the last Westerner to interview bin Laden, who was explaining that, in person, the terrorist financier comes across as neither mad nor demonic. Abruptly, someone at the station cut him off: "As important as it is to understand those who may have perpetrated these attacks, it's equally important to remember the victims." The station then began talking to a man whose wife was killed in the attack. And this was on NPR.

Back in the mid-1970s, the great filmmaker Jean-Luc Godard observed that while a French TV network would be willing to give over an evening to a five-hour documentary on Maoism, it wouldn't broadcast ten half-hour programs on ten consecutive nights. Why? Because the long film could be treated as something special, *exceptionnel*, a TV event, whereas a nightly show would make thinking about Maoism appear normal. And that was not permitted. A similar logic took over in the post–September 11 media's coverage of September 11, which took an "exceptional" day and reduced it to a ritualized set of intellectual clichés and emotional postures—especially on television. Early on, mainstream networks decided to show as little carnage as possible, playing down images of dead bodies or people jumping from the twin towers; at the government's request, they refused to broadcast the al-Qaeda tapes that the rest of the world was watching, although today's dish-savvy terrorist surely prefers Al-Jazeera to anything owned by Rupert Murdoch. Like the bird in T. S. Eliot's "Burnt Norton," our media elite believes that humankind cannot bear very much reality.

Nor very much complexity. Far from encouraging open discussion of what happened and how the U.S. should deal with it (one waited in vain to hear from anybody to the left of Hillary Clinton), TV almost instantly began pushing the idea that there was a national consensus on how to react to the terror attacks—the only question was *when* the U.S. would go into Afghanistan. Part of this consensus was not asking troublesome questions. On a PBS special, *Looking for Answers*, reporter Lowell Bergman talked to various Middle Easterners who offered political reasons why many ordinary Muslims might feel some sympathy with Osama. Then he interviewed U.S. Deputy Secretary of State Richard Armitage, a balding blob of scowls who looked like Robert Duvall's Colonel Kilgore after a quarter century of Twinkies. When Bergman asked how he would respond to the political arguments of those in the Middle East, Armitage growled, "You're playing ball in their court. Don't play ball in their court." Meaning, there could be no discussion.

One day on CNN, *The Capital Gang*'s resident mad dog Robert Novak wiped away his mouth foam long enough to ask Christiane Amanpour if she was "optimistic" that President Bush could put together a coalition as his father had. "Well, I'm not optimistic or pessimistic," she replied wearily. That is, she was being a reporter, not a propagandist. But such moments were rare. In a country where skepticism is often confused with cynicism, networks were terrified of appearing heartless, if not unpatriotic. Naturally, such delicacy didn't stop corporate bigwigs from using the sudden spike in ratings to launch new talent, like MSNBC's ill-starred attempts to turn groovy-glasses gal Ashley Banfield into a star, maybe even a replacement for smug Brian Williams and his Amazing Tilted Head. But it did mean that you heard no serious debate on big topics: Should Congress have passed the USA Patriot Act? Should the U.S. invade Afghanistan or start bombing Kabul, a city that already looked like a sand-wrapped village from the original *Star Wars*? In fact, one of the few passionate and detailed arguments I heard after September 11 came on ESPN Radio, whose guests disagreed strongly about whether the NFL should cancel its games or fill its stadiums with people chanting, "USA! USA! USA!"—assuming that, naturally, everyone there would want to.

During the Iraq war, when questioned about the mood of the Iraqi people, Donald Rumsfeld would always reply, "There is no 'Iraqi people.' There are only people in Iraq." While this facile formula let him refuse to answer how U.S. troops were being greeted, he was right—and the same is true here. The media reflexively falls into homogenizing language—"All of America mourns today . . ."—yet it's far too convenient to assume that Americans speak with one voice. We don't, even when we're trying to. Ten days after the attacks, all the major networks simulcasted the *Tribute to Heroes* telethon, a glumly sequestered event during which stars like Tom Cruise and Julia Roberts showed up in turtlenecks and NYFD caps to raise money for the victims of September 11. At the end of the show, everyone got together to sing "America the Beautiful," and it became clear that many of the celebrities had to be fed the lines. An offscreen prompter was desperately muttering, "Crown thy good."

You could almost hear William Bennett going, "Typical." Even as the TV networks were genuflecting before the idea of patriotic unity, while still milking images of the falling towers like a prize Guernsey, many self-styled high priests of virtue treated September 11 as a verdict on our national morality. That down-home Torquemada Jerry Falwell notoriously blamed the attacks on all "the pagans, and the abortionists, and the feminists, and the gays and the lesbians who are actively trying to make that an alternative lifestyle, the ACLU, People for the American Way, all of them who have tried to secularize America." This was so bonkers that Bush rushed to disavow it, yet Falwell was not alone in his sanctimony. A few days later, *Time* ran an essay, "The Age of Irony Comes to an End," by veteran sermonizer Roger Rosenblatt, who managed to find a silver lining in the deadly terrorist attacks on New York and Washington. America, he wrote, might enter "a new and chastened time" in which people would no longer believe that "detachment and personal whimsy were the necessary tools for an oh-so-cool life." Of course, if anyone on this planet ever deserved an irony enema, it's Rosenblatt, a former Harvard professor who now plays the Troubled Conscience of America for *Time* and PBS. Yet in the days that followed, I kept reading people who seemed to agree with him, be it *Vanity Fair*'s sleek editor Graydon Carter, who also came to bury an Age of Irony he'd clearly been happier praising, or *Newsday*'s conservative columnist James Pinkerton, aglint with grim satisfaction: "*Seinfeld* won't disappear, of course; it'll be rerun, somewhere, forever. But everyone now knows that there's more to life than nothing, that some things really matter." Thanks for clearing that up. Behind all these people you could hear the scolding voice of such well-paid Jeremiahs as Bennett and Tom Brokaw, who'd spent so much time flogging his own bestseller that he'd obviously started believing that he was *part* of the Greatest Generation.

These were the guys who had spent the previous decade refurbishing the old America-as-Decadent-Rome analogy—you know, the country had become so permissive and relativistic and trivial that its citizens would fall to pieces in the first stiff wind. They were wrong on two counts. Despite America's love of scandal (O.J., Monica, Gary

Condit) and fondness for *Who Wants to Be a Millionaire?*, such silliness hardly called down the attack on the World Trade Center and Pentagon. Al-Qaeda has no qualms about murdering devout Muslims in Istanbul or Jakarta who've never heard of Britney Spears. Anyway, it's not as if we had been given a fateful choice—"Would you rather watch *Survivor* or stop bin Laden from killing 3,000 people?"—and couldn't tear ourselves away from the next immunity challenge. Say what you want against *Seinfeld,* it is no more trivial than the radio escapades of Fibber McGee and Molly that my folks listened to during World War II. And no more corrupting: Lightheartedness is the saving flip-side of our national sense of rectitude. When the big moment came on September 11, most ordinary Americans behaved with admirable courage; it was Prince Hal who flew to Nebraska. The firemen raced into the danger just like their grandfathers on D-Day; brave civilians died helping one another escape the World Trade Center; hearing what was going on, the passengers on United Airlines Flight 93 tried to take back the airplane. These people hadn't been ruined by the sixties or the immoral Bill Clinton (given the geographical location of the attacks, many probably voted for him); no fireman refused to do his job because he'd been crippled by irony or was busy daydreaming about J.Lo. So much for the sick soul of America. As the British demonstrated during the Blitz, you can fight the enemy and be ironic at the very same time; in fact, humor helped keep things bearable when the bombs were hitting London. Only dullards think you must be earnest to be serious.

One of the most touching things in the weeks after September 11 was watching late-night comics figuring out how to reflect the national mood. David Letterman donned a paternal gravitas, an obviously shaken Conan O'Brien urged kids not to be cynical, and brainy Jon Stewart had an emotional meltdown. You couldn't blame them. Faced with death and destruction, they felt that making the usual jokes was obscene. They were just being decent. On his first show back on the air, Letterman was widely admired for his reassuring dignity—he struck the right tone. Yet even as he treated the attacks with deadly seriousness, he didn't so much help viewers understand them as certify their incomprehensibility: "They say that the terrorists were motivated by religious fervor," he said in his most admired line of the night. "If you live to be a thousand years old, will that make any goddamn sense?" Well, yes. The history of religion is inseparable from the history of righteous murder. And to think Dave's famous for being *cynical*.

Still, it would be unfair to single out Letterman's bafflement. All over America people were talking about the need to "understand" what had happened, but it was unsettling to realize what many of them meant. A week after the attacks, three of the six bestselling books at Amazon.com were about Nostradamus, e-mails zipped around the country explaining that the attacks were mystically linked to the number 11, and folks kept finding Osama's face (or was it Satan's?) in the World Trade Center smoke. Not that nonbelievers like myself were innocent of magical thinking. Following the attacks, I obsessively sifted through data, somehow believing that if I paid close enough attention, the next piece of information would bring revelation. I stared at each new shot of Mohammed Atta's grim visage, logged on to the alarmist Israeli website Debka.com (which was accurate just often enough to keep you coming back), and pondered the theological significance of jihad-inspired pilots running up tabs in a Florida strip bar. Each time a new factual shard was uncovered—some of the bombers came from San Diego! bin Laden has a limp!—I'd file it away in my head, building my shield against mortality. So much for the belief that being "Western" automatically protects you from being steeped in medieval stupefaction.

Then again, none of this was hardly surprising. In keeping with the logic of Bush World, the media were encouraging all of us to think mythologically about 9/11:

- You kept hearing that *America had been changed forever.* That sounded more convincing back when Ground Zero was still burning than it did two years later when cable TV grew fixated on the trial of Martha Stewart, Congress failed to appropriate enough antiterrorism funds for police and fire departments, and SUV sales boomed despite the proven perils of relying on Middle Eastern oil.

- People kept saying that *America had lost its innocence*, always an odd claim to make of a nation founded by immigrants who stole the continent, grew prosperous through slavery, picked a fight with Mexico to get California, fought a Civil War, withstood the shock of Pearl Harbor, dropped the atom bomb, and endured McCarthyism, the Kennedy assassination, the War in Vietnam, Watergate, and Florida 2000. In fact, on September 11, America lost not its imaginary innocence but its very real, if illusory, feeling of invulnerability.*

- There was the peculiar belief that *9/11 was an exclusively* American *event.* Yes, the jetliners *did* attack New York City and Washington, D.C., targeting buildings that symbolized (or the terrorists thought symbolized) the United States' commercial and military power. Yet September 11's shock waves went around the world. Not only did hundreds of foreign nationals and foreign-born immigrants die— the attack was on a *World* Trade Center, after all—but the attack has changed lives in Kabul and Jakarta, Singapore and Karachi, Sydney and Madrid. This is something that Americans, obsessed with our own losses, still find it difficult to remember. Even as our government asked (or dragooned) other countries into joining a War on Terror against a common enemy, we too often ignored our allies' suffering. The day the bomb went off outside the Jakarta Marriott, killing fourteen, its coverage was dwarfed by Kobe Bryant's seven-minute appearance in the courtroom where he spoke barely a handful of words.

- Most dangerous of all was the myth that *the United States was attacked because it is Good.* No one was more responsible for this than George W. Bush, who not only described the battle against al-Qaeda as "good versus evil" but explained the September 11 attack in much the same way: "They hate our freedoms: our freedom of

*America's love affair with its own innocence has been well-tweaked by contemporary novelists. James Ellroy's *American Tabloid* opens with the lines, "America was never innocent. We popped our cherry on the boat over and looked back with no regrets."

religion, our freedom of speech, our freedom to vote and assemble and disagree with each other." Now, this is not altogether wrong. Al-Qaeda *is* dangerously evil in its doctrine of divinely inspired murder. Militant Islam *does* have a strong fascistic tendency that abhors the values of democratic pluralism, values that I would certainly call good. And one *should* fight fundamentalist murder with every available weapon. But as the French critic Roland Barthes once pointed out, a myth isn't a lie but an inflection—a way of angling the truth—and the President's attitude encouraged Americans to feel morally superior without helping us understand Osama, al-Qaeda, or Islamic terrorism. After all, if these evildoers simply wanted to attack a "good" nation, why not go after Canada or New Zealand? Those countries have free speech and real elections. The answer, of course, is these countries did not spearhead the 1953 toppling of the elected Iranian leader Mossadegh; they do not have empires whose tendrils extend all over the world, sell high-tech armaments to repressive Arab regimes, operate Air Force bases near Mecca, or boast Israel as a client state; they do not symbolize globalization. The United States does. All that, rather than its virtue, is what made it a target.

In the days when September 11 was hardening into 9/11, merely pointing out such things was enough to make you a whipping boy for media fundamentalists, who twisted such words to suggest that you condoned the murder of American civilians. Perhaps no single response to the attacks earned more hostility than Susan Sontag's words in *The New Yorker:*

> Where is the acknowledgment that this was not a "cowardly" attack on "civilization" or "liberty" or "humanity" or "the free world" but an attack on the world's self-proclaimed superpower, undertaken as a consequence of specific American alliances and actions? . . . The unanimously applauded, self-congratulatory bromides of a Soviet Party Congress seemed contemptible. The unanimity of the sanctimonious, reality-concealing rheto-

ric spouted by American officials and media commentators in recent days seems, well, unworthy of a mature democracy. . . . Let's by all means grieve together. But let's not be stupid together. A few shreds of historical awareness might help us understand what has just happened, and what may continue to happen. "Our country is strong," we are told again and again. I for one don't find this entirely consoling. Who doubts that America is strong? But that's not all America has to be.

Given that they were still pulling bodies from the rubble, you can understand why many readers were put off—the piece sounded heartless and smug, and was not as finely tuned as one might hope (the word "consequence" is a tricky one). But you had to wonder why such words would prompt *The Weekly Standard* to launch a "Susan Sontag Award" for political stupidity or why *The New Republic* would write such loaded sentences as "What do Osama bin Laden, Saddam Hussein and Susan Sontag have in common?" After all, Sontag was neither saying that the United States "deserved" to be attacked (whatever that might mean) nor that the terrorists had been entitled to indiscriminately slaughter thousands of people. Rather, her complaint was over the way the media and government were busily balling up the vast, delicate interlacing of history into the coarser stuff of public myth—mythology that could be used to push American political life farther to the right by creating what C. Wright Mills once called "an emergency without a foreseeable end."*

Put Out More Flags

"America did not change on September 11," wrote the neoconservative pundit Robert Kagan in his nifty little book *Of Paradise and Power*. "It

---

*Two years later, in his belated pro-freedom speeches about Iraq, President Bush himself began suggesting that the United States had spent too long backing undemocratic regimes in the Middle East—implying (à la Sontag) that there *is* a connection between American policies and international terror.

only became more itself." That was easy for him to say. From the beginning, it was obvious that that terrible day was going to be a boon to the political right, especially those like Kagan, who advocated an aggressive U.S. foreign policy. The attacks turned the President into a wartime leader and tapped into Americans' traditional belief that Republicans are the defenders of national security. Naturally, Bush exploited the public's newborn fear and patriotism, and we shouldn't get priggish about it. Politicians learn to turn everything, even tragedy, to advantage. It's their job. And the White House did it well. Bush's publicity team loved all the talk about lost innocence, good versus evil, and the President's triumphant star turn as Prince Hal maturing overnight into Henry V. They were all for anything that might distract Americans from the backstory of 9/11, which had (to say the least) its embarrassments, including the financial connections between the Bush family and the House of Saud, Reagan and Bush I's support of Saddam Hussein (which eventually led to two wars, one for each George Bush), and the administration's own slipshod performance before and during the attacks. Far better to emphasize images of Bush with a bullhorn on the rubble at Ground Zero telling the rescue teams, "I hear you." Such moments worked wonders, and within days, the attacks gave the President such a boost that you could almost see why so many conspiracy theorists were hellbent on proving that the White House was actually behind them.

During normal times, most Americans scarcely notice the President's cohorts. Do you remember the name of Clinton's Secretary of Defense? But in the weeks after 9/11, television offered a parade of government officials who appeared to be contestants in an all-politico edition of *American Idol.* Some did splendidly. Mayor Rudy Giuliani, who was never more human than during the calamity, went from sanctimonious jerk and adulterer to national hero—though in the TV movie, he still got played by James Woods, the cockroach Olivier. Secretary of State Colin Powell, MIA during the early months when Bush's unilateralism was insulting the whole world, found his star reascending when the administration needed a plausible front man for alliance building. An even gaudier arc was traced by Secretary of

Defense Rumsfeld, whose career was resurrected after the attack on the Pentagon, when he physically helped with the rescue effort, and would skyrocket when the Afghanistan war revealed his genius as a briefing-room slam-poet. Less fortunate was well-meaning Tom Ridge, whose friendly-bulldog face made him look like J. Edgar Hoover's son (with Clyde Tolson?). But Ridge lacked the old FBI tyrant's bark, let alone his bite: The Department of Homeland Security was known for little beyond logo-unveiling ceremonies and color-coded alerts that made the public jumpy without giving it any practical advice. Yet even he fared better than Tommy Thompson, the Secretary of Health and Human Services, whose uncanny Homer Simpson impression during the anthrax scare—he claimed the first victim had died from drinking funny Carolina springwater—promptly got him yanked off TV.

The most sinister figure of the bunch was Wyoming-born Dick Cheney, erstwhile reactionary congressman, Secretary of Defense for George H. W. Bush, and CEO of Halliburton Industries—in short, the military-industrial complex made flesh. Holding an office that FDR's vice president, John Nance Garner, once compared to "a bucket of warm piss," he seemed unable to decide whether he was Mr. Clean or Dr. Evil, one of the few pop-culture figures that Bush is known to enjoy. Cheney had gotten his big political break when, in 1969, Rumsfeld hired him as his right-hand man at the Office of Economic Opportunity. He seized this opportunity to become Rummy's ideal Number Two—loyal, efficient, and as terse as his boss was loquacious. Ever since, part of the Cheney mystique is that he's the acme of hard-nosed competence, a soft-spoken man, his voice as low and dry as a disused well in Death Valley, who can fire up an underperforming bureaucracy the way Steve McQueen could hot-wire a motorcycle. Even better, he was reckoned a great, levelheaded advisor with a pro-found commitment to *omertà*. Think Tom Hagen in *The Godfather*. (In Showtime's inept *D.C. 9/11: Time of Crisis*, Bush tells Cheney, "I'm going to need you at my side at all times, *consigliere*." The Veep beams.)

As George H. W. Bush's Secretary of Defense, this cautious man advised his president not to overthrow Saddam Hussein at the end of Operation Desert Storm. That's one reason why "Poppy" was so happy when young Dubya chose him as his running mate. This loyal family retainer would help keep his hotheaded son out of trouble the way Cheney had kept himself out of serving in Vietnam because, though a hawk, Cheney had "other priorities." But here the elder Bush made a serious mistake. Having himself lived a charmed life, he failed to understand the riptides of thwarted ambition that tear at any politician who devotes years to deference. His own Tom Hagen, James Baker III, bristled with resentment at having to save Bush I from his own political ineptitude; he saw himself, wrongly, as a future president, not somebody else's go-to guy. Something deep in Cheney rebelled at playing second fiddle to a dabbler like George W. Bush who didn't know or even care all that much about governing. Far from serving as a steady éminence grise, he became an intimidating Veep who surrounded the President with the equivalent of a praetorian guard that kept dissenting opinions out of the loop. "That's the way Dick likes it," former Secretary of the Treasury Paul O'Neill told *60 Minutes*.

Cheney's doom-laden view of life as a dog-eat-dog struggle (like Alan Simpson, he's a Wyoming Hobbesian) was at best a mixed blessing for the administration, where he became the leading figure in the country's foreign policy. It was Cheney who was running Halliburton in the 1990s when its subsidiaries were doing business with Saddam Hussein (he claimed he didn't know), who launched his own do-nothing antiterrorism task force before 9/11 (thereby ignoring the existing proposals of the Hart-Rudman Commission), who sparked a bad-publicity firestorm when he not only sneered at energy conservation as "personal virtue" but blamed California's energy woes on environmentalists and government meddling, when energy companies had actually been fixing prices. Here is a man who always puts the rich first. When O'Neill doubted the wisdom of the second big tax cut for the well-off, a policy about which Bush himself expressed second thoughts, the Vice President replied, "Reagan proved that deficits don't matter. We won the midterm elections. This is our due." One could write a book on who he's referring to with that "we" and "our." As Daffy Duck once shrieked, "Pronoun trouble!"

None of this means that Cheney is especially skillful at business.

During his time at Halliburton, he made ambitious deals—including the acquisition of a firm with asbestos-lawsuit liabilities—that wound up damaging the company. Although shareholders have benefited a bit from the crony capitalist side of having their former CEO be vice president, *Slate*'s "Moneybox" columnist Daniel Gross concluded, "American citizens must hope they avoid the fate of Halliburton shareholders: at first glad to have the experienced Cheney at the top, then excited about his ambitious plans, and finally, dismayed to be left holding the bag when Cheney moves on to another job." Iraq, anyone?

On no issue was Cheney more hard-nosed than the Iraq war, where his opinion occupied front and center. In the early days of the administration, he was one of those who insisted that the greatest threat against America came from rogue nations with long-distance nukes—a claim that justified spending a fortune on missile defense. Then, having something of a conversion experience after September 11, he did the unthinkable: He began seeking advice from intellectuals. He took a crash course in Islam and the Middle East, getting advice from Bernard Lewis and Fouad Ajami, two scholars known for believing that the once-glorious Muslim world needed to be remade and that overthrowing Saddam would be a terrific start. Dick Cheney listening to eggheads—and trusting them! Long before the war, Cheney was shuttling around the Middle East trying to secure support for the invasion (nobody jumped aboard); during the run-up to battle, Cheney's office pooh-poohed intelligence suggesting that Saddam was not so dangerous and highlighted evidence that he was; after things had started to sour, he turned up on *Meet the Press* to imply that there were connections between Saddam and 9/11—a claim that, later the same week, Bush himself would explicitly disavow. He continued to take money from Halliburton even after the the U.S. government gave it a huge contract in Iraq. More than anyone else in the Bush administration, even Paul Wolfowitz, Cheney was responsible for making the conquest and rebuilding of Iraq sound easier than it actually would be. For all we know, he may still be expecting that hero's welcome when he blows into Baghdad. Each time he emerged from the shadows, you understood why he'd been wise to spend most of his career there.

Still, in the first months of the Bush administration, Cheney's half-faced smile made him appear enough of a hard-ass that many assumed he was the real president, captaining the ship of state by remote control while Bush sat at the helm listening to a Texas Rangers game. Appearing on *Meet the Press* five days after the attacks, he seemed to think so, too; after years of dutiful deference, he suddenly seemed stricken by Alexander Haig Disease. Then he vanished to an "undisclosed location," eventually becoming the spookiest vice president in our history. Where earlier vice presidents traditionally struggled in vain just to get office space in the White House—Walter Mondale became the first, in 1976—the secretive Cheney spent the years after 9/11 hiding in unknown rabbit holes, periodically popping out for fundraisers (he was a star on that circuit) or to say things that would keep the public in a malleable state of anxiety. He said that the War on Terror could last fifty years and that it was "inevitable" there would be another attack as bad as September 11. He beat the drum for war with Iraq by deliberately overstating evidence of Saddam's capacities and then, when these WMDs were not found, attacked those who dared question the administration's inflated claims of Iraq's danger. Employing one of those fake oppositions that define the Bush years, he suggested that if you weren't for the Iraq war you were against fighting terrorism. Even more than Rumsfeld, he's cursed with an oppressive sense of his own rightness.

In early 2004, Cheney began making public appearances, hoping to change the widespread perception that our Veep is spooky. But by then, he'd long since turned himself into one of Bush World's sickest jokes. *Saturday Night Live*'s Darrell Hammond played him as a maniac prone to bursts of mad glee. Eminem gleefully pretended to electrocute him with a defibrillator in his nose-thumbing video "Without Me." In a *Village Voice* parody that cast Hillary Clinton as Harry Potter, Cheney even turned up as a giant serpent who lived in the Hogwarts' drainage pipes: "His voice sounded like an iceberg in a sewer." Mocked if not reviled, Cheney served his president by becoming a lightning rod for criticism, a reality that in no way diminished his power: Asked about which members of his team would return for a second term, the

President responded simply: "Cheney, for sure." His dark mutterings had Bush's ear, and he used his influence to override the advice of both Colin Powell and Condoleezza Rice, whose calmer rhetoric had less purchase on a president whose own mind occasionally heard the angel choirs of The Rapture. (And to think that Cheney's wife, Lynne, is the scary one.)

When the Vice President suggested that the War on Terror could go on indefinitely—Rice termed it a "generational commitment"—he wasn't making a prediction but laying the template of U.S. policy and the administration's orchestration of fear to ensure continued power. The strategy harked back to the very origins of the Cold War, when the Republican Senator Arthur Vandenberg advised Harry Truman that to get extra funding for military expenditures from a war-weary populace, he'd need to "scare hell out of the American people." Truman did, and it worked. In a similar way, the Bush team quickly grasped that the terror attacks brought out the conservatism in most Americans—not the doctrinaire modern conservatism that yearns to privatize Social Security and ban abortion, but the visceral conservatism that's terrified of losing its way of life. They played to this desire to keep everything the same. F. Scott Fitzgerald famously said, "The test of a first-rate intelligence is the ability to hold two opposed ideas in mind at the same time and still retain the ability to function." One can imagine genuinely great leaders calling on America to display this ability, to both fight the proponents of Islamic fascism *and* examine ourselves to see what this country might have done to invite such attacks. Such a large-souled response might have eventually made the United States a greater nation. But the administration offered something far less noble, and as usual, it took the form of a bogus opposition. "We have two choices," said Rumsfeld with customary briskness: "Either we change the way *we* live, or we must change the way *they* live. We choose the latter." It would never occur to the administration to suggest that we do both.

Of course, preserving "the way *we* live" meant using the patriotism fueled by September 11 to promote the Bush administration and its agenda. On ABC's *This Week*, George Will lectured us on the patriotic need for corporate tax cuts. The White House pushed through funds for the "Star Wars" missile defense system, which wouldn't have saved a single life on September 11 but had been a pet right-wing project since the Reagan years. The Republican National Committee used photographs of the President aboard Air Force One on 9/11 as a fundraising tool (one wonders which direction he was flying) and pushed back the date of their 2004 convention so that Bush could be renominated in New York City in September and get that 9/11 bounce. Even worse, that tragic day became a trump card whenever the President needed to justify preemptive war on Iraq or counter a slide in his popularity numbers: "You know," he said grumpily in August of 2003 as things got messy in Iraq, "the American people should suspect that this administration will do what is necessary to win the war on terror. That's my pledge to the American people. They have got to understand that I will not forget the lessons of September 11. And these lessons are loud and clear: that there are people who want to inflict harm on the American people." True enough. Yet did even Ann Coulter seriously think a Democratic president would have tolerated the 9/11 attacks ("Do that again, and we're going to be *really mad*") or refused to protect the American people from fundamentalist murderers? Everybody knew this was serious business. But it was part of the right's tactic after September 11 not only to wrap itself in the flag but imply others were coming at it with scissors. When Senator Majority Leader Tom Daschle ventured a few modest criticisms of the President's handling of the War on Terror, then-Minority Leader Trent Lott assailed him for doing so when "we have boys in the field."

The left, with its usual genius for lunging into sucker punches, made questioning their love of country a bit too easy. Although conservatives have no greater claim to patriotism than do liberals, they feel much more comfortable with its symbols. The flag-waving orgy that followed September 11 didn't just drive many on the left nuts, it prompted them to say so out loud, often with a whiff of snobbery toward those who take Old Glory seriously. Writing in *The Nation*, Katha Pollitt told us that, when her teenage daughter wanted to hang a flag out the window, she refused, saying that "the flag stands for jingoism and vengeance and war." (She's evidently never needed to find a U.S. embassy in a dangerous country.) Even worse, a handful of high-profile comments on the terror attacks didn't merely "blame America first" (to use the abusive cliché favored by the right) but betrayed a staggering rhetorical blindness. Talking to *CounterPunch*, Noam Chomsky did Mr. Spock to a T: "The September 11 attacks were major atrocities. In terms of number of victims they do not reach the level of many others, for example, Clinton's bombing of the Sudan with no credible pretext, destroying half its pharmaceutical supplies and probably killing tens of thousands of people (no one knows, because the US blocked an inquiry at the UN and no one cares to pursue it). Not to speak of much worse cases, which easily come to mind." It didn't occur to him that, if you want to win Americans over to your cause, you don't take the most horrifying event of their lives and instantly add, "But . . ."

The vast majority of people on the left supported action against al-Qaeda—"Clearly, considerable use of force will have to be used to capture these motherfuckers," said Doug Henwood, publisher and editor of *Left Business Observer*—and began discussing the best ways to fight Islamic fundamentalism. But you wouldn't have known this from the conservative feeding frenzy each time some artist/celebrity like Oliver Stone or the Indian novelist Arundhati Roy said something fatuous. The right poured suspicion on anything that deviated from their official line; as if fear of terrorism wasn't bad enough, one had to worry about being branded unpatriotic. Daniel Pipes's egregious organization Campus Watch, which boasts the daunting slogan "Monitoring Middle East Studies on Campus," was busy singling out supposedly subversive teachers. Conservative journalist-turned-blogger Andrew Sullivan raised the specter of a decadent "fifth column" on the left, revealing vastly less tolerance for those who disagree with him about terrorism than he expects the Roman Catholic church to show his own minority views (correct ones, I would add) about sanctioning homosexuality. *Politically Incorrect*'s Bill Maher, whose radicalism largely stops at hanging out with Hugh Hefner, got in trouble for suggesting that earlier attempts to deal with Osama through missiles were "cowardly." Ari Fleischer scolded him with the chilling words "There are reminders to all Americans that they need to watch what they say, watch what they do, and this is not a time for remarks like that; there never is."

One might have thought the omnipotent left was somehow frog-marching the country toward capitulation or that the woman sitting at Bush's side in all those photographs was Alice Walker, not Condoleezza Rice. Even poor Al Gore, who'd simply been cheated in an election and then kept his mouth shut, found himself being slapped down. This process reached a surreal pinnacle of insolence in the October 20, 2001, *New York Times*, which devoted an entire article to suggesting that even Gore's biggest supporters were glad that Bush had been elected. Reporter Richard Berke quoted unnamed Gore backers who suggested, among others things, that the ex-Veep "may know too much" about foreign policy to manage a war properly. What a failing: to know too much. When Al saw this in the pages of the *Times*, the shock must have splintered him into 10,000 toothpicks.

Even allowing for hysteria after September 11, the assault on dissent was clearly an opportunistic shadow-play by a right wing eager to suggest that those who oppose the White House were threatening the security of the American people. Meanwhile, in the real world of power, the realm of congressional votes and mass media coverage, things were going just as the Bush administration wanted. The war in Afghanistan went ahead with no great protest. The Democrats bowed down before the President's agenda, giving money to the "Star Wars" system—the defense establishment was delighted—and bailing out the airlines. It didn't hurt that Senate leader Tom Daschle's wife was an air industry lobbyist. In the surest sign that American policy was being shaped by fear, Washington raced through passage of the preposterously acronymed USA Patriot Act (as in Uniting and Strengthening America by Providing Appropriate Tools Required to Intercept and Obstruct Terrorism), a 342-page document whose unconstitutional niceties Congress barely had time to scan, let alone ponder. It sailed through the Senate with only one Nay vote—we salute you, Russell Feingold.

America had entered the age of Homeland Security, a phrase so fraught with totalitarian overtones that one didn't know whether to howl with anger, fear, or laughter, especially when a full two years later, the nation's firemen and policemen were saying they still lacked the necessary budget and planning for another big terrorist attack. But that was later. In the weeks after September 11, the administration hoped to reassure people with the manly presence of the new head of Homeland Security. As a White House aide put it, "We want to brand Tom Ridge. When people see him, we want them to think, 'My babies are safe.'" But some marketing campaigns come to naught; some brands are stronger than others. Without anyone really wanting it, the symbol of Homeland Security became the U.S. Attorney General, who was not a man to make anyone feel secure.

The Witchfinder General

No member of the administration has inspired more active dislike than John Ashcroft, a man eager to break down the barrier between church and state while standing for what's worst in both of them. That oddest of creatures, a boring zealot, he's the most visible of the Republican fundamentalists who, when not depositing campaign checks from the crooks at Enron, calling Confederate soldiers "patriots," or wheeling victims' families in to witness the execution of Timothy McVeigh in the name of "closure," spend their days fretting over other people's sins. One of the funniest parts of his confirmation hearings was listening to GOP senators bending over backward to insist that the newly dappered-up Ashcroft isn't really a bad guy. Why, he even has a sense of humor.

This isn't altogether false. Although his beliefs are those of a right-wing extremist, Ashcroft, who hails from Springfield, Missouri, has a sociable side recognizable to those of us who grew up in small, conservative midwestern communities: He's the local church's overbearing deacon who tries to get along with people to save them from damnation. He makes corny, self-deprecating jokes. A music lover, he's played the piano on *Letterman*, joined his fellow Singing Senators in crooning "Elvira" along with the Oak Ridge Boys, and been seen singing one of his own compositions, "Let the Eagle Soar," of which the less heard the better. To humanize himself, he confided to CBS's

Sunday Morning that he's a big fan of *The Simpsons*, saying, "I like the irreverence." Maybe at home, but his customary killjoy demeanor recalls the pithy verdict of the English historian Macaulay: "The Puritan hated bearbaiting, not because it gave pain to the bear, but because it gave pleasure to the spectators."*

Nobody ever expected that Ashcroft, distinguished for little more than his ideological manias, would become a regular on American television. Certainly not the Bush White House. After pulling off the feat of losing his Senate seat to a dead man, he had been named Attorney General as payback to the Christian right for backing Bush in the 2000 election. The President had wanted to appoint former Montana governor Marc Racicot, now chairman of the Republican National Committee, but Karl Rove had put the kibosh on that. The son of a Pentecostal preacher, Ashcroft was a true evangelical. On being sworn in as Attorney General, he was anointed with Crisco (by Clarence Thomas) in the manner of King David. Once ensconced in the Justice Department, he not only held prayer meetings, but two statues, the female Spirit of Justice (for years known fondly as Minnie Lou) and the male Majesty of Law, were covered with blue draping to hide their indelicate parts. Best of all, he could be counted on to say intolerant things about homosexuality ("I believe that the Bible calls it a sin and that's enough for me"), sic the feds on Oregon's assisted-suicide program, and make a big show of cracking down on vice. As an unquestioned right-to-lifer, he gives the administration credibility on that issue, even as Bush, like Reagan before him, pointedly doesn't try to ban abortion. If Ashcroft represented a nod to the hard right, he also served as a certified extremist that the President could use to establish his own moderation on issues that might get him into trouble; his presence let Bush triangulate against his own attorney general. This was a key reason Dubya put him there in the first place. And Ashcroft,

---

*Ashcroft's fondness for *The Simpsons* shows the mercurial nature of pop culture. In the early nineties, the Christian right attacked the show for being immoral and subversive. But as the years went by, these detractors began to realize that it is not only funny and fair-minded—an equal-opportunity mocker—but in its cockeyed way has always shown an abiding faith in family values.

too, must have thought it a dream appointment. Although he paid lip service to battling terrorism early in his term, he actually refused requests for extra agents and resources to battle the threat. He had other plans. He would nibble away at abortion rights, battle gun control, minimize antitrust prosecutions (his DoJ went soft on his ex-contributor Microsoft), deemphasize civil rights laws, and employ federal muscle to crack down on sin. He backed a highly publicized sting on a Big Easy prostitution ring and sought to censor things he found offensive.*

All that changed when he suddenly became responsible for protecting American citizens against terrorists. Although Ashcroft says he likes having the ball when the game's on the line, his first appearances after September 11 didn't show it. You could feel (and even feel for) his dread and inadequacy. On the day he announced the first terrorism alert, he approached the lectern with the slumped shoulders, Doonesbury eyes, and white lips of a man who expects the alien to jump out of his belly any second. Nothing he said was nearly as terrifying as his body language, and at that moment, anyway, I empathized with him. Exuding hemorrhoidal despair, here was a limited man facing what appeared to be a limitless task: protecting U.S. citizens against a ruthless unknown enemy. After that disconcerting performance, which sapped the nation's confidence, one felt sure that Bush would quietly set him up with a cushy professorship at Bob Jones University. But again and again, there he was on the tube justifying the Bush administration's whittling away of constitutional rights—refusing to name detainees, eavesdropping on prisoners' conversations with lawyers, creating military tribunals in a presidential directive so slipshod that the rest of the so-called civilized world was shocked. The one right the Attorney General fiercely protected involved the ownership of guns, which he apparently considers the highest law: He even

*Sometimes you could sympathize. In the summer of 2003, the Justice Department went after the company that produced a video, *Ass Clowns #3: The Director's Cut*, which featured Christ coming down from the cross to sodomize an angel. Such a heroic use of free speech makes one proud to be an American.

kept the FBI from examining the gun-purchase records of illegal immigrants. You have your favorite amendment to the Bill of Rights; Ashcroft and the NRA have theirs. (At times the right's attitude toward civil rights resembled a joke cooked up by *The Daily Show.* Back in March 2003, Justice Antonin Scalia, the intellectual Freddie Kruger of Supreme Court conservatives, went to Cleveland to accept the local City Club's "Citadel of Free Speech Award." Demonstrating his love for the First Amendment, he banned broadcast media from his speech and refused to answer any questions from reporters.)

Along with an assistant attorney general, Vict Dinh, Ashcroft sired the USA Patriot Act, which gave the federal government unprecedented new power to secretly round up suspects, hold them indefinitely without charge, and "sneak and peek" into people's private lives (phone calls, credit-card bills, library records, even their homes) by invoking national security in a special closed court. Bad as this was, things would have been much worse had Ashcroft been allowed to run as wild as he desired. In his massive, thorough, breathtakingly anal *After: How America Confronted the September 12 Era*, Steven Brill shows how the Attorney General's initial proposals were so nakedly repressive (suspending habeas corpus!) that they stunned even Republican congressmen and White House staffers, none of whom he'd bothered to consult as he laid waste to the Constitution. Like many others, they were unnerved by the "frustrated and panic-stricken" Ashcroft (to use the words of conservative columnist William Safire), whose zeal kept running away with him. His proposals became so radical that the right itself had to slow him down. It was the wacko Texan Dick Armey, then the House Majority Leader, who helped lead the fight against the proposed Operation TIPS, a Stalin-worthy scheme designed to get millions of Americans reporting on one another to the authorities. It was the White House that intervened when Ashcroft, visiting Moscow, decided to personally announce the arrest of terror suspect Jose Padilla, claiming "We have disrupted an unfolding terrorist plot to attack the United States by exploding a radioactive 'dirty bomb.'" Aghast at such extreme language, the President's men tried to get him to soften claims that were both exaggerated and alarmist. The

Attorney General seemed to miss the point. While it was politically useful for the public to live with a low-level hum of fear—such things induce support for a sitting president—you didn't win swing voters by scaring them silly (not two years before the next election, anyway) or setting up programs that treated informing on your neighbor as the national ethic.

Despite all this, Ashcroft became the personification of the war at home. What made him frightening was that his manner expressed not optimism, which is the glory and opiate of the American people, but a haunted awareness of the fallen nature of man; he evoked a tradition of demagogic religiosity that goes back to the the origins of America itself. Awash in Holy Roller paranoias—even more than Bush, he is a Christian mirror-image of Osama bin Laden—Ashcroft embodied per-haps the oldest and most repressive of our national archetypes. He was the driven Puritan minister obsessed with ridding the countryside of evil, a refugee from *The Crucible* suddenly elevated to a position of vast power. The seventeenth-century fanatic Cotton Mather once said, "Never use but one grain of patience with any man that shall go to impose upon me a Denial of Devils or of Witches." Three centuries later, you saw the same mentality in Ashcroft: Asked a tough question, his first instinct was to suggest that you were in league with the "evildoers" (a term Bush himself got from the Fifth Psalm). Testifying before the Senate Judiciary Committee in late 2001, he sat uncomfortably at his table like Jabba the Hutt, chin melting into his shoulders, soft features taut with a hanging judge's icy rectitude, his whole attitude rejecting the Democrats' questions. "To those who scare peace-loving people with the phantoms of lost liberty," he said, "my message is this: Your tactics only aid terrorists, for they erode our national unity and diminish our resolve. They give ammunition to America's enemies, and pause to America's friends. They encourage people of goodwill to remain silent in the face of evil." When a cabinet member talks like this to the major-ity party of the U.S. Senate, one can only imagine how he would treat ordinary citizens who opposed his policies. Seeing Ashcroft treat Democratic senators as if they were al-Qaeda fellow travelers, you knew he smelled the brimstone stench of treason in simple disagreement.

Although his actions weren't as extreme as they often appeared he's actually a calculating politician—his Witchfinder General persona did much to ratchet up the general level of fear, not least among immigrants and Muslim-Americans who believed he was far too eager to lock them up. It finally didn't matter that far fewer Muslims were detained than initially feared (around 5,000) or that only a few high school kids were investigated for having antiwar posters. If you've spent any time in an authoritarian state, be it a "soft" one like Singapore, which goes after the opposition with libel suits, or the classic kind like the People's Republic of China, which simply chucks dissenters into prison, you know that the art of political repression lies in cowing the population, not arresting it. And that's what Ashcroft did. He was Bush's bad cop. Very bad cop: Of those 5,000 Muslims detained as terror suspects after September 11, only one was ever convicted.

Where the President would go to a mosque and urge tolerance for Islam, the Attorney General often behaved as if he'd just seen *Minority Report* and thought that the Department of Pre-Crime was a heckuva good idea, though that stuff with the mutants smacked of sorcery. Why wait until people actually *did* something? If you couldn't imprison young Muslim men indefinitely for minor visa violations, you were never going to stop terrorism. That's why we also needed Patriot Act II, which expanded government power in ways even more un-American than the first one. Luckily, many of Ashcroft's ideas never came to pass, sneered into oblivion by both left and right, and some of those that did pass were soon under fire: Three states and over a hundred cities voted, nonbindingly but pointedly, to reject certain provisions of the USA Patriot Act. By August of 2003, Ashcroft had begun what was termed "a sixteen-state, eighteen-city Patriot Act tour" to defend the original act, ordering all ninety-three U.S. attorneys across the country to launch a parallel effort in their regions. The years had dimmed neither his sense of righteousness nor the Bush administration's ritualistic use of the terrorist attacks to justify un-American methods. "To abandon these tools," Ashcroft told the conservative American Enterprise Institute, "would senselessly imperil American lives and American liberty, and it would ignore the lessons of September 11." Whether those "lessons" (what an abused term!) were moral or practical, he did not say. Nor did anyone ask him. He refused to grant interviews to print reporters, preferring to spread the word through local TV stations, known nationwide for being soft touches.

But by then things had changed anyway. Voltaire once observed that governments need both shepherds *and* butchers, and the Bush administration's interest in the tedious shepherding-work of Homeland Security had been overshadowed, and seemingly replaced, by its invasions of Afghanistan and Iraq. If one legacy of 9/11 was America's fearful sense of its vulnerability, another was an increasing militarism, the belief that, as Rumsfeld put it, "the best defense, and in some cases the only defense, is a good offense." His words were music to all the visionaries, neo-imperialists, and would-be nation builders who saw in the rubble of September 11 the chance to remake the world.

CHAPTER 3

The Disquieting American
or
The "Why Do They Hate Us?" Blues

It really is true that foreign affairs is the only important
issue for a President to handle, isn't it? I mean who
gives a shit if the minimum wage is $1.15 or $1.25, in
comparison to something like this.

—JOHN KENNEDY TO RICHARD NIXON,

AFTER THE BAY OF PIGS

few years ago in Ho Chi Minh City, known to the local kids as
HCMC, I was heading up Dong Khoi, the legendary downtown
street that, like a happy love affair, begins at a hotel and ends at a
church. A six-year-old boy in a faded Adidas T-shirt followed me,
shrieking, "You wan' grangree? Kwai mari can! Kwai mari can!"
Puzzled, I stopped and he forced a shrink-wrapped book into my
hands. It was a smeary bootleg paperback of *The Quiet American*, the
1955 novel that later became famous for predicting the United States'
crackup in Vietnam before it had properly begun. The title character,
Alden Pyle, is an archetypal Yankee do-gooder who believes he's helping build a society that transcends both European colonialism and Ho
Chi Minh communism. His creepy naïveté leads to disaster, including
his own murder. "Grangree" = Graham Greene.

It struck me as fitting that Saigon's hawkers should tout this book,
for in a city constantly redefined by different rulers, *The Quiet
American* has remained an enduring monument. Greene's ideas were
recycled by a thousand foreign correspondents during the Vietnam

War and, in the form of Philip Noyce's recent screen adaptation, has gone on shaping our mythology of that country to this day. Still, leafing through this faux Penguin back in my hotel room, not so far from where Pyle met his ugly end, I found myself wondering why the talismanic English-language book on Vietnam hadn't been been written by one of the several million Americans who once passed through that beautiful, unlucky land. Now, it's hardly unprecedented that such a landmark book would have come from an Englishman, for Britain's major export seems to be writers who travel the world and write damnably well about every single place. Over the last century or so, they've set the standard for recording the tricky truths of empire. From Conrad and Kipling to Joyce Cary and Paul Scott, their books capture the clash of cultures, the gin-and-tonic-fueled realities of expat living, the blinkered values of the rulers and rebelliousness of the ruled.

In contrast, American writers have barely registered that for decades we have been the world's dominant empire—our tendrils (to be benign) or tentacles (sinister) extend everywhere. Although one would think great writing would be born of this complicated reality— "Opportunity, adventure, sunsets, dusty death," as Don DeLillo elegantly summarized it—our global power has inspired shockingly little memorable fiction outside of war stories. There are no great American novels about the U.S. in the Philippines (which we took over in 1898), the postwar reconstruction of Japan and Germany, our military presence in South Korea (where, over fifty years, we've stationed hundreds of thousands of soldiers); no memorable novels about Iran, Saudi Arabia, Russia, or China; closer to home, no defining tales of Panama, Mexico, Brazil, Chile, Haiti, or the Dominican Republic (Mario Vargas Llosa wrote the showstopper there). When I think of Cuba, I instantly think not of literature but of Michael Corleone giving Fredo that killer's kiss in Havana. There are, of course, notable exceptions—Norman Rush's great novels of Botswana, Robert Stone on Central America and Israel, Paul Theroux (though he's something of an honorary Brit) on Southeast Asia, and William T. Vollman on hookers worldwide. (It's pitiful how many

Western novels about Asia, including *The Quiet American,* center on women paid for sex.) But what a meager crop from such a vast, fertile field. Few tales could be more compelling than that of Americans building a new kind of empire in the name of anti-imperial freedom, yet for every novel that tackles the subject—for instance, Henry Brommell's *Little America,* about a CIA brat's inquest into his father's role in the Middle East—we have hundreds of tired yarns about sub-urban adultery, dysfunctional families, or growing up zany in the South.

Such literary parochialism would scarcely matter were it not a cultural symptom of a blind spot whose consequences hit home violently on September 11, 2001. On the weekend after the terror attacks, CNN carried a report from Pakistan, whose crooked leader, Pervez Musharraf, was being browbeaten into helping the United States hunt down the terrorists. A snippet of footage showed a band of students in the streets of Islamabad raising a banner written in English for international cameras. "America," it read, "think why you are hated the world over." The sign read like a direct riposte to the millions of Americans—from nurses to athletes to professional journalists—who had spent the previous days saying they wanted to "understand" what happened on September 11. And their bluesy refrain was nearly always the same. How could they do this to innocent people? Why do they hate us so much? One simple answer to these questions remains true to this day: They hate us because we don't even know why they hate us.

For the last sixty years, it has been this country's luxury to be so big and strong that we haven't needed to worry about what our dominance might mean to the rest of the world, even to the many countries that like us. Americans take pride in our well-intended optimism, but this attitude has too often become the willful ignorance of prosperous people content to let their leaders do all the thinking about the rest of the planet. Kipling famously asked, "What do they know of England that only England knows?" We might ask the same about America, whose power touches every country on earth, even such hellholes as North Korea. When George W. Bush ran for president, it was reckoned a joke that he couldn't name the president of Pakistan. He can now, and so, one hopes, can we. After all, it is one thing for an uneducated Taliban fighter to know nothing about the working people murdered in the World Trade Center attacks. It's quite another for an American, who can tap into the world's storehouse of information with a mouse click, to be unable to find the Persian Gulf on a map or be unaware that, even as we seek to democratize Iraq, the U.S. government continues to back brutally undemocratic Middle Eastern regimes. "Innocence," says the Englishman Fowler in *The Quiet American*, "is a kind of insanity."

Our American innocence is largely inseparable from a clumsy, self-regarding sense of the outside world that, since the beginning of the republic, has been a homegrown form of isolationism. It's not that we don't care about other countries, but that, as good modern Romans, we expect all roads to lead *here*. That's why most Americans don't learn foreign languages and why, unlike earlier imperial powers, we have few citizens willing to live in disagreeable foreign lands where our nation has serious interests: The CIA can't recruit agents who speak Arabic or are willing to be posted in grim spots that are long on diarrhea and short on cappuccino. Although most Americans believe that the U.S. is conspicuously generous in giving foreign aid—and President Bush pushed through the biggest rise since 1962—it actually gives the lowest percentage of its gross domestic product (1/10 of 1 percent) of any donor country. (Even after the increase, foreign aid now receives $5 billion less per annum than under JFK—not even adjusting for inflation.) Such ignorance is thoroughly predictable in an era when our Congress is filled with know-nothings, many of them washed into office on benighted waves of Gingrichery and Christian fundamentalism. Evidently unaware that the People's Republic of China is officially atheist, a few years back a visiting U.S. congressman in Beijing flabbergasted a Chinese deputy foreign minister by asking him if he'd accepted Jesus Christ as his "personal savior." This obtuseness about the outside world is reinforced by our television newscasts, which, having long ago abandoned the idea of keeping serious foreign bureaus, often simply ignore such "irrelevant" events as the ethnic slaughter of 3,000 villagers in Congo. Even when the foreign news concerns international terrorism, it receives disgracefully little coverage unless most of the casualties are American. When a bomb blast killed nearly two hundred revelers in Kuta Beach, Bali, in the autumn of 2002, CNN could barely be bothered to show footage from Indonesia—it was devoting 24/7 coverage to the D.C. sniper. From watching American TV, you never would have known that in Australia the date October 12 instantly became a dark landmark in the national mythology to put alongside Gallipoli or that the Aussies were struck by the self-centered feebleness of U.S. coverage: The online *Miami Herald* noted, for instance, that two Americans died in the Bali blast, adding, "Most of the dead are foreigners."

We've spared even less feeling for al-Qaeda's innocent victims not of the West—the Kenyans, Tanzanians, Balinese, Moroccans, Israelis, Afghans, Turks, and, of course, Iraqis. George W. Bush *does* notice these victims, although he's rather bad at putting his empathy across. This is partly because he's never been very interested in the outside world. If any newly elected president ever embodied obliviousness toward world affairs, it was surely George W. Bush, who, despite family money and his father's globetrotting vocation, had done shockingly little foreign travel for a fifty-year-old millionaire seeking to become the most powerful man on earth; during the 2000 campaign, his PR team plumped up his foreign-travel résumé to make him seem less unworldly. But his blinkered provincialism kept showing through. At a joint press conference in Paris with Jacques Chirac, he sneered at an American reporter for asking the French president a question in French, an outburst that left international audiences incredulous. Months after invading Iraq, this man who proudly said he never reads the daily papers pronounced himself shocked to hear that moderate Islamic nations had grown more anti-American since 9/11, a fact most Americans already knew. (And to think we mocked LBJ for always having three TVs going on the different networks.) In Manila, Bush didn't exactly bowl over the Philippines' Congress when he compared invading Iraq to the Spanish-American War: "America is proud of its part in the great story of the Filipino people. Together our soldiers liberated the Philippines from colonial rule." He seemed perfectly unaware that, once the U.S. wrested the Philippines from the Spanish in what Secretary of State John Hay called a "splendid little war," it slaughtered many tens of thousands of Filipinos who didn't want America imposing its own regime (which naturally we did for over forty years). As ever, Bush's defenders try to spin this lack of knowledge as a kind of secret weapon. Under Secretary of Defense Paul Wolfowitz told *Vanity Fair* that the first time he met Bush it was clear that "he didn't know very much," then went on to praise him for being a good questioner who was unafraid of showing that he didn't know things—as if a president wouldn't ask even better questions about, say, Iraq if he already knew something about Sunnis and Shiites, or the hard facts of Britain's disastrous colonial experience there.

When he assumed office, Bush wasn't simply ignorant of other countries. He disliked them because they made him feel his ignorance. An orderly man who likes the security of home, he viewed the outside world with obvious mistrust, like a tourist abroad who, fingering his money belt against pickpockets, feels certain that the local merchants are always out to rob him. He hid this during the 2000 campaign when he pilloried Al Gore for the dream liberal idea of "nation building," winning my approval by saying that it was important for the U.S. to be "a humble nation." That attitude changed once *he* was the one being asked to be humble. Almost immediately, he plunged into a unilateralist foreign policy tinged with a Crawfordite's instinctive isolationism. He looked askance at international agreements that would stop him or the United States from doing what it wanted. He refused to sign the Kyoto protocol, campaigned against the International Criminal Court, and—in a decision whose larger consequences are not yet fully known—unilaterally decided to abrogate the Anti-Ballistic Missile Treaty in order to pour billions into the missile defense system that still deserves that snickering sobriquet "Star Wars." Such policies annoyed, indeed enraged most of the world, not least because of his way of presenting them. Bush's America was soon seen as a bullyboy throwing its weight around, like the jerk behind the wheel of a Hummer who always speeds through amber traffic lights knowing that, in case of collision, you're the one who's going to really get crunched.

As luck would have it, Bush's America received a second chance on September 11. Suddenly, this seemingly impervious giant of a country had suffered humanizing wounds that won the world's sympathy. Hundreds of thousands mourned on the streets of Europe, and foreign rivals used the occasion for positive, if not altruistic, diplomacy —they agreed to help in the newly minted War on Terror. When the U.S. took action against the Taliban, everyone understood why, and international protests were muted. But a man's character is his fate, as Heraclitus said by way of Augie March, and within a year, Bush had squandered the world's goodwill, replacing it with a free-form hostility no less significant for often being foolish or incoherent. European streets were now packed with anti-American demonstrators. Hundreds of millions, no, make that *billions* of people—including most citizens of our leading allies—began wondering out loud if the U.S. had become a rogue elephant of a state, an even greater threat to peace than Islamic fundamentalist wackos and Middle Eastern dictators. The cause of this about-face wasn't simply U.S. military action— although invading Iraq did up the ante—but the haughty, downward gaze with which the Bush administration addressed the world. Dividing the world between Usses and Thems, it blew Iran's post-9/11 sympathy by including it in the Axis of Evil, an idiotic phrase that not only named the wrong countries—if we're talking evil, what about Pakistan and Saudi Arabia?—but prompted North Korea's Kim Jong-Il to start flaunting his nukes. America is now widely viewed as a nation that doesn't merely want to change the world as it sees fit, but arrogantly insists on its right and even obligation to do so. Such moralism drives other countries as bonkers today as it once drove Kipling, who wrote: "I never got over the wonder of a people who having extirpated the aboriginals of their continent more completely than any other modern race has ever done, honestly believed in their godly little New England community setting examples to brutal mankind."

In *The Quiet American*, Fowler says of Alden Pyle, "I never knew a man who had better motives for all the trouble he caused." I wish we could say the same for the Bush administration, which has used September 11 and the idea of a perpetual war on terrorism to promote its own partisan interests. Still, the people who run U.S. foreign policy these days aren't wholly cynical, and they share much of Pyle's dangerous idealism, albeit without his becoming modesty. These guys think they know what's best for the world and feel no qualms about saying so. With its cocky words and cowboy strut, Bush World has created a distressing new national archetype: the Disquieting American.

Attack of the Fifty-Foot Neocons!

Terrible as it is to say, Americans can accept it when a handful of our countrymen are blown up in a faraway country that most of us will never see. But when terrorists kill 3,000 civilians on American soil— and would have happily killed far more—such violence demands a compelling response. Doubly so when the murder is committed in the name of totalitarian theocracy, the most dangerous ideology in the world today. "There is hardly such a thing as a war in which it makes no difference who wins," Orwell wrote. "Nearly always one side stands more or less for progress, the other side more or less for reaction." In the case of the struggle against fundamentalist terror, knowing which side was right required no great discrimination. For all its disappointments and betrayals, liberal democracy is worth fighting for; it holds open the possibility of a future that will live up to its values. Not so the starry-eyed, starry-chambered medievalism of Osama and Omar. These murderers aren't freedom fighters of any stripe. They are unfreedom fighters. They murder innocents, rich and poor. Their attacks on the West make me think of the boxer Joe Louis's immaculate reply when asked, during World War II, why he would fight for a country that treated African-Americans so badly: "There ain't nothing wrong with this country that Hitler can fix."

Being against Islamic totalitarianism has always been the easy part. The hard part is knowing how far to go in prosecuting a supposed "war" on "terror." It's worth pausing to grant Bush and his team a few moments of sympathy for what September 11 did to their lives. Faced with an enemy whose potentialities were unknown (remember when we thought every American city might be crawling with sleeper cells?), they had to pick their way through a shadowy terra incognita, unsure whether they were doing too much, yet terrified that doing too little would lead to catastrophe—they fell asleep hearing those dirty bombs go tick-tick-tick. The one incontestable move was going after al-Qaeda and the Taliban. Even though that invasion came accompanied by daunting historical analogies about Afghanistan as the graveyard of foreign invaders, the war itself looked like that famous scene in *Raiders of the Lost Ark* when an Arab stands there waving his scimitar menacingly and Indiana Jones just pulls out a pistol and plugs him. While the attempt to get Osama was something of a bungle—Bush was strangely fearful of casualties—these were the glory days for the War on Terror. The Taliban was quickly removed, there were surprisingly few deaths, and most Afghans seemed pleased to be able to paint their fingernails or get Leonardo DiCaprio haircuts. And why not? As Christopher Hitchens cleverly put it, they'd been bombed *out* of the Stone Age. Even for Bush-haters there was amusement to be had in the President suddenly championing women's rights (over there, anyway) and Donald Rumsfeld turning into Rumstud, as Dubya liked to call him.

But rapid victory bred what would just as rapidly become a national truism: Winning the war was easy; the hard part was winning the peace. Not that the Bush administration made a valiant effort. For all his prewar promises about rebuilding Afghanistan (and postwar references to an Afghan Marshall Plan), the CEO President was still thinking about the quarterly balance sheet. Having accomplished his goals for the end of 2001, he was already moving on. Afghanistan became a mere sideshow in the War on Terror, less dangerous but far from healed. More than two years after the fall of the Taliban, the country remains unstable and desperately poor, with an interim leader, Hamid Karzai, born to be played by Ben Kingsley, who's jokingly known as the Mayor of Kabul. True, the capital city now boasts an Italian restaurant. But vast reaches of the countryside are in the hands of warlords, outlaws, and surviving fighters from the Taliban and al-Qaeda. The nation's infrastructure remains a disaster, international relief agencies struggle to provide aid, local officials get assassinated, American soldiers are still involved in bloody firefights (the terrorists are coming back), and the country's finance minister fears the country may become a "narco-mafia state." While the U.S. spent $1 billion a month for its military presence, only 1/20th of that was earmarked for rebuilding a nation wrecked by decades of fanaticism and war. From time to time, the dapper Karzai brings a beggar's coat to Washington in search of money. (Although Bush initially left funds for Afghanistan out of his 2003 budget, he finally committed an extra $1 billion for rebuilding in September 2003, when things were going badly in Iraq.) To top it all off, the war failed to offer catharsis to a nation shaken by September 11. Osama had not been found either dead or alive. He simply vanished—from Afghanistan *and* President Bush's speeches.

Overthrowing the Taliban demonstrated the administration's seriousness, yet it hardly spelled the end of international terrorism. The War on Terror still needed a larger battle plan, an analysis, a theory. It clearly wasn't going to come from the Democrats, who were not only out of power but out of ideas. They harbored a mistrust of American power—a historically reasonable mistrust, it must be stressed—and had lost the romantic Humphrey Bogart liberalism that made them want to fight for underdogs everywhere in the world. Where once the left had championed social justice around the globe, it had long since grown, well, *conservative*—shaky, pragmatic, fearful of upsetting a post–Cold War status quo that appeared to be working rather well for America. Under Bill Clinton, the U.S. had eschewed grand visions in favor of what baseball people call "small ball." The results were mixed: disgracing itself in Rwanda, scraping by in Bosnia, doing okay in Kosovo. But the shock of September 11 demanded something bigger and more vivid—an overarching vision. Aside from the rare likes of Paul Berman, whose book *Terror and Liberalism* urged a long, Cold War–style struggle against Islamic fascism, the left often felt paralyzed. The Democrats, in particular, appeared to endorse Bush's foreign policy yet be waiting for him to make mistakes so they could whack him.

In keeping with our age, the Big Idea came from the right. Not from conservative "realists" such as George H. W. Bush and James Baker III, who notoriously said of the Bosnian genocide that the U.S. didn't have a dog in that fight, nor from Pat Buchanan–style Paleocons, who believe America shouldn't intervene beyond its own shores unless directly threatened. Rather, September 11 became a launching pad for the neoconservatives, a loosely knit group of thinkers, journalists, and politicos whose influence on the Bush administration has led some to view them as a conspiracy, if not a cabal—to use the anti-Semite's term of art for a group with many prominent Jewish members. (Absurdly enough, some neocons began accusing critics of anti-Semitism for simply using their own term "neoconservative.") In truth, the neoconservatives have worked in broad daylight for decades and laid out their worldview far more clearly than the leaders of either party.

Their ideas were first formulated in the 1970s by ex-liberals, most of them Democrats, disenchanted by what they saw as sixties amorality, welfare-state excess, and a weak-willed foreign policy traumatized with Vietnam Syndrome. They took (and still take) special pride in possessing "moral clarity," a habit of mind that usually comes down to creating spurious oppositions and then accusing opponents of "relativism" when they refuse to accept them. Early on, the neocon "persuasion" (as its doyen, Irving Kristol, calls it) was largely the work of embattled outsiders who'd grown up in lower middle-class households. But over the years, they came to disdain the liberalism that had once succored them and to embrace a right-wing version of revolutionary zeal. Hence the creepy alliance with the Christian Coalition; hence the foreign policy thinking that uses the word "realist" pejoratively. (In this, anyway, neocons are the direct heirs of the sixties radicals they're so proud of thinking foolish.) Since getting its first limited toehold during the Reagan presidency, neoconservatism has become a comfortable line of work thanks to the many well-funded right-wing foundations and the moolah of Rupert Murdoch, who bankrolls their house organ, *The Weekly Standard.* No longer embattled (or lower middle class), they now exude the smugness of the strong who have inherited the earth.*

The filmmaker Paul Schrader, of *Taxi Driver* and *American Gigolo* fame, once explained to me why seventies movies had been so daring: Back then, he said, people were so confused by what was going on— Vietnam, Watergate, Free Love, Black Power, Women's Lib—that for once they turned to movies to make sense of the world. September 11 gave much the same boost to American neocons. A public that normally yawned over foreign affairs suddenly became eager for ideas about what America should do. And after thirty years of rehearsing their rap, the neocons were hot to deliver it—they beamed with neon exuberance. The cover of *The Weekly Standard* told you that America had to fight to win (as if anybody was really saying the opposite). Defense advisor Richard Perle, who takes no small delight in being nicknamed "The Prince of Darkness," went on ABC's *Sunday Morning* and inveighed against "insipid internationalism." Over on PBS, David Brooks recited from the Gospel According to Irving Kristol: "Americans have always been alone when we fight since we became a superpower. In part because it's lonely at the top: We have responsibilities which nobody else has. But in part because we have the missionary zeal about spreading democracy around the world, which spooks other countries who are a little more cynical, a little more *realpolitik.*" Those foreigners just aren't high-minded like that nice Mr. Cheney.

If the networks wanted somebody rabid, they'd trot out saturnine Daniel Pipes of the Middle East Forum, who, when not writing articles claiming that the left loves Osama (say what?), was happy to badmouth the Islamic world. All this neoconnery was enthusiastically

---

*The mention of inheritance here is deliberate. Just as Bush was born a princeling, so were several of the brightest neocon lights, who became known as "minicons." For instance, *The Weekly Standard* is edited by William Kristol, the son of Irving Kristol and social historian Gertrude Himmelfarb; the magazine's cofounder, John Podhoretz, is the son of *Commentary*'s Norman Podhoretz and Midge Decter; foreign affairs pundit Robert Kagan (of *The Washington Post* and Carnegie Endowment for International Peace) is the son of Yale classics professor Donald Kagan.

backed up by the two academic fellow-travelers who were instructing Cheney in the ways of the Middle East. The enjoyably florid Fouad Ajami (does anyone else still speak so merrily of "brigands"?) kept telling Charlie Rose that all the Middle East understands is power. Meanwhile acclaimed orientalist Bernard Lewis accused the Islamic world of responding to its obvious failure by playing "the blame game"—rather than confronting its own flaws, it keeps claiming to be a victim of the West. Basking in all the newfound media attention, Lewis displayed a level of mandarin self-satisfaction that made Gore Vidal look as down home as Andy Griffith.

Although nobody would call Bush himself a neoconservative—in fact, he still bears a grudge against Kristol and *The Weekly Standard* for backing John McCain against him in 2000—the Bush administration is nonetheless well-stocked with second-tier figures who either are neocons or embrace their major ideas: Paul Wolfowitz (Under Secretary of Defense), Douglas Feith (Under Secretary of Defense for Policy), John Bolton (Under Secretary of State for Arms Control and International Security), Lewis Libby (the Vice President's Chief of Staff), not to mention Dick Cheney and Donald Rumsfeld, who share the neocons' hard-line assumptions if not their utopianism. (The Veep and Rummy are what the Brookings Institute's Ivo Daalder calls "assertive nationalists.") Working for a president who knew zip about international relations, these foreign policy "Vulcans" proved every bit as powerful and well-known as Kennedy's Best and the Brightest, who came a cropper in Vietnam.

What the neoconservative philosophy offered Bush (and the rest of us) was a *radical* foreign policy far more aggressive than the ones that had preceded it. It argued that, unlike the farsighted Gipper, Presidents Bush I and Clinton had not grasped a superpower's duties and obligations. Failing to understand our nation's "special role in the world," they had muddled along from event to event, wielding America's strength too timidly, as if unaware that this nation's might makes exercising power inescapable: "[I]f you have the kind of power we now have," wrote Irving Kristol, "either you will find opportunities to use it, or the world will discover them for you." According to the neoconservatives, George W. Bush's immediate predecessors had given America a "squandered decade." Bush I failed to topple Saddam back during Gulf War I, while Clinton's crimes were almost too numerous to count. At different times, neocons assailed him for not ousting Milosevic after the Kosovo campaign, for driving the U.S. military into dangerous decline, and for appeasing Islamic terrorism by merely lobbing a few missiles, much as Rome didn't face up to Hannibal's malfeasances after the First Punic War. ("The Romans looked away," concludes proto-neocon historian Donald Kagan, "then they took actions that were inadequate for their purpose.") They preferred to forget that it was neocon hero Reagan who hastily pulled American troops out of Lebanon after a truck bomb killed 241 U.S. Marines on October 23, 1983. It was that decision that first convinced terrorists that America was a paper tiger that would run if hit.*

It has always been part of our national self-image that Americans use our power in the name of a higher good, a belief that found a classic expression in the Monroe Doctrine. Even as President James Monroe was declaring that there would be no colonization in the Western Hemisphere, the very act of making such a declaration asserted the United States's intention to treat nearly half the world as its own huge zone of influence. That same blend of idealism and self-interest runs through neoconservative ideas. They disdain the U.N. (as if that corrupt, depressingly inept organization hadn't long been in America's pocket). They champion the aggressive use of U.S. power,

---

*While one can only share the neocons' contempt for Bush I's behavior in Iraq—in particular, calling for an uprising and then allowing the rebels to be massacred—history has not been altogether kind to their harsh judgments of Clinton. He may not have toppled Milosevic, but the Serbs themselves did: The dictator wound up deposed and in the docket, and the U.S. hasn't been forced to occupy that country as it now does Iraq. The military routs of Afghanistan and Iraq were accomplished with the supposedly decimated military that Clinton bequeathed Bush. As for his unwillingness to confront terrorism, Clinton's National Security Advisor Sandy Berger warned the Bush people on the first day that they'd spend much of their time dealing with terrorism, but his advice fell on deaf ears, a point forcefully underscored by the former counterterrorism chief, Richard Clarke.

not because Americans are eager to run the world but because U.S. dominance is good for everyone else, even if they don't know it. So good, in fact, that the Bush administration's 12,500-word policy paper, "The National Security Strategy of the United States of America," laid out a vision of an imperial America so unopposable that, if alive, Charles de Gaulle would have instantly declared war against the U.S. as a matter of honor. In truth, such vainglory didn't begin with Bush or the neoconservatives; keeping America inviolably preeminent has been the government's de facto policy since the end of the Cold War. Still, this 2002 document was shockingly naked in its declaration that the U.S. would allow no other country to rival, let alone equal, its power. Beneath its bureaucratic gobbledygook, the Bush team's paper read distressingly like the program for intergalactic domination one might find aboard a Romulan spaceship in *Star Trek*.

We received a defense of such thinking in Robert Kagan's *Of Paradise and Power*, an elegant, reasonable-seeming essay that is actually nothing short of a twenty-first-century imperial manifesto. It argues that America is obliged to run things precisely *because* our prosperity and military power make us uniquely qualified to do so. Where the self-absorbed, undermilitarized Europe is busy turning its own continent into a self-satisfied "paradise" (scoff, scoff), the U.S. is out doing the muscular work of keeping the world safe for democracy and freedom. Or as Kagan catchily summarized the difference: "Americans are from Mars, and Europeans are from Venus." Convinced of our national rectitude, he insists that it's in everybody's best interest that the U.S. lived by a double standard: "It must refuse to abide by certain international conventions that may constrain its ability to fight effectively. . . . It must support arms control, but not always for itself." Living above and beyond the rules governing ordinary nations, the U.S. will be the ultimate arbiter of the international good—rather like the U.N., but without the aggravation of other nations having a vote. No fool, Kagan realizes that not everyone will be happy with such a configuration of the world, but he's prepared to live with the world's unhappiness—which may be another answer to the question "Why do they hate us?"

One need not be a foreign affairs specialist to see the dangers in such a global vision, from the plain arrogance of insisting that American self-interest is in the world's best interest, no matter what other countries may think, to the deeper, more reprehensible megalomania that makes such an attitude possible. The neoconservative project presupposes a supersized United States entitled to possess the most wealth, use the most oil, eat the most food, emit the most destructive gases, and, of course, flaunt far more WMDs than any country could possibly need. It assumes that the planet is far better off *because* America spends enough on weapons to be the only superpower, even if (according to U.N. experts Jeffrey Sachs and Sakiko Fukuda-Parr) just one half of the United States's 2003 defense budget would do extraordinary things to fight world poverty: control the AIDS, malaria, and TB pandemics, ensure that children could go to school rather than work, increase the food productivity of poor tropical farmers, and let poor households get access to safe drinking water, energy, and markets.

During the run-up to what's now called Gulf War I, Margaret Thatcher sent an emissary to Washington to make sure that President George Bush didn't get "all wobbly." The neocons fretted that Bush II might lack the resolve to do what they thought needed to be done— for starters, treating Kabul as a sleepover on the way to Baghdad. They need not have worried. In the aftermath of September 11, the idea of America's historical mission (and exceptionalism) took on a new luster at the White House. The neocons' clarity and assertiveness were especially alluring to fidgety George W. Bush, who is more than slightly unnerved by ambiguity. Like John F. Kennedy before him, he takes pride in bold action, but unlike the JFK who spoke of "the long twilight struggle" against communism, Dubya's struggles require high noons and moonless midnights. You won't catch him muddling or playing small ball; he wasn't about to be known for the slow, dreary work of tracking down terrorist cells and making America's ports secure. Here was a man with a Destiny. To borrow the title from a fine book by Chris Hedges, war was a force that gave him meaning.

The neoconservative vision of history offered Bush the chance to swing for the fences, while reinforcing his natural disposition to tune out those who disagree with him. It insisted on America's right—nay, duty—to act unilaterally. It saw the value—nay, necessity—of fighting preemptive war. And in its utopianism about refashioning the world—and here one sees the neocons slipping into their Alden Pyle costumes—it argued that the U.S. could go beyond merely killing off a bunch of terrorists and, through a new improved version of the Domino Theory, turn the Middle East democratic. Such reasoning would eventually lead the President to go after the monstrous Saddam, a neocon target since before the Clinton administration. (Although Afghanistan had already been conquered, it was just too depressing to be the first domino.) Naturally, Bush insisted that there was nothing imperialistic about American plans for the Middle East. He kept saying, "We don't seek an empire," seemingly unaware that the U.S. already has one. But some neocons were not so shy of the E word. "No need to run away from the label," said Max Boot of the Council on Foreign Relations: "America's destiny is to police the world." At last, a man who lives up to his name.

Twenty-five years ago, it would have been almost impossible to sell such an idea to the American people. But 9/11 hadn't just filled the country with fear and a desire to strike back, it had given a jolt of energy to a transformation that had been going on for years—the militarization of American life.

From Prussia with Love

For much of our history, Americans have been a violent people but not a notoriously bellicose one. We have, of course, had our share of leaders betwitched by the glory of battle: "All the great masterful races have been fighting races," brayed Theodore Roosevelt. "No triumph of peace is quite as great as the supreme triumphs of war." Still, most ordinary citizens wanted the U.S. to steer clear of World War I, and FDR could only get the country to enter World War II after a direct attack on Pearl Harbor. Marvel Comics and Hollywood to the contrary, earlier generations of American soldiers were not famously aggressive (even by French standards), though they were always cocky.

During the First World War, the ill-prepared American military refused to take advice from allies who'd already been fighting for years. "If the Americans do not permit the French to teach them," Clemenceau said prophetically, "the Germans will do so."

All this changed with the Cold War. Beginning with Truman, America adopted a radically new international posture. Faced with a totalitarian threat from the Soviet Union and addicted to the growth made possible by a wartime economy, the government mobilized the country's material and psychological resources to create what Gore Vidal likes to call the "National Security State." No matter which party was in power, the U.S. stockpiled weapons, built up a huge conventional army, spent billions on gargantuan Pentagon budgets, and trained citizens in the faulty Newtonian geopolitics of the Domino Theory. Exercising the *droit du seigneur* claimed by every great power, it began using military action as a routine tool of foreign policy: Since 1945, we've engaged in two hundred such actions, some vast (the Korean War), others comically dinky (Reagan's invasion of Grenada). Although the taste for intervention was slowed by the Vietnam "quagmire," a Golden Oldie term that enjoyed a vogue in the Baghdad Summer of 2003, the Prussianization of American life began a vigorous renaissance under Ronald Reagan. By the time George H. W. Bush invaded Panama—for reasons that look even shoddier today than they did in 1989—it had become clear that our leaders, especially our Republican leaders, were in thrall to military force. But so were the Democrats. Intimidated by the military because of his fishy dealings with the draft, Bill Clinton deferred to the Pentagon, lavishing money upon it and laying the groundwork for the antiballistic-missile system. The money spigot was opened still wider by George W. Bush. Even before September 11, he had already proposed ratcheting up the military budget by $33 billion, not merely the largest increase since Reagan had decided to spend the Soviet Union into bankruptcy but a rise larger than Russia's entire military budget. The numbers are flabbergasting. Today, we have more than seven hundred foreign bases, and with a military budget of $401 billion, the U.S. spends more on defense than the next fifteen countries in the world combined.

This has as much to do with money as ideology. In *Catch-22*, the profiteering mess-hall officer Milo Minderbinder says he'd "like to see the government get out of war altogether and leave the whole field to private industry." American reality has done him one better—it's merged the two. Over the forty-odd years since President Eisenhower offered his warning about "the military industrial complex," the spiderweb has only grown bigger and stronger. As Minderbinder had hoped, many military functions have been privatized—companies like Halliburton now provide soldiers with their meals. At the same time, the Bush defense establishment has been embedded in Fortune 500 corporations. By now, the whole world can recite the litany of the administration's corporate links—Halliburton, the Carlyle Group, the bin Laden family. And these are only the famous cases. Over its first eighteen months in office, the administration named thirty-two appointees to top policy positions who were former executives, paid consultants, or major shareholders of top defense contractors. In the spring of 2003, *The New Yorker* published an article by Seymour Hersh suggesting that superhawk Richard Perle, known for his love of high living, was using his plum, albeit unpaid, position as chairman of the Defense Policy Board to promote his business interests. After first threatening to sue, Perle gave up the chairmanship—though not his place on the board—once other publications began questioning the ethics of taking several hundred grand from corporations obviously banking on his connections. *The New York Times*'s Paul Krugman jokingly proposed a game called "Six Degrees of Richard Perle" that would track his ramifying business ties. Naturally, Perle insisted he'd done nothing wrong, by which he meant nothing illegal. I believe him. So much, these days, is legal. But mere legality does nothing to diminish the stench of the defense world's well-heeled cronyism, a foul system of back-scratching now accepted as normal. In his classic 1956 study *The Power Elite*, C. Wright Mills noted that the top positions of the corporate, government, and military establishments are "increasingly interchangeable." Half a century later, a revolving door links private industry, the U.S. military, and the Pentagon bureaucracy, all of which have a vested interest in keeping the military machine running. This interest profoundly affects their psychology and their worldview: Republican or Democrat, these guys believe in the system. On the campaign trail in New Hampshire, Wesley Clark smilingly told a group of college students, "I'm a product of that military-industrial complex General Eisenhower warned you about."

The great American radical Randolph Bourne declared that war is the health of the state, and the War on Terror was like vitamins to our already-militarized government. Not only is the military now involved in domestic operations to an unprecedented extent, the Bush administration created a permanent, hugely expensive Department of Homeland Security, the dystopian name of which suggests a new era in American life complete with terror alerts, ubiquitous security guards, even higher levels of high-tech surveillance, and rollbacks of constitutional liberties. Naturally, this was an enormous windfall for all the corporations that would take in billions servicing that new department—the military-industrial complex sprouted brand-new limbs to grasp with. Abroad, the White House's thinking went far beyond working with other governments to wipe out terrorist training camps, roll up clandestine cells, and cut off their funding sources. From the moment the planes hit the World Trade Center, long before anyone knew who was actually responsible, several of Bush's top advisors wanted to use the attacks as a reason to make war on Iraq. Regime change! While such a desire was partly a strategic response to a potential threat and partly an expression of the neocon vision of a remade Middle East, it was also an almost inevitable consequence of possessing a fighting force that is, noted *The New Republic*'s Gregg Easterbrook, "the strongest the world has ever known, both in absolute terms and relative to other nations; stronger than the Wehrmacht in 1940, stronger than the legions at the height of Roman power." The internal logic of possessing (and paying for) such power means you will favor it as a way of solving your problems. As Robert Kagan put the matter: "A man armed only with a knife may decide that a bear prowling the forest is a tolerable danger, inasmuch as the alternative—hunting the bear armed only with a knife—is actually riskier than lying low and hoping the bear never attacks. The same man armed with a rifle, however, will likely make a different calculation of what constitutes a tolerable risk."

With no small prodding from the Bush administration, September 11 played to a fondness for the military that had already been on the rise in American culture for several years. Polls showed that Americans trusted the armed forces more than they have for a generation, and that young people showed the most faith of all. And why not? The U.S. military demonstrably *works*. It is efficient, egalitarian (in its practices if not its demographic makeup), and blessed with rockin' weaponry that can wreak astonishing amounts of damage on property with a comparatively small loss of life, especially for U.S. personnel. And because thirty years have passed since our media last presented grisly real-life images of U.S. casualties—showing military coffins has been banned since Gulf War I—Americans found it easy to embrace stories about battlefield heroism, the glamor of fighting itself. The hokey *Saving Private Ryan* was in, the cynical *Three Kings* was out; Tom Cruise learned to be a good samurai. Samuel Johnson once observed that "Every man thinks meanly of himself for not having been a soldier," and our pop culture bore this out. It coughed up an entire industry of war-hero wannabes: novelist Tom Clancy, the past master of armament porn; actor Tom Hanks, who often appeared to think he really *had* saved Private Ryan; the late historian Stephen Ambrose, who would have given his right arm to have lost his left one at Omaha Beach; and Robert D. Kaplan, a skillful reporter and scary thinker prone to sweat-lodge titles like *Warrior Politics: Why Leadership Demands a Pagan Ethos*. Hoo-hah!

Burnishing his image, the President also jumped on the bandwagon of Teddy Roosevelt, canonized in Edmund Morris's 2001 bestseller *Theodore Rex*. But one thing is clear. Dubya's drawn not to the reformer who busted corporate trusts but to the imperialist soldier who carried a big stick. There is, of course, something slightly nauseating about the denizens of this particular White House vicariously grooving on the charge up San Juan Hill. Where the rambunctious Teddy couldn't wait to get into battle, our President and Vice President (and countless neocon advisors) are pedigreed "chicken hawks." They were gung ho for America's involvement in the Vietnam War, but made sure they wouldn't have to fight it themselves. (Sneered retired General Anthony Zinni, "Perle! Ha! A paper cut was his biggest scrape.") One shouldn't be too surprised by this. We once lived in an America in which it was assumed that political big shots would have served honorably in the armed forces—fabled Vietnam dove George McGovern had been a decorated bomber pilot. That began changing with Ronald Reagan, a WWII noncombatant who pretended—believed?—that he helped liberate the concentration camps. Now, with the political passing of the WWII generation (its last gasp was Robert Dole's 1996 presidential run), our fixed ideas about the relationship between soldiers and civilians, warmakers and negotiators have been knocked for a loop.

The loser in all this has been American statesmanship—we are now better at waging war than negotiating to avoid it. Ever since the Nixon years, money and authority have been siphoned away from the State Department and delivered to the Pentagon. As Dana Priest shows in *The Mission: Waging War and Keeping Peace with America's Military*, today's real diplomatic power belongs to what she dubs the "Proconsuls of Empire"—the Pentagon's five regional Commanders-in-Chief (or CinCs), each of whom controls a huge swath of the world. Filling the void left by an enfeebled State Department, the rulers of these so-called CinCdoms shape policy, steamroll ambassadors, and spend money with no fear of rebuke. For his wartime press conferences during Operation Iraqi Freedom, CinC Tommy Franks spent $250,000 on a flashy set that was FedExed from Florida. In one of *The Mission*'s most revealing stories, Priest tells how at a big regional conference in Bahrain, America's seven Persian Gulf ambassadors stayed in ordinary hotel rooms, while then-CinC Anthony Zinni and his staff commandeered an entire wing, including a suite the size of a house. The proconsul's bill for two weeks? $550,000.

Of course, this is just milk money to a Defense Department that has never been more powerful or better entrenched. Secretary Rumsfeld is in his second tour at Defense, Vice President Cheney ran that department during Desert Storm, and even Secretary of State

Powell is himself former head of the Joint Chiefs of Staff—a company man who invariably stays with the program, from helping downplay the My Lai atrocities to overselling Iraqi military buildups before two different wars. In the old days, politicians had to rein in their military wild men: "Old Blood and Guts" George Patton; insubordinate Douglas MacArthur, who wanted to march from Inchon all the way to Beijing; cigar-chomping Curtis LeMay, who urged nuking Havana and Hanoi; even Stormin' Norman Schwarzkopf of the charging-hippo rages. Today, the generals are restrained—think of Powell, Richard Myers, or Tommy Franks—and keep trying to hold back the cracked civilians. Cheney, Rumsfeld, Wolfowitz, Perle—these men think of the *generals* as hidebound and overcautious. They mock the CIA for being wimpy, then, with staggering dishonesty, blame the skeptical intelligence services for overselling Iraq's WMDs. Although Powell's reassuring demeanor played a huge role in making the American people admire the military, the defense establishment hawks can't hide their disdain for him and his fellow State Department pantywaists who'd rather haggle than get the job done. You know the U.S. government has gotten militarized when a former four-star general is thought a pushover because he believes in having discussions with rival leaders before the air force starts bombing them.

Few in the Bush administration have faith in diplomacy, least of all those working at the Pentagon. Of course, it was infuriating that the very people who insisted on proof that Osama was behind September 11 were often the same ones who idolized him for pulling it off; of course, sometimes one needs to apply a few strokes of the big Rooseveltian stick. Still, one hoped that the shock of September 11 might have led America to a broad, public reappraisal of its foreign policy. Invade Afghanistan, sure, but rethink the U.S. government's longtime support for corrupt tyrannies, spend real money to improve the conditions in the underdeveloped world, sign on to fair-minded trade agreements, and begin a broad intellectual campaign in the Islamic world to win the war of ideas on behalf of Western values. Wiser minds might have convinced the President to stop calling Ariel Sharon "a man of peace" (an honorific that even the old warmonger's admirers don't believe) and spend a few billion creating an elite unit to fight terrorists inch for inch, tit for tat. The administration did pursue some of this intellectual agenda, often farcically: The State Department hired Charlotte Beers, a hugely successful adwoman who'd done campaigns for (among other products) Head & Shoulders, to market American values. Beers was soon gone, as was nearly all talk of peaceful ways one might combat militant Islam. Talking about Europe's carrot-and-stick policy toward Iran's nuclear program, Under Secretary of State John Bolton sneered, "I don't do carrots."

For Bush, being serious about terrorism meant using massive force to force "regime change" in Iraq and, from there, change the world—the Disquieting Americans packed major heat. Although the U.S. already had the most powerful military in history, the neocons kept grumbling that it was actually too weak. Months into the Iraq war, *The Weekly Standard* would chastise Bush (and no longer just Clinton) for his "parsimony" in maintaining "dangerously inadequate" levels of troop strength—only $400 billion! In their view, the U.S. needed at least twelve divisions (not just ten) to meet the Bush Doctrine's goal of preemptively stopping potential attackers, a strategy that could be implemented only at the end of a gun. This martial attitude achieved its self-parodic peak in an *Atlantic Monthly* piece by Robert D. Kaplan. Taking his inspiration from a cavalcade of colonialists and tyrants, he offered something of a user's manual for the American imperium. His ten handy rules spelled out the values implicit in the administration's policies, and when not unintentionally funny ("Rule No. 3: Emulate Second-Century Rome"), his advice was unnervingly warlike: "No mission," Kaplan declared, "should ever be compromised by diplomatic punctilio."

Believe it or not, other countries proved reluctant to get with this program, despite the sterling reputation of the so-called Pax Romana—at least among the Romans who weren't slaves.

Some Freedom Fries with Your War, Sir?

A few months before the bombs started hitting Baghdad, I was waiting in a taxi line outside the Barcelona airport. Behind me, a young

American businessman was greeting his newly arrived buddies by paying his own homage to Catalonia: "This is the best fuckin' party city in the world. You get home at 4:30 . . . in the afternoon. And the women are unbelievably sexy. But you gotta watch out for this Bush thing. Last week, I met this Swedish chick, unbelievably beautiful, and she started talking about how if Bush was there she'd, like, *kill* him. Which is bullshit." He paused. "Me, I *like* the guy. But if you want to get laid here, bro', you gotta say you voted *against* him."

The same was true all over the planet as the U.S. prepared to fight its most unpopular war since Vietnam. After September 11, the world had stood behind the Bush government's War on Terror, internalizing America's trauma so completely that even Indonesia's Megawati Sukarnoputri spoke of "9/11," although like the rest of the world, her vast Muslim country normally records that date as "11/9." But over the following months that changed. By the one-year anniversary, my foreign friends began pointing out that history hadn't actually begun on that ghastly day in September of 2001, however much we may like to think so. Chile, for instance, had already spent nearly three decades commemorating September 11. That was the day in 1973 when a CIA-backed coup toppled the elected President Salvador Allende and installed a brutal military dictatorship—one of those casually bloody fillips of U.S. foreign policy that led billions of people to mistrust President Bush's motives in the Middle East.

The world's antiwar fever was widely reported in the U.S., but you had to be in Europe to grasp its full virulence. America's allies could hardly have been more hostile. France acted badly, which was predictable. But so did Germany, where floundering Chancellor Gerhard Schroeder retained office by using glib anti-Americanism to distract voters from their economic woes—making him the antiwar alter ego of Bush, who was doing the same thing in the States. Tony Blair may have become Bush's better half in the war effort, but even on the right, the chattering British elite had its doubts. *The Daily Telegraph* insisted that Blair's much-touted dossier on Saddam's WMDs proved nothing; *The Spectactor* speculated on how an invasion might serve U.S. oil interests. Although Bush's vigilante act makes me cringe, I was driven equally crazy by Europe's practiced smugness. When the German justice minister compared Bush's tactics to Hitler's, I did want to point out that, well, actually the Guantanamo camp still has a ways to go to reach the highest Aryan standards. Reading Oxonian science professor Richard Dawkins's reflexively snotty remarks about the "illiterate, uncouth, unelected cowboy in the White House"—so it's back to the Couth Standard, is it?—I momentarily got in touch with my inner Bill O'Reilly. Long before the war started, resistance to Washington's power, as Timothy Garton Ash noted in *The Guardian*, had become so knee-jerk that millions of Europeans had lost the ability to tell good causes from bad when America was involved. To them, we were bloodthirsty barbarians. Two years running, Cannes gave big prizes to American movies about the student killings at Columbine, Michael Moore's *Bowling for Columbine* and Gus Van Sant's *Elephant*; refusing to be outdone, the British awarded the 2003 Booker Prize to *Vernon God Little*, a thudding black comedy on the theme of, you guessed it—Columbine. All this was enough to confirm the narrator's observation in DeLillo's novel *The Names*: "America is the world's living myth. There's no sense of wrong when you kill an American or blame America for some local disaster. This is our function, to be character types, to embody recurring themes that people can use to comfort themselves, justify themselves and so on. We're here to accommodate. Whatever people need, we provide. A myth is a useful thing."*

Of course, America's own behavior could hardly have been more impolitic, from Rumsfeld's slagging off of "Old Europe" to the cover

---

*America does feed its myth, often hilariously. During Bush's 2003 visit to London, where he took care to pronounce the word "nuclear" correctly, the White House went berserk in its demands. Not only did it bring 700 security men to supplement the 14,000 on-duty bobbies (the most since the end of WWII), but it sought to redo Bush's room in Buckingham Palace (adding concrete walls and bulletproof glass) and have two Black Hawk choppers flying overhead at all times. The English politely refused, although the U.S. security detail's electronic equipment still interfered with Queen Elizabeths's TV reception. "The poor dear," said a friend. "All she could do was watch Charles's old Benny Hill tapes."

of *The Weekly Standard* proclaiming, WE ARE THE WORLD. The Bush administration cleverly fanned the flames of anti-French populism, the better to discredit antiwar feeling. This is an old ruse in American political life—Patrick Henry once accused Thomas Jefferson of an excessive fondness for French food that led him to "abjure his native victuals." The White House was mightily abetted by the media, which, as ever, could resist everything except temptation: Like contestants on *Iron Chef*, they served up dish after dish of the same Gallic goose. No matter that, on September 12, 2001, *Le Monde*'s cover had carried the headline NOUS SOMMMES TOUS AMÉRICAINS (WE ARE ALL AMERICANS) or that Jacques Chirac, only eight days after the attacks, had been the first foreign head of state to a pay a memorial visit to New York. Bill O'Reilly pushed a boycott of French products, *The National Review* called the French "cheese-eating surrender monkeys" (a gag cribbed from *The Simpsons*), and *Saturday Night Live* ran a fake travel ad calling them "cowardly, yet opinionated, arrogant, yet foul-smelling, anti-Israel, anti-American, and, of course, as always, Jew-hating." I groaned when two Republican congressmen insisted on the House cafeteria serving "Freedom Fries," but I hooted when a few dim souls decided to show their patriotism by dramatically emptying bottles of burgundy and bordeaux that had already been imported and paid for. *Bien sûr*, there was foolishness to be had on both sides of the political divide. One afternoon I went to a lecture by Arianna Huffington, who spent the whole time puffing her latest book. During the Q&A, a young man asked a question in a heavy accent. "Where are you from?" Huffington inquired. "France," he replied, and the auditorium full of lefties broke into spontanteous applause.

While much of America's francophobia was delectably absurd, some people who should know better got into a snit. Outraged that other countries aren't as idealistic as the U.S. claims to be, *New York Times* columnist Thomas Friedman—who too often plays to the cheap seats in a grab for that next Pulitzer—couldn't get over France's cynicism in thwarting the Bush administration's efforts against Saddam. Still, that was less depressing than hearing my compatriots grouse about our allies' "ingratitude" in not supporting the Iraq war after the U.S. had saved them from the Nazis, helped pay for their post-WWII reconstruction, and saved them from communism. Here, Americans were trying to have it both ways—insisting on our national altruism in fighting for freedom yet also insisting that we're owed. In fact, there's something ignoble about expecting people to be grateful, especially for something our grandparents did. Sure, Chirac's advice was often lousy and self-serving—he was pursuing the interests of himself and of France—but it wasn't stupid to tell the Bush administration it was making a big mistake.

Although I myself opposed the war for unglamorous pragmatic reasons, the intellectual repertoire of the antiwar left was often depressingly small-minded, as if thwarting George W. Bush was the acme of progressive achievement. I myself had no quarrel with signs saying "NO BLOOD FOR OIL." One doesn't expect a sustained argument on a poster. Yet I snorted at placards comparing Bush to Hitler— carry a poster like that in a *real* fascist state, and you're dead, man. The left once stood for worldwide freedom and liberation, but by 2003, it had grown apt to begin its sentences, "Saddam is a bad guy, but . . ." This was precisely the kind of pro forma admission of an uncomfortable truth that let the Carter and Reagan White Houses to talk themselves into backing the goon. If you've ever spent any time in a dictatorship, or even read Kanan Makyia's *Republic of Fear,* you know better than to think this way. And Saddam's trial will underscore this point.

Still, those millions on the street provided a far more trenchant opposition to the war than the congressional Democrats, whose political strategy couldn't have been more supine. Terrified of bucking Bush's popularity, they could only hope he overreached. After first voting to give Bush the power to go into Iraq, they spent the next several months whining that he hadn't "made the case" for war—as if they themselves lacked the ability to scrutinize the evidence and make their own case, pro or con. Once it became inescapably clear that the President was going to start the bombs falling, Senate Minority Leader Tom Daschle threw the fit he should have pitched back when he was voting "Yea" on the resolution. Later, when John Kerry finally grasped that Democratic voters really hated the war, the presidential hopeful, who'd also voted yes, began grumbling that he'd been deceived by the White House. The guy never stops talking about having served in Vietnam, but didn't he *learn* anything there?

The Democrats' rhetorical ineptitude reached its nadir when ABC News's *This Week* interviewed two liberal congressmen, Representatives David Bonior and Jim McDermott, who were in Baghdad checking things out for themselves. It was bad enough that the pair stood before the cameras, sweating profusely and looking amiably befuddled, like trusting small-town ministers about to be swindled in the souk. It was worse that they kept saying the Iraqis assured them that U.N. inspectors could go wherever they wanted—even as the Iraqi government itself was publicly announcing that they couldn't. But things bottomed out when McDermott suggested that Bush might "mislead the American people" to get them into war. This wasn't an idiotic thing to say because it's untrue—heck, Bush was just joining the daisy chain of lying presidents—but because he said it on the streets of Baghdad while implying that he trusted the Iraqis more than his own leader. McDermott had no inkling how badly this would come across in America.

Although intelligent antiwar speakers occasionally turned up on TV—Tony Judt and Stanley Hoffman became regulars on the suddenly invaluable *Charlie Rose Show*—the media was overrun by prowar voices whose arguments for invading Iraq were basically of two kinds, one pragmatic and preemptive, the other idealistic, even utopian. Along with the White House, the former argued that Saddam posed a clear and present danger to the United States; the latter, that "regime change" would liberate the Iraqi people from tyranny and possibly set a democratic example for the whole region. Among the pragmatists, the one who enjoyed the greatest vogue was surely onetime CIA analyst Kenneth Pollack, whose book *The Threatening Storm: The Case for Invading Iraq* was the publishing version of a mayfly. Just as those insects enjoy a single day of adulthood, pass on their genetic message, and promptly die, so Pollack's book became obsolescent once the Coalition of the Piddling (as Jon Stewart dubbed it) actually *did* invade Iraq. But in the six months leading up to the war, you couldn't turn on NPR or CNN without someone intoning the book's portentous, pseudo-Churchillean title (this storm wasn't just *gathering*) and asking its author to share his expertise. In a world of talking head-cases, Pollack had the increasingly rare knack of coming off as a calm, honest broker with no hidden ideological agenda or Beltway-star narcissism. (I kept waiting for the obligatory debunking profile, but none ever appeared.) Insisting that Saddam did pose a serious danger in the long run, yet also insisting that an invasion would have to be done right, Pollack's seriousness appealed to readers on both sides of the debate: Neocons and liberal hawks such as *The New Yorker*'s David Remnick used the book to justify toppling Saddam; skeptical doves used its arguments to chide the Bush administration for racing into Iraq without thinking things through. The fierce irony of all this was that the very credential that made Pollack seem authoritative—his work for the CIA—proved to be the thing that made his judgments ultimately unreliable. For all his good sense and balance, Pollack wound up popularizing an assessment of Saddam's WMD program that American weapons inspector David Kay would eventually term "all wrong."*

Although the idealists included a great many liberal hawks (most notably, apostate leftist Christopher Hitchens), the most influential was the neocon Under Secretary of Defense Paul Wolfowitz, a quietly appealing figure who has been kindly portrayed in a Saul Bellow novel (*Ravelstein*) and affectionately nicknamed "Wolfowitz of Arabia" after the romantic English officer T. E. Lawrence, who imagined—to the point of delusion—that he was helping the Arab people, including today's Iraqis, win their freedom. With his honorable intentions and gentle speech, Wolfowitz had the makings of a tragic figure; at the least, he was the administration's closest thing to the original Quiet American (he even had a professor for a father, just like Alden Pyle). And his head was bursting with a big vision: By taking over Iraq, the U.S. would free the Iraqi people from a murderous thug, help rebuild

---

*Ever the honorable schoolboy, Pollack did something the Bush administration resisted. He admitted his error publicly and, in the February 2004 *Atlantic Monthly*, tried to figure out how he and the Company could have been so wrong.

the country's ravaged infrastructure, and show America's strength in the war of ideas against the Arab despotism and Islamic fundamentalism that are antithetical to the West's deepest values—values that should be universal.

Although friends shudder when I mention it, I myself feel the pull of this utopian vision and imagine that millions of my fellow Americans do, too. I've always loved this country for creating the Marshall Plan and pulling off the postwar reconstruction of Japan. (Yes, I know there were self-interested reasons for both.) While traveling in such ravaged countries as Zaire, Cambodia, and Romania right after the fall of Nicolae Ceauşescu, I've often found myself regretting that America couldn't just step in and take care of things—help the beleaguered people set up a decent government and start building a country that works. Such a savior mentality is, of course, disquieting, but a Quiet American does live inside me and finds something very seductive in Wolfowitz's dream for Iraq. There's a romantic grandeur to the whole conception—remaking a wounded country, if not the whole troubled world—that stirs something deep and good in our national soul, something that's one of the glories of America. The left has often shared it.

The trouble with this grandiose vision, of course, is that the man enacting it is not a thoughtful idealist like Wolfowitz or a devout internationalist such as Tony Blair, who articulates such ideals so eloquently that Paul Berman dubbed him the actual leader of the free world. Metaphorically, perhaps. But the President of the United States is George W. Bush. Jazzed by tax cuts and obsessed with secrecy, his corporate-elite approach to his own nation never augured well for freedom and justice in postwar Iraq. He made Afghanistan less hospitable to Islamic terror, then left it to suffer. He harped on Saddam's danger in his 2003 State of the Union address but never mentioned the word "democracy" in connection with Iraq. He sought U.N. approval for the invasion—to "kofi" the war, as the Brits slangily put it—but made it insultingly obvious that he wanted the world's rubber stamp, not its opinion. Most undemocratically, in making his case for an internationally unpopular invasion that would wind up costing the

American people hundreds of billions of dollars, he and his administration were (to be kind) disingenuous.

Before the war, you kept hearing about the bombing tactic known as "Shock and Awe," a name so catchy that video-game makers were fighting to trademark it. The plan was supposedly designed to cow into submission any Iraqis it didn't blow sky-high. The Bush administration didn't actually use it in Baghdad, but it did employ something similar on the American public. Even as government officials were claiming that war wasn't inevitable, the Bush administration flew 200,000 troops to the Middle East, tried to slip Turkey $15 billion for its help (the Turks refused the baksheesh), and warned Saddam that it was "five minutes to midnight." Seeking to forge a psychological link between Iraq and 9/11, the government cranked up the scare tactics— declaring orange alerts, putting antiaircraft missiles on the Mall, telling fantastic tales of Iraqi drone planes that could drop biochemical weapons on American cities. In an infuriatingly circular bout of self-fulfilling prophecy, Vice President Dick Cheney argued that we had to use our troops in Iraq precisely *because* we'd committed them—otherwise, we would seem weak. (The vile Henry Kissinger concurred.) This was the sort of reasoning that led to World War I, when military timetables became more powerful than political will. And once the war officially ended, the same reasoning persisted: Because we'd invaded Iraq, Congress *had* to give $87 billion to support the troops who *had* to invade Iraq because we'd committed them in the Middle East in the first place.

To convince the American people that they were in immediate danger from Iraqi weapons of mass distruction, the administration fobbed off plagiarized student essays as top-secret info, claimed a new bin Laden tape demonstrated al-Qaeda's connection to Saddam (when the recording suggested precisely the opposite), deliberately hid information that Iraq may have already destroyed its WMDs, and boasted about giving hard evidence of Iraqi weapons to U.N. inspectors—who termed this info "garbage after garbage after garbage." Through it all, the President kept insinuating that Saddam was linked to September 11. By my count, he did it seven different times in his single pre-war press conference. Of course, what do you expect of a man who, in an unintentional nod to Orwell, kept saying that we had to go to war because we are a nation of peace?*

Now, there is nothing shocking about a president, Republican or Democrat, misleading the public into war: LBJ did it in Vietnam, Ronald Reagan in Grenada, Bush I in Panama. Back in the early 1970s, the French social philosopher Raymond Aron noted that it's common for American leaders to employ the exaggerated rhetoric of "absolute evil" to win public support for complicated political decisions. Wolfowitz essentially admitted as much to *Vanity Fair* when he said that "for bureaucratic reasons" the administration settled on WMDs as the reason for war with Iraq "because it was the one reason everyone could agree with." He might have added that nobody in the administration, least of all the President, wanted to alert the American people to the true size and cost of the project. A mistake. Had Bush made that case frankly, the American people would probably have followed him. Instead, the administration chose to assert that American soldiers would be greeted as liberators and that, thanks to foreign aid and Iraqi oil income, the reconstruction of Iraq would be dirt cheap. A few weeks into the war, the head of the United States Agency for International Development, Andrew Natsios, did precisely that, telling *Nightline* that the cost to America would be $1.7 billion, a claim so brazenly spurious that Ted Koppel's toupee jumped an inch. "You're not suggesting," Koppel said incredulously, "that the rebuilding of Iraq is going to be done for one-point-seven billion dollars. . . ." In fact, Natsios was. But as with so much of what the Bush administration said in preparing America for war, it was ultimately hard to know how much was conscious hype and how much willful self-delusion.

Even today, I'm not even sure the White House itself knows for sure. You get a war like Operation Iraqi Freedom only when leaders' best and worst instincts are working in tandem. The decision to

---

*Months after the war, Bush finally admitted that there was no proven connection between Saddam and 9/11—this, a few days after die-hard Cheney suggested there might be.

invade Iraq was, to use the Freudian term, *overdetermined*. It was born of multiple reasons and motives—some admirable, some not. The Bush administration took the country to war because it wanted to guarantee that no Iraqi weapons of mass destruction would ever be used against the U.S. Because it wanted to liberate the Iraqi people, install democracy, and become a model for the whole Islamic world. Because it wanted to break up the anti-American status quo in the Middle East. Because it wanted to give America a perch in the Middle East that would cut us loose from Saudi Arabia and let us loom over Iran. Because it wanted access to Iraqi oil. Because bagging Saddam might offer a psychological substitute for not catching bin Laden (although when it happened, people began asking about Osama again). Because it would allow Donald Rumsfeld to ride his armored hobby-horse about rapid, high-tech warfare. Because it would reinforce Karl Rove's pet theory that Bush's presidency would begin a Republican period of dominance akin to that started by the imperialistic William McKinley. Because trouncing a monster like Saddam could make Bush invulnerable in 2004. Because it fed the President's post-9/11 sense of grandiosity. Because Bush is a man who's never happy sitting still—he always needs to do *something*.

So why not take out the sumbitch who tried to kill your old man? There were, of course, many compelling answers to such a question. They became far more urgent on March 19, 2003, when, to borrow a Churchillean locution, the Bush administration put its ideas to the proof. As in Afghanistan, the man providing the answers was not the President but one of the great political showmen of our era.

The Loudest Disquieting American

Although it is George W. Bush who must take credit or blame for the whole War on Terror, he wasn't its star performer. That distinction belonged to Donald Rumsfeld, the seventy-one-year-old Secretary of Defense who took a normally unglamorous job and, by dint of crazy personal charisma, became one of the most entertaining government officials in the last fifty years. Brainy, garrulous, funny, snappish, and supremely self-confident, he embodies everything seductive and dangerous about American neo-imperialism. Rumsfeld's rapid rise and slow, inexorable fall have made him the perfect symbol of Bush-era foreign policy in the years since 9/11.

That ghastly day resurrected Rumsfeld's career. Back in August 2000, he appeared to be a goner. *Slate* even ran a regular item called "Rumsfeld Death Watch." But from the moment he started briefing the media about the war in Afghanistan, his breezy assurance made him the administration's most electrifying presence—*Meet the Press*'s Tim Russert dubbed him "America's stud." In her delightfully worshipful biography *Rumsfeld: A Personal Portrait*, which reads a bit like a special issue of *Seventeen* magazine written for the AARP, the neocon Midge Decter says he incarnates "the return of the ideal of the Middle American Family Man." While I might feel the same if I'd spent *my* adult life married to Norman Podhoretz, she misses the quality that made Rummy so attractive: He's a hard-ass, Midge. Decked out in his gray suits and rimless glasses, he strolled into briefings like Wyatt Earp into the saloon—smart, poised, and absolutely positive he was the biggest swinging dick in the room. ("My whole life's a movie," he once said.) The rap against Rummy has always been arrogance, a quality much despised in bureaucrats. But in wartime, people want a cocksure leader, the kind of guy who enjoys sparring with reporters, grins when things appear to go badly, and shows occasional glimpses of our Middle American lunacy. Nixon devised the so-called Madman Theory to make communist nations think he might dementedly fire off nuclear weapons, and Rummy gave off some of that same wacko vibe. Months before the Bush people talked publicly about regime change, you could catch a gleam in Rummy's eye—*Hot damn, Saddam!* And who knew? While in the neighborhood, he might just decide to flatten Tehran, too.

Unlike his chicken-hawk colleagues, Rumsfeld has never been afraid to mix it up. Where Bush flew to Nebraska on September 11 and Cheney ducked underground, he helped the rescue workers outside the Pentagon. In the following weeks, most of the Bush team walked around wearing permanent expressions of annoyance or existential dread. Not so Rummy, who always looked to be having a blast. He toyed with his questioners ("I could answer, but I'm not inclined to"), employed admirably straightforward words such as "kill" and "corpse," and, as mentioned earlier, cheerfully mispronounced Osama's surname. Rummy invariably savors his words like a minor poet granted a reading at Harvard, and connoisseurs came to relish the moments when he jauntily punctuated his sentences out loud, referring to "Osama bin Laden, comma, mass murderer" or serving up perfect gems of zazen wisdom: "Nothing we have, nothing in the defense establishment, nothing you own in your homes is perfect. Your cars aren't perfect. Your bikes aren't perfect. Our eyeglasses aren't perfect. We live with that all the time. If you cannot do everything, does that mean you should not do anything?"

Although his runaway tongue tended to get the administration in trouble—"Every time Rumsfeld insults Europe," observed *New York Times* columnist Nicholas Kristof, "it costs us another $20 billion"— this freewheeling verbal brio seemed refreshing in an administration that was proud of wringing all personality from its public statements. As Tony Judt remarked, Rumsfeld may have infuriated other nations with his cracks, but at least his words let you see what the Bush people were really thinking. Not that reporters did anything worthwhile with his statements. A couple of weeks into the Afghanistan war, *Saturday Night Live* ran a funny sketch in which Rumsfeld kept telling Pentagon correspondents that their questions were stupid. What made the spoof so telling wasn't Darrell Hammond's spot-on impersonation but the deadly-accurate portrait of how the press let itself be kicked around. They accepted Rummy's bullying not only because he delivered the goods—nobody else in the administration was half so quotable—but because his derision tapped into their own self-loathing. These journalists knew that they kept showing up to hear official statements from officials who made no pretense that their words were true. For all the talk of its liberalism and cynicism, the media respects officials who are good at their jobs, and nobody stonewalled or twisted the facts half so memorably as Rummy. Like the TV audience, they relished watching him perform, and in return, he looked down on them with a kind of exasperation one might bestow on a particularly hard-to-train pet.

Of course, Rumsfeld has always preened himself as being able to defeat anybody *mano a mano*. He's spent a lifetime showing off his toughness. In his youth, he did one-armed push-ups for money. As a wrestler at both Princeton and in the navy (where he won the championship), he was known for straightforward aggression: "Rumsfeld was the kind of wrestler," recalls an opponent from Cornell, "you knew what he was going to do and he'd do it anyhow." His take-charge style led him to become a naval flight instructor, just like Tom Skerrit in *Top Gun* (although Rummy actually had the good looks of Tom Cruise), and his combativeness did not dwindle as he got older. He ran for Congress and won. He became a protégé of Richard Nixon, refusing to take on assignments that wouldn't advance his career. And he established himself as a punishing political infighter. If Kissinger moved through the White House bureaucracy like a brilliant broken-field runner, James Mann noted in *The Atlantic*, Rumsfeld was Jim Brown—he'd run right over you. And he would never willingly take a bullet. The leaked "long, hard slog" Iraq memo of October 16, 2003, wasn't simply Rummy's meditation on fighting terrorism. Finding its way into print a week after articles began blaming Rummy for the faltering reconstruction, it was designed to prevent his enemies from suggesting that America's troubles in Iraq had been created by any of *his* illusions.

Rumsfeld's macho style led military historian John Keegan to gush in *Vanity Fair*: "He does not bargain, he does not negotiate, and his mental processes are devoted entirely to calculating how he can successfully inflict violence on those he hates." Everything about the man bespeaks the will to power—he whipped out fifteen-pound dumbbells and began doing curls for a *Time* reporter—and one can only imagine the frustrated ambition that throbs mightily within his secret self. He made a hopeless run at the 1988 Republican nomination, aborting his campaign in April 1987. It must gall his soul that well-born schmoozers like the two George Bushes should both have been elected president while a man of his caliber didn't make it out of the starting-gate. But Rumsfeld could never have won such an office—his gifts are inseparable from his abrasiveness. In fact, his need to be the smartest guy in every conversation makes him an heir of JFK's Secretary of Defense, a statistical brainiac mockingly known as Robert "I Have All the Answers" McNamara. The military hated him as it now hates Rumsfeld, who makes it far too clear that he shares Clemenceau's belief that war is far too important to be left to the generals. But McNamara's brilliance was always lashed with neurosis; he slicked down his hair so tight that one feared his head might explode if a single hair got blown out of place. Rumsfeld has never revealed any such inner turmoil. He's been too busy browbeating generals and dashing off "snowflakes," as the military brass calls the despised memos that keep falling on their desks. He would never see the benefit of participating in a film like Erroll Morris's engrossing documentary *The Fog of War*, which finds McNamara defensively picking at the unhealed psychic scabs from his role in the Vietnam War.

Unlike most of those he works with at Defense or in the White House, Rumsfeld is not really a conservative ideologue. As a congressman, he voted for the Freedom of Information Act and sneered at the lazy minds of far right-wing groups; heading the liberal-minded OEO, he fought to make it (and, therefore, himself) stronger; advising Nixon, he warned the President that staying in Vietnam was a losing proposition. (In all of these things, he was right.) But while he's not a hard-core right-winger, he is an instinctive radical who shakes up things wherever he goes. When he became president of Searle Pharmaceutical Company in 1977, he decided to decentralize its operation, quickly firing 150 employees at the central office and transferring 150 others. Taking over Defense for the second time, he made it his mission to reshape the military against the generals' wishes by developing missile defense and making the armed forces smaller, faster, and more technically sophisticated. For him, the key to everything is transformation. As he once remarked, "I don't find it hard to change, but some people seem to. And some countries seem to. And some institutions seem to. But it is particularly important." Rumsfeld's instinctive desire to reinvent every institution he touches (an odd echo of Trotsky's Theory of Permanent Revolution) explains why he's meshed so well with his under secretaries Wolfowitz and Feith, plus the radical right-wingers in the Bush administration. They gave shape to his desire to reform the world—and to do it now.

If Rumsfeld's often pedantic impatience makes him a pain to work for (who likes having his grammar corrected for no good reason?), it also makes him the kind of icon that people love to send up. Frank Gannon wrote a hilarious *New Yorker* fantasy about Rummy ordering breakfast at Denny's ("Bacon is, we all know, and nobody seriously doubts it anymore, very similar to sausage"). Hart Seely compiled a wonderful book, *Pieces of Intelligence: The Existential Poetry of Donald H. Rumsfeld*, that revealed his mastery of our native tongue by putting his statements in verse form. Even straight reporters got into the act, treating his press conferences as gaga pieces of performance art, running half-minute clips instead of the usual six-second sound bites. A British group called the Plain English Campaign mockingly gave him its annual "Foot in Mouth Award" for perhaps his most famous remark: "There are known knowns; there are things we know we know. We also know there are known unknowns; that is to say, we know there are some things we do not know. But there are also unknown unknowns—the ones we don't know we don't know. And if one looks through the history of our country and other free countries, it is the latter category that tend to be the difficult ones."

In fact, this is a perfectly lucid statement and, like so much of what Rumsfeld says, was fun, smart, and true. What makes him dangerous, though, is that he often says things that are fun, smart, and false. The first member of Bush's team to use Churchill's famous line about how, in war, truth must be surrounded by a bodyguard of lies, he kept that bodyguard hopping. During the war in Afghanistan, he denied civilian casualties from U.S. bombing long after international reporters had documented them, and then began attacking groups (including Doctors Without Borders) that reported on the noncombatant dead and wounded. When it came to Iraq, his lies grew even balder and more self-protective. Before the invasion, he was asked by PBS's Jim Lehrer if he expected the invasion to be welcomed by most of the Iraqis. "There's no question that would be welcomed," he said crisply. "Go back to Afghanistan. The people were in the streets playing music, cheering, flying kites, and doing all the things that the Taliban and the al-Qaeda would not let them do." After the war ended and American forces were under guerrilla attack, he was asked about his prediction. "Never said that," he snapped. "Never did. You may remember it well, but you're thinking of someone else. You can't find, anywhere, me saying anything like those things you just said I said."

In fact, by the beginning of the Iraq war, Rumsfeld's star had begun to plummet. Part of this was simple overexposure: His act got tired. And once the official war was won, his aura of invincibility began to be frayed by the ongoing troubles. While he'd received rapturous kudos for the war plan—the kind of technical challenge on which he thrives—he had no instincts at all for the nation-building process that he insisted on overseeing. Perhaps because the idea of an extreme Middle East makeover was Wolfowitz's, Rumsfeld lost sight of what Clausewitz termed the *zweck*, the political purpose of the war. He was all bluster, and the world—starting with the Iraqis themselves— quickly grasped that the Pentagon's peace plan was a botch. Asked about the looting of Baghdad, Rumsfeld jauntily answered, "Freedom's untidy. Free people are free to make mistakes and commit crimes and do bad things"—sanguine words one didn't really picture him uttering about, say, the L.A. riots. One reason the soldiers hadn't stopped the looting was that the U.S. didn't have enough boots on the ground (as the idiom has it) to maintain civic order, a problem that became increasingly obvious—except, apparently, to Rumsfeld. As the guerrilla attacks mounted and U.S. soldiers died, his press conferences began to feel increasingly unglued from reality. Consider the follow- ing exchange about a Baghdad rocket attack recorded by the *Village Voice*'s James Ridgeway:

QUESTION: Mr. Secretary? . . . At the same time, Mr. Secretary, your Deputy, Paul Wolfowitz, was there last week at the Al Rashid Hotel and there was an attack and, in fact, one American officer was killed. Mr. Wolfowitz was shaken up. Isn't that evidence that in fact things are not as peaceful there as sometimes you would like to see them portrayed?

RUMSFELD: It seems to me that doesn't really follow. The fact of the matter is in any major city in the world, there are attacks of various types that take place.

Nor did his October 16 memo restore confidence. In it, he raised the question of whether the Defense Department was doing the right stuff to a win the War on Terror, asking: "Are the changes we have and are making too modest and incremental? My impression is that we have not yet made truly bold moves, although we have made many sensible, logical moves in the right direction, but are they enough?" Which sounds sensible enough, except for one thing: At that point, the U.S. had already invaded two countries. How much bolder and less incremental did Rummy expect to get?

Even during these dark days, he was always a treat to watch, but hearing him talk, I found myself remembering one of the ten lessons McNamara learned from Vietnam: You must be prepared to reexamine your reasoning. For all his big talk about change, Rummy was not, and by the autumn of 2003, *The Weekly Standard* was dubbing him "Secretary of Stubbornness" and *Time* was asking, "Is Rumsfeld Losing His Mojo?" William Kristol had no trouble answering yes: "Rumsfeld lost credibility with the White House because he screwed up the postwar planning. . . . For five months, they let Rumsfeld have his way, and for five months Rumsfeld said everything's fine. He wanted to do the postwar with fewer troops than a lot of people advised, and it turned out to be a mistake." (Of course, Kristol was looking for someone to blame for the troubles in Iraq lest we start remembering the neocons' foolish predictions about how smoothly things would go there.) Through it all, Rummy's sense of being right never wavered. He maintained the stoic attitude expressed in an earlier poem:

> *Opinion polls go up and down,*
> *They spin like weather vanes.*
> *They're interesting, I suppose.*
> *I don't happen to look.*

Perhaps he should have. For bit by bit, his arrogance in the face of the facts and the world's opinion came to seem a potent metaphor for the Disquieting Americans' know-it-all approach to international affairs. Like the President himself, Rumsfeld hates admitting he's wrong—you won't find him apologizing for glad-handing Saddam back in the eighties. He plays to *win*, and if he cannot, he will still pretend that he has, fighting until the last grain of sand finally slips down the hourglass.

Rummy's son once remarked that his father "doesn't ski as if he's *on* a mountain, he skis as if he wants to *move* it." He has always greeted the world in much the same spirit. While such an attitude may be helpful in ousting a tyrant such as Saddam Hussein, it hardly seems the wisest approach to showing an increasingly skeptical world the graces and charms of the American way of life. As every good skier knows, you'll go faster and farther if you respect the mountain rather than trying to show it who's boss.

Ten Quick and Easy Lessons from a Long, Hard Slog

1. Remember Pearl Harbor. In the first six months of the Pacific War, the Japanese grew so euphoric over their seemingly effortless success that they began to suffer from what they termed "victory disease"—an overconfident sense of well-being quickly shattered by the realities on the ground. Much the same happened to the U.S. in Iraq. Blessed with incomparably superior firepower, its military enjoyed a cakewalk that, at least temporarily, vindicated Rummy's theories about modern warfare. Saddam fled, Baghdad quickly fell (no new Stalingrad, this), and by May Day, President Bush was landing on the *Abraham Lincoln* to declare "Mission Accomplished." The Greeks had a word for this: Enter HUBRIS, stage right. Even as the administration exulted, the seeds of trouble were sprouting. The Pentagon had underestimated the hidden opposition and overestimated its own control over events. U.S. forces stood by as looters decimated Iraqi government offices, protecting only the Oil Ministry—a public relations catastrophe. The Coalition of the Willing went months without providing water, electricity, jobs, or public order, a problem that became deadly obvious during the subsequent months of guerrilla attacks—a bloody drip-drip-drip of shootings, roadside explosions, and monstrous suicide bombings. Even before Saddam's capture, nobody thought the insurgents would win, although it did seem possible that everyone might lose. But by the time the administration asked Congress for $87 billion for Iraq, victory disease had given way to a pained awareness that "winning" in Iraq would never be as triumphant as the administration had once dreamed. By the time Bush's *Top Gun* landing finally appeared in a campaign ad, it was being run by John Kerry.

2. **Never oversell a war.** In urging the invasion, Disquieting Americans like Dick Cheney did what any smart football coach would warn you not to do—they raised expectations sky-high. They didn't just claim that Saddam was an imminent threat, wallowing in WMDs, but implied that those who disagreed were naive or cynical. They didn't just say he was a fascist gangster who deserved to be overthrown but suggested that oppressed Iraqis would welcome U.S. troops with open arms, if not blizzards of rose petals. The hard sell backfired. When those WMD stockpiles didn't turn up, the world believed the U.S had deliberately exaggerated the danger; just as bad, the prediction that Iraqis would embrace coalition soldiers only made the guerrilla attacks appear more dire. As I write, seven hundred soldiers have died in Iraq, many of them in accidents. This is an incredibly small number for such a massive invasion (in Vietnam, five hundred soldiers sometimes died in a single week), and had the administration prepared the country for a difficult, drawn-out occupation rather than a love-in, the public might have been impressed by how well things were going. As it was, officials were forced to practice the alchemy of transmuting bad news into good. Who will forget the day when Bush defensively insisted that increasingly violent attacks were proof of the coalition's *success*? Within weeks, he'd sped up the timetable for ceding power to the Iraqis, begun asking the U.N. for help, and, despite his continuing support for repressive regimes all over the

planet, started giving Wilsonian speeches about America's need to embrace democracy: "Sixty years of Western nations excusing and accommodating the lack of freedom in the Middle East did nothing to make us safe—because in the long run, stability cannot be purchased at the expense of liberty." Such sentiments are admirably correct, although one would trust Bush's sincerity more if he hadn't been using principle as his fallback position.

3. Nobody loves an occupier, however benevolent. Although the rose-petal scenario didn't materialize, many Iraqis did greet Americans as liberators. But they were also torn by a welter of other, more painful emotions. *Shame* that in over a quarter century they hadn't been able to dispose of Saddam themselves. *Mortification* at the state of their country. (Watching tapes of the captured Saddam, a middle-aged Iraq man told *The New York Times*'s John Burns, "I hate this man to the core of my bones. Just seeing him sitting there makes the hairs on my arms stand up. And yet, I can't tell you why, I feel sorry for him, to be so humiliated. It is as if he and Iraq have become the same thing.") *Resentment* that their country was being run (and seemingly overrun) by foreign invaders. *Suspicion* that the coalition forces wanted to take over Iraq's resources. *Anger* that a nation so willing to topple the mighty Saddam was so unwilling to use its awesome resources to give the people water, electricity, employment, and safety.

The administration could and should have predicted this, for such feelings are a recurring theme of the literature of occupation. Consider Norman Lewis's September 23 diary entry from his book *Naples '44:* "I have arrived at a time when, in their hearts, these people must be thoroughly sick and tired of us. A year ago we liberated them from the Fascist Monster, and they still sit doing their best to smile politely at us, as hungry as ever, more disease-ridden than ever before, in the ruins of their beautiful city where law and order have ceased to exist. And what is the prize that is to be eventually won? The rebirth of democracy. The glorious prospect of being able one day to choose their rulers from a list of powerful men, most of whose corruptions are generally known and accepted with weary resignation. The days of

Benito Mussolini must seem like a lost paradise compared with this." Although I doubt that non-Baathist Iraqis would look back on Saddam's reign as halcyon, Lewis's words haven't lost their sting.

4. What utopians start, realists finish. In dreaming up the Iraq war, the neocons (and their vice presidential advocate) made a series of mistakes born of cocky enthusiasm. They assumed that Iraq wasn't as shattered, materially and psychologically, as it actually was. They believed that Iraqis would warm to the Defense Department's favorite exiles, such as slippery Ahmad Chalabi. Condemning the State Department as defeatist, they ignored its carefully designed "Future of Iraq Project" plans, cut out its experts such as Thomas Warrick (who knew vastly more than they did about that country), held up appointment of its staff members even as the Coalition Provisional Authority was 50 percent understaffed, and trusted reconstruction to people chosen more for their ideology than their practical experience. Aren't Republicans supposed to be the competent ones? Describing the postwar planning, one senior administration member told *The New Yorker*'s George Packer: "It isn't pragmatism, it isn't Realpolitik, it isn't conservatism, it isn't liberalism. It's theology." The peace plan was such a mess that the neocons fell out of favor; the White House began heeding the advice of the previously disdained foreign policy "realists." You knew that the President had grown weary of utopianism when he sent "He Who Must Not Be Named"—James Baker III—jetting around the globe to arrange debt relief for the Iraqis. One of the most cynically efficient political operators in modern American history—if only the left had someone half as skillful—Baker is too shrewd to make the Bush administration's fundamental error. You would never catch *him* believing his own propaganda.

5. You can manufacture myths, but you can't control their meaning. Although the invasion of Iraq produced endless hours of video footage, it was defined by carefully orchestrated mythic moments: the rescue of Jessica Lynch, U.S. soldiers pulling down the Saddam statue in al-Firdos Square, the photographs of the dead Uday and Qusay Hussein, the President serving turkey to the troops on Thanksgiving, and Saddam Hussein in his Jerry Garcia beard having his teeth inspected.* Each of these oft-replayed scenes went haring across the screen accompanied by suitable sighs and coos from the media, but once surpassed by the tortoise crawl of history, they no longer mean what they once did. While there's nothing to add about the irony of Bush's "Mission Accomplished" landing (except that the forty-dollar action figure of Bush in his flight suit did accomplish *its* moneymaking mission), one should recall that toppling the Saddam statue was also a choreographed media event. This wasn't the fall of the Berlin Wall with throngs of liberated souls spontaneously dancing for joy; it was a couple of hundred Iraqis, carefully framed by the cameras and surrounded by American tanks, taking part in a symbolic gesture designed to be shown on television.

Never did a pop myth change its meaning more profoundly than the saga of Lynch, the likable nineteen-year-old army private who became a national heroine when the military and a credulous media turned her into a Grrrl Power G.I. Jane. According to the myth, Lynch was captured only after fending off *fedayeen* with the alacrity of Buffy the Vampire Slayer; later she was rescued by the U.S. military in a midnight raid whose daring was hugely exaggerated. In a slower, more innocent time, that fantastic tale might have survived for years. Yet even before official combat ended, Lynch's story began looking less like *True Lies* than Preston Sturges's WWII comedy *Hail the Conquering Hero*, where 4-F Eddie Bracken pretends to be a war hero to wow his small town. Only here, Pfc. Lynch was the scam's victim, not its perpetrator. Within seven months of her capture, this once-glorious myth had guttered and died. CBS's *Saving Jessica Lynch* may have been the first TV movie in history to be less inspirational than official news coverage of the same event. Lynch herself spoke out, too,

*American forces shaved the beard but left his mustache: It was crucial that the man not merely be the real Saddam but *look like* the real one, not some hirsute Wizard of Oz figure with a bad dye job. Such are the semiotics of tyrant branding.

revealing herself to be a woman of estimable decency and candor. She wished the U.S. army hadn't been in Iraq; she said the military shouldn't have given footage of her rescue to the TV networks; most of all, she disliked having her flesh-and-blood wounds turned into myth (in this case by *The Washington Post*). "They used me in a way to symbolize all this stuff," she told Diane Sawyer. "It hurt me in a way that people would make up stories they had no truth about."

6. Being wrong before doesn't mean you are wrong now, but . . .

Over the last half-century (at least), America's Middle East policy has been a feast of cynicism, blowback, and faith in foolish aphorisms— my enemy's enemy is my friend. The U.S. government backed the repressive Shah of Iran and House of Saud, embraced the Afghanistani *mujahideen* because they fought the Soviet enemy, and now gives free rein to bloody-minded Ariel Sharon because he's a hard-liner against terrorism, not to mention a surrogate tough-guy dad for Dubya. Back during the Reagan years, the U.S. turned a blind eye to Saddam's butchery because he was fighting our Iranian enemy—and cutting deals with Bechtel. This wretched history was often brought up by those who opposed administration policy in Iraq. "We supported Saddam back when he was gassing his own people," they said, "so why should we topple him now that he's stopped?" The prowar camp's answer was simple: The old policy was wrong and the new one is right. As Hitchens tirelessly pointed out, getting rid of Saddam was all the more justified because it rectified the ghastly error of sanctioning his barbarity in the first place. Although Hitchens's reasoning here is correct, waging a just war isn't merely a question of policy but of trust. After all, many of the men involved in ousting Saddam—notably, Rumsfeld—were the very ones who had winked at his actions during the presidencies of Reagan and Bush I. That's one reason that so many people worldwide reacted with such furious suspicion to George W. Bush's sanctimonious rhetoric about America's high ideals—they knew the U.S. had dishonored those before. If the President had come out and admitted that his father, Rummy, and others had been dangerously wrong about Iraq—maybe even apologized for our country's role in propping up a particularly vile dictator—he might not have swayed anyone to the prowar side, but he would have displayed the moral clarity that he and the neocons take such pride in possessing.

7. A conquered nation is not a fire sale. I wouldn't dream of denying that Iraqis are better off without Saddam. But in an eerily ideological version of "mission creep," President Bush's early talk of freeing Iraq morphed into a policy of installing a "free market" economy in Iraq: privatizing all the major state industries except for oil, encouraging multinational corporations to set up shop, allowing foreign investors to buy up to 100 percent of domestic businesses, and paying a fortune to American firms for reconstruction. For all the endless complaints one hears about Halliburton's $7 billion contract, the problem goes beyond the fact that this particular company is making a small fortune in Iraq. (That's mainly a PR bungle, especially abroad: News of the deal ran on front pages throughout the Middle East.) The real problem is that the administration is imposing its free-market religion on a conquered people who may not want it. While this policy might speed up reconstruction in the short run, it also means that much of the country's wealth will belong to investors based outside Iraq, many of them with risk-free investment deals paid for by U.S. taxpayers. While President Bush likes to compare Coalition efforts in Iraq to postwar Japan, the preeminent historian of that earlier occupation, John W. Dower, flatly rejects the analogy. Writing in *The Los Angeles Times*, Dower notes that such policies as the Iraqi privatization measures were "simply unthinkable" during the occupation of Japan, which encouraged national self-sufficiency by allowing the Japanese government to protect and promote its domestic industries. The Bush administration has chosen the precisely opposite course and runs the risk of duplicating some of the worst features of post-communist Russia, where state industries were snapped up cheap by a handful of powerful moguls, giving them inordinate power and leaving the average citizen with almost nothing.

8. Winning a war doesn't necessarily make you safer from terrorism. A couple of days after L. Paul Bremer's famous "We got him,"

Howard Dean was pilloried for his claim that capturing Saddam Hussein hadn't made America any safer. Like so much of what Dean said (*Yearrgggh*), it was an off-the-cuff provocation; but like so much of what Dean said, it also expressed a truth recognized by honest people on both left and right, including the top U.S. military official in Baghdad. Days after Saddam was caught, America went to "orange" alert, teams searched for dirty bombs in five major U.S. cities, the government began canceling some flights from Europe and Mexico to the U.S., and Iraq saw countless more guerrilla attacks. The great illusion of the phrase "War on Terror" is that it makes one think it can be fought like a proper war. In the months leading up to the invasion of Iraq, the Bush administration assured the American people that victory would help protect the U.S. from terrorist attacks; the Pentagon insisted that the war wouldn't distract it from the relentless pursuit of al-Qaeda and other Islamic militant groups. In fact, one thousand Special Forces were pulled out of Afghanistan where they'd been pursuing al-Qaeda and bin Laden and put on the trail of Saddam. But that was the least of it. Bush's own special assistant for combatting terrorism resigned five days before the Iraq war, saying, "The difficult long-term issues both at home and abroad have been avoided, neglected, or shortchanged and generally underfunded." While spending scores of billions of dollars in Iraq, the administration has devoted too little money to making America's ports, bridges, trains, electrical infrastructure, or nuclear power plants more secure. It has failed to give firemen, police departments, and hospitals the money they need to handle a major emergency.

War, in fact, is always a huge distraction. It devours resources and thinking—just as Dean suggested. This was tacitly acknowledged in Rumsfeld's "long, hard slog" memo, which wondered whether the Islamic world, especially its madrassas, may be producing terrorists faster than we catch them and fretted that the government lacked "a broad, integrated plan to stop the next generation of terrorists. . . . The U.S. is putting relatively little effort into a long-range plan, but we are putting a great deal of effort into trying to stop terrorists. The cost-benefit ratio is against us! Our cost is billions against the terrorists' cost of millions. . . . Is our current situation such that 'the harder we work, the behinder we get'?" What made this scary wasn't Rummy's recognition that the War on Terror isn't a normal war but that he was bringing up these questions six months after the U.S. had invaded Iraq in the name of battling terrorism and two full years after everybody in America knew about madrassas, learned the phrase "asymmetrical warfare," and realized what a terrorist could do with a mere half million dollars—flatten skyscrapers, murder thousands, cripple an airline industry, and cost the American economy tens of billions.

9. It's the Iraqis, Stupid. Even those who opposed the war should acknowledge that the one undeniably good consequence of Operation Iraqi Freedom was liberating the traumatized Iraqi people from Saddam. Yet it's part of our narcissism that, even when we invade and occupy another nation, we still view the story as being about ourselves: American power, the G.I. body count, the political fallout back home, the state of our national soul. While Bush's defenders hailed him for extending freedom—even when the occupation was going terribly wrong—his detractors greeted each new explosion and casualty with the chilly satisfaction of a cosmic prosecutor preparing a legal brief against a star-spangled Grim Reaper. What was missing in all this talk was the fate of the Iraqis, who spent decades being ground to dust by one of the world's most ruthless regimes, and even now are too often treated as tokens in a larger geopolitical struggle. European powers have skimped on aid to punish Bush for his unrepentant unilateralism. Fascist guerrillas have murdered hundreds of ordinary Iraqis in their attempt to chase out the Americans and prevent the country from becoming a modern, democratic state. Even as neocon ideologues have treated the country as a test tube for their theories about American power, much of the left still views Iraq solely as proof of America's turpitude. For his part, the President sees the country as both a source of glory (George W. Bush, Liberator of Iraq!) and of political danger, which is one reason he put Iraqification on fast-forward: He didn't want negative headlines spoiling his reelection campaign. For anyone of humane instincts, the fundamental question is simple: Will the Iraqis eventually wind up having a decent society? If so, the whole huge investment of blood and treasure (as military folks like to call it) will not have been wholly in vain, whether or not it starts the dominoes falling in the countries around it. If not, the war is a far bigger misadventure than one may already fear. For those who oppose George W. Bush, the galling irony is that we must devoutly hope his decision is somehow vindicated—for the Iraqis' sake, not ours.

10. Time will tell just who has fallen (and who's been left behind). Art critic Harold Rosenberg once remarked that American time has become the dominant tempo of modern history. Of course, one problem with our rushing sense of speed is that it makes us impatient—for results, for meaning, for certainty. But there is no certainty in history ever. When the CIA helped topple the Iranian prime minister Mohammad Mossadegh in 1953, they could not have guessed how things would play out: His replacement, the Shah, would inspire such a level of fundamentalist extremism that he eventually was overthrown and replaced by the Ayatollah Khomeini, a theocrat whose hatred of America led President Jimmy Carter to encourage Saddam Hussein to invade Iran, launching a long, nasty war that killed so many people that the ayatollahs bribed mothers to have children—prompting an Iranian baby boom whose twentysomething members now prefer democracy to fundamentalism—while back in Iraq, America's wayward "ally" Saddam became such a menace that the U.S. fought two wars against him. Could anyone have predicted such blowback? From the start, one of the most exasperating things about the Iraq war has been the way that almost everybody, prowar or anti-, sounded so damned sure about what they were saying at any given moment. That Saddam directly threatened America with his WMDs. That Baghdad was going to be a bloodbath. That reconstruction would pay for itself. That the Arab street would erupt. That the looting didn't matter. That you can't install democracy in a Middle Eastern country with no democratic traditions. That you *can* install democracy in a Middle Eastern country with no democratic traditions. That the timetable was too fast. That the timetable was too slow. *Enough!*

Back in the 1970s, Richard Nixon asked Zhou Enlai his verdict on the French Revolution. The Chinese premier famously replied, "Too early to tell." The same is true of Operation Iraqi Freedom. It would be an act of foolish arrogance for anyone to predict with any certainty what will happen in Iraq—civil war, another dictatorship, or, just maybe, some frail, struggling move toward democracy. But now that even neocons have been issuing mea culpas for their blindness in promoting the invasion, one thing is clear. Nobody with any sense could call the war a triumph or propose waging such an action again.

CHAPTER 4

Idols and Survivors:
Populist Social Darwinism

By trying we can easily learn to endure adversity.
Another man's, I mean.

—MARK TWAIN

PUDD'NHEAD WILSON'S NEW CALENDAR

In 1972, *Harper's* sent America's bounciest misanthrope, Kurt
Vonnegut, to cover the Republican Convention that renominated
Richard Nixon. He came back with his mustache at half-mast. "The
two real political parties in America," he mourned, "are the Winners
and Losers. The single religion of the Winners is a harsh interpretation
of Darwinism, which argues that it is the will of the universe that only
the fittest should survive."

Things have changed a bit over the last three decades. Thanks to
the Christian right, none of our politicians dares mention Darwin,
except to say he shouldn't be taught in schools. ("Religion has been
around a lot longer than Darwin," our president has noted helpfully.)
Beyond that, the Winners' agenda is now far harsher than it ever was
under Nixon, whose social policies would strike today's Republicans
as downright socialist. The Bush administration has given the rich
hundreds of billions in tax "relief," while excluding millions of less-
favored Americans (including U.S. troops) from other forms of tax
relief. Even as it gave $80,000 write-offs to businessmen who buy
Humvees, it sought to change the Fair Labor Standards Act in a way
that would cost countless hourly workers their overtime. Just redefine
their work as administrative and the extra hours are *free*. Underlying

such behavior is the President's embrace of a philosophy (or more accurately, an outlook) I call Populist Social Darwinism. Bush boasts about returning power to ordinary people—"We want to give you back *your* money"—then pursues policies that produce a class of highly visible Winners while unraveling the social safety net. Anytime you so much as mention this, you're accused of waging class warfare.

Originally conceived in the mid–nineteenth century, Social Darwinism was fathered by the English positivist Herbert Spencer. He, not Darwin, actually coined the phrase "survival of the fittest." But he did find confirmation of his ideas in *Origin of Species,* using the Theory of Natural Selection to provide both a biological justification for the savage inequalities of laissez-faire economics and a reason to hope for the future—the truths of evolution would lead, in distant generations, to a superior form of man. Spencer's ideas proved especially popular in the United States after the Civil War, partly because they tapped into America's fascination with Darwin (there was a time when we took pride in scientific know-how), but mainly because they dovetailed with the arriviste ethos of the Gilded Age. At the very moment the rich were growing richer and the poor more exploited, along came a theory that served as the perfect ideological fig leaf. Although Spencer emerged from a modest background (his father was an antiestablishment Methodist schoolteacher), he and his acolytes held that vast discrepancies in wealth and power were part of a "natural" process unfolding so slowly that conscious attempts to change it were foolish and possibly counterproductive. Just as Marxism replaced old-fashioned morality with a "scientific" theory of dialectical change, so Social Darwinism provided a "scientific" picture of evolution that explained away the immorality of sweatshops, child labor, working Chinese immigrants to death on the railroads, and conquering supposedly inferior races. The mere idea of the state helping the poor was anathema. Like one of our Republican congressmen who still think that Medicare is Bolshevism, Yale's homegrown Social Darwinist, William Graham Sumner, dourly insisted in 1885 that socialism extended to "any device whose aim is to save individuals from any of the difficulties or hardships of the struggle for existence and the competition of life by the intervention of the state." Needless to say, the rich lapped this up, especially when it came accompanied by high-minded religious nostrums. As historian Richard Hofstadter argued, "Darwinism was seized upon as a welcome addition, perhaps the most powerful of all, to the store of ideas to which solid and conservative men appealed when they wished to reconcile their fellows to some of the hardships of life and to prevail upon them not to support hasty and ill-considered reforms."

Naturally, such a doctrine was vehemently rejected by reformers, including the followers of William Jennings Bryan, who railed against the misery caused by untrammeled laissez-faire attitudes.* In an irony Spencer might have appreciated, though Sumner certainly would not have, the ruthless capitalism of the nineteenth century created a labor movement that rebelled against it, even threatening socialism, gradually pushing America toward the gentler welfare capitalism of the twentieth century. As Franklin Roosevelt created programs to help protect citizens against the harshness of unemployment, old age, and economic change, it became clear that the fittest capitalism was the modern welfare state. By the time Aaron Copland wrote "Fanfare for the Common Man" in the early 1940s, Social Darwinism had been thoroughly discredited.

Or so one thought. But ever since Ronald Reagan took office in 1980, Spencer's vision of Winners and Losers has been sneaking back. Shorn of its previous Darwinian claims to science but still robed in a Victorian-style moralism, it has found justification in the writings of neocon historian Gertrude Himmelfarb, who views the nineteenth-

---

*Bryan's case says a lot about the changing political face of religion in our national life. Although Bryan became notorious for opposing Darwin's theories in the 1925 Scopes Monkey Trial, Garry Wills's *Under God: Religion and American Politics* points out that what turned the good Evangelical against Darwin wasn't religious dogma but his horror, on visiting Germany in the early days of the Nazi Party, to see how ideas of evolution were being used to support repugnant ideas about eugenics and racial superiority. If only today's anti-Darwinians had as much concern for social justice as the often-mocked Bryan, who cared about the living as much as the unborn.

century attitudes as being in many ways superior to modern liberal social engineering. Decades of prosperity had let everyone forget what the New Deal had done for America. Suddenly, government welfare was treated as the cause of social ills, not the solution, and the state had become the enemy of the people. Onetime FDR-worshiper Reagan slashed the top income tax rate by 60 percent, to its lowest level since the beginning of the Great Depression. (It had been as high as 90 percent during the Eisenhower boom years.) The process of distributing the wealth upward continued under Bill Clinton, who affected to regret it, and carried over to the presidency of George W. Bush, who does not. His compassionate conservatism is content with a two-tier society whose levels drift farther apart all the time. One shouldn't be fooled by the right's loud populism. Off the air, Rush Limbaugh brags of his fondness for $2,000 bottles of wine and illegal Cuban cigars. One prefers the honesty of the new magazine *Robb Report Worth*, which boasts about being "strictly for the super-affluent," meaning people who make over half a million a year.

America is increasingly a country where Winners' kids attend private schools and the Losers' go to fading public ones, where Winners shop at specialty grocers and Losers buy their food at Wal-Mart or Costco, where Winners fly business or first class while Losers are stuck in economy sections and treated with flagrant, lunch-in-a-doggie-bag contempt, where Winners choose from a smorgasbord of jobs and Losers like Jessica Lynch enlist in the military because they couldn't get a job at Wal-Mart. The chances of upward mobility have shrunk vastly in the last thirty years; *BusinessWeek* says the odds have dropped by 60 percent. In that same period, the richest 1 percent of the population has doubled its ownings. It now possesses as much as the bottom 40 percent, and the richest 13,000 families own as much as the poorest 20 million households. As Al Franken vividly put it, this is like Bemidji, Minnesota, having more income than all the residents of New York, Los Angeles, Chicago, Houston, Philadelphia, and Phoenix combined. While Bush didn't create this situation, his policies are making the divisions far more extreme. He's institutionalizing a New Gilded Age in which the state gives financial assistance to the very wealthy—Bill Gates personally saved $82 million in the first year of the dividend tax cut—while showing little concern for those who do not. What compassionate leader could preside over the loss of more than two million jobs—many among the middle class, whose positions have permanently moved abroad—and still be obsessed with cuts to the estate tax? In 2003, Bush racked up a $480 billion budget deficit while cutting programs like Head Start and AmeriCorps, the entire budget of which was only three times Gates's dividend tax cut. Convinced in the inherent goodness of the free market—a religion he embraces more deeply than Christianity—he evidently thinks it normal for Winners to take what they want. The Losers be damned.

In this, he merely reflects the prevailing values of what Robert Frank has dubbed the "Winner-Take-All Society," in which a small number of star performers reap ever-greater rewards while the majority receives less and less. You can see it in the retail world, where the Wal-Mart store on the outskirts of a small city devours the business of its entire downtown. You see it in pop culture, where the sales of one *Harry Potter* novel dominates bookstore revenues for an entire summer, and a single hit franchise like *Law and Order* can keep an entire network in the black. ("There are only two kinds of TV shows," an industry honcho once told me. "Hits—and the ones that don't matter.") You see it in the media, which keeps churning out Power Lists, Hot Lists, Cool Lists, and It Lists, makes sure every kid knows which movie is #1, and even bombards us with stories about precocious young Winners like the eighteen-year-old novelist Nick McDonell, who wrote the 2002 novel *Twelve*, a Manhattan knockoff of *Less Than Zero*, and fifteen-year-old Nikki Reed, screenwriter of the rancid girls-gone-bad teenflick *Thirteen*. And naturally, you can see it in business, where (depending on the source) corporate CEOs make 282 to 400 times more than their hourly workers, seven times higher than when Reagan took office. *The Onion* captured the spirit of our time in a headline: CONGRESS RAISES EXECUTIVE MINIMUM WAGE TO $565.15/HR.

Nowhere was the Hobbesian war of the few against the many keener than at the President's favorite crooked company, which will be studied for years as a prime example of runamok crony capitalism. Enron's ethos was superbly portrayed by the *Houston Chronicle*'s Greg Hassell, whose postmortem on the company painted a memorable portrait of Enron's glory days, laying bare a corporate culture that almost gleefully tossed its vanities onto the bonfire. Beyond the in-building health club and free Starbucks coffee, silver Porsches became an obligatory status symbol, and traders were known to freak out when their annual bonus was only half a million bucks. This conspicuous consumption was encouraged by an evangelical leadership that one former executive compared to the Taliban—either you were for the company or you were an infidel. To call down an Enron *fatwa*, you needed merely ask for proof of its extravagant claims of profitability. This same casual amorality turned office politics into one endless struggle for survival in which a policy nicknamed "rank and yank" had employees give one another annual ratings, with the bottom 15 percent being fired. Given such a cutthroat culture, it was hardly surprising when so many of the top Enron execs sold off their own shares for a fortune but prohibited underlings from doing the same, even after it became obvious that the value of Enron stock was dropping faster than an Irish heavyweight. Such is the fine art of Darwinian bankruptcy.

When I first told a friend about rank and yank, she said, "It sounds like a reality game show." And though she was kidding, she also wasn't. Populist Social Darwinism sends long spokes through the heart of Bush World in all its triumphalism and resentment. It informs our pop culture, feeds the arrogance of Winners, calls down disrespect on Losers, and inspires an attitude toward celebrity that is at once slavish and embittered.

The Law of the TV Jungle

Although running for renomination unopposed, President Bush wanted to enter the primary season with a $200 million war chest. He spent much of 2003 popping into Republican fundraisers at which guests would ante up $2,000 for a meal that was sometimes no more nourishing than hot dogs and presidential homily. These events were invariably packed. Bush knows that people love a front-runner, and so do Rupert Murdoch's minions at Fox. That's why their hit show *American Idol* doesn't merely grab millions of viewers—it keeps reassuring them that they're sharing in its glory. There was an amazing moment in the program's second season when smarmy-cute host Ryan Seacrest, who resembles a tree slug impersonating the emcee in *Cabaret*, greeted the audience with exciting news: *American Idol 2* wasn't merely the highest-rated program, but the contestants' catchy-shameless cover of "God Bless the U.S.A." was the number-one single and *Thankful*, the album by the first season's champion, Kelly Clarkson, had just debuted at the top of the charts. The studio audience roared, thrilled to feel itself riding atop the cultural bandwagon—they, too, got to be Winners.

American Idol is far from the only hit program of its kind. One of the defining features of Bush-era culture is the way that Populist Social Darwinism has been reflected in the deluge of Reality TV game shows—*The Apprentice, Fear Factor, Big Brother, The Great Race, Joe Millionaire, The Bachelor, Boy Meets Boy, The Bachelorette, America's Next Top Model*, and, of course, the aptly named *Survivor*—all of which are faux Darwinian games of selection, extinction, survival, and victory. While the premise of such shows is far from original (think of *Ted Mack's Amateur Hour* or ABC's *The Superstars*), an old idea has been pushed to extremes. For starters, these shows promise huge rewards. The contestants are no longer hoping to win Amana freezers or the chance to call on Paul Lynde in the center square. They want to be millionaires (a standard prize in the post-Regis world), nab high-profile recording contracts, get a job with Donald Trump, or marry somebody rich. But with great rewards come great humiliations, and these Reality game shows have mercilessly played up one aspect of the Darwinian struggle for survival: degradation.

To compete on these shows does not merely require your talent, physical prowess, or intelligence. You have to be prepared to eat night crawlers, have your physique sneered at by experts, get called an idiot by a snide host, have your dishonesty revealed (*Meet My Folks* wired contestants up to lie detectors), or permit your tears, rage, jealousy, self-pity, petulant weakness, and pathetic bickering to be broadcast all over the land. As a final fillip, the greed and humiliation are often provoked by a huge popularity contest. You win such games *politically*, by convincing the other competitors, a potential romantic partner, or the home TV audience that somebody else should be voted off the show and you deserve to stay. The Darwinism of such programs really *is* social, because what finally matters is your skill at surviving within a human ecosystem, a revelation that first wowed the public when the Machiavellian Richard Hatch unexpectedly won the first *Survivor* (even as Bush was winning the presidential election) by employing the manipulative skills he'd acquired as a corporate trainer. Almost immediately the phrase "the tribe has spoken" became a reigning national metaphor.

The reflexive habit of attacking Reality TV as voyeuristic trash strikes me as fuddy-duddyism at its most misguided. What matters is that such shows offer a glimpse into our national psyche. The most revelatory of the bunch is *American Idol*, whose transcendent junkiness has been so successful that one can't decide whether to tear one's hair or genuflect. The program has taken the hoariest of ideas, the old-fashioned talent contest, and transformed it into a mirror of our national life—38 million viewers watched the finale of *American Idol 2*. One can only envy the cunning or luck that led its producers to scuttle the first word of the original British title, *Pop Idol*, and replace it with "American," a depleted adjective unexpectedly replenished by September 11. As it turned out, that patriotic flourish could hardly have proved more fitting.

At the beginning, two things were clear. First, *American Idol* dealt in commercial white pop-music taste—there was no indie rock, no folk music, no hip-hop, no r&b. Second, the show got its kick from the headlong collision between the show's star-is-born populism and the nastiness of English panelist Simon Cowell. What a masterstroke to make the show's Dr. No a bitchy Brit! Where his sidekicks, Randy Jackson and Paula Abdul—revealingly, an African-American man and an Arab-American woman—made an annoying point of being sunny, Cowell constantly did that most un-American of things: He said what he thought. The contestants' singing was "dreadful." They wore "ugly" outfits. They had "no chance to win this competition." His words gave the show its sting, sparing viewers the usual *Star Search* dreariness, and because Cowell uttered his waspish truths in a British accent, his words packed a peculiarly contradictory charge: While his criticisms carried real force—Americans still, unaccountably, cede cultural authority to the Brits—they were softened because his manner carried no small whiff of self-amusement. Cowell was, after all, the only non-American on *American Idol.* An American who said such things would have seemed like a mean son of a bitch. The audience would have lynched a Frenchman.

Still finding its way in the post–September 11 culture, the first year's series came down to a battle between amiable, frizzy-haired Justin Guarini, who resembled a Richard Simmons stretched thin, and eventual champion Kelly Clarkson, whose generic-belter voice suggested a one-octave Mariah Carey. Hailing from the President's home state of Texas, where she sang in the state choir and performed *Brigadoon* in high school, Clarkson was precisely the sort of contestant you'd expect to win a national popularity contest in an America that had recently decided that George Bush was the real deal. Unlike her archrival, Nikki McKibben, the show's "bad girl," Kelly had good Christian values and an air of unfeigned sweetness. She looked eerily like a small-town Monica Lewinsky who'd never put out for a president—at least not a Democrat. You could feel her brassy sincerity when she sang the show's official song, "A Moment Like This," a song of answered yearning that deliberately announced the show's fantasy of a nobody becoming somebody overnight. She sang on the show about how it feels to win the show:

> *Oh, I can't believe it's happening to me*
> *Some people wait a lifetime for a moment . . . like this.*

If Clarkson's victory was a simple populist tale of a nice Texas girl making it big, *American Idol 2* offered a far richer picture of the country's complicated cultural values. It was broadcast during the war in Iraq, and to know exactly what that meant, you need merely have listened to the singing of contestant Joshua Gracin, hailed for his "Garth

Brooks twang," a phrase that must have had Brooks dancing like Rumpelstiltskin on that fifty-gallon hat of his. There was only one striking thing about the twenty-two-year-old Josh: He was a terrible singer. Yet week after week the public voted to keep him on the show, even as the upbeat panelist Randy Jackson (who was cagily moving into Simon territory) declared that his pitch had been sharp through an entire song and Cowell wondered aloud how a guy this rotten hadn't been kicked off the first week. Josh had two things going for him. He was a Marine, and this was wartime. That was enough. "When Josh crooned the first few lines in the group's 'God Bless the U.S.A.' performance," wrote *Entertainment Weekly*, burbling with jingoistic fervor, "he left no doubt that he's proud to be an American. And we should be proud to have him as an Idol." Josh may not have had the musical stuff of an idol, but he did have the uniform to prove he was an American. So were the other contestants, of course, but some Americans were proving more equal than others.

One of *American Idol 1*'s creepiest features had been watching the country's invisible voters boot off accomplished black performers in favor of lousy Caucasian ones—survival of the whitest. The best singer, Tamyra Gray, didn't even make the final. None of this meant that voters made an overt attempt to knock black singers off the show, although such feelings were doubtless part of it. The show's skewed balloting hinted at the insidiously casual racism that's based on relative comfort levels. Just as NFL owners routinely pass over promising African-American coaches in favor of white retreads with whom they feel socially at ease, so *American Idol*'s voters probably tend to vote for singers who seem more like themselves—or their dreams of themselves. Which tells you something about the demographic for flag-waving "event" television. If the show had been broadcast on today's wigga-happy MTV—which before Michael Jackson's *Thriller* was itself slammed for being lily-white—both the voting and the music would have taken on a radically different racial slant.

The second season was a different story, although things looked dire when the talentless Josh was voted one of three "safe" contestants while the two dark-skinned African-Americans, single-named Trenyce and mountainous Ruben Studdard, were made to sweat—one of them had been voted off. The shocker was the near elimination of Ruben (one came to call them all by their first names), a huge, sweet-faced sub–Luther Vandross who to that point had so clearly been the best performer that the panelists were rolling their eyes and suggesting, not all that subtly, that the public needed to, you know, put aside their prejudices and vote honestly. This theme was picked up by *Good Morning America* and *The View* to such an extent that there was a counterreaction, with viewers suggesting that the P.C. media wanted to bully them into voting for Ruben by suggesting that they were racist if they didn't.

By the end, nobody was talking about race (until the "3 Divas" turned up the following spring). Even though the white runner-up, Clay Aiken, actually outsang him in the final shows, Ruben won *American Idol 2* and the series was a populist triumph. As a twelve-year-old girl gushed after attending the final show at the Universal Amphitheatre, "You feel like you're a celebrity, too." (She'd been taught our modern equivalent of "Every man a king.") But Ruben's victory proved far muddier than Kelly's. He was soon mired in a lawsuit with 205 Flava Inc. over the bright jerseys he wore on the show, a sponsorship deal that reportedly violated the show's ground rules; then his first album, the soulless *Soulful,* was outsold by Aiken's debut, *Measure of a Man,* which instantly shot to number one. Despite finishing second, Clay proved to be the show's de facto winner.

If Clarkson's post-9/11 victory felt like a vote for Bush, Aiken's enormous popularity became something of a public uprising. In a show designed to manufacture a pop idol, the ungainly Clay—who got a makeover deep into the series—was so resolutely *unmanufactured* that something amazing happened: He was carried aloft by an audience that genuinely cared whether he won. A moment of commercial pop culture suddenly took on a huge emotional dimension. And inspired unexpected controversy: Not only did some fans think Clay had been unfairly torpedoed by speculation that he was gay, the final tally was so close and so ineptly explained that some viewers began claiming that Fox had tampered with the results. You kept waiting for Katherine Harris to show up to certify the vote. The belief that Aiken was robbed in the contest's finale spawned gigabytes of Internet recrimination and debate, even prompting the creation of a People's Republic of Clay website, where his devotees could express their passion. As a friend joked, the only difference between the 2000 election controversy and the one on *American Idol* was that Clay Aiken's supporters really *did* like their man.

As always in these Darwinian game shows, of course, the biggest winners were those who owned and operated the franchise. The contestants did their part to fatten the Murdoch fortune. It's part of the genius of the *American Idol* series that the competing singers don't merely provide free entertainment. They're also enlisted into doing commercials for the show's sponsors—Ruben and Clay crooning for the Ford Focus—and used to cross-promote other Fox "product." One week during *Idol 2*, Josh, Ruben, Clay, and Trenyce were filmed at the premiere of *X2*. Afterward, they told viewers how fabulous this 20th Century Fox movie was (which suggests they may not have seen it), and their praise was folded into the show itself. In Trenyce's last hurrah before being bounced, the show used digital effects to turn her eyes milky-white, just like Halle Berry's character Storm. As she walked off the stage for the last time, listening to Josh mangle one last song, she wore a lovely, brave smile. She seemed as nice as pie, precisely as one must seem to win a popularity contest like *American Idol*.

But nice isn't the winning ticket in Populist Social Darwinism. Good-hearted, half-talented singers come and go, but the show's biggest name continues to be smug judge Simon Cowell, who has parlayed his cut of the *Idol* shows and recordings, both here and in Britain, into enormous profits—the British press gasps that he's worth £30 million. Is he really as heartless as his put-downs suggest, or is he just playing a role? It doesn't matter. Having made his fortune by treating other people as Losers, he's a member of a supremely recognizable modern group:

Sore Winners

Halfway into the 2002 NFL season, 49ers wide receiver Terrell Owens scored a touchdown against the Seahawks in Seattle. Crossing the goal line, he flabbergasted everyone by pulling a Sharpie from his sock, autographing the ball, and handing it to his financial advisor in a nearby box seat. The next day, the sports media were shrieking about hotdogging, bad sportsmanship, today's spoiled athletes—and what kind of example is this for our kids? Me, I just laughed out loud. Owens's silly stunt was simply routine braggadocio that was inevitably topped one year later when the Saints' Joe Horn celebrated a TD by pulling out a cell phone he'd planted in the end zone and making a celebratory call. The next day, the sports media were shrieking about hotdogging, bad sportsmanship, today's spoiled athletes—and what kind of example is this for our kids?

It's long been part of our national self-image that Americans are Good Winners. When Yankee soldiers triumphed over Burgoyne's army at the 1777 Battle of Saratoga, British prisoners were impressed by the victors' polite silence—there was no gloating or jeering. When U.S. troops entered Germany after World War II, they didn't indulge in an orgy of rape as did the Soviets but helped rebuild the country, winning a caricatured reputation for being beaming men with chocolate bars. And when the U.S. Olympic hockey team won its famous "Do you believe in miracles?" victory over the Soviets in Lake Placid in 1980, the players exulted in their triumph without getting in the Russians' faces. In truth, no country always behaves well in victory. Sometimes our Winners have been gentlemanly; at others, vulgar and ruthless. Just ask the foreign basketball players flattened by Charles Barkley at the Barcelona Olympics. During the heyday of Social Darwinism, capitalists worked people to death without the slightest qualm and made no apology for it—try to form a union and goons would come after you with clubs. Meanwhile, the rich exulted in their wealth. The delightfully named Mrs. Stuyvesant Fish held a 1904 dinner party in honor of her dog, which turned up in a $15,000 diamond collar at a time when the average annual income was $380. Standard Oil tycoon John D. Rockefeller explained his fortune to a Sunday school class by declaring, "God gave me the money."

The Bush years may be the coarsest period in our nation's history since those days. To my amazement, I sometimes find myself nostalgic for the comparatively modest ill manners of the Reagan years, when the U.S. invaded countries like Grenada and "Junk Bond King" Michael Milken was on the prowl. Today's Winners don't simply win, they win *badly*: bragging, sneering, lording it over the Losers, and promoting themselves with a crassness that would leave Duddy Kravitz blushing. When Hurricane Isabel knocks out the power in much of Washington, D.C., the Redskins' billionaire owner doesn't just get a huge generator to restore his own electricity but turns on all his lights, so that his house glows like the Vegas strip while his annoyed neighbors sit in the dark. Practicing the "look out for yourself" philosophy preached in his books, Bill O'Reilly gloats about how many copies he's sold, accuses critics of "envy," and uses his media platforms to pitch his books and "The Spin Stops Here" tchotchkes. Seventeen-year-old hoops phenom LeBron James drives to high school in his $50,000 Hummer, not even bothering to pretend that he's a regular student. And careerist wiseass Dennis Miller, who now embraces George W. Bush on CNBC the better to kick the underdog, justifies a bellicose U.S. foreign policy by saying, "We are real good at what we do and the whole world is going to hell in a handbasket. As that gap gets wider, they'll hate us more and more and more. We are simultaneously the most hated, feared, loved, and admired nation on this planet. In short, we are Frank Sinatra, and you know something, the Chairman didn't get to be the Chairman lying down for punks outside the Fontainbleu." On the worst day of his life, Ol' Blue Eyes, who grew up poor in Hoboken, was more idealistic about America than that.

Such Bad Winners aren't simply found in the media. We encounter them every day, from the workplace where higher-ups treat employees like "the help" to the service industries where "the help" is treated as something even lower: I recently watched an Armani-besuited woman park her Mercedes SUV in the middle of a busy street near a restaurant, dodge through traffic, and toss the keys to the busy valet parker, snapping, "I don't have time to wait for you." Granted, this was in Beverly Hills, but once such behavior was for spoiled teens. Now you find such thuggishness everywhere. It's certainly out front in business, whose leaders pride themselves on their brutality, as Donald ("You're fired") Trump made clear while pitching the stretch-limo fantasy *The Apprentice*: "I think there's a whole beautiful picture to be painted about business, American business, how beautiful it is but also how vicious and tough it is. The beauty is the success, the end result. You meet some wonderful people, but you also meet some treacherous, disgusting people that are worse than any snake in the jungle."

For decades, we were told that company owners and CEOs made a lot more than their employees because they were taking enormous risks. If they made bad decisions, they'd lose their jobs, while workers could just punch the clock and collect their paycheck. That fantasy has been turned upside down in a world in which CEOs of failing companies get extra stock options even as they lay off workers and bankrupt their pension plans. In October 2003, *The Economist* ran a cover story about executives that pictured a gargantuan carrot and asked, "Where's the Stick?" Yet what makes today's business leaders galling isn't simply their greed—that's always been part of the picture—but their shamelessness.

Consider the much-bruited case of Peter Olson, chairman and CEO of Random House, who goes through the publishing world brandishing his big balls as proudly as a gaucho his *boleadora*. So pleased is he with his bullying that he allowed *The New York Times Magazine* to record his regal behavior at the 2003 Book Expo America in Los Angeles:

> On his way back to the Random House booth, Olson stopped to chat with a man who now runs the Frankfurt Book Fair. "I fired him," he said a moment later. "I recognize hundreds of people here. Many of them worked for me. Many of them I fired personally." He did not seem upset by this. In fact, he seemed amused. He walked a few steps farther. "I fired him," he said as two men passed by. "There are so many people here that I've fired that we could have a reunion." Olson's smile broadened.
>
> By the time Olson showed the reporter his stuffed lion—"I can't help it, I always gravitate toward the predators"—he wasn't merely being a Bad Winner, he was making a production of it, like one who'd

studied old tapes of *Goldfinger* to see how a crowd-pleasing supervillain behaved.

When Tyco chairman and CEO L. Dennis Kozlowski was indicted for fraud and conspiracy, it emerged that he not only defrauded the state of New York of more than $1 million in sales tax on purchases for his art collection but got Tyco to fork out more than $135 million in largely forgiven loans and personal expenses. As James Stewart observed in *The New Yorker*, "The less he actually needed Tyco's money, the more he felt entitled to take it." He's not the only one. On NPR's *Fresh Air*, antitax zealot turned Beltway powerbroker Grover Norquist stunned the host, Terry Gross, by actually comparing the estate tax to the Nazi persecution of the Jews.

Such vaulting brutishness can't be blamed on George W. Bush, but he's nothing to humble the Winners. He couldn't be less like his hero, Teddy Roosevelt, no small egomaniac himself, who helped knock apart the Gilded Age because its ignobility gnawed at him: "Of all forms of tyranny the least attractive and most vulgar is the tyranny of mere wealth." The Bush administration is a veritable hive of bad winners, whether it's the President scowling peevishly at questions that Reagan would have dispatched with a joke, the Vice President sneering that energy conservation is no more than "personal virtue," or Rummy treating everyone from reporters to generals as if they were no brighter than whelks. Nothing betrays such arrogance more than Republican big shots' public boasts that the GOP is becoming the "natural" party of power—a *norteño* version of the PRI, the kleptocracy that ran Mexico for seventy-one years. They brag about placing Republicans in key lobbying slots of K Street, freezing out PACs that don't ante up, and using congressional redistricting to ensure that the GOP keeps winning more seats. Such political hardball is hardly unprecedented. Although less ruthlessly, the Democrats played many of the same tricks for years. What's new is how flagrantly Bush and his party flaunt tactics it was once thought politic to keep hidden. It's no longer enough just to *do* these things, one must make a public meal of it.

The rich and powerful aren't the only ones who have grown flush with pleasure at their privilege. Marx famously declared that the ruling ideas of any age are those of its ruling class, and conservative intellectuals have been busily crafting the Winners' postmillennial ideology, from elaborate arguments for American militarism to defenses of high-end consumerism. Over the last few years, we've been inundated with tomes such as Kagan's *Of Paradise and Power*, which insists that the United States has the duty to run the world; Joseph Epstein's smug *Snobbery: The American Version*, in which the Northwestern prof riffs on status-mania (from the seat of his $45,000 Jaguar); and James B. Twitchell's sharp *Living It Up: Our Love Affair with Luxury*, a volume urging us, not quite ironically enough, to think of luxury as "the necessary consumption of the unnecessary." Now, that's a phrase I bet L. Paul Bremer didn't try out on the Iraqis.

The most amiable of these works is David Brooks's *Bobos in Paradise: The New Upper Class and How They Got There*, a self-described piece of "comic sociology," which argues that our new upper class represents sort of a Hegelian synthesis of bourgeois aspiration and bohemian lifestyle. As you'd expect of the *New York Times*'s house neocon, Brooks is a master at giving us right-wing politics with a human face. I recognized many of my own foibles in his descriptions. Free of the reflexive contempt for middle-class life that weakens so much cultural analysis, he fills his book with astute social observations, good-humored swipes at the Bobo taste for pricy water and T-shirts—"We spend our money on peasant goods that are created in upscale versions of themselves"—and self-deprecating asides: "I sometimes think I've made a whole career out of self-loathing." It's an amusing line, although Brooks doesn't strike one as being another Roy Cohn. The Pangloss of patio culture, he seems eminently satisfied with the world and his place in it—he hadn't been an editor at *The Weekly Standard* for nothing. *Bobos in Paradise* is finally far less eager to question the values of today's Winners than to endorse them. "Bobos have reasons to feel proud of the contributions they have made to their country," Brooks tells us. "Wherever they have settled, they have made life more enjoyable (for those who can afford it)." An entire vision of the world reveals itself in those parentheses.

Early on, Brooks argues that our new ruling class, which replaced the old WASP version, is a creation of America's modern meritocracy. Individuals rise through their accomplishments, not inherited status. And this, conservatives insist, is as it should be. That's why they oppose preferential systems such as affirmative action—except, of course, for members of the elite. One of the most preposterous examples of such thinking came in *In Praise of Nepotism: A Natural History*, by Saul Bellow's son, Adam, an extremely thick book of thin propaganda. Vaclav Havel once remarked that there's always something fishy about an intellectual on the winning side, and the younger Bellow does nothing to prove him wrong. The book's basic idea is pretty much what we've come to expect from conservative writers—a defense of the ruling order and its perks. Bellow argues that our so-called New Nepotism is a good thing because the privileges of birth have become bound to "the iron rule of merit." Although the children of the rich and powerful clearly have more opportunities than the rest of us—posh schools, open doors, powerful allies, a sense of comfort with the elite—this is still a far cry from traditional nepotism, in which parents hired their kids outright or pulled strings to land them a good position. Whatever your connections today, Bellow insists, you still have to earn your success. This is certainly true of the NBA, where Bill Walton can't just call up David Stern and get his son Luke a good contract with the Lakers. But what of Colin Powell's son, Michael, whom Bush appointed chairman of the FCC? What of Dick Cheney's daughter Elizabeth, a deputy assistant secretary of state? What of Secretary of Labor Elaine Chao, who's married to Senator Mitch McConnell and had as acting solicitor for the Labor Department Eugene Scalia, the son of—oh, no one in particular.

And then, of course, there's the Nepotist-in-Chief, with whom Bellow wisely dispenses very quickly. Dubya's cushy rise from hot-tempered party boy to underqualified president is not exactly a career that leaves one wanting to praise nepotism. Nor did a lacerating *Los Angeles Times* exposé that chronicled corporate America's latest trick for buying up votes in Congress: Companies simply hire as their lobbyists the children of U.S. senators whose votes affect their industry. For instance, John Breaux Jr. and the distinguished Chet Lott (a pizza-parlor manager in Kentucky) suddenly landed high-paying jobs as lobbyists for BellSouth. What stellar achievements landed them these gigs? Their fathers, Louisiana Senator John Breaux and Mississippi Senator Trent Lott, just happened to be on the Senate committees that voted on telecommunications legislation.

Predictably, Breaux and Lott and the many others in Congress with lobbyist relatives swear that they would never give a special break to a corporate cause just because their own flesh and blood happened to be representing it. Just as predictably, cases like this don't get a whole lot of play from Bellow, who, with the suaveness of one who can declare the Borgias "a remarkable family," seems blind to the elitist corruption at the heart of his argument. On the side of the Winners, he's too busy declaring nepotism an "art" that can be practiced well or badly. Then, too, so is winning. Part of doing it gracefully is knowing how to have your own way without making everyone else feel small.

I'm a Loser, Baby
(so why don't you kill me?)

When Arnold Schwarzenegger first went on *The Tonight Show* to announce that he was running for governor of California, he said three silly things. He joked that choosing to run was his toughest call since deciding to get a bikini wax in 1976—a lame quip that promptly got him thumped by pundits for not being "serious." He wheeled out his old tagline, "Hasta la vista, baby," seemingly unaware that it had gone moldy a decade earlier. And he uttered a surreal campaign promise: "We have to make sure that everyone in California has a great job, a *fantastic* job." Fantastic jobs for everyone! Now, there was a piece of utopianism to make Karl Marx seem as pinched as Sam Walton. One pictured millions of Californians deciding that their jobs weren't fantastic *enough*—why not own the Lakers or costar in the next Julia Roberts movie? But while it was easy to mock Schwarzenegger's blindness to the realities of work, it was hard to be surprised by it. Not only did he personally enjoy a life purring with privilege, but he was part of a culture that has less and less interest in people who don't.

This is most obvious in our attitude toward our 35 million poor—up 8 percent, or 2.8 million, since 2000. Four decades ago, Michael Harrington wrote *The Other America*, which helped focus public attention on the vast numbers of Americans still living in poverty during the greatest economic boom the world had ever seen. "The millions who are poor in the United States," Harrington wrote, "tend to become increasingly invisible. Here is a great mass of people, yet it takes an effort of the intellect and will even to see them." Over the last quarter century, a similar effort of intellect and will has gone into making them invisible again: *What* other America? When homelessness first became an obvious problem during the Reagan administration (not a coincidence), most people were horrified and ashamed to see America go the way of the Third World. Editorials were written, newscasts were filled with poignant stories. But a quarter century later, we've grown so accustomed to stepping over people on sidewalks that we do it without looking—we've accepted the fact that there are people beneath our feet. Our city governments have gotten efficient at rousting the homeless from our pavements and making them move on . . . somewhere. And our politicians have retreated so far that pundits were dazzled when John Edwards began talking about "the poor" (normally, like Howard Dean, they would do this only in a glossy piece for *Vanity Fair*). Neither side wants to scare off middle-class swing voters by bringing up an unpleasant topic that might demand spending tax money. Anyway, trying to end poverty was part of the "era of big government," and Bill Clinton officially declared that over years ago.

This renewed invisibility of the poor was predictable. Most middle-class people, especially those kingmaking swing voters, are geographically segregated from poverty. They live far from disadvantaged neighborhoods and rarely if ever enter them; the working poor enter their consciousness not as people but as "service personnel." They're also insulated from the poor by history. Few middle- and upper-class Americans under sixty have firsthand experience of severe economic hardship, and when confronted with news of layoffs or mass firings—even in the executive offices—they tend to act like those arrested in Stalin's Soviet Union. They think there must be some mistake. It was far different for those, like my parents, who lived through the Great Depression. Having survived economic collapse, they grasped the value of the social safety net and the moral urgency of trying to end poverty. They knew that unemployment, bankruptcy, and hunger didn't only befall other people.

Nor did having an uncool job. Most people did. That's why for most of our history, there was honor in ordinary labor. Farmers saw farming as a superior way of life, coal miners prized the manliness it took to brave those dark shafts, autoworkers felt like trailblazers working the assembly lines and setting the forty-hour, nine-to-five standard we still largely embrace; my grandfather Bergstrom was damned proud to be a railroad man for the Rock Island Line and would have slugged any SOB who condescended to his place in society. And this pride was mirrored in popular culture, especially the movies. Even as the Hollywood dream factory produced elegant phantasms like Fred Astaire and Ginger Rogers, it churned out hundreds of movies about truckers, store clerks, oil riggers, waitresses, soldiers, itinerant laborers, cowpokes, and policemen (back when crime movies weren't simply a pretext for lots of spectacular action-picture pyrotechnics). Warner Bros. built an entire studio on working-class characters, and it wasn't alone. Hollywood was filled with stars—cocky bantam Jimmy Cagney, sexy Jean Harlow, the sweatily virile Clark Gable, the ambitious shopgirl Joan Crawford—who embodied a romanticized version of blue-collar style and aspiration.

But just as today's corporations lay off older workers and renege on retirement benefits—the idea of loyalty in business feels positively ancient—so American culture now inundates us with the implicit message that to be ordinary is to be a loser. In this age of Power Lists, Hot Lists, It Lists, our media can hardly be bothered to notice anybody who isn't rich, famous, or willing to go on Reality shows, which are filled with people plucked from their real environments and then stuck into artificial ones like the house on *Big Brother*. When we are given such stories, they're likely to be an upper-middle-class horror show like one of those *New York Times* articles about a fiftyish corporate executive with a big mortgage and young child who loses his

$300,000-a-year job and winds up selling khakis at The Gap. You never find big newspaper articles about the men and women who *rise* to manage clothing stores in malls. The Sundance fantasy that "independent film" would explore the real America has all but died, done in by indie filmmakers who made Hollywood knockoffs as a calling card for the studios, by producers who discovered that prizewinning pictures didn't necessarily make money at the art house, and by studio execs who quickly coopted the best talent for the mainstream industry. Meanwhile, Hollywood clearly finds ordinary people a downer. Forget 1979's *Norma Rae*, the true story of a single mother who helped unionize her textile factory in an Alabama milltown—it won Sally Field an Oscar. Hollywood's current notion of a populist heroine is *Legally Blonde*'s Elle Woods, a rich girl who (assisted by costar Sally Field) must rise above the stigma of her hair color and pet Chihuahua.

Or consider *You've Got Mail*, Nora Ephron's remake of *The Shop Around the Corner*, the 1940 Ernst Lubitsch classic that is perhaps the most sublimely loving of all romantic comedies. The original was about two bickering, lonely salesclerks who don't realize they're actually in love. Well, those characters may have been fine for 1940, but you won't find a studio today making a movie about "insignificant little clerks" (to borrow Margaret Sullivan's description of Jimmy Stewart in that film). It's too depressing—they're *nothings*. Which is why Ephron bumped her characters up to the front of the plane. In the process, Lubitsch's story of ardent workers became the yuppified tale of a boutique bookstore owner on the Upper West Side who ultimately hooks up with a man whose book chain is driving her out of business. You've Got Money!

In the days after September 11, the whole country bowed down before New York City's firemen and policemen, regular guys who sacrificed their lives saving other people. Each time you turned on the TV, some politician and celebrity in America seemed to be wearing a FDNY ballcap or jacket. Yet this short-lived respect only served to accentuate the fact that today's biggest pop-culture heroes have very little to do with ordinary life. We've long passed the point when heroism assumed the human scale you found in a delectable piece of romantic hooey like *Casablanca*. Aside from the antics of the *Jackass* crew, whose buddy-buddy bravado is magnificently American in its homespun goofiness, ours is an age that demands *super*-heroism. That's why George W. Bush has his own action figure, Jessica Lynch's fight to survive a wartime attack was inflated into an Iraqi-whacking feat worthy of all three of Charlie's Angels, and the major pop-culture events are centered on superheroes—Spider-Man, the X-Men, The Terminator, *The Matrix*'s Neo, and, of course, Harry Potter with his lightning-bolt scar that's like an upbeat mark of Cain. These days, we want our heroes to be bigger than we ever could be—we want them to be extraordinary.

This is hardly a cultural disaster. Personally, I would rather be Humphrey Bogart than Tobey Maguire, but there's no evidence that those who watch *Casablanca* are more likely to save a drowning child than those who watch *Spider-Man*. In fact, one of the most embarrassing outbursts in recent years was English novelist A. S. Byatt's screed in *The New York Times* attacking adults who enjoy the Harry Potter books for wallowing in adolescent fantasy. Going after good books didn't simply make her a killjoy (no wonder the public has turned against literature) but also missed the point. What makes today's superhero yarns distinctive is that they have very little to do with their protagonists' superpowers and everything to do with their neuroses, discomfort with their gifts, and need to learn how to handle their supremely unconventional talents. They're pop versions of the classic bildungsroman—they put ordinary feelings in extraordinary garb. And they're often more truthful than such supposedly down-to-earth projects as *King of Queens*, a faux blue-collar sitcom, or Steve Martin's condescendingly minimalist novels, *Shopgirl* and *The Pleasure of My Company*, in which this fine Hollywood comedian tries to show that he understands the struggles of The Little People. When movies or TV *do* try to portray ordinary people in ordinary garb, they usually flatten things out, removing the social texture from daily life and dwelling on purely personal matters of family, friends, and love. If you ask an entertainment executive why today's portraits of ordinary life are so muzzy and general, he'll tell you that personally he loves things with the sociological eye of Tom Wolfe (if not Balzac himself), but viewers want fantasies. They want the amazing car chase in *Bad Boys 2* with automobiles tumbling like dice down the freeway; they want to see Jack Nicholson pretend he would consider hooking up with a woman his own age; they want the aging adolescents in *Sex and the City* to live in cool apartments, wear expensive clothes, and eat fabulous meals without the baggage of real work or living parents. But fantasies come in many kinds, and during the Bush I years, *Roseanne* became the number-one show by rooting its comedy in the post-Reagan realities of everyday life: deadening jobs, unemployment, lack of money, teenage sex, child abuse, marital exhaustion; when the American economy went bad, the show's characters felt the pinch. Almost the opposite of *All in the Family*, whose loutish portrait of Archie Bunker was liberal Hollywood's revenge on the Silent Majority, the show was all about trying to live with the indignities of blue-collar life without being a fool. In fact, what made *Roseanne* the greatest of all situation comedies was that it spoke directly about the great dirty secret of American life—social class. But talk of class is as scary to industry executives as it is to *Wall Street Journal* editorialists (who see class war looming in a tiny increase in the top tax rate), and once *Roseanne* went off the air, TV lost all interest in the workings of class.

But years into Bush Culture, it's not only showbiz types who have trouble capturing the social truths of ordinary life. The failing even colors works trying to do just the opposite. That's precisely what happened with *American Splendor*, an enjoyable, touching, well-made film based on the autobiographical comic by Harvey Pekar. When the movie appeared in 2003, it won big prizes at Sundance and Cannes, received rave reviews, and had audiences cackling with pleasure. And Pekar was suddenly everywhere, chatting on NPR, talking to Charlie Rose, publishing his comics in *Entertainment Weekly*. One Saturday morning, there was even a drawing by Harvey on *The New York Times* Op-Ed pages telling readers about his beloved Cleveland. He and the movie had seemingly tapped into a deep yearning for stories about everyday people. And no one could be more extraordinarily ordinary than Harvey: "I'm not a superhero," his ten-year-old self says at the start of *American Splendor*. "I'm Harvey Pekar."

American Splendor tells the story of an irascible, eccentric loner—the Underground Man, junior division—who lives in a blue-collar Cleveland neighborhood, works as a filing clerk in a VA hospital basement, and burns with a desire for everything: freedom, justice, love. He also longs to be famous, to project the shadow of his daily life on the skies like his own private Bat Signal. But he wants all of this on his own terms—no eating night crawlers for him, thank you. And so he writes a series of autobiographical comics intended to capture his everyday reality—the decline of Cleveland, the tediousness of his job, the addictiveness of his drug of choice (record collecting), the annoyance of standing behind poky, talkative old Jewish ladies in the supermarket checkout line. Gradually those comics change his reality. Through them, he meets his wife Joyce Brabner, a comics reader who's almost as nutty as he is, becomes known nationwide for his eighties appearances on the *David Letterman Show*, adopts a young girl, and winds up appearing as himself in the movie *American Splendor*. Whether he's successful or down on his luck, we always feel Harvey's odd, angry integrity. When we see vérité footage of his retirement party after thirty-five years at the VA, the moment is heartbreaking because it has the authority of truth. Thirty-five years in that basement! This isn't aestheticized slumming, this is his life.

Or at least part of it. Even as the movie takes care to show us Harvey's ultimate triumph, it ignores much of what his triumph was *about*. For starters, it makes him too likable—cute even. Pekar's enduring aim was to reveal his experience in all its jaggedness, fury, and crushing smallness, and in his comic—which won the American Book Award in 1987—he does that: When Harvey feels rejected by a woman, he'll think "you cunt!" and then go on to pick a fight with a totally different woman just because she's female, too. That unsavory side of Harvey is largely missing from the movie. So, too, are his ideas. Pekar describes himself as "a working-class intellectual," but the movie largely ignores both his stridently peculiar left-wing politics and his tender feelings about the decline of the Cleveland he loves. For all his self-absorption, Pekar has always been able to see beyond himself. Even as the movie hit the theaters, he was releasing the beautiful

American Splendor three-parter, "Unsung Hero: The Story of Robert McNeill," about a young black man's experience fighting in Vietnam. Its power came from its insistent ordinariness.

Pekar's appearances on *Letterman* used to make me squirm because Dave, still in his snide older-brother mode, always treated Harvey as an oddball to be goofed on rather than as a man with something to say. That scenario eerily repeated itself during the film's PR blitz. When Pekar appeared on *Charlie Rose*, Charlie did a Letterman, greeting his guest's words with the giggles he normally saves for guys like Jackie Chan whose English is hard to follow. He didn't take him seriously, not even when Harvey said that all he wanted from life was enough money to have a decent retirement and send his stepdaughter to college. Even outsiders want the best for their kids. Charlie's whole attitude was *What a character.*

Although *American Splendor* is innocent of such condescension, it's very much the representative product of a culture shot through with Populist Social Darwinism. Harvey Pekar has the stuff of a great seventies movie loner whose alienation should offer a snapshot of a whole society—he's equal parts Ratso Rizzo, *The Conversation*'s Harry Caul, and The Man Who Fell to Earth. But for all its virtues—and resolutely "indie" vibe—this film is finally no great act of rebellion, nor even a pointed rejection of the social order. Rather, this story of an ordinary guy becomes a Bush Era fantasy in which the unhappy outsider not only winds up with a family but winds up becoming a celebrity, and not a bleak one like Travis Bickle or Rupert Pupkin. No wonder audiences loved it. Harvey becomes an American Idol starring in a movie about himself, a Rocky Balboa for today's bohemian.

Celebrity Justice Syndrome

If one had to identify the beginning of celebrity culture in America, one might well begin with the twentieth century's *first* Crime of the Century—millionaire Harry Thaw's 1906 murder of architect Stanford White for having, a few years earlier, debauched his wife, Evelyn Nesbit Thaw, a fabled beauty and onetime Gibson Girl. A nice juicy story, the crime inspired a tabloid fiesta that held the country enthralled. By now, of course, such media events have become old hat. We've had many such extravaganzas, from the 1924 Roxie Hart murder trial that inspired *Chicago* to the Kobe Bryant rape case, leading countless pundits to chastise the public for being addicted to celebrity, sinking into voyeuristic triviality, and not being able to tell reality from entertainment. While one hardly wants to defend nonstop coverage of Gary Condit or Scott Peterson—who knew that Modesto was so immodest?—I'll leave others to fight that lost battle. My concern here is the way that, in the polarizing Bush Era, America's perennial love-hate relationship with fame has been pushed to new extremes: Never have we been so overwhelmed by the sheer visibility of celebrities, but never have we felt such unconcealed delight in watching them fall.

There may be no more enjoyable celebration of this fierce ambivalence than *Celebrity Justice*, a nightly program devoted to the legal wrangles of the famous, the well-known, and the many hundreds of half-familiar faces who inhabit the fringes of contemporary consciousness like the ghosts in *The Sixth Sense*. Here, in exuberantly skimpy detail, you will learn why Kate Jackson sued her hair company, how Cameron Diaz dealt with a man who wanted to blackmail her with topless photos, or what led that Manhattan taxi driver to sue P. Diddy for millions. But one shouldn't think the show is all celebrity gossip. It offers a smattering of psychobabble, too. One night, it solemnly reported, "According to the website of the *Journal of Nervous and Medical Diseases*, CWS, or Celebrity Worship Syndrome, affects up to 30 percent of the population." Of course, coming on a show like *C-J*, as it affectionately calls itself, this quasiscientific claim felt more self-congratulatory than cautionary. Still, the item did hint at an awareness, in the very belly of the beast, that there may be something not altogether cool about our increasing bombardment by stories about the rich and famous.

The reasons are largely economic. The last fifteen years have seen a boom in the number of networks and glossy magazines dedicated to telling stories of the rich and famous. Their demand for people to cover has prompted an unprecedented proliferation of celebrities (who, as

Daniel Boorstin famously defined them, are well-known for being well-known). Even as a handful of idols achieve astonishing levels of international renown (Schwarzenegger, say, or Michael Jordan), our culture has become flooded with pseudostars like Brad Pitt, a good-lookin' fella, to be sure, but one who's a star only to magazine editors. Like recent "It Boy" Colin Farrell or Ben Affleck (whose disaster with J.Lo in *Gigli* became a national laughingstock before the film was even released), Pitt has yet to provide the one sure proof of stardom—that audiences will flock to a movie just to see him. And there's increasingly less distance between these A-List pseudostars and the teeming ranks of the B-List so gleefully mocked by snarky magazines such as *Radar*, which exist to mock them. The Bush years may have cost millions of ordinary people their jobs, but it's been a seller's market for minor celebrities. They enjoy an overwhelming demand for faces to put on magazine covers, celebrate in arts sections, or chronicle on shows like *Biography*: A show that once profiled Winston Churchill is now doing Luke Wilson. The desperation for star-related material has reached the point that *Access Hollywood* once interviewed me about an interview I'd done with Nicole Kidman. They couldn't get *her*.

As the gap between Winners and Losers has grown larger, so our celebrity coverage has become more bipolar along the line of the English tabloids (perhaps because we're starting to have the same kind of class structure as Britain). This is especially clear in the glossy magazines. On one side is *In Style*, which makes not the slightest pretense of saying anything meaningful about the celebrities whose houses it shows you. The magazine is a publicist's dream, the kind of carefully orchestrated puffery that, one might think, could be believed only by dreamy small-town shopgirls half a century ago. It's easy to see why famous people were happy to appear in it and why other publications, aping its success, would create breathless new sections like *Entertainment Weekly*'s News and Notes ("Hope Davis, you are the best!"). But in *In Style*'s gushy wake came the glossy gossip mags, the suddenly popular *Us Weekly* (edited by marketing genius Bonnie Fuller, who is equal parts Jackie Collins and Ma Barker) and the astonishingly successful *In Touch Weekly*, whose juicy short items, scads of photos, and $1.99 cover price make *People* look as substantive and classy as *The Atlantic Monthly*. Seeking freedom from the tyranny of legendary gargoyle publicists such as Pat Kingsley, they employed full-court-press tactics that changed the rules of how respectable publications treated celebrity. Suddenly, cover-girl actresses like Gwyneth Paltrow were yearning for the good old days when the American paparazzi had a sense of proportion and weren't always around to grab a shot of stars looking crappy at the mini-mart. The Internet has pushed things even further. Ever since Matt Drudge scooped *Newsweek* on its own story about Monica and Bill, it's been part of the Net's mission to do what the mainstream shies away from. It was a website that first revealed the name of Kobe Bryant's accuser; another broke the story of Schwarzenegger's seventies gangbang-and-drugs interview with *Oui*; yet another reprinted the divorce papers of Billy Bob Thornton and Angelina Jolie. So many sites broadcasted Paris Hilton's sex tape that even I feel I've slept with her. Predictably, this helped make a hit of her rotten, one-note Reality show *The Simple Life*, in which she and Nicole Ritchie became surrogates for the Bush daughters. Born to party, they seemed oblivious of lives unlike their own.

In a 1965 memoir, Elizabeth Taylor commented on the paradox of stardom: "The public seems to revel in the imperfections of the famous, the heroes, to be in the position of attacking—which I guess makes them feel a little bit superior." But the sheer inescapability of celebrity in our lives has pushed these feelings of hostility to a new level. Bush Culture has become one long *schadenfreude* spree. We enjoy seeing even minor celebrities get theirs, whether it's money-grubbing Bill Gates being pied, poor-little-rich-girl Winona Ryder getting convicted for shoplifting, or Iowa State's basketball coach—embarrassingly, the state's highest-paid government employee—being forced to resign after photos showed him at a postgame party in Missouri guzzling beer and nuzzling a coed. (Never kiss the chick whose boyfriend is holding the camera.) When HBO aired its documentary *Born Rich*, about kids who'd been just that, a CNN commentator said the show proved that the well-off "are just as tacky and gauche as the rest of us." Or more so, like Ally Hilfiger and Jaime

Gleicher on MTV's *Rich Girls*, who wander through high-end Manhattan like the stars of *Clueless* redone by Diane Arbus. Such shows made me fond of the honest, relatively good-natured cruelty in MTV's *Punk'd*, where hip young celebrities are deliberately embarrassed or freaked out by other hip young celebrities—a concept that is, I guess, *groundbreaking*. The fun of the show is watching the victims' mask of cool start to crack, revealing something of their real selves. If the same thing happened to people with no public persona to shatter, the only point would be malice.

Of course, there's something petty about taking joy in another's misfortune. But you'd have to be nobler than I not to have grinned when Rush Limbaugh got nailed for illegally buying the "hillbilly heroin" to which he was addicted: On his first day back from rehab, he told his audience, "I am no longer trying to live my life by making other people happy"—precisely the sort of narcissistic announcement he would have mocked Barbra Streisand for making. And I chortled when it turned out that William Bennett, America's former drug czar, ex–Secretary of Education, and morality profiteer—he gets fifty grand for a speech and made a small fortune from *The Book of Virtues*—had gambled away up to $8 milllion over the previous decade, most of it in the dehumanized realm of the slots and video poker. (I don't know what grandiose fantasy Mr. Morality thought he was living in those casinos, but it wasn't exactly 007 at the chemin de fer table in Monte Carlo.) Unlike Limbaugh, the problem wasn't that Bennett had done anything illegal. It was that, like so many on the sanctimonious right, this apostle of self-control was so selective in his piety. The only victimless vice that this pharisee didn't denounce just happened to be his own—he seemed plenty happy to imprison poor drug addicts.

Then again, such hypocrisy doesn't stop with Limbaugh and Bennett. A similar bad faith underwrites the current explosion of what Nietzsche called *ressentiment*—a twisted feeling of envy that comes mixed with moral superiority toward those one is envying. That feeling is the key to the success of such high-profile bestsellers as the breezily enjoyable *The Nanny Diaries* and the ill-written *The Devil Wears Prada*, which follow a predictable formula: They take a bitchy rich employer who cares more about her wardrobe than her kids, slather on name brands and status details, and filter it all through the mind of a heroine who, despite her innate decency and proper education, clearly yearns to have those same upper-class accoutrements. Playing to the worst intincts of their readers, these novels show that the devil who wears Prada is no more sinister than the one who hopes to yet feels superior to the one who already does.*

While the majority of stories about celebrity justice unleash feelings no nobler than malicious delight in another's ill fortune—they're finally about nothing more than bad behavior—a handful move beyond mere gossip to reveal enduring truths about American life you don't find in our novels, movies, or TV shows. Like the best pop culture, they become a way of grappling with personal and social issues that official culture can't or won't address. The O. J. Simpson trial became a so-called media circus not because the public is a collection of boobs (to use the tired locution of Mencken and his imitators) but because it was a great story that was about *everything*—love, sex, violence, race, money, fame, athletics, social class, the peculiar sociology of Los Angeles, the dark whorls of the psyche. *And* he got acquitted. Any good novelist would kill for such a tale, and only a toffee-nose would find it beneath him.

The same holds true of Michael Jackson, whose arrest for child molestation bumped Iraq off TV screens and brought him back, yet again, into the public's curious eye. Although much was made of his post-arrest interview on *60 Minutes* in late 2003—a pro-Michael infomercial surrounded by charges that CBS had paid him to appear—this wasn't even his most revelatory TV appearance of the year. That came in ABC's broadcast of a British documentary, *Living*

The Devil Wears Prada's villain is an infernal fashion-magazine editor who snaps at her beleaguered assistant because her latte is too cold. Can you imagine such wickedness? Much of America obviously did and took no small pleasure in hearing that Manhattan fashionistas are shallow, selfish, and mean. But compared to the Hollywood of Scott Rudin and Joel Silver, where the term "you stupid cunt" is an accepted form of address, this book's idea of the Boss from Hell feels positively quaint.

with Michael Jackson, one of the Bush era's major media events. The show drew 27 million viewers and had folks yakking all over the country; though no one knew it at the time, it even contained footage of the young boy whose family would eventually press charges. You could hardly blame audiences for watching. I certainly did. After all, from his bad plastic surgery to the way he treats his children, Jackson's whole life seems like a train wreck. Even by today's hallucinatory standards of celebrity, Jackson is the mother lode of *schadenfreude*-inducing follies—his oddball marriages, Neverland Ranch, friendship with Liz Taylor, chimp named Bubbles, silly glove, spectral visage (which itself became the subject of an hourlong *Dateline NBC*), and, of course, the accusations of pedophilia.

None of this can be separated from the fact that he's a brilliant musician. If his songs had not been so popular, he would never have tried to transcend ordinary categories—black and white, male and female, young and old. Then again, if he'd been more self-conscious about his desire for self-transformation, he might now be viewed as an avant-garde hero rather than written off by many as a tragic loon. (Nobody was nearly as mean to David Bowie.) Starting from the childhood stardom that so clearly sent him off the rails, Jackson's story is so rich in poignancy and social meaning that one could easily spend years plumbing its depths: Why his face (like Greta Garbo's in Roland Barthes's acclaimed essay) is the stuff of myth. How his Peter Pan fetish is a metaphor for millions of contemporary children forced to shine (entry exams for kindergarten!) in an Ever-Everland culture in which achievement-mad parents dream of perfecting their kids. Or what fantasy white America was embracing when they made him a god in the early 1980s, and what it says about his middle age that he's still trying to turn white in an era when even that cute Justin Timberlake is cannily heading in the other direction—with help from the endlessly replayed bare breast of Michael's sister at the Super Bowl.

All this makes the man a fascinating phenomenon. But *Living with Michael Jackson* boasted a different level of drama: It inadvertently revealed the ressentiment hidden in celebrity journalism itself. Early in the program, the forty-four-year-old star watched film of his ten-year-old self singing "ABC," and the canyon dividing the two Michaels was so heartbreaking you might have thought that, despite its superficiality, the show was going to be sympathetic. Guess again. It didn't teach America much about Michael Jackson, but it sure taught us a lot about its filmmaker-interviewer Martin Bashir, who was piggybacking on Jackson's fame to enhance his own. Working in the self-aggrandizing documentary mode made famous by Nick Broomfield, Bashir spread himself like oleo over the movie—his voice-overs brimmed with "I," "I," "I." He cajoled and wheedled to get what he wanted, put words in Jackson's mouth, and then treated the results as a "gotcha." Worst of all, he ended up sounding like a D.A. prosecuting a child-abuse case for which he himself had no evidence. Bashir asked Jackson easy questions onscreen, then nailed him with the filmmaker's ultimate weapon—the toxic voice-over. Afterward, Bashir was interviewed by *PrimeTime Thursday*'s Chris Wallace, who listened with a scrupulous deadpan as Bashir, suddenly all moral concern, talked about how "disturbed" and "worried" he was by Jackson's relationship to kids: "I never saw him do anything offensive to a child ever. BUT . . ."—and here came the insinuating payoff—"goodness knows what goes on in the boundaries of Neverland when no one is there." How true. Goodness also knows that such an approach is the classic style of the London tabloids, which milk every drop of prurience from a story even as they moralize about it. An entire journalistic code springs from this double-helix of hypocrisy, which dominated the British media long before invading our own.

That same mixture of exploitation and moralism greeted what may have been the Bush Era's most resonant new melodrama: the indictment of mogul-homemaker Martha Stewart for engaging in insider trading in shares of the biotech firm ImClone. The real villain in the piece was ImClone CEO Sam Waksal, who was subsequently imprisoned for his role in the financial jiggery pokery. But he was just a faceless social climber (*Time* ran a photo of the poor schmuck beaming alongside a sardonically grinning Mick Jagger). In contrast, Stewart had already finished her climb, hanging out with the famous, changing America's sense of style, transforming herself into a cultural archetype—and lightning rod. Her legal woes drew snickers around water coolers, was discussed live on her regular segment of CBS's *The Early Morning* as she grimly chopped vegetables, got replayed in a TV movie on CBS (*Et tu, Brute*) that turned her life into a cheery cartoon, and was treated with no small glee by the press. *The New York Times* coined the term *blondenfreude.*

None of this was surprising, for Stewart is a strong, aggressive, conflicted woman in a society still unnerved by such creatures. Her biography contains within it a history of American womanhood in the last half century, capturing nearly all its cross-currents: In twenty years, she went from being a married Westport caterer to becoming the divorced CEO and walking logo of a billion-dollar company, her work aggressively remaining in a realm traditionally thought of as "feminine." In one sense, her take-charge cooking and decorating was a response to the changes in women's lives after the feminist 1960s, changes that found more women than ever going into the workplace but also left millions feeling that they had lost something—the down-home skills once passed on from mother to daughter. Stewart helped revive that knowledge, linking the traditional pleasures of arts-and-crafts to post-WWII ideas of home economics. She taught America how to make "good things" in an era of ugly, prefab vulgarity—crappy strip malls, supermarket baked goods, craftsmen who no longer give a damn. Martha did give a damn, always, and urged everyone to do the same.

Then, having made herself the synonym of old-fashioned home comforts, she updated the whole shebang for days when even Costco sells fine wines: She went corporate. Her landmark deal with Kmart was a turning point in popularizing modern American design culture; indeed, Stewart was something of an aesthetic heroine. She helped liberate millions from the tyranny of ugly, ill-conceived goods—low-thread-count towels, Day-Glo colored ceramics—that had long been one of the most depressing features of not having much money. Her way of changing mass taste made her a far more culturally significant figure than, say, Eminem, Martin Scorsese, or any dozen novelists you might choose to name. In her blend of the homespun and the hypercapitalist, she embodied aspirations that were every bit as typical of the nineties economic boom as dotcom mania. Where creeps like Jack Welch merely wanted to own the world, Stewart strove to remake it in line with utopian ideas of country coziness unsurprising in one who'd escaped working-class roots. There was nothing eccentric about this. Her ideals touched something deep in millions of Americans, mainly women, who yearn to know how to arrange flowers or decorate a Fourth of July cake.

Along the way, her vision of the world generated a profound ambivalence. I have many women friends who like what she does and admire her business acumen, yet still can't stand her personality or the idealized *über-hausfrau* she has come to represent. Martha embodies women's economic power but also binds that power to traditional female roles. A volatile connection. After all, it's one thing to teach the audience how to make a moist bundt cake, quite another to purvey the image of the domestic goddess in an age when most women have jobs. The contradictory sexual politics of Stewart's work may help explain why—although she's a well-known backer of the Democratic Party— her most vigorous defenders were on the right, from MSNBC's rancid Joe Scarborough to the editors of *The Wall Street Journal* (who have a seemingly infinite tolerance for shady stock dealings) to the libertarians at *Reason* who put her on the cover as the martyred Saint Martha. Of course, it's easy to understand why the right-wing media would embrace Stewart. Not only does her work refurbish old-fashioned feminine roles, but it rakes in a fortune doing it: This onetime model is the symbol of skyrocketing upward mobility, which made her both attractive and daunting. You can picture a Wall Street type dreaming of a wife like Martha keeping the house shipshape, at least so long as he could have some hot-blooded mistress back in his Manhattan pied-à-terre. And you can also picture Martha, having married that kind of guy before, having none of it.

For ordinary Americans, Stewart's high-flying success raised tricky questions of gender and social class. In the beginning, Martha-ism was all about democratizing the promise of worldly perfection, but this promise took on a spooky new aura once she turned into an infomercial with legs, boasting, "I am a brand." She became widely disliked for a bossy authoritarian manner that hinted at the elitist superiority that she once promised to overturn. Frozen in her control-freak persona, she began to seem madder and madder—Ana Gasteyer's lethal *Saturday Night Live* impression gave us a sociopath whose chosen weapons were piecrusts and Christmas ornaments. Through all her travails, Stewart clearly paid a price for being the classic Type A woman (think of *American Beauty*'s contempt for Annette Bening's character), and in a world where most celebrities make like Oprah and let it all hang out, Martha had spent her whole life refusing to do that. Although her legal problems had visibly aged her, they hadn't broken her will. Even telling Barbara Walters of her fears, her upper lip remained so stiff you could use it to scrape ice from a windshield. Walking from the courthouse after her conviction, her face a Kabuki mask of impassivity, she was chided by many reporters for her hauteur and lack of remorse. But her stoicism wasn't aristocratic pretension. It was an expression of the blue-collar toughness that let Polish-American Martha Kostyra rise above a background that she found imprisoning.

Although Stewart's self-reinvention should have made her a free-market heroine, it put her in the political crosshairs, especially in the topsy-turvy reality of Bush's America, where populism is nearly always as phony as a glass eye. These days, nobody wants to seem like a toff. Coming off as the platonic WASP bitch, this genuine child of the working class made the perfect fall gal for an elitist administration that wanted to pretend it was doing something about corporate malfeasance. Although faced with the sort of tactics once used against gangsters like Al Capone—she was convicted of obstructing justice in the investigation of a $50,000 "crime" for which she wasn't charged—she was forced to pay for the incomparably greater sins of Enron's Kenny Boy Lay and the other business execs whom the Justice Department chose not to prosecute. Even those who decided her fate viewed her trial in symbolic terms. Juror Chappell Hartridge, a forty-seven-year-old computer technician, said he hoped the verdict sent a message to big corporations, adding, "Maybe it's a victory for the little guys." (In its startling haste and eagerness to teach a lesson, Stewart's conviction was almost the flip side of the O. J. Simpson jury's verdict on the LAPD.) As ever, Martha was helping to keep things nice and orderly—in this case, the Bush World status quo—by becoming a sacrificial lamb in the court of celebrity justice.

But Lady Justice's scales go up and down, and her sword cuts both ways. While Martha Stewart was on the East Coast paying for the sins of others, the West Coast was writing a very different story:

Ahnold: The Rise of the Anti-Machine

In his magnificent anti-Maoist polemic *Chinese Shadows*, Simon Leys tells how the Communist Party ruined Chinese opera, perhaps that culture's greatest popular art form. Before the revolution, opera houses were rowdy, slovenly places in which the audience's boos, cheers, and raucous applause became part of the show. Ever mistrustful of spontaneous outpourings, Party officials decided to "reeducate" the public, training it to applaud only after the curtain fell, and to keep people in line, flashing "Silence" signs in all four corners of the theater. In the process, they killed the communal joy of opera-going, turning it into a dead academic spectacle.

The same party-pooper spirit reared its head during the California recall election, surely the most media-saturated governor's race in history. Although it began as a partisan hustle by an ambitious San Diego Republican, Darrell Issa, who spent a fortune getting signatures urging the incumbent's ouster, the event promised to be something extraordinary—an electoral Saturnalia in which the normal rules didn't apply. Voters had the unprecedented chance to toss out their sitting governor, Gray Davis, a self-promoting cold fish who had made a career of being the lesser of two evils. In his place, they were offered a cornucopia of potential replacements—not just the usual Democratic and Republican apparatchiks, but an acid-house menagerie of porn stars, porn barons, billboard sirens, diminutive sitcom actors, ex–baseball commissioners, talk-show divas, dreamers, idealists, cranks, and lost souls who, for just once in their life, wanted to see their name on a ballot. The day after Arnold Schwarzenegger joined their number, I went to a party where everybody was, as we say in L.A., totally *stoked*. There's a reason people like me adore California—it seems to have been created by L. Frank Baum—and the 2003 recall had voters more excited than any election in decades. Our dreary old politics was becoming as much fun as *Survivor* or *American Idol*, and each time some outsider bragged that his state would *never* vote for a movie star like Schwarzenegger, we smiled at their envious, unstoked self-delusion.

But if the public enjoyed the recall, hard-core politicos and the mainstream media did not; they smelled mob rule. It was assailed by such conservatives as William Safire and by the famed liberal conglomerate BillandHillary; Cokie Roberts, that delphic oracle of Beltway banality, invoked the Founding Fathers to bludgeon the recall: "Jefferson and his friends," she told Chris Matthews, "are rolling in their graves right now." (Maybe so, but they've done so much rolling over the years, they must think they're on a rotisserie.) No matter that ex-governor Jerry Brown said the job wasn't all that hard to do. The guardians of official culture hated the recall's carnivalesque brio, its way of refreshing the democratic spirit by standing the status quo on its head. They saw it as the latest proof of California voters' irresponsibility, if not further dire confirmation that our entire culture is being devoured by entertainment. In an attempt to restore order—and flash their own "Silence" sign—the media set about whittling down the field of 135 candidates to an acceptable size. They quickly trashed a couple of well-known contenders (sharp-tongued Arianna Huffington never recovered from *The L.A. Times*'s exposés of her tax records), wrote others off as election-day no-hopers (good-bye Peter Ueberroth), and buried all but a handful of contenders deep in the news section, when they covered them at all. Only five candidates were asked to appear on the televised debates, sinking any dark horse's chance to reach a statewide audience. They made things respectable when the whole joy of the enterprise was precisely the opposite. Who didn't want to hear what Larry Flynt would say in a TV debate? Could Gary Coleman actually have more on the ball than Ahnold? By the time the winnowing had been done, the only truly imposing candidate was zealous State Senator Tom McClintock, who, unlike his celebrity rivals, actually did know something about the state of California. But he had one liability. Gazing straight at the voters with mad eyes—an L.A. columnist compared him to Tony Perkins—he proposed policies so retrograde they would have turned the nation's most modern state into The Land That Time Forget.

Amid such dreariness, Schwarzenegger glittered like a diamond in a bucketful of lard. Although not the most articulate of men—his sentences trail off into phrases like "and all dis stuff"—he's famously shrewd. Back in 1976 when he made *Stay Hungry*—a movie that marked his passage from side-of-beef bodybuilder to side-of-beef actor—director Bob Rafelson was telling people that Arnold was the sharpest person on the set. Rafelson might have added that he was also the most ambitious, for Schwarzenegger's defining feature is his obsession with power. During the campaign, he was briefly hassled for an old remark about admiring Hitler's ability to make the crowd love him. Yet what he admired about Der Führer wasn't the Holocaust—there's no evidence that he's anti-Semitic—but the whole hero-worship business. From the early days when Arnold resembled the provincial hero of a nineteenth-century European novel driven to make it in the big city, he pursued his goals with discipline and guile, whether popping steroids and doing endless reps to build up his undersize calves or cannily using his comical accent ("Fuck you, asshohr!") to turn a laughably ungainly name into a worldwide brand. His was the immigrant saga writ large for the media age. Knowing that California's largely apolitical electorate wanted little more than to be led, he used his own record of hard work and voluminous success to offer voters a soaring idea of leadership free of the ballast of saying exactly what that might be.

His politics work just like his movies. Although I've often enjoyed his performances—*The Terminator* wouldn't have been nearly as original without his droll, robotic vibe—Arnold's film work, like his gubernatorial campaign, is resolutely content-free. He has said that he tried to model his career on Clint Eastwood's, shuttling between action pictures and comedies, yet their approaches to filmmaking couldn't be less similar. After making it big as an iconic tough guy, Eastwood spent the next thirty years exploring masculinity, violence, social justice, and his own screen stardom—he consciously worked at knocking apart the persona that made him famous. Aside from a calculated worship of violence, the only meaning you find in Schwarzenegger's work is his desire to make money and enhance his brand. All his mystic rivers lead back to the greater glory of Arnold. His self-reinventions—including running for office—have been about nothing larger than repositioning himself to succeed in a changing marketplace.

For those terrified of a Schwarzenegger governorship, such self-centeredness was actually reassuring. A born businessman with ties to the Kennedys and Hollywood, he's far too pragmatic to become an ideologue. Even more than Ronald Reagan, Arnold is bored by the details of government; his real knack is for promotion. His run for office brilliantly tapped into public anger about politicians, although I might have hanged myself if I had to hear him quote that "mad as hell" speech from *Network* one more time. Yet watching him on the high-tech stump you could tell this was all an act. He didn't share that anger any more than he was fascinated by the nuances of pension-fund financing. His decision to run had nothing to do with principles, policies, or even California. It was all about himself, which means that he was actually a lot like the governor he was replacing.

With one lurid difference: Where Gray Davis's Achilles heel was his addiction to campaign money—you could almost hear the cash registers go *ka-ching* inside the governor's office—Schwarzenegger's was his sexual behavior. Once *The L.A. Times* broke its huge "Groper-gate" story, the election turned into a bad-faith jamboree. Weirdly declaring, "Where there's smoke, there's fire," Arnold said he couldn't remember the incidents in question, then apologized for doing them anyway. Liberals who once defended Clinton were suddenly treating Arnold as Caligula, drawing cavernous distinctions between a president enjoying Oval Office analingus from a starstruck college-age intern and a gubernatorial candidate pulling a woman onto his lap and asking if she's ever had a man stick his tongue up her backside. Such a refined moral calculus would have brought tears to the eyes of Immanuel Kant. Meanwhile, hypocritical Republicans switched off their sanctimony-packs once they saw a chance of their party winning. David Dreier, the same Congressman who voted to impeach Bill Clinton, not only served as the Schwarzenegger campaign's cochair, he turned up on CNN's *Late Edition* to vouch for Arnold as a sterling family man. Evidently, having consensual sex is a major no-no but groping women who don't want it is fine—because it's not really about sex but power.

Perhaps the most stunning response to the raft of sexual-harassment charges was the deathly silence from the famously liberal film industry. Paramount chairwoman Sherry Lansing made a much-quoted public declaration that there's no sexual harassment on movie sets, adding that "Moviemaking is a very gender-blind business"—a line that sent bitter female laughter echoing from Studio City to Beverly Hills. (Quick now, name three women directors in Hollywood.) Still, if anyone should have felt mortified, it was those well-known actresses—including Jamie Lee Curtis, Rita Wilson, Kelly Preston, and Linda Hamilton—who wrote letters to *Premiere* complaining about a March 2001 article ("Arnold the Barbarian") that chronicled Schwarzenegger's notoriously crude sexual antics. They all said they'd never experienced or witnessed any such thing. Well, of course they didn't. Arnold wasn't going to squeeze Mrs. Tom Hanks's breasts or tell the wife of his director, James Cameron, what he once allegedly told a waitress: "I want you to go in the bathroom, stick your finger in your pussy, and bring it out to me." These actresses are his peers—or at least he thinks their husbands are. Assuming they weren't lying to protect him, you could only marvel at the cocoon that would keep them from grasping that Schwarzenegger would be charming to them and save his barbarism for those he could harass with impunity.

Had the ruling Democrats fielded a strong candidate such as Senator Dianne Feinstein, Arnold would still be desperately hoping to make *Terminator 4*. But they did not, and so he was able to play by his own rules, doing an end run around the traditional political media. He gave most of his face-time to outlets like *Oprah, Access Hollywood,* and *Entertainment Tonight*—the puffery circuit he'd been manipulating for years. News reporters didn't like it, but why submit yourself to tough questions when Larry King is happy to give you free publicity? Besides, the print media were already giving him plenty of coverage, recording his every move and churning out tiresome headlines based on his movie titles—if only he'd never been in *Total Recall.* Not only was Arnold on the cover of *Time* and *Newsweek,* but every major paper in and out of California devoted incomparably more space to his campaign than to anybody else's. His campaign drew so much international media attention that a British documentary crew started making a film about the other crews making films about Arnold.

From beginning to end, Arnold was given the star treatment, and star treatment is what got him elected. He ran, in fact, a clumsy race, lying about taking special-interest contributions and hiring Republican consultants whose presence diminished his claims of independence. His campaign only looked skillful because, like George W. Bush in 2000, he transcended low expectations—he didn't blow the debate. Under the circumstances, that was sufficient. Since President Harry Truman upset challenger Thomas Dewey in 1948, there hasn't been a single important American election in which an unpopular incumbent defied huge odds to win a dramatic victory. The public always votes for the new guy or the exciting new story line, and Schwarzenegger realized this. His Hollywood background proved his grasp of pop storytelling. He knew that the recall was his only chance to win the big prize—he could never have won a Republican primary—and he was savvy enough to position himself as a tribune of The People versus the "special interests." Using his stardom to claim he was automatically above the grubbiness of partisan politics, Arnold married Republican economics ("to make better duh business climate") to a Democratic liberalism on questions of lifestyle; he played the outsider able to take California beyond the strident oppositions that have defined the Bush era. And precisely because he was preposterous and seemingly omnipotent, he made voters feel that everything is possible. The election became a lesson in the law of natural selection.

Given the choice between politicians and a movie star, the public naturally selected the star. And it did so in numbers that made the naysayers appear foolish. Not only did Schwarzenegger alone get more votes than the anti-recall vote for Davis (roughly 4.2 to 4 million), but he received 750,000 more votes than Davis had gotten in the 2002 ballot.

On election night, Arnold was introduced by emcee Jay Leno—now, *there* were two jaws you could use to crush boulders—and from the moment he bounded on stage, you saw why he'd won such a resounding victory. Strutting confidently and grinning with pleasure more genuine than any he'd shown in the previous weeks, Duh Gubna radiated the qualities that Californians eternally think their due: star power, optimism, and fun. True, he'd said nothing substantive on the campaign trail, as a full two-thirds of his supporters freely acknowledged. True, he was no man of The People, unless the Kennedy family counts. His key backers were real-estate developers, corporate millionaires, and political hacks who'd worked for former Republican governor Pete Wilson. No matter. In keeping with this era of Populist Social Darwinism, his was a populism of attitudes, not policies; he promised joy, unity, *action.* His mere presence in the race made California feel exciting and hopeful again. Heck, he even upstaged Iraq! And beaming Arnold wasn't a sore winner but a gracious one, although there remains a question of whom he's being gracious to. His first acts as governor came straight from the Bush Era manual. He canceled the car tax increase (pushing California $4 billion deeper into debt), fired the head of the Department of Motor Vehicles (a fraud-buster disliked by auto dealers, who contributed $500,000 to the Schwarzenegger campaign), and pushed through a $15 billion bond that would, in the impeccable manner of the new conservative populism, pass the state's debt on to a later generation, while still leading to major cuts in, naturally, programs for the poor and the ill. As for the rest of us, we're still waiting for our jobs to become fantastic.

CHAPTER 5

Meta-Media Madness:
We Distort, You Deride

From new transmitters came the old stupidities.
— BERTOLT BRECHT

In Barry Unsworth's *The Songs of the Kings*, an ironic novel about the run-up to the Greek invasion of Troy, Odysseus—the villain—startles himself with an epiphany: "The driving force in human society was not greed or the lust for power, as he had once thought, but the energy generated by juggling with concepts, endlessly striving to make perceptions of reality agree with them, to melt things together, iron out problems, harmonize warring elements. . . . They would rule the world who knew this and used it." To that end, he decides to twist the arm of the Singer, a Homer-like figure who's equal parts artist and journalist, to make sure his public songs will goad the Greeks into eagerly doing their kings' bidding. But it turns out that the Singer doesn't need to be cajoled or threatened. He already knows what side his bread is buttered on.

The Singer has countless heirs in the modern media. Their low point surely came on March 6, 2003, when the President held his lone press conference before taking the country to war with Iraq. Bush and his control-freak handlers dislike such unscripted events because, as Communications Director Dan Bartlett told *The Washington Post*, "If you have a message you're trying to deliver, a news conference can go in a different direction." You betcha: A few glimpses of truth always manage to slip through. One such moment came late in that conference, which was otherwise a small masterpiece of redundancy and evasion. Asked why so much of the world was protesting U.S. policy toward Iraq, Bush's face assumed its trademark glower. "You know, I appreciate societies in which people can express their opinion," he said, uttering these words with such transcendent sourness that you could tell he wished America weren't one of them.

Not that the White House press corps was itself any advertisement for independent thinking. Aside from ABC's Terry Moran, who had the guts to suggest that Bush had ducked an earlier question about the world's opposition to war, these high-profile reporters groveled like a roomful of Gollums—but without the cunning. They didn't call the President on his bait-and-switch references to September 11, slippery linkages of Saddam and "al-Qaeda–type terrorist groups," or refusal to discuss the cost of impending war with the citizens who were going to wind up paying for it. Instead, they were content just to be in the same room with the big guy. None dared risk the fate of eighty-two-year-old correspondent Helen Thomas, who had recently declared Bush the worst president in U.S. history and become persona non grata. She wasn't called on. Nor were *The Washington Post*'s Mike Allen and Dana Milbank, who had peeved the White House by asking comparatively skeptical questions. That charge could never have been leveled against the American Urban Radio Networks' reporter, April Ryan. After establishing her racial bona fides by mentioning the Congressional Black Caucus, she tossed him a question so squishy that even Larry King would have thought twice, or maybe I mean once. "How," she asked, "is your faith guiding you?" Bush was not unhappy to tell her. Deploying the moist eyes he often calls upon to prove his sincerity, he said he prayed that war could be averted, as if God, and not he, got to make the final call.

Afterward, Terry Moran, who began his career toiling in the honorable vineyard of Court TV, expressed his horror, noting the President's flat performance and comparing his fellow reporters to "zombies." But in fact, the whole occasion was much scarier than *Dawn of the Dead*. America had been offered something of a Potemkin Village press conference, a scripted event complete with reporters waving their hands as if to spontaneously catch the President's eye, even though they knew, and *The Washington Post* reported, that Bush was working from a prepared list of handpicked questioners. Back when Eastern Europe was communist, workers used to say, "We pretend to work and they pretend to pay us." Our press corps has its own version: "We pretend to ask questions and they pretend to answer us." Both sides find this arrangement perfectly satisfactory.

In the days to come, I kept meeting people who wondered how so many reporters could have been so rotten. "How would you describe that performance?" a friend asked. "Prone or supine?" And that question led to others. Where was the so-called liberal media (or SCLM, as Eric Alterman has dubbed them)? Had they lost their self-confidence and begun skewing their coverage to the right? Were they cowering before the Everest of the President's approval rating? Or were they simply driven by careerist fear that behaving like proper journalists might cost them their access, their reportorial lifeline, and with it their chance to wind up as a high-priced pundit? In one way or another, the answer to all these questions was "Yes." In keeping with the tenor of the Bush years, we must now brave a culture in which Fox News keeps rising, liberal journalism keeps floundering, and the reigning journalistic metaphor is being "embedded."

Bias, Slander, and Lies

When I was teaching at Georgetown University in the eighties, I once witnessed a bitter political argument between an earnest Catholic jock from the Midwest and an aggressively brainy young Englishwoman who attacked his logic with all the leniency Uma Thurman shows her enemies in *Kill Bill*. After a few minutes, the young man gave a frustrated sigh:

"You obviously don't understand what I'm saying."

"I understand it perfectly," came the crushing reply. "And I'm saying you're *wrong*."

He looked at her, stunned, and didn't open his mouth again for the rest of the hour. The other students, all American, stared at the haughty English interloper with palpable dislike: When it comes to debate, Europeans are from Mars and Americans are from Venus. Raised on British notions of logic and evidence, she had violated one of our most powerful punctilios, the unspoken belief that if everyone would only speak clearly, honestly, and with perfect goodwill—if we were all *nice*—there would be no need for arguments or fights. We could all, finally, settle on a common truth, and nobody would have to be wrong.

This deep-seated fantasy of consensus was born of many causes: our practical-minded culture's worship of "the facts," which supposedly exist free of opinions or ideologies, our rejection of explicit (and divisive) class politics, and our *e pluribus unum* dream of assimilation, in which immigrants of many lands swan-dive into the melting pot and emerge as one united people. Even our two-party structure, which would seem to imply opposition, has tended to encourage the notion that truth lies somewhere between two not-very-extreme poles; hence the tedious worship of bipartisanship one so often finds on the Op-Ed pages. For most of the last sixty years, this fantasy of harmony was fed by our news media, which, during the prosperous, corporatizing Cold War culture of the 1950s and early 1960s, came to celebrate the idea of an American consensus—we'd reached, Daniel Bell told us, the "End of Ideology." Treating middle-class experience as universal, journalism went from being a faintly disreputable line of work (think of the boozy, wisecracking reporters in thirties movies) to a self-styled "profession" whose big names were increasingly drawn from prestigious universities and espoused the high ideals of objectivity that Joseph Pulitzer had introduced to the *St. Louis Post-Dispatch* and *New York World* in the late nineteenth century.

The rise of the three big television networks—which quickly became the public's main source of news—nourished this sense of consensus. Not only did they remain avowedly apolitical (unlike newspapers, they never endorsed presidential candidates), but their coverage hewed to what they perceived to be the values of an imaginary *civilized center*—the Democrats or Republicans that Chet Huntley or David Brinkley could imagine having dinner with. Such was the definition of "neutral." TV conferred national stardom on its

newsmen, which only reinforced the sense that they transcended partisanship. The anchormen who spent all those evening hours in your
living room were seen as being above mere politics—Rockefeller
Center Olympians. My parents always turned on CBS News not
because Walter Cronkite expressed their political views more fully
than NBC's Huntley and Brinkley or sharp-tongued Frank Reynolds,
marooned on the then-forlorn island of ABC. They watched him
because they'd watched Edward R. Murrow before him, and anyway
Uncle Walter had a reassuring vibe. Still, it would never have occurred
to them to wonder if a rival network was cooking the coverage. The
gods didn't do that.

By the mid-1960s, this media consensus was already under a twin-
track assault from the *two* huge counter-countercultures to emerge
during that decade. The more immediately visible of these was the
longhaired one, which took yipping delight in mocking "straight"
publications and began creating an alternative press of its own—most
famously, *Ramparts* and *Rolling Stone*. At the same time, largely out of
the spotlight, the Goldwater right (remember the shunned Young
Americans for Freedom?) was sowing the seeds of a right-wing movement that would eventually produce not only Ronald Reagan but
the Christian Coalition, Newt Gingrich, George W. Bush, and John
Ashcroft. One of its prize tactics was a systematic attack on "the liberal
press," later upgraded to "the liberal media." Nobody did this more
relentlessly than the Nixon team—his crooked Veep Spiro T. Agnew
relished working the refs—but in an amusing reversal, their
flamboyant dishonesty momentarily put the mass media in a heroic
new light. After Watergate, young people were pouring into J-schools,
and Cronkite topped the polls as "the most trusted figure in American
public life."

Today, it seems otherworldly that any journalist could enjoy such a
title. The honor now belongs to Oprah, and frankly, she deserves it
more than Cronkite ever did. Although the dream of consensus lingers,
especially among Americans who can't stomach the partisan vicious-
ness of the Clinton and Bush years, we live in a society polarized by
political attitudes and fragmented by a surfeit of media outlets. It is

one of the invigorating paradoxes of the new millennium that, at a time when America's mass media becomes ever more centralized and gargantuan companies such as Viacom (CBS), General Electric (NBC), Disney (ABC), Time Warner (CNN), and News Corporation (Fox News) control staggering amounts of information, the public's relationship to the media is more decentered than ever before. People now get their news not only from the broadcast networks or their hometown paper but from cable news, talk radio, webzines, e-mail newsletters, and bloggers, not to mention scores of out-of-town (even French) newspapers they can instantly pull up online. But as the Australian poet Les Murray once wrote, "Nothing's free when it is explained." Just as the proliferation of blurbs in movie ads has made all critics appear to be idiots or flacks, so the rabbitlike proliferation of news sources—many of them slipshod, understaffed, or insanely partisan—has inevitably devalued the authority of any individual source.

We've entered the age of meta-media. CNN legal analyst Jeffrey Toobin reports on how media coverage could affect the Kobe Bryant rape trial. *The Washington Post*'s Mike Allen gets interviewed about covering President Bush's secret Thanksgiving trip to Baghdad. After the 2003 NCAA basketball final, talk radio isn't buzzing about Syracuse's victory over Kansas but about CBS reporter Bonnie Bernstein repeatedly asking the losing coach, Roy Williams, if he was going to take another job at the University of North Carolina, prompting his startling on-air reply: "I could give a shit about North Carolina right now." In such an atmosphere, the saga of Stephen Glass's phony articles for *The New Republic* is deemed worthy of a feature film, *Shattered Glass*, that would never have been made twenty years ago, and Simon & Schuster eagerly publishes his bad semi-autobiographical novel, *The Fabulist*. When Jayson Blair's fakery sparked a palace coup at *The New York Times*, he landed on the cover of *Newsweek*, spawned an episode of *Law and Order: Criminal Intent*, and nabbed a deal for *Burning Down My Master's House*, a memoir that let him paint himself a villain (for the first paragraph, anyway) and enjoy still more coverage (but no sales). Like Blair, the media world is boundless in its narcissism.

Given all this, it's no surprise that there are now scads of official media critics (*The L.A. Times* has two) who earn their paychecks by assessing *The Wall Street Journal*'s redesign, anatomizing the White House's manipulation of the press, or grousing when *Nightline* postpones a report on Bush's visit to Blair to cover the latest news about Michael Jackson. "Entertainment is taking over the news," goes the plaintive cry—words I've been hearing all my conscious life. These critics' analyses are supplemented by both *Reliable Sources* on CNN and *Fox News Watch*, shows that often rise to a level of meta-meta-media self-referentiality: They analyze how others have analyzed how a story is being covered. (The last sentence, by the way, is a majestic piece of meta-meta-meta-media criticism—ruminations on ruminations on ruminations on journalism—which makes me feel as if I've wandered into that hall of mirrors in *The Lady from Shanghai*.) Many of today's media critics are sharp cookies, and reading them dissect news coverage is reminiscent of watching an NFL game in the early days of instant replay when you suddenly saw for sure just how many calls the referees got wrong.

The official media critics are far outnumbered by amateur obsessives. Out on the Internet, being a media watchdog isn't a job but a calling, one that has already changed the structure of authority in American journalism by subverting the hieratic power claimed by so many major newspapers and networks. Just as Martha Stewart helped bring stylish design to the masses, so cyberspace has democratized political commentary and media criticism—anyone can make like George Will or Howard Kurtz. And the culture is far better for this explosion of lively new voices. During the Bush years, blogs have gone from being largely the province of bored, lonely, or troubled souls (nearly all male, interestingly) to a new form of public expression so precise, timely, and linked to real information that it makes the Sunday morning pundits seem like stumps in the petrified forest.

These days, many blogs are written by brainy, tireless people engaged in what one might call "asymmetrical warfare" with established media outlets. Lacking the resources of big news organizations, they seemingly wake each morning hellbent on showing how *The New*

York Times has grown less liberal under Bill Keller (quite true), unearthing the ideological bias of a headline, catching a reporter's laziness or inaccuracy, or simply "fisking" a news story that bugs them.* The best sites cast a hard, steady light on stories the official media have ignored or mishandled; for instance, Trent Lott's fall from power was directly due to bloggers such as Josh Marshall and Andrew Sullivan. This was no aberration. Like Atrios, Kos, or *Opinion Journal's* proudly reactionary "Best of the Web Today"—whose James Taranto I read with the aghast fascination of a child watching maggots devour a dead cat—today's Internet stalwarts have huge followings among those who make and cover the news. The leading bloggers are actually far more powerful than they'd be if they merely wrote traditional columns in the powerful dailies. What they write now shapes other people's columns.

Like most things on the Internet, these daily forays range from the exhilarating to the depressing, and for every intelligent site like Kausfiles or Atrios, there are dozens of web-pages dedicated to the blogorrhea of small-souled nitpicking. Opinion rules. With rare exceptions like Marshall's TalkingPointsMemo.com, most bloggers aren't I. F. Stone digging up information that nobody else has noticed and then revealing the unspoken workings of power. It's blaming George Bush or "the liberals" for everything that goes wrong in America, shrieking "Gotcha!" at tiny factual errors in articles written on short deadlines, or accusing *The New York Times,* day after day, of deliberately misleading readers by covering news from a too-liberal perspective—as if that NFL referee wasn't just wrong about an incomplete pass but deliberately made the wrong call because he had money on the game.

Of course, the battle cry over slanted journalism has been sounded for years on the right: If Rush Limbaugh couldn't complain about the liberal media, his daily show would run only five minutes. Still, the

---

*"Fisking" was named after the left-wing British journalist Robert Fisk, whose vehement opposition to American policies in the Middle East made him a frequent target of bloggers eager to show his bad faith, prejudice, and dishonesty.

Bush years have given rise to an explosive escalation of the bias wars. Former CBS reporter Bernard Goldberg had a bestseller with *Bias: A CBS Insider Exposes How the Media Distort the News*, in which this self-declared man of the left ("I'm a liberal the way liberals *used to be*") insisted that the media, including his old network, are too liberal, slanting their coverage to make the flat tax look bogus or pretend the homeless problem went away under Bill Clinton. More dim than malevolent, Goldberg was quickly surpassed by right-wing scourge Ann Coulter, the sort of baleful, leggy blonde you expect to see in bed with James Bond just before he kills her. Her own hit book, *Slander: Liberal Lies about the American Right*, starts off by saying, "It's all liberals' fault," and grows cruder after that. (One savors the irony of her calling Gloria Steinem a "termagant.") Coulter's sales marked something of a sea change in publishing. In the past, such books tended to be brought out by right-wing houses such as the lamentable Regnery, which is *still* releasing books attacking Bill Clinton. But after the success of *Slander*, the Crown Publishing Group (a division of Random House) got hungry for those right-wing dollars. It didn't merely sign her up for another hot-button jeremiad, *Treason: Liberal Treachery from the Cold War to the War on Terrorism*, it launched a whole new imprint, Crown Forum, devoted exclusively to feeding conservative readers their ideological Alpo. In the process, *Slander* became the first book in history to radically change its publishing house without managing to change a single reader's mind.

Both *Bias* and *Slander* are astonishingly rotten books—partial, self-serving, egregiously unfair, and addicted to formulations so cheap that trying to argue with them can only make you dumber. Really, what can one say in response to Goldberg's claim that "everybody to the right of Lenin is a 'right-winger' as far as the media elites are concerned"? Perhaps he means Lennon. For all their heady scent of accusation, the right's attacks on the media are rife with a sense of victimization—the very quality that conservatives often accuse minorities of exploiting to win undue sympathy. Poor us, they moan, our viewpoint is not being represented in the mass media. Evidently, it's not enough to have held the presidency for sixteen of the last twenty-four years, to control the

Congress and the Supreme Court, to dominate talk radio and the gargantuan Clear Channel (which helped organize pro-Iraq war rallies), to boast a network mouthpiece in Fox News, to have twice as many daily papers endorse Bush as Gore, and to watch vaunted liberal publications such as *The Atlantic Monthly* and *The Washington Post* slide steadily to the right. As Michael Kinsley laughingly observed, rightwing pundits apparently want some sort of affirmative action for conservatives in the media—the only social bias they care about. You don't find Coulter, Goldberg, or the Media Research Center's Brent Bozell insisting that the ultraconservative Heritage Foundation hire more Harvard liberals or demanding that more Greens be put on the board at Halliburton.

Eventually, the left fired back with several media books of its own, from Conason's *Big Lies* to Franken's *Lies and the Lying Liars Who Tell Them.* The most detailed of the bunch was Eric Alterman's useful *What Liberal Media? The Truth about Bias and the News,* which noted that, despite its supposed bias, the "so-called liberal media" did manage to put Ann Coulter on the *Today* show, *Hardball,* and *Crossfire* and to profile her in *Newsday, The New York Observer,* and *The New York Times.* Alterman does the valuable, time-consuming work of reminding readers just how few liberal-left pundits are allowed to push their agenda on TV: "Who among the liberals can be counted upon as ideological, as relentless, and as nakedly partisan as George Will, Bob Novak, Pat Buchanan, Bay Buchanan, William Bennett, William Kristol, Fred Barnes, John McLaughlin, Charles Krauthammer, Paul Gigot, Ben Wattenberg, Oliver North, Kate O'Beirne, Tony Blankley, Ann Coulter, Sean Hannity, Tony Snow, Laura Ingraham, Jonah Goldberg, William F. Buckley Jr., Bill O'Reilly, Alan Keyes, Tucker Carlson, Brit Hume, CNBC's roundtable of the self-described 'wild men' of the *Wall Street Journal* editorial page, and on and on?"

From my own experience, I know for certain that right-wing journalism is far more murderously partisan, going nuclear at the least provocation. If *New York Times* columnist Paul Krugman had outed a CIA agent as did retro-thug columnist Robert Novak, conservatives would have been demanding his arrest for treason. At the same time,

I agree with conservative critics that journalists tend to be more politically liberal (especially on lifestyle issues) than the country as a whole, which over the last twenty years moved so far to the right that *Democrats* balanced the budget and pushed through welfare reform. Yet it doesn't necessarily follow that reporters or their publications deliberately misstate facts or slant stories. Especially on the left, they often overcompensate and have frequently done so during the Bush years. The "liberal media" may be preponderantly pro-choice, but their dislike for Al Gore helped George W. Bush get elected. Watching *The New York Times* spend years pounding Bill Clinton, I often wondered: Would *The Wall Street Journal* go after a Republican president's lies and malfeasances with the same ferocity? Deep into the Bush presidency, we all know the answer to that one.

The point here is not to declare a winner in the bias wars, but to point out its centrality to Bush culture. For the first time in decades, it's become transparently clear that America has an ideological media, that our TV networks, newspapers, magazines, and radio talk shows all represent particular points of view. On the whole, the growing awareness of this is a good thing, although many Americans, including rabid partisans, instinctively rebel against it: Why else would conservatives flay *The New York Times* for being the voice of liberalism yet be outraged afresh each time Krugman calls Bush a liar? Why else would my friends flip on Fox News, then flip out when it proves to be exactly the pro-Bush network they thought it was in the first place? Mao Zedong once said that the American moon and the Chinese moon are the same moon. He's right, but Fox News's Iraq and *The New York Times*'s Iraq often appear to be, as it were, very different moons.

Europeans have lived for decades with the knowledge that there's no such thing as a neutral media. When Londoners pick up the blimpish *Telegraph*, the trendy-left *Guardian*, or Rupert Murdoch's *Sun* with its moralism and big bare breasts, they know the paper's editorial angle and read accordingly. Americans are learning to do the same thing, which is one reason liberals now have Air America Radio and Al Gore wants to start up a likeminded cable channel. Traditionally, European newspapers have taken their political attitudes from the parties they support, whereas what's driving American media toward overt ideology is less political conviction than money. Like everything else, from sexual perversions to team jerseys, ideology has become a marketing niche. This is hard on media liberals, who prefer to think of themselves as fair-minded souls attuned to values higher than commerce. Despite their recent angry books, lefties feel uncomfortable with the notion that their values may not embody the national consensus. Not so conservatives, who not only venerate the profit motive but are still hooked on their exhilarating sense of being embattled even as they claim to represent majority opinion. For the right, the only thing better than bashing a liberal or grousing about bias is getting paid to do it.

No place pays you better than Fox News, which, in the years since George W. Bush came to office, hasn't merely become the most nakedly partisan network in the history of American television but the harbinger of a new, politicized media that many on the left find terrifying.

Crazy Like Fox

To talk of Fox News is to begin with its founder and owner, Rupert Murdoch, the seventy-three-year-old Australian mogul who created the network in 1996 as a huge outpost in a media empire that has made him hated on five continents. Like so many of the men who dominate the Bush Era, Murdoch is a faux populist member of the elite. The scion of a newspapering family, young Rupert went to Oxford, then set about amassing his billions with a two-pronged attack: Even as he used his media holdings to bully and sweet-talk those in power, his various outlets pandered to mass taste. In the half century since he took over the family firm, this strategy has turned him into the very symbol of the wicked media tycoon.

"I call my cancer Rupert," said the English TV writer Dennis Potter (he wrote *The Singing Detective*) in his last interview before dying of the disease in 1994. "I would shoot the bugger if I could. There is no one person more responsible for the pollution of what was always a fairly polluted press." The left decries his baleful influence on America, where his company News Corporation owns (among many other things) Fox

News and the quintessential right-wing tabloid, *The New York Post*. Even his more intellectually respectable properties, such as *The Weekly Standard*, express Murdoch's conservative politics. Yet as James Atlas noted in *The Atlantic Monthly*, the man is no dedicated ideologue. Murdoch uses his media power to promote—his media power. He's all about business, even at the hugely unprofitable *Post*, which assures him a large and valuable presence in New York City. Where Ted Turner's goofball idealism dulled his sharklike instincts, Murdoch has never let the sentimental attachment to principle disrupt the orderly making of money. He fits perfectly Oscar Wilde's definition of a cynic as one who knows the price of everything and the value of nothing.

His massive holdings led the head of Common Cause to dub him "the poster boy of media consolidation," but this cheats the man of his true dimension. Murdoch is actually the poster boy of the cultural contradictions of capitalism. Probably the most radical single figure in American life, he is a political conservative whose enterprises subvert the very institutions and values he claims to be conserving. It was this defender of family values, not Turner, who gave America *In Living Color*, *Married with Children*, and *Paradise Island*. On the one hand, Murdoch is an astonishing source of vitality, building Fox News from nothing, transforming Fox Broadcasting Network into by far the most exciting of our broadcast channels—home to *The X-Files*, *American Idol*, *The O.C.*, and, supremely, *The Simpsons*, the great Middle American epic that far surpasses the fiction of Dos Passos or Sinclair Lewis. On the other hand, he's a partner in totalitarian repression, dropping the BBC from his Asian Star TV satellite system to placate China's murderous leaders who didn't want any networks that criticized their policies. On yet another hand (it takes far more than two for a cephalopod like Rupert), he's perhaps the world's most successful purveyor of right-wing ideology, nowhere more triumphantly than at Fox News, which has not only established itself as the Bush administration's house organ but has shown that there are massive profits to be made in ideologically driven TV. At a time when CNN and MSNBC are battling to maintain their ratings, Fox News's audience has increased by leaps and bounds—40 percent from 2002 to 2003. Its success prompted *The Daily Show*'s Jon Stewart to make a joke many liberals identified with: "*We* need a twenty-four-hour fake news channel. Fox can't be the *only* fake news channel out there."

Most liberals revile Fox News and wonder why anyone—other than yokels and snarling conservatives, of course—would ever watch it. Some of this is the merest snobbery, the sort of class superiority that the right justly pummels the left for harboring. If you tune in to the network for even a few hours, the reasons for its success quickly become apparent. The network clearly preaches to the conservative choir—championing Bush, bitch-slapping foreigners, vilifying Sean Penn as if he were a spokesman for something more than his own ego. Yet beyond this, Fox's allure is that its programming has the breezy, crass vitality that typifies the Murdoch media universe. It takes the eye-catching energy of the newspaper tabloids, tosses in a hard-faced blond anchorwoman or two, and then stirs in hours of the volatile bombast that made talk radio a national sensation. It gives you news inflamed with emotion. As one rival network head said to me: "I can't stand the politics, but it's much better *television*." *Monday Night Football* forever changed sports telecasting with its multiple cameras and oddball triumvirate of announcers. Fox is doing the same to TV news with its gleeful outrage, unabashed nationalism, finely tuned sense of drama, *whooshing* graphics, and rousing theme music (is that a cowbell?). This is a network with a sense of fun, and even at its commentators' angriest, the Fox studio makes you feel the people there are having a good time.

One person who understands Fox's success is Michael Wolff, *Vanity Fair*'s grandiose but still canny media critic. During Operation Iraqi Freedom, he went to one of the daily press briefings at CENTCOM's media center in Doha and directly asked Brigadier General Vincent Brooks if there was any point in listening to his denatured answers. Predictably, this got him attacked by Fox News. But as Wolff told the authors of *Embedded*, an oral history of the media in the Iraq war, he didn't take it seriously: "When Fox said I was a 'traitor,' did they really think I was a traitor? No, they don't really care. They're doing their thing. It's all about taking sides and in a sense it's all about conflict, and we have fun in conflict. Good television is made out of conflict. The interesting Fox subtext is that you have two factors going on here—you have ideology and you have good televison."

The dark huckster behind all the fun is Fox News's chairman and CEO, Roger Ailes, a master provocateur who combines a great instinct for what works on television with the overbearing personality to make it happen—Bill O'Reilly compares him to Patton. Of course, the general didn't have much feel for pop culture, while Ailes possesses a gangsta sense of aggression and payback that's perfect for the era of sore winners. Under Ailes's guidance, Fox mocked former employee Paula Zahn when she jumped to CNN, ran a commercial insinuating that MSNBC reporter Peter Arnett was a traitor, and spent one entire morning comparing CNN anchor Aaron Brown to a dentist, a gibe deadly in its cruel accuracy. This last attack was revenge, Ailes told *The New Yorker*'s Ken Auletta, for Brown's slighting words about Fox. It wasn't for nothing that Ailes once worked for Richard Nixon. In fact, he first made his name by putting together Nixon's campaign telecasts, a role that established him as the best character in Joe McGinnis's *The Selling of the President 1968*. From the beginning Ailes has been deliciously quotable, and virtually nobody who writes about him can resist quoting his great riff on Tricky Dick:

> Let's face it, a lot of people think Nixon is dull. Think he's a bore, a pain in the ass. They look at him as the kind of kid who always carried a bookbag. Who was forty-two years old the day he was born. They figure other kids got footballs for Christmas, Nixon got a briefcase and he loved it. He'd always have his homework done and he'd never let you copy.
>
> Now you put him on television, you've got a problem right away. He's a funny-looking guy. He looks like somebody hung him in a closet overnight and he jumps out in the morning with his suit all bunched up and starts running around saying, "I want to be President."

What's unforgettable isn't simply Ailes's cold-eye—he knew exactly the kind of guy he was backing and didn't care—but the Daumier verve of his portraiture. Ailes actually makes far better copy than the guys who work for him, and each time I read one of his interviews, I rue the fact he doesn't have a show of his own on Fox. Who could resist it? He wouldn't have to fire Brit Hume, who's as smart as he is dour, or O'Reilly, who's the franchise, but I'd rather see Ailes on my screen than smug jerks like Tony Snow, Sean Hannity (who seems like the guy who *didn't* get hired to replace Jimmy Kimmel on *The Man Show*), or Hannity's quasiliberal munchkin Colmes.

Ailes spent years working for Republicans (he also helped elect Reagan and Bush I) and has both feet planted in that ideological world. After 9/11 he even sent a letter of advice to George W. Bush. Perhaps because he's so flagrantly of the right—no other future network head has made anything like the infamous Willie Horton ad—he's tireless about insisting that Fox really is "fair and balanced," even as its core audience relishes the fact that it *isn't*. Ailes has a magical knack for slogans, and I never stop being impressed by the terse poetry of "We report. You decide." It's a great tagline. Of course, as an old professor of mine once said about Rousseau's protestations of candor at the beginning of his *Confessions*, "If you have to keep telling us how honest you are, you're not."

By now, you may be as weary as I am of people gung ho to prove that Fox news is biased. Of course it is: That's the point. Fox is the network that trumpeted the untrue story that the Clinton staff had trashed the White House. It's the network that sent Oliver North to Iraq as a war correspondent and interviewed Pat Boone about his new album of patriotic songs. It had a graphic calling the French the "axis of weasels," sneered at antiwar protestors, and offered war coverage that waved the American flag like a cheerleader's pom-pom. The soldiers' families loved it. After Bush's surprise Thanksgiving visit to Baghdad, CNN's Walt Rogers called it a "stirring story" but cautioned that, even as Bush was feeding the troops, reporters in the Iraqi capital were hearing explosions. Predictably, things were rosier over on Fox, which was wowed by the trip: "It's got to demoralize the bad guys. . . . What they're familiar with is a show of power. *This* is a show of power." It sure is, but I'm not sure who's showing what to whom.

I see no problem with a news channel presenting things with a partisan slant. If the right wants to hear Pat Boone pondering America's moral decline, they're more than welcome to him. Yet one does wish Ailes's squadron would cover the news a quarter as well as *The Wall Street Journal*, the reporting of which is as renowned for its accuracy as its editorial page is for its Neanderthal grunting. In the autumn of 2003, the University of Maryland's Program on International Policy Attitudes released the results of a nationwide survey. It showed that 48 percent of Americans believed that U.S. troops found evidence of close links between Saddam and al-Qaeda, 22 percent believed U.S. troops found weapons of mass destruction in Iraq, and 25 percent believed that international public opinion backed the Coalition's war with Iraq. None of these things was true. What made this survey telling wasn't the public's misperception but its correlation with their media outlets: Where only 23 percent of NPR/PBS consumers held at least one of these mistaken beliefs (compared to 55 percent for CNN and NBC viewers), the number among Fox viewers was a whopping 80 percent. Ailes can say, "We report. You decide" 'til kingdom come, but something about Fox's reporting makes its viewers decide *wrong*.

In the end, however, Murdoch and Ailes's greatest triumph has been to convince the world that Fox News is a major force. The right takes the network's growing audience as proof that its values now occupy the political center; the left often behaves as if nobody would have ever voted for Bush had they not been bamboozled by Murdoch's medicine men. Meanwhile, its competitors have been in a dither. TV execs are not the bravest or most visionary of souls, and in the wake of Fox's rise, CNN had something of an identity crisis. Even as it cast its lot with anchorman Aaron Brown—almost a parody of the thoughtful liberal—it was sprucing itself up with sexier graphics and music, dredging up Connie Chung from TV's collective unconscious (she soon sank back down), and hoping that graying-but-groovy Anderson Cooper would make the network less geriatric—no easy task with Larry King being popped from his sarcophagus every evening at nine. MSNBC was worse, falling to its knees before what it considered the runaway Republican zeitgeist. Although MSNBC has

TV's most biting newscaster in irony-drenched Keith Olbermann, the ex-*SportsCenter* anchor who spearheaded ESPN's reinvention of sports news, its execs preferred to go the yahoo route. Certain that the royal road to success was populating the screen with right-wing blabbermouths, they first hired serial bigot Michael Savage, who often seemed like the world's only homeless man with a nationwide TV show, then essentially fired him for being Michael Savage. (He urged one "sodomite" caller to "get AIDS and die, you pig.") Going the extra mile, MSNBC also signed on Joe Scarborough, who is, I believe, something that fell out of Roger Ailes's ear during a tour of Florida. His show, *Scarborough Country*, is a smeary Xerox copy of *The O'Reilly Factor*. *Vanity Fair*'s James Wolcott noted the strangeness of NBC diluting its reputation as a serious news organization in a pathetic attempt to court conservatives too toxic for Fox. If CNN or MSNBC had to retool themselves, they would have been wiser using Cooper and Olbermann to woo the huge audience of disaffected liberals who crave a network that's fair and balanced in *their* direction.*

The strangest thing about these desperate attempts to keep up with Fox News is that, for all its buzz, the network is still eons from being a cultural juggernaut. Fox's top dog, O'Reilly, draws 2.7 million viewers, which isn't simply far fewer than Rush Limbaugh's 14 million radio listeners, it's only one-third of the 8-million-plus who tune in to watch poor old Dan Rather, an outdated figure of fun who increasingly resembles newscaster Kent Brockman on *The Simpsons*. Granted, drawing nearly three million viewers is not nothing; then again, in a country of 293 million people, this means only one person in a hundred watches *The O'Reilly Factor*, not exactly a groundswell. If the show were on broadcast TV, those numbers would get it canceled. The only reason Fox is now considered a cultural bellwether is that, within the self-absorbed, trend-obsessed world of media movers and shakers,

*The one MSNBC figure who came closest to figuring this out was Chris Matthews, a man torn between the gee-whiz liberal romanticism that led him to join the Peace Corps and the ambition that has made him adopt a blowhard persona. Tonsils in tatters from shrieking through the Clinton years, he was the only major TV pundit to speak out repeatedly against the Iraq war.

gaining a few hundred thousand cable TV viewers a year is reckoned an epic achievement—proof that Ailes has his finger on the pulse of America. And because these same people fit Orwell's definition of the power worshiper, they think that what's happening now will happen forever; hence their desire to emulate whatever is working at any particular moment. Which means Fox.

Naturally, the network takes care to boast about every achievement it can. Bragging of its popularity and prowess, it's even taken to calling itself "The Channel of Political Record." And maybe it is—in Crawford. No matter. Like so much at Fox News, the power of such a slogan lies not in its accuracy but in its cockiness, audacity, and air of absolute conviction—precisely the qualities that define its gaudiest personality.

Talent on Loan from Roger Ailes

You might think Bill O'Reilly has it made. He fronts a nationwide radio program. He hosts cable news's biggest show, *The O'Reilly Factor*. He has published three short books with very large print, and each has become a huge bestseller. But that just shows how little you know. The guy feels slandered, mistreated, misunderstood—so abused, it seems, that he must seek the consolation of ceaseless self-promotion. Click on his TV show and he'll try to sell you his new book. Click on his radio show and he'll try to sell you his new book and refer you to his website, BillOReilly.com. Go to "Bill's Home on the Web" and you'll be urged to visit the Bill O'Reilly Store, where you can purchase such fabulous items as gift packs of his books, and for the paltry sum of $49.95 (plus $10.96 for shipping and handling), a doormat bearing the legend "The Spin Stops Here!" So, it seems, do the bucks.

There's a certain irony to O'Reilly selling doormats, for his whole shtick is about not being one. It's about cutting through all the "spin," taking charge of your own life, being a blue-collar guy who doesn't b.s. When O'Reilly rails against Hollywood liberals or CIA Director George Tenet, you know he's calling it exactly as he sees it. And if you don't know, he'll tell you, then tell you again. This tends to drive his detractors crazy (my wife flees the room when I click on his show) because the "No Spin Zone" all too often becomes a "No Facts Zone." There's an entire book, *The Oh Really? Factor: Unspinning Fox News Channel's Bill O'Reilly*, devoted to nothing but demonstrating the man's promiscuous relationship to the truth. O'Reilly tends to throw out specious statistics (fifteen of the September 11 hijackers came through Canada), deny he's said things he's on record as saying (comparing the Koran to *Mein Kampf*), and insist that if he's wrong about a fact he'll issue a correction—which he then doesn't bother to do. Granted he's a commentator not a reporter, but if fellow conservative pundits David Brooks or William Safire made half so many errors at the despised *New York Times*, they'd lose their jobs (luckily, they could always find work at Fox News). Then again, like Ronald Reagan, O'Reilly draws strength from believing that his common sense is truer than mere facts. If he thinks the Reason Foundation is "left wing," who cares that it's actually libertarian? In ratings terms, he's probably right not to care.

I first saw him back when he was anchoring *Inside Edition* and even then felt the pull of his domineering charisma. Tabloid journalism requires the shameless shuffling of sleaze and morality, and nobody is better than O'Reilly at serving up trash with a hearty dollop of sanctimony. This gift obviously caught the eye of Ailes, who did for O'Reilly what Sergio Leone once did for Clint Eastwood: He took a performer of limited range but unexpectedly grand ambition, then put him in a situation that turned his persona mythic. Where *Inside Edition* squandered O'Reilly's gifts, burying them in rubbish about stars and serial killers, Ailes grasped that he'd found a guy whose "grandstanding egomania" (as novelist James Ellroy has admiringly called it) only came to full flower when commanding the whole screen, the whole show. In this, O'Reilly resembles Rush Limbaugh, who is incomparably more effective running his own radio program than he was struggling to be heard during his short-lived gig on ESPN's NFL pregame show. Although the two men share a similar stance—they're the American guy whose every nerve-end shrieks at the madness of modern culture, with its free contraceptives, Ivy League Bolsheviks, and telecasts of *Angels in America*—their talents are radically different. On radio, O'Reilly's not nearly as good as Limbaugh, a right-wing agitprop master blessed with a strangulated musicality of voice, a keen sense of humor, and manic bursts of inspiration—his synapses start firing like popcorn. On television, though, everything flips. Straitjacketed by a fat man's inescapable self-consciousness, Limbaugh seems uneasy, even a tad Heepish, and much smaller in the flesh than in the AM version. But put the camera on Bill O'Reilly and the guy keeps getting bigger. With his "I dare you" gaze and flaring nostrils (one sometimes wonders if his guests are flatulent), he has a face made for injecting drama into talking-head TV. He's the molten core of a famously cool medium, and if you think that's easy, just watch Matthews and Scarborough laboring to catch fire over there on MSNBC.

"We are all born with natural talent," wrote O'Reilly in *Who's Looking Out for You?*, "but we must tap into it with a vengeance in order to reach our full potential." Vengeance, indeed. A friend of mine from Chicago says the guy reminds him of the genially brutal priests at his high school who would smile as they knuckled you on the head ("Anything in there?"), and it's true that O'Reilly's first job after college was teaching at a Catholic high school in Florida. Although one of his gifts is distilling outrage into brief, lucid pellets—which is what makes his "Talking Points Memo" so aggravating to liberals—his success is ultimately built on his capacity for head-to-head showdowns. *The O'Reilly Factor* can be profitably seen as the populist answer to *Meet the Press*, a show that proudly promulgates the myth of the ruling elite's seriousness and decorum, while scrupulously avoiding troublesome questions of ideology. Where beefy Tim Russert is famous for digging up that irrelevant quotation from 1994 that will make John Kerry squirm ten years later on the campaign trail, O'Reilly has no time for the small potatoes of catching somebody out on a few piddling facts. He's into bottom lines and worldviews and righteous conclusions. He once told *Esquire* that "90 percent of the world's problems are black-and-white," and you can see that in his exasperation with nuanced conversation. A very sharp guy, he employs a barrage of tricks, from his way of saying the word "professor" (imagine Tom DeLay saying "homosexual") to his fondness for rhetorical chicken. Rather than ask a guest what he thinks of George Tenet, he'll give his own firm opinion of the CIA head and then ask, "Am I *wrong*?" Even if the guest agrees, O'Reilly's combative style has made the moment *dramatic*; if not, he's instantly forced the guy into a head-on collision. And this he knows is good TV. Physically, O'Reilly is a big, intimidating guy and clearly thinks it a selling point that viewers think he might just leap across his desk and start pounding a guest.

This thuggishness puts him in a long line of Irish gasbags that includes Senator Joseph McCarthy, and even further back, Father Charles Edward Coughlin, the priest whose angry 1930s radio broadcasts ("Somebody must be *blamed*!") were a scary mix of populist economics and pro-fascist anti-Semitism.* Although O'Reilly does not share these men's worst ideas, he does employ their rabble-rousing trick of promoting himself by going after supposed enemies of The People—in his case, the same "liberal elite" assailed by McCarthy and Nixon. This has long been a successful tactic, for it taps into deeply felt status anxieties, feelings neatly summarized by Garry Wills in *Nixon Agonistes*: "Since America has an 'open' social system with no stable classes, men do not have fixed social identities; they must earn their position in society, their status. Yet in a fluid world of opportunity, status is insecure, always slipping, unless men earn it again, perpetually reestablishing themselves. This leads to resentment, the desire to be more American than the next man, more superlatively common, less questionably alien." If you read O'Reilly's books, you realize that Bill has a bleak Irish soul. He can easily picture his success slipping away. Such feelings explain why he becomes furious when Al Franken debunks the Horatio Alger myth of his rise from humble, working-class origins in Levittown to his current position as a millionaire TV

---

*Nativist Pat Buchanan is another of McCarthy and Coughlin's heirs—you can still hear strains of the old music. The Democrat versions of this type are Russert and Chris Matthews.

star. O'Reilly's whole persona is built on his gutbucket American honesty, so it saps his credibility to talk up his hard childhood, then have
it come out that his family lived in middle-class Westbury and vaca-
tioned in Florida—a far softer childhood than, for instance, Dan
Rather's. It makes him sound like, well, a liar. And this spooks him.

But only his harshest critics really care about this not-uncommon
piece of personal mythologizing. "Class is a sensibility," O'Reilly says,
and just like George W. Bush, he's chosen his class identity rather than
passively accepting the one he was born with. He genuinely feels that
he grew up humbly, and his whole manner suggests a man who
doesn't just sympathize with blue-collar machismo and petit-
bourgeois resentment but feels it in his belly. One suspects that these
feelings come from his relationship to his father, a strict, sometimes
brutal man who, as his son puts it, "would have won praise from
Mussolini for his, uh, child-rearing practices." O'Reilly duplicates that
style on his show, where he often plays the paternalistic Il Duce. In
perhaps the all-time classic *Factor*, he furiously went after Jeremy
Glick, whose father had been killed in the World Trade Center attack,
for dishonoring his dad's memory by opposing American foreign
policy:

> O'REILLY: I'm sure your beliefs are sincere, but what upsets me
>   is I don't think your father would be approving of this.
> GLICK: Well, actually, my father thought that Bush's presidency
>   was illegitimate.

O'Reilly eventually threw Glick off the show, saying, "Cut his mike.
I'm not going to dress you down anymore, out of respect for your
father."

But in his hard feelings, O'Reilly's also the son who feels that he's
been unfairly knocked around by the whole world. You can see this in
his anger toward those who would scoff at his family background or
cock their snoots at *Inside Edition*. He got an M.A. from Boston
University, and he obviously still smarts from how all those Harvard
and MIT kids looked down on the school; hence, in part, his blood

hatred of Al Franken, Harvard '73. It's not accidental that O'Reilly left broadcasting at one point to get a degree from the Kennedy School—like Dubya, he was laying claim to a credential he both admires and detests. Unlike so many right-wing politicians who run against Washington while wanting to move there forever, O'Reilly's rancor toward the elite isn't phony, which is why it resonates with viewers who know in their gut that he feels about things the way they do. Sensing this, he feels himself entitled to make huge, unprovable proclamations about the country—for instance, that America loves Julia Roberts but doesn't like George Clooney. Actually, America is fine with Clooney. It's O'Reilly who can't stand him, warning his audience against the actor's Hollywood liberalism: "We are living in a time where perception is reality and impressions are formed from rank propaganda and outright deception."

Although O'Reilly is clearly a man of the right (one of his many fibs is that he's not a registered Republican), his politics are slightly less knee-jerk than you expect to find on Fox News; he's anti–death penalty, for instance. Yes, he reamed Clinton for Monica, which was OK by me, accuses "secularists" of trying to destroy "traditional" values (tell that to Bart Simpson), and like many a nouveau riche has the unlikable habit of grumbling about high taxes. But none of this gives him any faith in politicians, even the Republicans his network backs: "George W. Bush genuinely likes people," he has written, "and would help you, I believe, if you could get his attention. But Mr. Bush is not a micro kind of guy—he leaves most details to steely-eyed assistants who will not be getting the Dr. Tom Dooley Medal for compassion anytime soon. The President is not a reformer, nor does he get very upset about injustice in our society. He is a child of privilege and brings a sense of entitlement to his job."

These words come from *Who's Looking Out for You?*, probably the purest expression of the stark philosophy one might call O'Reilly Existentialism. The book's underlying message is that, ultimately, we all must look out for ourselves. No matter how loved we think we are, we will still die alone. If the book makes anything clear, it's that Bill O'Reilly has learned to look out for Bill O'Reilly. For with him everything is *personal*. He savages Al Gore for not coming on his show but has a soft spot for Janeane Garofalo because she had the courage to appear on *The Factor*. He does a "Talking Points Memo" defending Mel Gibson's film *The Passion* against *New York Times* "secularist" Frank Rich and casually mentions that he and Mel have a business deal going. During the period when he and Fox were pushing to get Tenet fired, you could tell that Bill didn't really care who runs the CIA. He just wanted to see if his show had the power to get the guy canned.

In his afterword to *The No Spin Zone*, James Ellroy alludes to the O'Reilly "wit." Perhaps I missed the episode when he showed some. Few things are grislier than O'Reilly's beaming attempts to pretend he's good-humored. The closest thing to being merry I've ever seen him was in the summer of 2003 when he hosted Ann Coulter, who was promoting *Treason*, an egregious book—and Big Bill knew it. After arguing briefly about her hero Joe McCarthy, he asked about her famously vitriolic manner and she denied it. "You don't have any vitriol?" he yelped. "What is this, *The Wizard of Oz*?" As they talked on, he looked at Coulter with genuine bemusement, not because she was saying anything funny but because he could tell that his own act was a whole lot better than hers.

Bubble Wrap

When Roger Vadim made *And God Created Woman* in 1956, critics praised its approach to sexuality (embodied in the carnal young Brigitte Bardot) for being so avant-garde. Jean-Luc Godard demurred. Vadim wasn't ahead of the times, he said, everybody else was *behind*. I often feel the same way about our media culture, where Fox News can seem like the future because the left-leaning media are still struggling to escape the past. While Murdoch's two Bills—O'Reilly and Kristol—burst with confidence that they're surfing the very crest of the zeitgeist, their liberal-left counterparts lack any such assurance. They're still paddling out in hopes of catching a wave, glumly aware that history's riptide might wash them out to sea.

No one has paddled any harder than Aaron Brown, CNN's flagship anchorman—and Dr. Jekyll to O'Reilly's Mr. Hyde. It was always part of the network's Ted Turnerized aura that it was liberal—not liberal-bias liberal, of course, but open-minded enough that it could play in hotel rooms all over the planet. When he first caught our eye on September 11, Brown seemed the network's ideal front man. He is wry, sensible, and to all appearances a very nice man; if he has any vanity, it's that he's not vain. Clearly repelled by Fox News's partisan bombast, he nightly turns out something of a meta-newscast that frequently offers reasons for doing particular stories and arranging them in a certain order. Having learned from Fox that format is all, he's given cute names to the newscast's sections. His show begins with The Whip™, in which Brown gets teasers from reporters stationed around the globe, and winds up with "Morning Papers" (complete with crowing rooster), a brief finale that one fears he thinks hip: He goes through the front pages of the next day's newspapers with the diluted wryness of a third-generation Mort Sahl. (I half expect to see him doing this segment in a sweater.) From start to finish, Brown clearly wants to give his newscast the soothing, civilized air that good liberals like himself prefer. The night Mary Matalin thanked him for having such a "smart show" (she'd just finished steamrolling him), he fought against looking as tickled as he obviously was. Like so many in the media, he really, really wants to be given an A+.

The only trouble is, he works in a medium that's usually looking for smart ways to be dumb. Irving Kristol famously defined a neoconservative as a liberal who's been mugged by reality. Brown is a liberal journalist who's been mugged by Reality TV. For all his attempts to be droll, low-key, and serious, he's still working in twenty-four-hour cable news, which means that he spends a good deal of time wringing his hands over what he's putting on the air. Talking to students in Oklahoma, he admitted, "The events of 9/11, sadly, have blunted some of our instincts," especially in covering the Bush administration. "I wouldn't say we gave them a free ride, but I don't think we put many speed bumps in their path." I guess not. In fact, Brown's war coverage, at once eager and "sensitive," led to a savage parody in Aaron McGruder's comic strip, *The Boondocks*.

The night that actor Robert Blake was arrested for murder, Brown approached the story with all the fretfulness of a preacher explaining adultery to a nymphomaniac. "As we sit here tonight, there's a ton and a half going on in the world, and all of it is, in the larger scheme of things, really important. This is interesting and this is breaking and this is news, but at some point there are these other things that need to be dealt with too, and that's one of the things that, I hope, we'll see, will make it different from our end, from the media's end in how we approach this thing." And then, having said all this, Brown proceeded to do exactly what he'd been hired to do. He peeled off his cleric's collar and hopped into the sack with the Blake story—bouncing up and down for hours. He compared the actor to O. J., ran old clips from *Baretta*, interviewed lawyers, celebrity journalists, and lawyers who've turned into celebrity journalists. In the process, one saw the crisis—and capitulation—of today's weak-willed liberal journalist who deplores the world's wrongs in wry, sensible, humane tones yet somehow never gets around to righting them. Watching Brown keep his head above a story he was cramming down America's throat, I was torn between irritation at the way he was betraying his principles and sympathy with his flailing attempts to remain honorable in the current journalistic world.

It is, of course, terrifyingly easy to flail in the opposite direction—refusing to change long after the world has moved on. This is precisely what appears to have happened to *The Nation*, which, for as far back as I can remember, has been the journalistic lodestar for those leftists who think the Democratic Party middle-of-the-road. Now in its 139th year, the magazine looks to be thriving. Thanks to George W. Bush, its subscriptions have climbed to record levels—more than 150,000. Its finances may eventually break even, a small miracle in the world of political magazines. And its publishing adjunct, Nation Books, has put out twenty books, including two very hot titles: Gore Vidal's *Perpetual War for Perpetual Peace* and *Forbidden Truth* by Jean-Charles Brisard and Guillaume Dasquié. Everything's going so well, in fact, that I feel kind of churlish in pointing out what most on the left are unwilling to say out loud: *The Nation* is a profoundly dreary magazine.

One need merely compare it to that other thin, ideologically driven publication, *The Weekly Standard*, the neocon house organ that's 130 years younger. About halfway through Bush's term of office, I began putting new issues of each side by side on my end table and, to my surprise, discovered that while unread copies of *The Nation* invariably rose in guilt-inducing stacks, I always read *The Weekly Standard* right away—even though I routinely disagree with nearly all of it. Why? Because seen purely as a magazine, *The Standard* is far more alluring, and not only because Rupert's big bucks pay for slick paper. As gray and unappetizing as homework, *The Nation* makes you approach it in the same spirit that so many leftists have voted for Walter Mondale, Michael Dukakis, Al Gore, and John Kerry—where else can you go? In contrast, *The Standard* woos you by saying, "This is a magazine that's in touch with what's happening. We're having big fun over here on the right."

Back in the sixties, the left was the home of iconoclasm. Even today, its biggest star is weisenheimer Michael Moore and its most effective news outlet *The Daily Show*, which is peerless at capturing Bush Era absurdity, whether it's highlighting Henry Kissinger's qualifications for heading the 9/11 investigation commission ("The man nailed Liv Ullmann!") or praising Homeland Security: "You haven't lost your freedoms," purred fake news analyst Stephen Colbert, "you've *gained* limits on your civil liberties." But these are exceptions. Over the last thirty years, the joy has dribbled out of the left—it now feels hedged in by shibboleths and defeatism. Meanwhile, the right has been having a gas: Lee Atwater grooving to the blues, Rush Limbaugh chortling about Feminazis, grimly gleeful Ann

Coulter serving up bile as if it were chocolate mousse. These same high spirits course through *The Standard*. Even when he should be drenched with flop-sweat about Iraq, its editor, William Kristol, always shows up on TV grinning like a catfish. His magazine features catchy covers (Democratic lemmings diving off a cliff), jaunty-unfair headlines (a hit piece on Brazil's popular leftist president was called "Brazil's Nut"), and in addition to the usual kennel of foaming militarists, a core of first-rate writers, including Christopher Caudwell and David Tell, perhaps the country's most compelling editorialist. Although driven by a Disquieting American's devout ideological agenda, Kristol knows how to mix things up, running a parody page (it dreamed up mock Medicare cards sponsored by drug companies), funny articles by the likes of P. J. O'Rourke (who reminds us that conscience-free reactionaries tend to make better humorists than well-meaning liberals), and short, sharp items designed to keep readers amused during those long, fearful nights trapped inside the Baghdad Sheraton. Many of the magazine's attempts at humor fall flat, but at least Kristol and Co. know they're supposed to try. Snappy and pointed, *The Standard* is designed to compete for attention in a world that has many magazines, many newspapers, many TV shows.

Not so *The Nation*, which presents itself as an obligation. In his book *Design and Crime*, the left-wing critic Hal Foster attacks the contemporary obsession with well-designed objects, claiming "design abets a near-perfect circuit of production and consumption without much running room for anything else." The same asceticism is obviously at work in *The Nation*, visually mired in the same mentality that kept documentaries slathering on folk music decades after Dylan went electric, as if being out of touch were a badge of integrity. In a day when the clever Canadian magazine *Adbusters* attacks corporate culture by standing advertising techniques on their heads—it's wisely hoping to attract some readers under fifty—*The Nation* specializes in anti-corporate anhedonia. While its covers have recently grown more striking and combative, the rest of the magazine feels deliberately unsexy. Jokes are largely limited to Calvin Trillin's doggerel, headlines are warnings not enticements—do *you* want to read a piece about John

Lee Malvo's trial called "A Killing Nation"?—and too much of the writing is muffled by low-word-rate padding and fear of offending the magazine's many vocal, easily offended constituencies. Reading the average *Nation* editorial is like trying to gobble dry muesli. Although the magazine still has some compelling writers, from film critic Stuart Klawans to neighing Stalinist warhorse Alexander Cockburn, its most visible figure, the polymathic Christopher Hitchens, theatrically resigned during the Iraq war run-up, whacking the publication for thinking John Ashcroft more dangerous than al-Qaeda.

Hitchens had already offended many on the left by attacking Bill Clinton. During the impeachment scandal, he signed an affidavit contradicting Sidney Blumenthal's testimony about the President calling Monica Lewinsky a stalker. This brave, honorable act got him unfairly labeled, in some quarters, as "Hitch the Snitch." Still, it was one thing to go after a Democratic president from the left, another to support George W. Bush in his War on Terror and invasion of Iraq. In the months after September 11, you heard Hitchens's old friends lamenting his transformation into a blimpish, Blimpish Tory. You heard nasty jokes about his boozing and vanished elegance (*The Onion* ran a headline: Christopher Hitchens Forcibly Removed from Trailerpark after Drunken Confrontation with Common-Law Wife). You heard whispers that he had been corrupted by all those huge paychecks from *Vanity Fair*, a gig that surely had made him the highest-paid left-wing journalist in the world.

For reasons that elude me, Hitchens almost seemed to encourage such attacks. He gave obnoxiously cocky interviews, called the Dixie Chicks "fucking fat slags," and sneered at those who opposed invading Iraq, often content to rout the dumbest antiwar protestor rather than engage the arguments of the smartest. His righteousness brimmed with self-aggrandizement—as if all of history had conspired to create this dramatic moment in which Christopher Hitchens would play the embattled Voice of Truth. In Hitchens's behavior one saw distorted reflections of the literary-hero-worship on display in his 2002 book *Why Orwell Matters*. But where the man born Eric Blair had deliberately made himself a genuine outsider, living poor and eschewing the benefits of his social background, Hitchens's way of playing the honest truth-teller fit all-too-neatly into the ethos of Bush World. Forever living high, dropping the names of his well-connected comrades, and writing mock-heroic, but still self-congratulatory pieces about breaking the law by smoking in Manhattan, he became the Rich Man's Orwell.

Still, Hitchens is one of the two or three smartest journalists I've met, and what got lost in the kerfuffle was that Iraq had inspired some of the sharpest writing of his career. He's always been a superb polemicist, and his work was especially fine in his pieces for the on-line magazine *Slate*. His defense of invading Iraq as a *progressive* cause proved far more compelling than any justification for the war offered by the White House (or *The Weekly Standard*, for that matter). Even when Hitchens's arguments didn't persuade you, they made most of the debate on the subject look simpleminded and doctrinaire; his analysis of terms like "regime change" and "drumbeat to war" forced those who opposed the war to sharpen our arguments. They left you smarter. Looking back over those pieces today (they're collected in *A Short Long War: The Postponed Liberation of Iraq*), you realize how much poorer *The Nation* is not to have him in its pages.

When Hitchens quit, he railed against the stupidity of those who refused to see the dangers in Islamic fascism. He might equally have complained that the magazine had little sense of America. *The Weekly Standard*'s editors grasp that most Americans now talk about politics in the guise of culture, which is why they would print a piece linking Tocqueville to the BCS rankings in college football, or run David Brooks's wry sociology pieces about such conservative archetypes as "Patio Man"—the king of the outer-ring suburbs. In comparison, *The Nation*'s editors seem pleased to have no pop instincts. They cranked out endless earnest policy pieces and book reviews with no drama or verve. In his book about Stalinism, *Koba the Dread*, Martin Amis shrewdly observed that the fall of communism liberated his pal Hitchens's writing by ending its ritual genuflections and obligatory defensiveness. *The Nation* enjoyed no such liberation. Like too much of the left, it keeps waiting for history to start running backward so that it can regain its old stature. Given the opportunity to rethink the possibilities of a "progressive left" (to use one of its prize terms) in an era when Americans are genuinely threatened by Islamic terror, Republicans are scheming to take a permanent grip on power, and the electorate is so conservative that idealistic youths think Howard Dean a radical, the magazine has continued preaching to a choir that seems to have been sitting skeletal in its dusty robes since the Spanish Civil War. It belabors points that its readers already agree with (e.g., Bush is the very devil) and avoids tough-minded journalistic coverage of a liberal agenda that seems to have added no new programs or ideas since the failure of communism. It keeps getting lost in internecine debates and naive boosterism. It covered Jesse Jackson's ass for years, and, Hitchens aside, wasted page after page defending Clinton as if he were a sexual martyr. To judge from the work of regular correspondent John Nichols, who writes like a gaga press agent, failed Clinton Cabinet member Robert Reich was a bold tribune of The People and yapping, bad-hair Dennis Kucinich had a prayer of becoming the Democratic nominee in 2004.

To his credit, Nichols does travel around the country, whereas those in charge of *The Nation* seem to have been swaddled in bubble wrap and locked in Patty Hearst's old closet. A depressing symbol of this is a writer I've long admired, Katha Pollitt, whose most memorable pieces in years—the fatuous post-9/11 column saying that she sees the American flag as a symbol of tyranny and a *New Yorker* confessional about cyberstalking her ex—suggested that here was a person who needed to get out more. One might say the same of the magazine's editors, who are evidently content to keep appealing to the same small group of like-minded people who can't believe that anyone could watch *The O'Reilly Factor* or believe CBS guilty of liberal bias. They need to talk to some folks who own guns.

Nobody needs it more than the magazine's editor and public face, Katrina vanden Heuvel, who often turns up representing *The Nation* on the talk shows. Smart, well-informed, and attractive, she seems the ideal person to do it. There's only one problem: Her style couldn't be worse for this era of rightwing populism. Tense, humorless, and utterly oblivious of how her words might play between the coasts, vanden Heuvel comes off as less a champion of ordinary people than a cold, exotic, outer-space alien—the editor from Planet Leftron. She either doesn't know this or doesn't care, for rather than attempting to win over the public, she joylessly intones what she has to say—and it always sounds negative. Obviously, nobody ever taught her the crucial lesson enunciated by Frank Sinatra. "An audience is like a broad," said that great man of the people. "If you're indifferent, Endsville."

A la recherche du *Times* perdu

America's two most powerful liberal media outlets, *The New York Times* and National Public Radio, *do* pay attention to the audience. Both have a nationwide reach, an editorial style designed for prosperous, well-educated whites, and a sense of aspiration that makes most of their competitors look lazy. While NPR boasts the most consistently intelligent programming in America—its 15 to 20 million listeners make it a necessary counterweight to Rush Limbaugh and Clear Channel, especially in the heartland—*The New York Times* is one of the world's finest newspapers and certainly the most ambitious. When the paper won seven Pulitzers for its coverage of September 11, media critics pointed out that newspapering had become haunted by the specter of Steinbrennerism—the rich franchises win because they can afford to spend the most money to win. NPR and the *Times* share one other big thing in common: They're attacked from both the right and the left, though not quite in the way one might suppose. The most stinging criticisms come not from conservatives, who dream happily of closing them down, but from bohemians and leftists who find their centrist liberalism annoyingly friction-proof and their cultural coverage too "middlebrow" (a word that, in classic American fashion, was invented by twenties publishers to woo readers who wanted books that were neither too literary nor too pulpy). For all their virtues, it is the frustrating destiny of NPR and the *Times* to leave much of their natural audience disappointed. They're imprisoned in politeness: When Bill O'Reilly walked out on an interview on *Fresh Air*, NPR's ombudsman determined that the host, Terry Gross, had pushed too far with unfairly aggressive questioning. But what's wrong with sometimes asking questions that make a guest furious? When O'Reilly gets mad at his guests, he throws *them* off. I wonder what Fox's ombudsman—as if—has to say about that?

Normally, NPR seems the more precariously situated, yet the Bush years have been good to it. September 11 demonstrated the value of enlightened talk shows, the network's listenership keeps growing, and McDonald's heiress Joan Kroc bequeathed it $200 million. The road has proved rockier at the *Times*, which, for all its prosperity and Pulitzers, endured a period of enormous public embarrassment that for several months left the Gray Lady looking as slobbery and lost as one of the Bush girls. In the spring of 2003, the whole country learned about Jayson Blair, the twenty-seven-year-old reporter caught faking material in more than thirty stories, a hardly unprecedented piece of journalistic dishonesty that anti–affirmative action ideologues tried to pump up into a dire parable about promoting minorities too quickly. (In fact, the real reason for Blair's overhasty rise was American newspapers' desperate search for with-it, young reporters of any color who attract "the kids," though anyone who wants to go into print is, almost by definition, too square.) Blair became the icon of media corruption during the very heyday of the bias wars. Suddenly worried about its credibility, the *Times* suspended Pulitzer Prize–winning reporter Rick Bragg when it came out that some of his empurpled prose was based not on firsthand research but on the work of an unpaid stringer who received no credit. At first Bragg insisted such selfishness was standard industry practice, but after his colleagues vehemently attacked him for saying so, he resigned in a huff and went off to write the Jessica Lynch bio. Although neither the Blair nor the Bragg incident was in itself catastrophic or even particularly surprising, the scandal wound up toppling editor Howell Raines, who, in less than a year, had alienated most of the *Times*'s staff by employing a management style borrowed from Alabama coaching legend (and sumbitch) Paul "Bear" Bryant. This newsroom putsch caused no small ideological aftershock, for the right had spent months accusing Raines of giving the paper a lefty slant in everything from biased headlines to its obsession with getting women admitted to the Augusta National Golf Club.

Had such upheaval taken place at Fox News or *The Los Angeles Times*, the story would have been a two-day wonder. But *The New York Times* occupies a privileged spot in the ruling elite's psyche. It is *the* establishment organ, the paper that must be reckoned with by anyone interested in wielding power, or even in distributing a tiny art movie. For conservatives, the *Times* is an indispensable target and emotional crutch; it lets them feel permanently disenfranchised even when they are running things. To them, the *Times*'s tailspin was pure *jouissance*, the giddy B-side of Fox News's orgasmic ascent, and they were still breathing hard about it months later. This was not without its comic side, for as media critic William Powers (no relation) pointed out in *The National Journal*, many of the paper's detractors were bashing it for no longer being "the paper of record," as if it, or any daily, could ever truly be such a thing. Meanwhile, the paper's troubles landed like a body blow on establishment liberals, who have long treated the paper as the one sure pillar of media wisdom—a barrier between themselves and a world in which Matt Drudge is the new Edward R. Murrow (another Walter Winchell would be bad enough). One can only imagine the head-clutching that greeted the discovery that *Times* reporters could be as loosey-goosey with the facts as Rush Limbaugh.

Of course, facts are stupid things, as the noted epistemologist Ronald Reagan so aptly observed, and some journalistic crimes more dangerous than others. Just consider the case of another *Times* bigfoot, reporter Judith Miller, well-known for her anthrax-period bestseller, *Germs*. Even as the Blair fiasco marched across front pages and magazine covers, media critics as diverse as *The Nation*'s Alexander Cockburn and *Slate*'s Jack Shafer, a libertarian, were dismantling her coverage of Iraqi weapons of mass destruction. Before the war, Miller had swayed public opinion with big front-page exclusives about Saddam's stockpiles of biochemical weapons. Trouble was, her key unnamed sources turned out to be Ahmad Chalabi and various defectors, the selfsame Iraqi exiles who were also the leading source for many of the Defense Department's statements about WMDs—statements that the *Times* itself would later suggest had been manipulated to justify preemptive war. Naturally, the editors didn't mention that their own reporter had presented the same information to readers as if it were true. But as Shafer noted, "Miller, more than any other reporter, showcased the WMD speculations and intelligence findings by the Bush administration and the Iraqi defector/dissidents. Our WMD expectations, such as they were, grew largely out of Miller's stories."

After the war, her maneuvering was even dodgier. She cut a devil's bargain with the U.S. military weapons-inspection team, MET Alpha, gaining exclusive access to an Iraqi scientist's revelations about illicit WMDs. In exchange, she accepted "terms of accreditation" that included letting her copy be checked by military officials. In her search for the career-enhancing glory of exclusive access, Miller was treating hard-news reporting as a slightly grander branch of celebrity journalism, where similar deals are routine. Yet her egregiously bad judgment received far less attention than Blair's modest fictions for one simple reason. His mistakes were safely "personal" (read: nonpolitical), while Miller's were shot through with troubling implications for the Bush administration *and* the media. Her big WMD scoops now read a lot like propaganda. By comparison, Blair's inaccurate description of a suburban driveway or Bragg's sub-Faulknerian fustian about Gulf Coast oystermen feels positively benign. Where these guys were simply promoting themselves, Miller wound up flacking for the war.

Her case serves as a useful reminder that *The New York Times* is far from the unwavering liberal beacon that so many friends and detractors want to believe it is. For all the anti-Bush columns by Frank Rich, Maureen Dowd, and Paul Krugman, the paper is less America's voice of progressive news and comment, as many naive readers hope it to be, than the sounding board of the national elite—as its management fully intends it to be. Wanting those blue-bagged papers dotting suburban driveways like so many sapphires, it never tacks far from the center. That's why no newspaper can claim two better conservative columnists than cagy old William Safire and sensible David Brooks, why its arts coverage lurches from the stodgy to the giddy while being denied an energizing identity, and why it has recently created so many stand-alone sections dedicated to consumerism—"Dining Out/In," "House and Home," "Sunday Styles." *Times* editors know that their prosperous readership sees no contradiction between elite news coverage and long pages devoted to what William Powers calls "Lifestyle Voyeurism"— reports from furniture fairs in Milan, rib-eye steak recipes from super-star chef Alain Ducasse. The two have actually melded in the career of political reporter R. W. Apple Jr. As his political analyses sink deeper into lazy, after-dinner-speech banality, he'll jet anywhere to write *engagé* pieces about Tiptree marmalade, Miami's top cubano sandwiches, or the Singaporean hawker stall serving the best *laksa*.

These bows to elite consumerism should not be confused with Raines's much-decried decision to run front-page stories on Britney Spears or St. Louis Rams running back Marshall Faulk. That was actually a good call. Unlike previous *Times* editors, the impatient Rumsfeldian Raines was quick to grasp that such pop-culture stories often reveal more truth about American life (for instance, teenage girls' sexuality) than do such crushingly dull newspaper staples as the three-part report on our troubled educational system. His vision of things was ideal for Frank Rich, whose years as a film and theater crit-ic provided him with ways to "read" the whole culture. Although his prose too often sloshes around in self-satisfaction, his own and the *Times*'s (it must be exhausting to speak for the cosmos), Rich's columns have been singularly attuned to Bush Culture. He finds the political significance in the things that his readers are actually talking about—be it pornography chic, Richard Clarke, or Mel Gibson's Jesus movie, which had Rich manning the barricades months before that wretched film came out.

Still, it would be a mistake to take Rich's column, however liberal-minded, as representing the soul of *The New York Times*, which is still living off publishing *The Pentagon Papers* in the same way *The Washington Post* is still basking in the afterglow of Watergate. Although it waxes leftish on Bush's budget, this is the same establishment paper that wrongly hounded Bill Clinton over Whitewater, gave Miller's inflammatory WMD articles front-page play, ignored the antiwar movement until it became unignorable, and contributed mightily to the 2000 campaign coverage that helped defeat Al Gore. Why didn't the *Times* look as hard at Bush's military and business record as it did at Clinton's? One of the chilling moments in Frank "Panchito" Bruni's *Ambling into History* comes when he explains how he and the *Times* decided to play down last-minute revelations about Bush's 1976 guilty plea to a DWI charge—a damaging fact that he'd never mentioned even when asked about past bad behavior. Why? Turns out the country's most powerful liberal paper didn't want to be accused of skewing the election with a last-minute revelation, even one casting important new light on a conservative candidate who was supposedly more honest than the fudger Al Gore. The Bush team appreciated this discretion, Bruni tells us with exquisite institutional vanity, "because they felt that the major television networks took their cues from the *Times* more regularly than they did from anything else. This was why, on the second morning after the story broke, Bush sauntered toward me as I cadged a bagel from the refreshment table between first class and coach and said, most originally, 'You're a good man.'"

Instead of resigning on the spot in shame, Bruni promptly asked for an interview. He got turned down, of course. The Bush people had already gotten what they needed from this good man. And who actually broke the story about Bush's DWI? The right-wing rabble-rousers over at Fox News, who *don't* take take their cues from the *Times*. If nothing else, Roger Ailes knows that his network's strength lies in not being muzzled by supposedly civilized niceties.

The Lonely Passion of Paul Krugman

If the *Times*'s coverage of George W. Bush has a reputation for toughness, this is largely due to Paul Krugman, the bearded, fiftyish columnist whose attacks on the administration give him a cultural wallop to rival O'Reilly's. His brains, lucidity, and increasingly bare-knuckled style have made him something of a cult figure, admired or disparaged in roughly equal measure. While *The Economist* has dubbed him "a thinking person's Michael Moore" and Robert Silvers of *The New York Review of Books* compares him to left-wing hero I. F. Stone,

Punditreview.com has declared him "the Babe Ruth of Partisanship" and *The Wall Street Journal*'s daily blog sneers at the left's "Krugmania." His collection of columns, *The Great Unraveling*, became a bestseller during the book world's great anti-Bush gold rush, and readers avidly scrutinize his line-inches for hints of revelation. When he slyly revealed near the end of one column that his wife is black, it became the stuff of dinner-party conversation.

Back when everyone else was talking about Raines's firing, a friend joked that the real story of *The New York Times* was Krugman's battle with fellow columnist Thomas Friedman for the soul of Maureen Dowd. We both had a good laugh, but a few months later, Friedman and Krugman appeared in successive segments on *Charlie Rose*, and aside from both having unfashionable facial hair, they could hardly have been less alike. As always, Friedman was smug, gee-whizzish, and anecdotal, like the beloved high school civics teacher who could never finish his history Ph.D. thesis but really wows sixteen-year-olds by explaining the Middle East using Nextel slogans—"Good things come to those who don't wait." In contrast, Krugman was cool, analytical, prickly—and angry at Bush. When Dowd's name came up, Krugman said, "She's gotten mad, too. . . . From the way it was a couple of years ago, a bit after September 11, a lot more people are seeing the world the way I do, and Maureen is one of them." While this wasn't altogether gallant—suggesting that Dowd finally caught up to *his* perception— his words did have the virtue of being accurate. They also offered a glimpse of his vanity.

Krugman has reasons to be vain. He teaches economics at Princeton, is widely admired for his work on currency crises and international trade, and possesses the John Bates Clark Medal, an award reputedly harder to win than the Nobel Prize; thanks to his spot at the *Times*, he is the most famous liberal economist since John Kenneth Galbraith. His training has made him a rare bird in the world of media pundits, for unlike nearly all his peers, who landed their gigs after working as reporters or political aides, Krugman takes a professional approach to economic matters. He knows how to do the math. And he knows that others do not. Watching him on TV, you can see that he does not suffer fools gladly and feels that most everybody else is one of the fools. Early in his journalistic career, this self-described "soggy liberal" (he admires Sweden) was frequently smacked by the left for being too procapitalist, too proglobalization. He called *The Nation*'s William Greider "thoroughly silly" and "foolish" for his acclaimed book *One World Ready or Not: The Manic Logic of Global Capitalism*, accused Clinton's Secretary of Labor, Robert Reich, of dealing in wishful "fictions," and lambasted the French Socialists for their economic policies in terms that would delight O'Reilly: His piece was called "Liberté, Egalité, Inanité." It's a measure of how far American politics have swung to the right that this centrist liberal economist is now thumped for being a left-winger, even a socialist, and that many on the left (though not the dead-enders at *The Nation*) now adore the fact that he's a world-class economist. Nobody was smarter about how market manipulation fueled the California energy crisis. When Krugman attacks Bush's tax policy or talks of the long-term consequences of the new Medicare bill, he knows better what he's talking about than the administration's handpicked bean-counters who insist that everything will be just fine.

Although the *Times* hired Krugman before Bush took office, his name is as inescapably bound to this particular presidency as Dowd's was to Clinton's. Rereading his early columns (or the pieces he wrote for *Slate* before that), you're struck by their air of slightly amused, professorial detachment. The current administration shattered that fast. Part of his column's fascination has lain in watching Krugman's measured Ivy League cool turn into the acrimony and clenched teeth of partisan politics; he has gone from thinking in terms of idiots and smart people (the terms one might expect of an ivory tower economist) to employing the supercharged political lingo of truth-tellers and liars. Krugman has tirelessly argued that "the U.S. government has been seized" by the avatars of Populist Social Darwinism—"an extremely elitist clique trying to maintain a populist façade." He accuses the White House of "looting the future" and indulging in Orwellian doublethink, beginning one memorable column, "War is peace. Freedom is slavery. Ignorance is strength. Colin Powell and

Dick Cheney are in perfect agreement. And the Bush administration won't privatize Social Security." As his charges against the Republicans have grown more sulfurous, his rhetoric has become more openly populist. Writing after the 2002 congressional election, he declared, "We're going to have an extended sojourn in the political wilderness"—and Krugman has never struck anyone as a "we" kind of guy. Ever more partisan, he even became a political tactician, telling Democrats the best way to oppose Bush's tax policy: selectively roll back tax cuts for the wealthy, while preserving those for the middle class. His battle cries resounded all the louder as they bounced off the civilized marble of the *Times*'s Op-Ed pages.

While Krugman's ideas heartened those on the left, they drove millions on the right bananas. He became subjected to constant sniping from *The Wall Street Journal* and the swarming mosquitoes of Blogville (Krugman calls them his "stalkers"), who chart and deride his tiniest mistakes, such as using a quotation from a *Washington Post* article that the *Post* later corrected—after Krugman's column already appeared. He became a favorite target of tall-poppy chopper Mickey Kaus, whose Kausfiles website ran a Krugman "Gotcha" contest to "review the writings of this once-sensible Princeton economist . . . and find the dire assessment that looks the most embarrassingly wrong in light of the recent strong economic data."

Naturally, all this sits rather poorly with Krugman, who, when he began writing for the *Times*, was unaccustomed to the mud wrestling that has become political journalism. As far back as the introduction to his 1998 book, *The Accidental Theorist and Other Dispatches from the Dismal Science*, he was already nostalgic for his earlier days as a professor who talked only to the cognoscenti and let others explain the truth to the outside world. "To be honest," he says, "I would go back to those innocent days if I could; in a way I feel that I have been expelled from Eden. But there is no going back, for I have become all too aware that the truth does not, in fact, always prevail. . . ." Nor is it always pretty. One unhappy cost of Krugman's expulsion from his academic paradise has been the coarsening of his thought, which has grown blunter the farther he's moved into the partisan free-for-all.

He's become the Angriest Economist in the World, bound so tightly with tension and anger that he almost seems to sputter. Where his writing in *The Accidental Theorist* displayed the intellectual elegance you expect of a filigreed mind, *The Great Unraveling* melted it down to make bludgeons. Forceful but annoyingly repetitive, the latter was less a proper book than a huge, fragmented political pamphlet whose author stays on message as unshakably as the president he's opposing. Taken one after the other, Krugman's collected *Times* columns don't grow in your mind; they start feeling monotonous and jarringly apocalyptic, even intoxicated with self-importance.

Such egotism is predictable in a pundit who feels that he's not merely opposing a lousy president but battling a dangerous regime that would destroy the nation. Still, it got to be a bit much when he described himself to *Der Spiegel* as "a lonely voice of truth in a sea of corruption"—one imagined Frank Rich muttering, "Gee thanks, Paul." He tweaked columnist Michael Kinsley's tardiness in noticing Bush's lies when, since the beginning, Kinsley had been one of his key allies (and therefore rivals) in exposing the President's duplicity. One suspects the same arrogance gives Krugman his juice. He has used his bully pulpit at the *Times* to do something that nobody else in the mainstream has had the courage to do with such adamantine urgency. He hasn't merely assailed the administration's lies but also "the kid-gloves treatment Mr. Bush has always received from the news media, a treatment that became downright fawning after Sept. 11." His irritation with the media's laziness doesn't stop with its White House coverage. In discussing three deeply unnerving facts about the widely used Diebold electronic voting machines—they are easily hacked, leave no traceable paper trail, and are manufactured by a company whose CEO declared himself "committed" to a Bush victory—Krugman posed the question one wishes an important *Times* columnist *would* ask: "Why isn't this front-page news?" One only hopes he asked it of his own editors with the same force he did in the paper, for predictably, the *Times* was one of the media outlets that had given the whole subject short shrift.

Beyond the lacerating intelligence of his particular columns on the Bush administration's policies, it may be Paul Krugman's great achievement that, like Pauline Kael in William Shawn's *New Yorker*, he offers readers the sort of aggressive, strong-willed personality that the *Times* has long seemed bent on suppressing. Against the odds, this chilly academic has injected fighting passion into a newspaper so steeped in decorum that it muffles whatever liberalism it may actually desire to express. For many readers, his two-fisted liberalism comes as no small relief—especially in *The New York Times*. As that paper's retired columnist Russell Baker put the matter with customary grace: "It seems slightly scandalous that Krugman has persisted in noting that the present administration has been moving the lion's share of money to an array of corporate interests distinguished by the greed of their CEOs, an indifference toward their workers, and boardroom conviction that it is the welfare state that is ruining the country. Krugman has been strident. He has been shrill. He has lowered the dignity of the commentariat. How refreshing."

Embedded in What?

1. Boots on the Ground

When Randolph Bourne said that war is the health of the state, he might have added that it's also the health of the Fourth Estate. War sells papers, boosts ratings, builds reputations, and helps networks establish their brand: During Gulf War I, CNN was made on the rooftops of Baghdad. Small wonder, then, that the media bowed down before Bush's plans to invade Iraq as compliantly as they had hailed his new gravitas following September 11. This was infuriatingly true on television, where CNN and the broadcast networks all but ignored antiwar voices, and Fox News put them on only to doubt their patriotism. Making war in Iraq raised moral questions that a virtuous nation ought to address: How many people is the U.S. willing to kill in order to feel safe from *potential* danger? If nearly the whole world thinks we're engaged in a wrongheaded war, what are the implications of prosecuting it anyway? But Americans traditionally care more about technique than philosophy, and once it became clear that war was coming, the coverage grew obsessed with the details of *how* the U.S. would fight it. There were hours of reports on "shock and awe," spiffy tanks and brainy missiles, proposed electronic attacks on power grids, and anti-Saddam pamphlets being dropped from the sky like Rumsfeld's snowflakes. One afternoon I heard a radio segment on the army's anticipated use of "ruggedized" Phrasalators, talking handheld devices that U.S. soldiers could use to give commands in Arabic— "Get down on the ground." They sounded really neat, but judging from the results, they will not soon replace interpreters.

The first few days of the war spelled a return to the post-9/11 days of fluttering electronic flags and patriotic fervor. When they weren't showcasing retired military officers in love with their own flinty analyses—after fifty years of Cold War, this country has regiments of them—the networks built their programming around live battle coverage, especially the bombing of Baghdad. One Saturday morning in Los Angeles, just after nightfall in Baghdad, I clicked on the television and, seeing the already familiar image of that city shrouded in darkness and silence, felt sure that it was about to be bombed. I waited, but a strange thing happened: nothing. No sirens, no antiaircraft fire, no buildings bursting into flames. After a few minutes, ABC anchor Charles Gibson ruefully said that they'd heard that something was about to happen in Baghdad, but since it obviously hadn't they were going back to regular programming. Full coverage, he added, would return the moment there was Breaking News—meaning, presumably, that day's fireworks. While there was something breathtakingly bald about such opportunism (Don't worry, you'll get to see the bombing *live*), it captured the voyeuristic spirit of the first digital war of the Entertainment Age. Along with millions of Americans, I spent the invasion's first few days glued to my set, as if having to catch a replay would mean I'd somehow missed out. I did this while knowing, as Susan Sontag pointed out in *Regarding the Pain of Others*, only the educated elite in rich countries enjoy "the dubious privilege" of treating war, injustice, and terror as a spectacle. Most of humanity knows these things firsthand and doesn't feel inured or immune to them.

After freezing out journalists during the last several wars, the

Pentagon thawed them with its policy of "embedding" reporters with the troops. While this decision gave journalists direct access to the fighting, and let a lot of middle-aged men live out their fantasies—who knew that Ted Koppel dreamed of being Ernie Pyle?—it guaranteed that news coverage would lack scope. Rummy is no dummy, and even as he boasted about giving reporters unprecedented access (co-opting the news media by letting them feel "inside"), he described the limitations of their work with his usual pithy pizzazz. "What we're seeing is not the war in Iraq," Rumsfeld said, "but *slices* of the war in Iraq." I was reminded of Alfred Hitchcock's old quip that he didn't make slices of life but slices of cake. In its opening days, the gung-ho TV coverage incessantly replayed the hypnotic son-et-lumière of bombs hitting Baghdad (an urban echo of the flaring palms in *Apocalypse Now*) and celebrated the geek-boy exuberance of reporters like CNN's Walt Rodgers, who gushed about the "steel wave" roaring across the desert. If Rodgers had been more deeply embedded within the U.S. military, you would have had to pry him from the mattress with a crowbar.

Although the "embeds" promised to show the unadorned face of war—Reality TV, only real—what Americans actually saw was sanitized. The most disturbing footage was broadcast on Al-Jazeera, which received the bounce from this war that CNN got from the last. Unlike American networks, which labor to create a good "advertising environment," it showed dead Iraqi civilians and U.S. soldiers who appeared to have been shot in the head. I hate looking at such grisly pictures, but I felt morally obliged—nasty death is one bottom-line reality of any war. Just ask Anthony Swofford, whose hard, finely observed Desert Storm memoir *Jarhead* became a wartime bestseller. The glory stuff is mythology, and if our networks were going to cover Operation Iraqi Freedom twenty-four hours a day, then they should have covered it without blinking; otherwise, they were just prettifying ugly things to comfort their viewers. I didn't want to be "protected" from the reality of limbless kids or soldiers' corpses, especially not by the sort of TV execs who claim they're looking out for me. These were the same guys who shoehorned their squeaky-clean war coverage into the Oscar telecast and the time-outs of the NCAA basketball tournament.

For all its immediacy, TV offered no reporting to match the print work of John Burns's passionate reporting in *The New York Times*, Jon Lee Anderson's *New Yorker* dispatches (and gripping trunk calls from Baghdad on *Charlie Rose*), or the tales of ordinary Iraqi citizens by *The Washington Post*'s Anthony Shadid, who actually spoke their language. Tellingly, none was an embed. Their intelligent, committed journalism was light-years from the exuberant jingoism at Fox News, which Roger Ailes seemingly modeled on Hearst's work during the Spanish-American War. If he thought any of his viewers had ever heard of it, he would have doubtless resurrected the old cry "Remember the Maine!" The only thing more shameless than Fox's coverage was the other networks' attempts to emulate it. At the annual dinner of the American Radio and Television Correspondents Association, no less than Dick Cheney praised the networks' Iraq coverage: "You did well," he told them. "You have my thanks."

They deserved them. Rather than telling their viewers what Operation Iraqi Freedom was getting them into, the networks highlighted the same handful of spectacular moments—the bombing of Baghdad, the toppling of the Saddam statue—and giddily displayed all the nifty new equipment they were using to cover the invasion. If the first Gulf War had been criticized for making battle feel as distant and detached as a video game, the promise of the second was that, with cameramen accompanying the troops, the war would be like, well, a video game, too—but one of the cool new PS2 numbers that plunge you right into the middle of the action. Only they forgot to provide the action, and the live coverage provided by embedded crews achieved a tediousness that would have excited only Andy Warhol. Still, the anchormen's thrill at their compact digital equipment erupted during the battle of Umm Qasr, when an obviously exhausted Aaron Brown stopped talking about what was happening with the soldiers and declared the event a great moment in journalistic history: "This is literally the kind of thing that we, in the business, have talked about for twenty years, thirty years probably, that someday we would have the ability, the technical capacity, to cover war live. And on this day, at 2:35 in the morning Eastern Time on a Sunday, that which we used to talk about . . . has come to be."

The Pentagon was revved up by the same technology, too, using its own camera crews to tape the Lynch rescue mission and, later, the footage of Saddam's spider hole. This footage was dutifully celebrated by the networks, which prompted Stephen Ives, director of a three-hour PBS documentary on American war reporting, to worry about the dangerous precedent: "It's not too big a stretch," he said, "to imagine an ever increasingly sophisticated Pentagon shooting more and more of their own 'news.' If that happens, it will challenge the media to avoid becoming a mouthpiece for propaganda."* But there were other challenges, too. The *Times*'s great war correspondent John Burns has spoken bitterly of how some rival American newsmen sucked up to the Saddam regime—buying $600 mobile phones for the family of Iraq's Minister of Information and soft-soaping the "essential truth" of the Hussein family's barbarity—in order to keep themselves in play. "There is corruption in our business," he said angrily, and his words were borne out by CNN producer Eason Jordan, who admitted that his staff didn't report everything they knew, lest they be thrown out of the country or get their Iraqi assistants punished. You could almost hear Roger Ailes chortling as these words reached the public ear.

2. Singing for Your Supper

If nothing else, Operation Iraqi Freedom made clear the cost of embedded reporting. Coverage becomes so fixated on individual reporters' slices of war that it rarely steps back to see the big picture. Then again, in a much larger sense, having news people traveling along with the troops is comparatively straightforward and harmless compared to the metaphorical embedding that underwrites everyday media life. For all the complaints about ideological bias, what shapes modern journalism are the dominant professional values, attitudes, and structures that affect how nearly all mainstream reporters, pundits, editors, producers, and anchors go about making their living. Almost everyone in journalism is some kind of embed, part of a

---

*The same thing happened on the home front, where the Bush administration produced and distributed fake news reports praising the President's Medicare package.

media culture in which truth, ideology, and careerism start to become one big blur, and the levels of embedding overlap like a poker hand in a game of six-card stud.

• **They are embedded in major corporations.** Virtually every media figure you have heard of gets his or her paycheck from a company owned by a huge corporation. This doesn't necessarily mean that journalists pursue an overtly pro-corporate agenda, but it does provide a useful hint as to why there was such stingy, belated TV coverage of the FCC's attempt to loosen rules on media conglomeration and why you're unlikely ever to see NBC do a major investigative piece on the nuclear power plants owned by its parent company, General Electric. It's also why national newscasts often seem reflexively "liberal" or "P.C." on questions of race, sexuality, and lifestyle. Because they're in the business of reaching the widest possible markets, media owners and advertisers want publications or programs to be *inclusionary*. Bigotry, or even the appearance of it, is bad for business.

• **They are embedded in their social class.** Although countless struggling freelancers work hard throughout the United States, the journalists employed by major media outlets tend to be highly educated and very well-paid, especially by comparison with average Americans. While their reflexive political values are usually liberal on issues like abortion, Medicare, or good funding for public schools (though naturally they don't send their own kids), they are at bottom deeply conservative. Because the system works for them, they have a vested interest in keeping things essentially the same. Well-off and well-connected, they don't feel personally threatened or outraged by government giveaways to corporations or tax breaks for the wealthy (Tom Brokaw makes $13 million) and the way workers are treated in factories and service jobs that nothing in their experience has made real to them. On the contrary, they are far more likely to feel on the same social level as the politicians and businessmen they cover, which is why you get such mortifying moments as reporters grumbling because Howard Dean never asked about *them*. In the TV documentary about the 2000 campaign, *Travels* *with George, The Financial Times*'s Richard Wolffe remarked that the journalists on that plane are "really well-paid people trying to convince other really well-paid people what's going on in ordinary people's minds." And this is general throughout mainstream journalism, whose news coverages reflects its cosseted practitioners' sense of privilege. Think how often you've heard it called "good news" when a strike is settled—even if management won a crushing victory. Have you ever heard an anchorman say, "Good news, tonight. The janitors have gone out on strike because of intolerable working conditions"?

• **They are embedded in the political-media elite.** In his trenchant autobiographical essay, "How a Caged Bird Learns to Sing," the critic John Leonard talked about his experience in what he calls "the information-commodities racket," where political reporters hang out with politicians, critics are friends with those they review, and the whole media universe forms one large, self-reinforcing chorus line of opinions and alliances that set the limits of acceptable thinking. Without forgiving his own compromises, he mapped the moral contours of that universe:

> I can't tell you for sure whether Tom Friedman, when he covered the State Department for the *Times*, should have played tennis with the Secretary of State. Or if Brit Hume, when he covered the White House for ABC, should have played tennis with President Bush. Or if Rita Beamish of the Associated Press should've jogged with George. Or if it was appropriate for George and Barbara to stop by and be videotaped at a media dinner party in the home of Albert Hunt, the Washington bureau chief of the *Wall Street Journal*, and his wife, Judy Woodruff, then of the *MacNeil/Lehrer NewsHour* and now of CNN. Or if one reason Andrea Mitchell, who covered Congress for NBC, showed up so often in the presidential box at the Kennedy Center was that she just happened to be living with Alan Greenspan, the Chairman of the Federal Reserve Board. Nor can I be absolutely positive that there's something deeply

compromised about George Will's still ghostwriting speeches for Jesse Helms during his trial period as a columnist for the *Washington Post*, and prepping Ronald Reagan for one of his debates with Jimmy Carter, and then reviewing Reagan's performance the next day, and later on writing speeches for him. Or about Morton Kondracke and Robert Novak's collecting thousands of dollars from the Republican Party for advice to a gathering of governors. Or John McLaughlin's settling one sexual-harassment suit out of court, facing the prospect of at least two more—and nevertheless permitting himself to savage Anita Hill on his *McLaughlin Group*. Or, perhaps most egregious, Henry Kissinger on ABC and in his syndicated newspaper column, defending Deng Xiaoping's behavior during the Tiananmen Square massacre—without telling us that Henry and his private consulting firm had a substantial financial stake in the Chinese status quo.

• **They are embedded in the demands of their jobs.** Explaining why his opinions differ so greatly from the rest of the elite "commentariat," Krugman says that it is partly because he's an outsider who doesn't rely on inside sources. Most topflight journalists do—the name of the game is access. That's why White House correspondents let themselves be pushed around by the disciplined, vindictive Bush administration, which treats them (in Ken Auletta's words) "as simply another interest group and, moreover, an interest group that's not nearly as powerful as it once was." If they rebel, they get cut off—which means losing a career-making gig. Although most of what they cover are pseudo-events that exist only to be shown on TV, they still contribute to the fiction that Bush's fundraising trips are state business, treating these promotional photo ops with the weary professionalism of streetwalkers pretending to be fascinated by a lovestruck john. And because they're faithful to this dumbshow, they are profoundly irked when the President's staff changes the rules on them. The White House press corps showed more outrage over being fibbed to about Bush's secret Thanksgiving trip to Baghdad than they did when he ducked their questions at that scripted pre–Iraq war press conference. As Randall Jarrell put it in *Pictures from an Institution,* "The really damned not only like Hell, they feel loyal to it."

• **They are embedded in the logic of careerism.** In the film *Shattered Glass,* the crooked young reporter Stephen Glass complains, "There are so many show-offs in journalism, so many braggarts and jerks." He's quite right, yet the real problem goes beyond creepy individuals to the system that encourages their behavior. The media world now obeys the same brutal logic of winning and losing that prevails elsewhere in Bush World. Winners become famous, get handsomely paid, land the prestigious and glamorous assignments—they become stars. Everyone else fights to hold on, knowing their bosses think them replaceable hacks in the information commodities racket—skilled workers, yes, but not powerful enough names to sell a magazine, cause viewers to switch channels, or even land a better job elsewhere. If you write, success means being invited to talk on TV; if you're already on TV, success lies in having your own show, or turning up as a talking head on a network telecast. But you can't do this unless you somehow separate yourself from the pack. The pressure to be bold, unique, dazzling leads not only to frauds like Stephen Glass and Jayson Blair, or corner-cutters like Bragg; it leads Miller to do shaky reporting in her search for the big scoop. Shrewd careerists know that they were much wiser engaging in the marketable hijinks of deriding Al Gore's stiffness than doing the dull work of unmasking George W. Bush's shifty statements about his health care record in Texas. Media types spent weeks moralizing about Blair and Bragg's dishonesty without ever grappling with the underlying reality that Michael Wolff pointed out in *New York.* Caught up in ferocious competition with faster, more sensational media, the print world cares ever less about precise reporting and ever more about crowd-pleasing prose; hence the ongoing epidemic of overwriting. Reporters' careers rise or fall on what Wolff calls "tradecraft," the ability to sweeten reality with stylish writing, even if that sometimes means pushing a bit beyond the literal facts to a more artistic "truth."

• **They are embedded in the immediate moment (where what's happening right now will happen forever).** No matter how much one may fight against it, the media are ruled by trend and buzz, and aside from a few lucky or irrepressible talents, those who prosper bring their offering to their temple in the marketplace. Few contemporary journalists have done this more brilliantly than *Vanity Fair*'s editor, Graydon Carter, whose career offers a distillation of the media elite's prevailing ethos. Back in the eighties, he was one of the masterminds behind *Spy*, a groundbreaking Snide Generation publication that made its name by lampooning the rich, powerful, and famous. But like his predecessor, Tina Brown, Carter has mastered the fine art of "transitioning." He parlayed *Spy*'s success into a job editing the sharp but less-snarky *New York Observer*, which in turn took him to *Vanity Fair*. While running a great many excellent articles in that magazine, he has also specialized in fawning over the very people he once mocked.

Carter is obviously a superb editor, one of whose enduring strengths is a lack of enduring principles. As the head of William Morris told *New York* magazine, Carter "has transcended being a great editor—he's really a celebrity." Just so. In the months after September 11, his magazine was appallingly eager to kiss the backside of the Bush administration, yet one shouldn't think this reflected any actual belief in Dubya or his policies. He'd just held his finger to the wind. Once elite opinion shifted, so did Carter. He began promoting Hillary for president, fretted to reporters about "the fragile state of U.S. democracy" (he'd matured, he said), and wrote a *Vanity Fair* "Editor's Letter" sneering at the vulgarity of the President's trip to London while boasting about a dinner he'd had at Sue Mengers's house in Beverly Hills whose "cast was David Geffen, Fran Lebowitz, Mel Brooks, Anne Bancroft, Kelly Lynch and me." Inevitably, he joined the parade of those authoring a Bush-bashing book, in part, one suspects, because he finds Dubya unspeakably annoying: He's deliberately rejected the aristocratic airs that Carter has spent a lifetime trying to take on. One doesn't imagine the conservatives trembling at his newfound anti-Republican wrath. Everybody knows that Graydon doesn't really mean it—you can tell, because he *thinks* he does—and that *Vanity Fair* will continue to salaam before the rich, powerful, and famous. Probably even Dubya if he gets that second term. After all, Carter is no fool, let alone an ideologue. Like the Singer in Barry Unsworth's novel about the invaders of Troy, he has internalized the deepest truth of meta-media morality: "There is always another story. But it is the stories told by the strong, the songs of the kings, that are believed in the end."

CHAPTER 6

The Small Pleasures of Big-Box Culture

We could just say: "Okay! You're right! Art is bad, silly
and frivolous. So what? Rock-and-roll is bad, silly and
frivolous. Movies are bad, silly and frivolous. Basketball
is bad, silly and frivolous. Next question?" Wouldn't
that open up the options a little for something really
super?—for an orchid in the dung heap that would
seem all the more super for our surprise in finding it
there?

—DAVE HICKEY

Although I can't recall the precise moment—it was after Tonya
Harding thumped Paula Jones on *Celebrity Boxing* yet before
Jennifer Aniston nudged J.Lo in that poll for Best Ass—I remember
turning to my wife and saying, "You know, maybe America *wasn't*
changed forever by September 11."

Sure, some things are different. Our palms get a bit sweaty as we
approach the airport—they're *still* not X-raying the stuff in the cargo
hold?—and millions of us could now identify Jacques Chirac in a
police lineup, which is where some Americans hoped to see him after
he besmirched the first lady's hand with his snail-slurping lips.
(DAMSEL IN DISTRESS—LAURA BRAVES WEASEL KISS, shrieked the
front page of Murdoch's *New York Post*.) But we're a long way from the
heroic age, back in 2001, when boning up on the Taliban or buying
your own copy of *Germs* felt like a matter of life and death. When was
the last time you thought about Cipro? Even as terrorists blow up

civilians, U.S. soldiers die overseas, and middle-class jobs pack their suitcases for India, Americans keep reveling in the goofy pop culture that is one of the great charms and occasional follies of our national life. Far from finding our lightness of being unbearable, we instinctively agree with George Bernard Shaw's remark that "seriousness is only a small man's affectation of bigness."

One might confirm the truth of this observation by watching George W. Bush, whose joyless menagerie of smirks and scowls befits a man whose ignorance of pop culture borders on the Gumpish, if not downright un-American. During the 2000 election, he thought the smash sitcom *Friends* was a movie and grew angry when asked about *Sex and the City*—he thought the interviewer was prying into his personal life. As President, his favorite movie is reportedly *Black Hawk Down*, which seems less a personal enthusiasm than a cinematic pep rally, rather like Nixon watching *Patton* over and over. (Of course, World War II turned out better than the U.S. mission in Somalia, which is why Ridley Scott's movie about Mogadishu was one of Saddam's favorites, too.) Bush hasn't even engaged in the Culture War salvos of Dan Quayle assailing *Murphy Brown* or Tipper Gore bewailing rock lyrics. Even though it's his nation's most successful export, the guy clearly thinks of culture as a waste of time. He's no more likely to rhapsodize about *The Simpsons* (the finest American work of art of the 1990s) than to start quoting Matthew Arnold on acquainting ourselves with the best that has been known and said in the world.

Then again, what would you expect? Pop culture is all about being cool, but being president is all about being square. John Kennedy was a hero to the young partly because he felt like an exception to this rule, even though ring-a-dinging it with Frank and Dino would be passé as soon as the Beatles hit America. But like Ronald Reagan, who was more a creation of popular culture than a consumer of it, JFK came steeped in glamour. Not so our other presidents, who usually seemed marooned on some personal theme park. Ike played golf during the heyday of Elvis, Kerouac, and Miles, walking out of Robert Mitchum movies because he hated the actor for smoking weed. LBJ fell asleep in films that weren't documentaries about himself, which was actually more embarrassing than Nixon showing up on *Laugh-In* to pretend he was really a good sport: "Sock it to *me*." While born-again Jimmy Carter presided over the rise of punk (I like to think of him pogoing up and down to "Oh Bondage, Up Yours!"), George H. W. Bush over-saw the heyday of Public Enemy and gangsta rap; if you'd told Poppy that a group called NWA had done a song called "Dope Man," he would have assumed it was staffers at some liberal PAC doing a satir-ical ditty about Quayle. By comparison with these predecessors, Bill Clinton's out-of-date affection for Elvis and Fleetwood Mac—and savvy willingness to talk boxers or briefs on MTV—made him seem as hip as, oh, Carson Daly.

With rare exceptions, a president's relationship to the broader American culture is a matter of aura and metaphor, counterpoint and parody—like the way that charges of voting fraud on *American Idol 2* became a parody of Al Gore's defeat in Florida. During the Bush years, there has been no spectacular cultural flowering as there was during the Gay Nineties, the Jazz Age, or the Swinging Sixties. In fact, the most striking cultural development has been the one that *didn't* hap-pen. It was predicted—and sometimes prescribed—that the bracing slap in the face of September 11 would get a country stoned on frivol-ity to sober up, remove its party hat, and get down to the hard busi-ness of being the last great hope of mankind. We would once again become patriotic, unified, serious—the Second-Greatest Generation.

Some of this did occur, especially the surge in patriotism. I felt it myself. In my first visit to Washington, D.C., after the attacks, I found myself walking down 17th Street. Passing Farragut Square, where gag-gles of office workers sat eating dismal carry-out lunches, I sliced east to Pennsylvania Avenue. There before me, swathed within a maze of armed security but gleaming bright in the midday sun, stood the White House. Like millions of others, I'd laughed when its famous columns were blown sky-high in *Independence Day*. But those were simpler times. That day, I didn't feel corny in thinking how nice it was to see it still standing. Collectively, the country showed its patriotism in countless ritualized ways—newly purchased flags adorning people's houses and cars, "God Bless America" becoming de rigueur at sports events, Budweiser commercials playing Hendrix's version of "The Star-Spangled Banner" over images of NASCAR drivers. Yet it was heartening how little jingoistic rancor and racism was actually unleashed by that September 11. As a nation, we seem to have lost some of the instinct for rah-rah patriotism that could make *Patton* an Oscar-winning hit at the very height of the Vietnam War; the closest today's Hollywood could come was glazing *Seabiscuit* with a nostalgic-sheen revisionism about Depression-Era America (which liberals too often treat as a golden age because of the New Deal). For every movie like the Bruce Willis action picture *Tears of the Sun*, which made a supremely violent case for foreign policy interventionism, there were two movies like *Spy Game* and *The Recruit*, which showed the CIA to be a deadly hall of mirrors—and none of them caught on with audiences. The military drama *JAG* got a ratings uptick from 9/11 but never became any kind of touchstone; nor did such amped-up antiterrorism shows such as *Threat Matrix*. On the contrary, the hot terrorism thriller was *24*, which employed a catchy gimmick—capturing a twenty-four-hour day in twenty-four episodes that unfolded in real time—to present a vision of political life so prodigal in its paranoias (scheming bureaucrats, warmongering oil barons, white-bread Islamic terror-chicks) that it made *The Manchurian Candidate* look as reportorial as *All the President's Men*. This was not a show to make viewers feel comfortable with the U.S. government or the War on Terror. In the show's second season, the African-American president played by Dennis Haysbert, who thoroughly trumps Martin Sheen as a liberal fantasy, barely squeaked through machinations involving a potential A-bomb explosion in L.A., then lectured his cabinet on ultimate values: America should declare war only if it can meet "the strictest standards of proof." The line packed a retrospective wallop as the months passed, and it became clear that, while Saddam may have been many wicked things, he was clearly not an immediate threat to the U.S.

Whatever patriotic groundswell followed September 11, it did little to increase the sense of national unity. How could it? Even as the country was being polarized politically by Bush and his war in Iraq, it continued to be culturally splintered by the ceaseless rush of books, magazines, movies, blogs, TV networks, and consumer products—a Niagara Falls of "product" that feels overwhelming. Do people actually see, read, or listen to all this stuff? When I was growing up, there were far fewer media options, giving Americans a far larger body of shared cultural experience. Although we're more closely wired to the world than ever before—I now grouse because I receive the BBC's TV newscasts only *five* times a day—that unifying range of common reference has dwindled. *Saturday Night Live* spoofs TV shows that most viewers have never watched (only 400,000 people tune in to Chris Matthews on *Hardball*), and Robert D. Putnam's phrase "bowling alone" has become a mournful metaphor for the loss of community. The two great pop-culture moneymakers of our time, video games and pornography, are things you do at home alone with your hands. It is one great paradox of the early twenty-first century that, at a time when the mass media is ever more centralized, and big-box stores like Wal-Mart dominate sales of CDs and DVDs—studio honchos make frequent pilgrimages to the company's headquarters in Bentonville, Arkansas— American culture feels more decentered than at any point in the last fifty years. Wal-Mart offers only a comparatively small number of the most popular DVDs, yet for all the chain's massive sales, this doesn't mean that all of America is buying and watching the same things. Network ratings are shrinking; trendsetting shows like *Queer Eye for the Straight Guy* are watched by only one in every 150 Americans; even those 9/11 books didn't sell. In *Time*'s 2003 year-end issue, the incisive James Poniewozik posed the question "Has the Mainstream Run Dry?" And he was right to ask. The so-called mainstream has become a niche, only one stream among many.

As countless bloggers could tell you, we're now freer to follow our own bliss than human beings have ever been: Let 290 million flowers bloom. As a teenager in Omaha during the sixties, it killed me that I couldn't see the foreign movies that I read about in Pauline Kael's *I Lost It at the Movies*. These days, some of them would probably turn up at the city's fancy new multiplex, and if not, I'd just rent them by mail from Facets or order them from Overstock.com, the online Wal-Mart. I recently received in the mail a videotape of *Play While You Play* by Hou Hsiao-hsien, the Taiwanese director who may be the world's finest filmmaker over the last twenty years. This particular film is so obscure that, when I went to interview Hou in Taipei in late 1989, there wasn't a print to be found in all of Taiwan. I left the country thinking I would never see it. Now I *own* it—for the cost of going with my wife to see Johnny Depp play an Oscar-nominated pirate for Disney. I've got my niche, and you've got yours. If you want to watch only shows about food, there's a channel that appears to broadcast Emeril twenty-four hours a day. If you want to read only right-wing screeds, you can join a book club that will sell you an endless supply of books demonizing the Clintons. If you want to enjoy only your favorite sexual kink, just click on the Internet and you'll quickly find a website that will replay your fantasy over and over—no need to spend even a single second watching somebody else's turn-on. We're free to be as quirky in our tastes as we want to be, and 9/11 did nothing to slow our love of mix-tape idiosyncrasy.

Nor did it launch America into a new era of gravitas. Perhaps daunted by the need to comprehend—and compete with—an apocalyptic attack witnessed by the whole world, our officially designated "high" artists have produced so little work responding to this historical moment that *The New York Times*'s Frank Rich lamented the artistic silence that let liars in the White House be the creative center of American life. Although popular culture did make a few stabs at capturing the texture of Bush World, it rarely did so head-on. Forget about Americans sobering up or growing more intellectual. If audiences wanted to see a revenge saga, they didn't want a 9/11 drama with real-world killing. They preferred the do-it-yourself payback offered by video games (our most popular entertainment) or the Asian fantasyland panache of Quentin Tarantino's *Kill Bill*, starring Uma Thurman as a wronged wife and mother (and metaphor for America herself), whose story wasn't so much the new millennium's bloodiest movie as its *reddest*. They hoped to deal with scary new realities the way *Sex and the City* dealt with the attack on Manhattan—acknowledging the city's wounds by making its shops, restaurants, and streets more glamorous than than ever. Post-9/11 America has revealed a seemingly insatiable taste for things that are often considered trashy or adolescent, from Reality TV and Hello Kitty to earnest cop shows with snazzy digital effects that let you follow a bullet's path through somebody's brain. Attempts to get really serious have rarely risen above feel-good spirituality or a self-proclaimed sincerity that's often too naked or anti-intellectual for its own good. These will not be remembered as years admired for their artistic resonance.

Ava Gardner famously said, "Deep down, I'm pretty superficial," a line that proved she was anything but. One might say the same of American life during the Bush years, which have shimmered with the contradictions born of the free market. Even as the White House set about creating an old-school administration committed to hierarchy and control—the Establishment back in charge!—the commercial logic of the marketplace was creating a demotic, big-box culture that flaunted its lack of respect for authority, centrality, and traditional standards of value. We live in an era that has put a cheerful new spin on Jack Palance's classic line from Godard's *Contempt*: "When I hear the word 'culture,' I reach for my wallet."

Righteous Shopping

One month before his inauguration, George W. Bush nominated Melquiades R. Martinez as his Secretary of Housing and Urban Development. Introducing the nominee, the President-elect told the audience, "There's no greater American value than owning something." This startling line went unnoticed by everyone except the *Austin Chronicle*'s nonpareil columnist Michael Ventura, who observed that, by placing ownership over democracy and the Bill of Rights, Bush gave you a pretty clear idea of where he was coming from. It also pointed to where the country was heading. Many Americans would doubtless agree with the President's values all the more strongly after September 11, which prompted a quantum leap in the impulse toward acquisitive "nesting." Shopping bags became imprinted with the stars-and-stripes; walking through San Francisco in late 2001, I saw a huge department-store banner declaring,

"America: Open for Business." With its emphasis on creating an "Ownership Society," the Bush years have crystallized the idea that consumerism is not simply a mock duty—"otherwise the terrorists will have won"—but an expression of creative democracy.

Ever since the early days of the republic, foreign visitors have been struck by our national addiction with getting and spending. Tocqueville was obsessed by our obsession with money, yet as far back as Thoreau, the respectable thinking about consumption was shadowed with disapproval. From Thorstein Veblen to *Babbitt* to Thomas Frank's *The Conquest of Cool: Business Culture, Counterculture, and the Rise of Hip Consumerism*, there's long been a tendency to see the average consumer as a dupe driven to buy things for unworthy reasons—flaunting wealth, keeping up with the Joneses, displaying one's bourgeois bona fides, succumbing to desires manufactured by cunning capitalists. Such ideas started out popular with conservatives terrified of mass culture, but ever since the heyday of the Frankfurt School, this dire conception of shopping has become left-wing boilerplate. As Herbert Marcuse put it in his influential, if clotted, little volume *An Essay on Liberation*, "The so-called consumer society and the politics of corporate capitalism have created a second nature of man which ties him libidinally and aggressively to the commodity form. The need, for possessing, consuming, handling and constantly renewing the gadgets, devices, instruments, engines, offered to and imposed upon the people, for using these wares even at the danger of one's own destruction, has become a 'biological' need."

Most of us would admit that this passage contains no small admixture of truth—the market culture has written consumerism into our emotional DNA. Who among us hasn't gone shopping to battle unhappiness? Who hasn't purchased an item of clothing we thought would make us look cool only to discover that cool can't be bought? Bamboozled into thinking that the "improved" Mach 3 would somehow make scraping off whiskers a pleasure, I recently spent several months miserably shaving with a new three-bladed razor that wasn't half as comfortable as the two-blader I'd abandoned. Buying things isn't exactly the ultimate expression of a large soul, and it's hard to picture Moses, Socrates, Christ, Mohammad, or the Buddha urging followers to shop 'til they drop. Then again, even those of us who think of the local mall as a gulag with a Starbucks should finally get over our knee-jerk rants about a consumer culture that hasn't merely been around for more than a century but has become what most of the world wants. Reading Marcuse or Frank, you understand Ellen Willis's shrewd perception that "anticonsumerism is the puritanism of the left." There is something joyless in a vision of the world that treats your beloved new Ford Focus as merely a symptom of alienation or sees only pathology in purchasing a pair of sunglasses that makes you look fabulous; this is a materialism that despises the material things of the world, at the historical moment when more people than ever are able (and eager) to enjoy them. As Virginia Postrel witheringly notes in her recent book *The Substance of Style*, *Newsweek*'s Anna Quindlen declared it "depressing" that the Afghan people, just released from Taliban tyranny, celebrated their freedom by buying consumer electronics—as if acquiring things they'd been long denied failed to meet the high standards of a prosperous journalist who, one suspects, did not herself live in a mud hut with no radio, TV, or Internet.

The decades of attacks on consumerism had never done much to stop ordinary people from buying what they wanted when they wanted it; after all, hundreds of billions of advertising dollars have been spent encouraging us to do just that. By the Reagan Era, even bohemia had shaken off some of its anticonsumerism and started feeling entitled to the better things in life. These days, even devil-worshipers wear Prada. I recently attended a dinner party in the Hollywood Hills with a screenwriter and a book editor who had been lefty students at Berkeley during its rebellious peak. They laughingly agreed that the most enduringly valuable thing to emerge from these days was the extraordinary restaurant Chez Panisse, founded by erstwhile student radical Alice Waters.

Still, even during the limos-and-furs eighties, an awareness was percolating that the desire to buy things was, if not exactly unsavory or wrong, an impulse that should be held in check. That vestigial moralism has now dissipated. We've grown accustomed to seeing

Michael Graves' tea kettle for Target treated with the same seriousness that one might apply to a work of art. The study of consumerism has evolved from a slightly disreputable academic specialty (like writing dissertations on Madonna's "Material Girl" phase) to the stuff of breezy sociological bestsellers. Today, Bush culture has made it intellectually respectable to celebrate shopping.

In *Bobos in Paradise*, David Brooks explores the middle-class consumerism satirized in *Babbitt*, but for all his wryness, he clearly sees such acquisitiveness as okay. In *Nobrow*, John Seabrook shows how the creation of cultural products (CDs, magazines, items of clothing) has become inseparable from the process of marketing them, and though he treats his own refusal to buy a $200 Helmut Lang T-shirt as a small, ironic triumph, his general approach is to lie back and enjoy marketing culture. Even as Thomas Hine's *I Want That!* shrewdly dissects what he calls "the buyosphere" for the nine major reasons people shop (power, insecurity, etc.), Hine cheerfully reminds us that although there "are millions of people on earth who live in circumstances where they cannot shop, most of them would do so if they could." The embrace of consumerism has taken over the whole culture—just think of all those "makeover" Reality shows devoted to new furnishings, new clothes, new hair, even new bone structure. (Sears, Roebuck recently paid a fortune to be the branded centerpiece of ABC's *Extreme Makeover: Home Edition*.) Where novelists once treated businessmen as figures of irony or pathos, the heroine of William Gibson's hip 2003 novel *Pattern Recognition* is a "cool hunter" with an almost mystical ability to discern whether a trend will be marketable. As individual character is increasingly defined by the objects we choose to buy, name brands have become the equivalent of Proust's madeleine. Disneyworld's new 2,880-room Pop Century Resort presents itself as a time capsule of the twentieth century, devoted to celebrating such commercial lines as Silly Putty, Duncan yo-yos, and the Mighty Morphin Power Rangers—there's a fake Play-Doh can that stands two stories high. These days, even nostalgia comes bearing a logo.

Nothing has symbolized the unabashed triumph of shopping more than Condé Nast's *Lucky* ("The Magazine about Shopping"), the bastard great-great-great-grandchild of the mail-order catalogues, often known as "dream books," that started mass market consumerism in the late nineteenth century. Launched in late 2000, just as Bush was being named President, *Lucky* has altered the publishing landscape. It was named *Advertising Age*'s Magazine of the Year for 2003, prompted Hearst and Time Inc. to develop their own versions, and has gotten inside the heads of "serious" magazine editors, who now offer pages of carefully presented products. Attuned to the cultural moment, *Newsweek*'s first-ever design issue was as sunny as an orange juice commercial: "On the following pages, you'll encounter not just cool new objects but a welcome optimism"—especially welcome, one imagines, to its advertisers. Magazine writers often joke that their articles are only there to separate the ads. With *Lucky*, this filler is unnecessary. The whole magazine is one uninterrupted advertisement. You buy the magazine to be told how to buy something else—and you thought capitalism couldn't be perfected. But taken on its own terms, *Lucky* is quite good—crisp, confident, alluring. It covers the terrain well, offers regional editions for greater usefulness, and is far more democratic in its tastes than *The Robb Report*, most fashion magazines, or even *The New York Times*'s "House and Home" section, which showcases the status-porn of $6,000 coffee tables and $2,500 copies of an antique jewelry box that "looks as handsome on a desktop as on a dressing table." Next to *Lucky*, *In Style* looks positively literary.

Marilyn Monroe once remarked that shopping was fun—"It's such a feminine thing to do." Every single episode of *Sex and the City* agrees. But such an attitude smacks of the 1950s, when the activity was thought a bit unmanly. Today, shopping is being deliberately masculinized. Not only has Condé Nast followed up *Lucky* with a guy version, *Cargo*, but as Simon Dumenco pointed out in *New York*, Bravo's *Queer Eye for the Straight Guy* is essentially the most charming infomercial ever aired. With fully half of its running time a conga line of product placements (Ralph Lauren, Illuminations, West Elm, etc.), the show is all about teaching men to transcend the fear of shopping: "Whenever I do go out," said an overgrown fratboy named Andrew, "I don't know what to get and I don't know where to go." *Queer Eye*'s Fab

Five helped the poor guy solve these problems, presumably easing his graduation into a metrosexual (to use the tired English term the media elite beat to death before 95 percent of America ever heard of it). Each time I go to a bookstore, I keep expecting to see the male versions of "chick lit" novels like *Confessions of a Shopaholic* or *The Nanny Diaries*, in which name brands replace characterization—but without *American Psycho*'s nastiness.

If anyone is happy about this triumph of consumerism it is surely Postrel, the libertarian futurist whose badly argued but enjoyable *The Substance of Style* is the most breathlessly seductive manifesto of righteous shopping ever written. You won't find Postrel agonizing over Plato's allegory of the cave: Those flickering shadows are real enough for her. Starting from the premise that "surfaces matter"—human beings naturally care about how things look—she claims that today's design culture represents a new and valuable realm of human freedom and pleasure. And in a sense, she's right. We're living through one of the greatest periods of design in human history. Objects are far more satisfying than the traditional arts—the look of my iMac offers more originality and joy than any ten books by John Updike. And this style explosion is profoundly democratic: We can create our own taste without fear of being looked down on. Not only have once-homely objects taken on affordably fine forms—we can buy a Philippe Starck–designed wastebasket at Target, get our Martha Stewart gear at Kmart—but the very act of choosing such products has taken on a positive new meaning. If I had to choose between a culture that produced only Chekhov or a Philippe Starck flyswatter, there'd be no contest. But the point is, one doesn't have to make such a choice. In the renaissance of fabulous consumer goods, individuals are free to pursue what Postrel terms "aesthetic identity," in which selfhood is linked to one's personal taste in products: "*I like this* becomes *I'm like this.*" More than ever before, she argues, shopping has become a form of credit-card utopianism, a way of saying who you are—or want to be.

Of course, with a good libertarian's worship of capitalism's imaginative bounty—she appears to believe that each branch of Starbucks is as unique as a snowflake—Postrel often loses sight of the social realities that make possible what she's enshrining. Target's employees belong to a different class than most of those likely to read *The Substance of Style*, and their freedom to choose styles or selves is accordingly far less substantial. They can't afford the $500 photo of Andy Warhol by Dennis Hopper that she finds an exciting example of "wall decor." Awash in such obliviousness, *The Substance of Style* is an almost perfect exemplar of the Bush Era's attitude to culture, both in its guilt-free giddiness about shopping as a form of self-creation and in its keen awareness that the reigning artifacts of our day are consumer objects. They are what we think, talk, and argue about.

The most passionate cultural debate of the last few years didn't focus on books, movies, TV, or architecture, but whether it's morally wrong to buy a sport utility vehicle or even a Hummer—the official vehicle of the sore winner. SUV haters have made owning such oversized gas-guzzlers a measure of political virtue, insisting that they are not only dangerous but immoral, devouring the world's resources and making America more dependent on Middle Eastern oil at the very moment it's fighting enemies financed by petrodollars. Defenders treat such reasoning as further proof (if any more was necessary) that liberals are an uptight drag, claiming that the real issue is Americans' freedom to express themselves. "Buying an SUV," Brooks has written, "is partly an act of fantasy. It's a way to connect imaginatively with a more inspiring life than the one you actually lead. Like every muscle car before it, SUVs are big, dangerous, and superfluous, but they're also poetry made of metal. They're symptoms of a latent spiritedness, even in a sedate suburban world. There's nothing wrong with having a little poetry in your life."

So which did America choose: virtuous self-denial or the metallic poetry of consumer pleasure? In the Bush years, you didn't have to be a genius to guess which of these arguments was going to get voted off the island.

Reality TV Isn't Reality (But Then, What Is?)

In 1998, Neal Gabler published *Life: the Movie, How Entertainment Conquered Reality*, which argued that all of modern life—politics, art, celebrity, sports, *la vie quotidienne*—is being transformed into grist for the mill of show business. What made the book fascinating wasn't its argument, which traveled ground already covered by such thinkers as Daniel Boorstin and Jean Baudrillard, so much as Gabler's conflicted tone. Although he clearly believed the reign of sleek entertainment a very bad thing—a retreat from human values in all their messy complexity—he was too savvy to come out and say that the public is filled with nincompoops who prefer living in a dreamworld. And so he left it as an open, albeit stacked question: "Is life, as traditionally construed, preferable to the movie version of life?" Others have been less shy about answering the question. It has become a truism that the mass audience out there—although not you and me, of course—can no longer tell the difference between real life and showbiz artifice. Why else would California have elected Arnold?

Telltale evidence of this has supposedly been the popularity of Reality TV, an oxymoronic term for one of Bush culture's defining obsessions. Turn on the tube at any time during the last three years and faux-vérité shows have been as inescapable as sales tax. *The Apprentice, Survivor, Big Brother, The Amazing Race, The Bachelor*—they keep mutating like the creatures on *The Island of Dr. Moreau*. And viewers have kept watching in such startling numbers that the media have never tired of pondering What It All Means. "The Reality Trip: How Far Can It Go?" asked *TV Guide*, then got too preoccupied puffing the shows to answer its own question. Even as *Entertainment Weekly* ran a long article demonstrating how some Reality shows actually fiddle with reality (daring stuff, that), *Time*'s James Poniewozik was comparing the shows' participants to Rupert Pupkin, the psychotic would-be star of Martin Scorsese's *The King of Comedy*. Noting the ties between Reality TV and the "reality" promoted by the White House, Frank Rich said Bush was like *Joe Millionaire*, the show about the sweet-talking con man who falsely promised his female suitors love and millions of dollars. I personally think Bush is more like self-righteous ballistics fetishist William Petersen on *C.S.I*—both are even, in their different ways, hard of hearing—but men of goodwill can disagree about such complex issues.

Like all pop-culture movements since the rise of the novel back in the eighteenth century, the Reality TV explosion at first triggered the hoary cry that the barbarians are at the gates. Even *The Washington*

Post's wisecracking Tom Shales seemed to treat each new Reality show as the End of Civilization—the same civilization, it's worth noting, that found entertainment in gladiatorial slaughter, bearbaiting, and *Let's Make a Deal.* Shuddering over *Joe Millionaire*'s success, *The Wall Street Journal*'s defiantly square Daniel Henninger, who appears to be waiting for his starring role in the next Whit Stillman film, grumbled at how today's "hypermass" entertainment keeps wooing our old pal, "the lowest common denominator." One wasn't really sure what kind of game show he'd expect in a country run by the free-market capitalists his paper so tirelessly champions: *Name That Aria? Who Wants to Be a Millionaire's Financial Planner?* Even television itself got snooty. Bravo ran a meta-Reality show, *The Reality of Reality*, that presented itself as an investigative report. It used clever editing and the lure of easy fame to mock shows that use clever editing and the lure of easy fame. Underlying all these criticisms was the (often unstated) complaint that Reality TV is unrespectable, irresponsible, vulgar. Which is, of course, one big reason why people like it. As the late Pauline Kael never tired of pointing out, audiences go to the movies (and other forms of popular entertainment) in no small part to enjoy irresponsible, unrespectable pleasure. Besides, American television has never been exactly a bastion of cultural dignity. (Ah, the Athenian Age of Milton Berle, Joe Pyne, Dean Martin, and Chevy Chase.) It's not as if SpikeTV pulled the latest Comédie-Française production of Racine from the schedule to free up a slot for *Joe Schmo.*

There are, of course, many crass and stupid things about Reality TV. It did, after all, give us *Temptation Island* and made a hit singer of Kelly Clarkson. That's why many smart people pass it off as a guilty pleasure. After all, it's one thing to dig these shows, quite another to let people think you're one of the proles they're supposedly aimed at. I wish there were far fewer bad shows. Lousy is lousy. But as one who has gotten hooked on watching a few of them, I'm struck that most critics spent so much time abusing the genre for being lowbrow, voyeuristic, exploitative, and malicious that it became easy to overlook the most obvious thing. The best shows are superbly contrived works of pop culture.

For starters, they recognize their own goofy evanescence. Where old-school television was all about creating flagships that keep going for years—which is why NBC paid the stars of *Friends* the price of six F-116s to preserve a Thursday-night dominance that nobody else gave a hoot about—Reality shows often have the giddily brief shelf life of pop songs. In an ironic parallel to such tony HBO shows as *Six Feet Under* and *Curb Your Enthusiasm*, they run a few weeks instead of a full, long-haul season, putting a premium on catchy immediacy. Nobody ever expected that *Fear Factor* or *Joe Millionaire* would still be going in 2010—their formulas have a clear sell-by date—so producers have had no qualms about cross-pollinating programs or playing fast and loose with familiar rules. That's why we had *Celebrity Fear Factor*, the gender-war switches in *Survivor 6: The Amazon*, and the spectacle of Matt on *Joe Schmo*, who was competing on a fake Reality show and didn't know it—then won everybody's hearts by being the world's nicest guy. In the original *Joe Millionaire*, a group of women competed to land a handsome schnook they'd been tricked into thinking was a moneybags. Trashy and hilarious, it played like a Molière satire updated by the Snopeses. And its follow-up, *The Next Joe Millionaire*, added a seemingly nifty topical fillip: A rodeo rider pretended to be a cowboy millionaire (Dubya?) to befool money-grubbing Euro-chicks whose nations had opposed the Iraq war. (It flopped: Americans really *don't* want to know about other countries, especially from a program so indebted to early Henry James.)

Although hardly as witty as *The Importance of Being Earnest* or *His Girl Friday*, such programs have been far more interesting than what they've been replacing—humdrum sitcoms and dramas whose one-liners and plot twists viewers can hear creaking a mile away. By comparison, a good Reality show offers a seductive premise, builds excitement with crackerjack editing, and, by thrusting ordinary people into extreme situations, ingeniously manufactures drama and unpredictable climaxes. Just look at how carefully *Survivor* breeds tribal loyalties and personal resentments or the way that *Trading Spaces*'s suburbanites start fuming when their once-tasteful living room suddenly looks like a bordello for Smurfs.

Television has always been about making viewers feel intimate with those on the screen—that was the genius of letting contestants take their agonizing time on *Who Wants to Be a Millionaire?* Over the last few years, Reality TV has provided what scripted programs so often fail to deliver. It's the rare fiction program that creates archetypal figures to match *Survivor*'s Richard Hatch, who flaunted his sneaky gamesmanship, and conniving Johnny Fairplay, *The Apprentice*'s grandiose Omarosa Manigault-Stallworth (Condi's satanic secret sharer?), the bellowing blue-collar family on *American Chopper*, or *Newlyweds*' archetypally dim Jessica Simpson—a walking Blonde Joke whose empty-headed amiability had people talking about "doing a Jessica." It's become a sneering cliché that these programs' participants are sad little people hoping for their Warholian fifteen, but in fact, what makes these shows appealing is that they're *democratic*—by media standards, anyway. The folks who turn up on-screen are far more representative of today's America than the formulaic characters you find on scripted TV (or in George W. Bush's cabinet). Reality shows offer gay men who aren't witty, African-American women who don't wear nail extensions and say "You go, girl," old folks who aren't adorable and homely, fat people who get to become stars rather than get stuck in character roles. Has any show ever captured the psychological reality of the workplace better than *Survivor*? It gives you the daily grind, the pressure to perform, the interpersonal jockeying for success, the niggling sense that one is falling in and out of favor—even a smirking, godlike boss, Jeff Probst, above and beyond the regular characters. For this very reason, these shows actually *do* reveal aspects of reality we seldom see on TV, whether it's ageism, class snobbery, racial tension (*The Real World*'s trademark), or the different power stratagems employed by men and women. Ph.D. theses are doubtless being written on the gender-role differences between *The Bachelor* and *The Bachelorette*, whose biggest star, Trista Rehn, appeared on both shows and scored a ratings bonanza with her televised wedding.*

*On TLC's popular *Faking It*, people with no qualifications are coached to trick people into thinking they're actually sommeliers or interior designers. The same premise appears in Steven Spielberg's hit movie *Catch Me If You Can*, in which Leonardo DiCaprio plays a teenage con man who convinces people that he's a pilot, doctor, and district attorney. All of which takes on a droll resonance when one looks at the careers of George W. Bush and Arnold Schwarzenegger. Catch *them* if you can.

With its various levels of "reality," Reality TV quickly provided a useful metaphor for the PR-mad ethos of Bush World, from the calculated use of the President clearing Texas brush to the hypnotically dull real-time footage from the networks' embeds in Iraq. This shuffling of the real and unreal probably reached its most vertiginous on *K Street*, George Clooney and Steven Soderberg's disastrous vérité drama. Promising viewers a juicy look at hustlers inside the Beltway, it wound up as a study of anomie among Washington insiders. James Carville and Mary Matalin played fictionalized versions of themselves as lobbyists who interacted with such well-known figures as Orrin Hatch, Joe Klein, Barbara Boxer, and, inevitably, William Kristol—those neocons are *everywhere*. In the show's most topsy-turvy sequence, Howard Dean underwent an imaginary coaching session with Carville, whose joke about Trent Lott was then used by Dean in an actual political debate, which was then watched on a TV monitor by Carville and the actor who plays his colleague. Dismayed by such a cavalier disdain for literal truth, unhappy critics and pundits began sounding like stoned college sophomores during a dorm-room rap session. Really, dude, what is reality?

Ratings, of course. That's why networks became eager to recycle popular contestants from earlier shows. The Reality world gradually started resembling Faulkner's Yoknapatawpha County, in which characters who have small roles in *As I Lay Dying* become leading figures in *The Hamlet*. For instance, Jerri Manthey—known to all of America as "the bitch" from the Outback season of *Survivor*—later turned up on *The Surreal Life* sharing a candy-colored SIMS-style house with six other low-level celebrities. What a motley crew. There was Vince Neil (who actually was from Motley Crüe), *Webster*'s chuckling Emmanuel Lewis, rapper-turned-minister MC Hammer, Gabrielle Carteris from *Beverly Hills 90210*, faded Goonie Corey Feldman, and 2001 Playmate of the Year Brande Roderick, whose first name looked like a misprint. The whole gang might have been engaged in a dress rehearsal for the California recall.

In his novel *Gilligan's Wake*, Tom Carson conjures a universe in which all of American culture becomes a gigantic blur—Gilligan,

Daisy Buchanan, Richard Nixon, Holden Caulfield, Homer Simpson, Bob Dole, and Maynard G. Krebs all live in the same space-time continuum. Something similar, albeit less extreme, is happening on our TV screens, where Dana Carvey's impression of George Bush comes to seem more real than the actual President, Senator John Edwards pops up on *The Daily Show*'s fake newscast to announce his presidential candidacy, Donald Trump plays The Donald on *The Apprentice*, and nutso North Korean leader Kim Jong-Il is mainly known as the butt of gags—Letterman joked that he keeps fit through "Torturecise." Such leveling was the theme of *The Surreal Life*, which thoroughly proved Emily Dickinson's dictum that "Fame is a fickle food/Upon a shifting plate." The show's best moment came when Jerri's six housemates grumbled because she was allowed on the show at all—Brande wanted a *real* celeb like Robin Givens. "She's not part of our society," muttered Feldman, and you kind of got what he meant. After all, they had once had hit movies, hit TV shows, hit records—or sat on Hef's lap. All Jerrie had ever done was get voted off *Survivor*. The great joke was that, these days, such an achievement made her the most famous one of the bunch. Years from now when people think back on the Golden Age of Reality TV—and they will—she'll be remembered fondly.

Of course, showbiz has-beens weren't the only ones eager to dine on fickle food. In one of Reality TV's most hilarious twists, Beltway pooh-bahs who clearly feel superior to the chumps who would appear on *Fear Factor* or *Big Brother* (not to mention those who would watch them) turned out to be every bit as starstruck as the average Joe Schmo. To the amusement of everyone who doesn't live there, these big shots knocked themselves out to land even a piddling cameo on *K Street*, a show nobody outside the Beltway even noticed. Such is the sorry state of D.C. cool—and Hollywood insight into politics. Even more amusing, these senators, lobbyists, and media hounds often wound up giving up more vivid performances than the professional actors who were stuck playing dull fictional characters. If nothing else, the show reminded you that successful politicians are gifted actors. Like the image masters at the White House, they know you're more likely to win over the public by seeming real than by merely being so.

Ghost Worlds

1. Inside the Pineapple

Deep into Alice Sebold's surprise blockbuster *The Lovely Bones*, the narrator—a fourteen-year-old named Susie Salmon who has been raped and murdered by a serial killer—gazes down at her neighborhood from heaven. "Our house looked the same as every other one on the block," she says, "but it was not the same. Murder had a blood red door on the other side of which was everything unimaginable to everyone."

In the weeks and months after September 11, when the blood red door was suddenly 107 stories high, many Americans didn't want to think about what lay on the other side. They preferred, not unnaturally, to think of happier, more innocent things. A few days after the terror attacks, I asked a TV critic I know if he'd seen anything on TV I should know about (I was still in my "you have to know everything about global terrorism or you'll die" mode). He said that he only turned on the set to watch *SpongeBob SquarePants*, the popular Nickelodeon cartoon about a goofy yellow sea-sponge who lives in a pineapple under the sea. Newscasts, he told me, were too depressing. What was the point of watching the same scary stuff over and over? It wasn't going to change things anyway.

He was hardly alone in abandoning the sinister confusions of the War on Terror for the company of SpongeBob, whose innocent tales of giving valentines or having bad breath have made him a Bush Era icon. In the post-*Simpsons* universe, cartoons have become incomparably sharper—like Reality shows, they're vastly more sophisticated than supposedly serious programming—and this meshes perfectly with a cultural moment in which more and more adults under fifty are enjoying the delights of childhood. They read Harry Potter, line up to buy cupcakes, and watch the Cartoon Network in greater numbers than they do CNN. If you go to the online newsgroup alt.sex.plushies, you'll discover that they've even made an erotic fetish of stuffed animals, both as costumes and as partners. Naturally, marketers and academics have jumped on this apparent yearning for regression, and as Christopher Noxon noted in a 2003 *New York Times* piece on what he termed "rejuveniles," researchers have produced a bumper crop of neologisms to describe the phenomenon: Today's *kidults* are enjoying *Peterpandemonium* or are trapped in *adultolescence* (to use the term favored by a MacArthur Foundation study). Predictably, such willful regressiveness has produced an orgy of scolding, from A. S. Byatt's *Potter*-bashing to the harsh words of *Time*'s usually calm Michael Elliott, who, after protesting that "these aren't just the mutterings of an old curmudgeon," muttered like an old curmudgeon that the idea of adults celebrating Halloween is proof of "the infantilization of American culture."

Meanwhile, ordinary Americans did what they always do when faced with such complaints. They ignored them, if they noticed them at all, and kept on doing what they wanted to. And what they wanted to do was walk the road to the consumer paradise we might call Cuteopia. Stroll through a mall and shop windows are bursting with Hamtaros, Powerpuff Girls, and Precious Moments dolls. Log on to the Net and you're caught in a blizzard of saccharine. There are websites for cute cats, cute dogs, cute girls, cute boys, not to mention the "cutecutecute ring," a network of sites linked by the international obsession with you know what. Over the years since September 11, Cute has gone from being the province of small chidren and teenage girls to an aesthetic idea embraced—and, of course, exploited—by adults. Louis Vuitton sells $3,000 handbags adorned with lovable figures by Takashi Murakami. Paul Frank sells fuzzy slippers adorned with his trademark, Julius the Monkey. Visit West L.A.'s flourishing Giant Robot shops and you'll find the angry anti–Cute Cute girls of Yoshitomo Nara (part of MoMA's "Superflat" show), whose work appears on ultrahip T-shirts that adorn movie actors at fancy Hollywood restaurants. There's dysfunctional Cute (*The Osbournes*), sweet-boy Cute (Justin Timberlake), sitcom-bedroom Cute (the Nick and Nora cloud-motif pajamas that keep turning up on TV), even midlife crisis Cute, as during the scene in *Lost in Translation* when Bill

Murray sits in a hospital waiting room with a gigantic plushie owl on his lap. This last takes place in Tokyo, which is fully appropriate, for that city (especially the legendary 109 Building in Shibuya) is ground zero of the international Cute explosion.

It doesn't take Freud or Weber to figure out the reason for such a boom in days when people are living under terror alerts. Although the word "cute" comes from "acute"—as in sharp like a needle—it now suggests precisely the opposite. The pleasures of Cute lie not its power to penetrate but in its blithe superficiality, its unabashed caress of the skin-deep. Because it's built on stock emotional responses (*Awww*) and easy, charming surfaces, Cute is a deliberate rejection of maturity, complexity, intellect, passion—all the tricky things that lie at the heart of life. In place of deep-dish meaning, it offers fuzzy good feelings. (Imagine Pop Art—but cuddly.) The ultimate in this must surely be Cute's reigning queen, Hello Kitty, who has become, to mix the metaphor, the golden calf of the new millennium. A billion-dollar earner for Japan's Sanrio Corporation, which even licenses her image for vibrating dildos, this cat's mouthless visage can be found staring at you everywhere from small East Village shops to your local Target. In fact, it is Hello Kitty's genius to take the zen of meaninglessness to a new level of vacuity. Even Mickey Mouse and Justin Timberlake *do* something. Hello Kitty just is. And this utter passivity is part of her appeal. "Hello Kitty seems to need your care," a fan once said, "but Mickey Mouse doesn't. He's fine without you." While I'm amazed that anyone could find Mickey Mouse too macho and robust, these words hint at one of the essential features of the Cute: People can find refuge in its inexpressiveness. The reason Hello Kitty has no mouth is that she has nothing to say.

Like so much Bush Era pop culture, Cute is an affront to elite taste. Intellectuals have long railed against kitsch, of which Cute may be the most flagrant (and lucrative) example. "Kitsch is mechanical and operates by formulas," Clement Greenberg wrote in a landmark 1939 essay. "Kitsch is vicarious experience and faked sensation. Kitsch changes according to style, but always remains the same." A similar indictment of kitsch (and by extension Cute) appears in *The*

Unbearable Lightness of Being, where Milan Kundera (who also disdains rock music) lambastes it for sugarcoating reality: "Kitsch is a folding screen set up to curtain off death," he fulminates. "Kitsch is the absolute denial of shit." In fact, the world of Cute kitsch is way ahead of him. A few years ago, a Taiwanese company introduced a line of products, Bang² Feces—known as Bang-Bang Feces—whose icon was a spiraling turd with a beaming worm inside.

Every vision of the world, no matter how trite or humble, contains an element of utopia, a dream of paradise. Cute offers an imaginary world free from crudeness or cruelty, one that wallows in our tenderest feelings. This helps explain why our culture has become so obsessed with an aesthetic style that, until recently, was largely aimed at teenage girls, a vulnerable group that feels force-fed into adulthood (thirteen-year-olds are now routinely expected to be cool about oral sex), lacks Buffy's ability to kick vampire ass (or its real-world equivalent), and winds up looking for refuge. These days, many Americans want that same fantasy of safety.*

This desire for safe harbor extends beyond the grave. During the 2003–2004 season, four different television shows (five, counting Claire Fisher talking to her dead father in *Six Feet Under*) took the *Buffy–Charlie's Angels–Powerpuff* Girl-Power boom in an unearthly new direction. They focused on young women who weekly get involved

---

*Precisely because it's drenched in youth and innocence, cuteness has always carried shadowy suggestions of its opposite—corruption, kinkiness, pedophilia. Back in the 1930s, Graham Greene created a scandal when he wrote about Shirley Temple's "neat and well-developed rump" and "dimpled depravity," concluding: "Her admirers—middle-aged men and clergymen—respond to her dubious coquetry, to the sight of her well-shaped and desirable little body, packed with enormous vitality, only because the safety curtain of story and dialogue drops between their intelligence and their desire." Twentieth Century Fox sued him for libel—and won. But Greene was right to see the connection between the cute and the prurient. It's made explicit by bestselling Bratz dolls (for eight- to twelve-year-olds) who dress like hookers, Japanese *anime*, in which saucer-eyed girls are routinely violated by tentacled space creatures, and the "Hit me, baby, one more time" rise of that semitalented, midriff-baring, ex-Mouseketeer, Britney Spears.

in supernatural events—being visited by God (*Joan of Arcadia*), communicating with dead people (*Tru Calling*), communing with gift shop knick-knacks (*Wonderfalls*), or helping the newly deceased pass smoothly into the next life (*Dead Like Me*). While there's nothing new about Hollywood dealing in soft religion—think of Jimmy Stewart and his angel in *It's a Wonderful Life*—there's been a flowering of such stories ever since the huge success of two 1999 movies: *American Beauty*, with its Buddhisty trash-bag-in-the-wind finale, and *The Sixth Sense*, the first film of the Ghosts' Rights Movement. Suddenly everybody was seeing dead people. Alejandro Amenabar's film *The Others*, starring Nicole Kidman, even told its story from the point of view of ghosts being haunted by flesh-and-blood humans, ending with a spectral "can't we all get along" speech—about the living and the dead.

From the beginning, this country has been swamped by religious feeling—the Founding Fathers were an exception—and while most Americans don't go to church, the vast majority still believe in heaven, hell, ghosts, and Satan. And millions believe in Jesus, as was made clear by the startling (to the elite) box-office triumph of Mel Gibson's *The Passion of the Christ*, a film so painfully literal-minded that the Redeemer's great gift to humanity seemed not to be his moral teachings but, like the battered Irish heavyweight Jerry Quarry, his ability to take a beating and keep going. Yet it would be a mistake to think that Gibson's renegade Catholicism (he thinks John Paul II a false pope) and obsession with ultra-violence are any more typical of contemporary American Christianity than the half-baked ideas put forth in the huge-selling thriller *The Da Vinci Code*, which turns on a millennia-old conspiracy to hide the truth about Christ's life (including his wife and kids). This is not a fundamentalist nation.

As sociologist Alan Wolfe shows in *The Transformation of American Religion*, today's believers don't inhabit a religious world dominated by sin and damnation. They're far from doctrinaire. Rather like George W. Bush, they treat faith as a kind of "mind cure," a way of healing one's soul, and this makes them ripe for stories that serve up muzzy supernaturalism. They've become especially receptive in these days when hard-line religion too often seems linked to earthly controversies and problems—retrograde restrictions on sexual behavior, violent dreams for reclaiming lost holy lands, men of the cloth who molest children and are then protected by their superiors. If you're going to tell a religious story for the mass audience these days, you're much wiser steering clear of the potentially troublesome details—all those specific beliefs and rituals.

Such vagueness made a bestseller of Mitch Albom's corny *The Five People You Meet in Heaven* and explains the vogue of *The Sixth Sense*'s writer-director-producer, M. Night Shyamalan, whom *Newsweek* dubbed "The Next Spielberg." Shyamalan is nothing if not commercially minded, and his 2002 *Signs* played to the widespread dread of terrorism and quasi-religious longing for Something More. Beginning with an eerie scene in which a family wakes to find that an enormous crop circle has been created in their cornfield overnight, the movie soon turns into the story of an alien invasion—one can't fail to think of September 11. Yet unlike such recent blockbusters as *Independence Day* or *Armageddon*, which never met an explosion they didn't want bigger and louder, *Signs* falls into a moral sententiousness worthy of a campaign speech. For the movie isn't ultimately about crop circles, space invaders, or even expanding consciousness—it's about that old Hollywood chestnut, redemption. Mel Gibson's paterfamilias regains the religious belief (and clerical collar) he abandoned when his wife died in a meaningless car crash, allowing him to again become a Proper Father. It's this rebirth that allows him to save his family from the aliens. (Now, *that's* a faith-based initiative.) But rather than have his hero regain his faith the old-fashioned way—by making peace with his wife's death and finding God's hand in the worldly signs that surround him—Shyamalan manipulates the plot details so wantonly that the movie winds up feeling like a cheap fundamentalist sermonette. "Except," as *Slate*'s David Edelstein noted in a splendidly crushing review, "Shyamalan has been careful to make his Almighty nondenominational." Taking care to offend no one but, possibly, us nonbelievers, *Signs* serves up the ultimate in calculated, bullying religiosity; it suggests that merely believing in some sort of Supreme Being can save us from the world's ills. It instructs us to put our faith in faith itself, as if the crucial thing isn't what we choose to put our faith *in*. With such a message, the movie harks back to Dwight Eisenhower's famous remark, "Our government makes no sense unless it is founded on a deeply held religious belief—and I don't care what it is."*

Although *Signs* was a hit, I have yet to meet anyone who cared much about it. The same is emphatically not true of *The Lovely Bones*, a beloved novel whose chipper cosmic melancholy echoes through all those TV shows about teenage girls in touch with the supernatural. Sebold's book sold over a million hardback copies and, more tellingly, was passed from hand to hand. It became the beneficiary and balm of an historical moment that is worth briefly recalling, for in its disorienting brew of fear and sorrow and media hysteria, it caught one emotional chord of the Bush years.

2. The Summer of Stolen Children

Years later, one can only wonder what terrible imaginings nourished the nationwide outpouring of grief for Samantha Runnion, the five-year-old girl from Orange County, California, whose abduction, violation, and murder prompted a funeral ceremony in which private mourning turned into a public spectacle joined by absolute strangers who drove for two days to attend. Feeling ran high at the Crystal Cathedral that evening in late July 2002, and had I been present, I might well have been caught up in its ecstatic display of communal grief—a moment of catharsis in what was being treated as the Summer of Stolen Children. But watching it on TV, I could only cringe at our networks' genius for turning sorrow into bathos.

Television news is all about triggering emotion. No channel did so more egregiously than CNN, which oscillated between "sensitivity" and hucksterism, often from sentence to sentence. Larry King introduced Dominick Dunne with his usual delicacy: "We're an hour away

---

*Gibson does care. Yet for all his insistence that he's doing justice to Jesus' sacrifice, *The Passion of the Christ* offers a hard-edged but soft-minded version of the Christian ideal—medievalism without the philosophy.

from an emotional funeral service for little Samantha Runnion. Hear his take on her awful murder." Quoting the dead girl's words about loving her family, reporter David Mattingly ordered the camera to zoom in on one of Samantha's drawings. And Aaron Brown served up maudlin pseudo-profundity: "This is a child who was just weeks from the second grade, who will never know the most simple things of life—a new bicycle, a first date, the anxiety of a final examination, or a broken heart." If Samantha had been an old woman, her funeral would have dwelled on what she'd done with her life, but as she was only five, it could only make a fetish of her death.

Although the murder of a child is always devastating, it's not often that one is deemed particularly newsworthy, let alone granted live national coverage in a world of trapped miners, beached whales, and Michael Jackson. What made the Runnion case a media event was how neatly its story line filled the needs of cable-TV news. Samantha was a cute little white girl of respectable parents (unlike the murdered Danielle van Dam in San Diego, whose folks were swingers) and lived in an apparently safe neighborhood in Orange County. Her avenger was media-savvy Sheriff Mike Carona, who seemed to have stepped from Central Casting with script in hand—he dubbed her "America's little girl." Her tale was perfectly calibrated to satisfy our dwindling national attention span. The crime didn't unfold too quickly, as happened with St. Louis's Cassandra Williamson, whose abduction and murder thirty-six hours after the Runnion funeral gave sympathy-weary viewers too little time to identify with the characters involved. Nor did it drag on like that of Elizabeth Smart, stolen from her home in Salt Lake City and not found for months. Elizabeth's story played out to a slower rhythm, a cause célèbre that ultimately became one of Bush World's signature media events. Only six months after her safe return, the story of her plucky innocence sank into the cynicism of a shouting match between CBS, which made an Elizabeth Smart docudrama, NBC, which had an "exclusive" Smart interview with purring Katie Couric, ABC, which ran clips from an Oprah interview with the poor girl, and the publisher Doubleday, which was bringing out a book on the kidnapping. Bathetic and inept, the Elizabeth Smart TV movie was aired directly opposite NBC's *Saving Jessica Lynch,* about another stolen young woman, a competitive battle that may explain why Elizabeth's parents spent the preceding weeks on seemingly every talk show. They became so ubiquitous that *The Daily Show's* Rob Cordry offered deadpan praise for their heroically loving efforts to make sure that the tale of their daughter's ordeal got boffo ratings during the network "sweeps" period. "These days," he added with mock rue, "a lot of parents wouldn't."

Everything about the Runnion and Smart stories made it easy for ordinary people to say, as they often did, that each of them had become "like our own little girl." While such expressions of empathy were often touching, it was creepy getting this from broadcasters busy using the tragedy to jack up their ratings. Every time I heard it, I was reminded of a line from Ian McEwan's novel *The Child in Time,* about a father whose daughter is snatched from a store: "The lost child was everyone's property," McEwan writes, and part of the horror of the Runnion case was watching America's little girl become the property of those who would bend her life to their own purposes and then abandon her.

Of course, American broadcasters are hardly the first to exploit a child's death to win an audience. Back in the 1840s, Charles Dickens's *The Old Curiosity Shop* contained the fabled death of Little Nell, a scene of a dying girl so extravagantly mawkish that Oscar Wilde joked that you'd have to have a heart of stone to read it without laughing. But at least Dickens was a sincere sentimentalist who gave Nell a life to lose. Today's storytellers haven't the slightest compunction about treating dead kids as simple narrative devices—trigger for easy emotion or shorthand for parental motivation. In *Minority Report,* a kidnapped young son became the excuse for Tom Cruise to believe ardently in the Department of Pre-Crime (which, as a good Hollywood liberal, he should have despised).

Still, none of this was as pernicious as the relentless news coverage of stolen children, which kept the media's Ministry of Fear humming. Parents I know live in eternal dread that their briefest lapse of attention could have fatal consequences—"I'm already overprotective," a friend told me about her seven-year-old—and cable news did them no favors by making stories of kidnap and murder the wallpaper of daily life. We were force-fed paranoia, as when Bill O'Reilly claimed that 100,000 kids in America are grabbed every year by strangers when the correct number is around 600 (welcome, once more, to the No Facts Zone). Nor was the damage undone when Aaron Brown assured us that "we're not in some epidemic of kidnapping" and then spent the next several minutes dwelling on the case of yet another kidnapped child. Brown's behavior made a mockery of his words, as when a woman asks her husband if he loves her and he answers "yes" without looking up from the ballgame.

Although the Summer of Stolen Children was a creation of excessive media coverage—obvious kin to 2001's Summer of the Shark—its spate of child kidnappings and murders naturally took on a particularly frightening resonance in the aftermath of September 11. It wasn't so long ago that suburban America felt untouched, protected. Now, no place felt safe. This connection appears to have been grasped by Sheriff Carona, whose initial words to the kidnapper ("We will be relentless. . . . We will hunt you down and arrest you") neatly echoed President Bush's threats to Osama bin Laden. One reason the Runnion case produced such an emotional release is that Carona got his man, Alejandro Avila, bringing about what people have taken to calling "closure." But no matter how often the President vowed to get Osama or Samantha's mother raged against the jurors who set Avila free in an earlier case, heartbreak cannot be cured with either justice or vengeance. Anger will not save you, nor will innocence.

This is one of the implicit themes of *The Lovely Bones,* which owed its popularity to being so gracefully attuned to the spiritual yearnings of a culture discovering that prosperity cannot protect you from loss. Rather than trapping us inside the unhappiness of parents tortured over losing their child, Sebold took a more imaginative path. She gave us the world through the voice of the young victim who, blessed by being outside time, looked down on Earth from an extremely pleasant heaven that smells ever so slightly of skunk; to readers she wasn't really dead. The result was the cheeriest and most life-affirming work ever written about child murder. Sebold herself is no stranger to very bad things—her first book, *Lucky*, was about her brutal rape as a college student—and *The Lovely Bones* guided us through the painful steps of a violent crime, steps that came to feel universal: Susie Salmon's encounter with the killer, her father's guilt at not protecting her, the not-quite-Runnionesque memorial service that lets her community feel better, the fracturing of her family under the pressure of death. Yet even as the novel charted the human cost of a teenage girl's murder, it also presented a vision of healing that, in its lavish doses of wish fulfillment, soared free of realistic constraints. Rather like *The Sixth Sense*, Sebold's book offered a reassuring pop-religious fantasy for a secular age. It told us that those we've lost aren't completely gone—"the line between the living and the dead could be . . . murky and blurred"—and that the dead may help the living to find peace. Pure anti-noir, it gave you death without the finality of death. True, Susie may have been raped and murdered by a serial killer. But she still was not one-tenth as sardonic as the teenage chicks in the film *Ghost World*, much less William Holden lying in that pool in *Sunset Boulevard*. Despite her deft storytelling, or perhaps because of it, one was tempted to chide Sebold for turning the bleakness of a young girl's murder into a book so likable and strangely upbeat—Sunrise Boulevard.

In a summer when newscasts routinely made the world seem much worse than it actually is, Sebold's winsomeness struck many readers as something of a blessed relief. No novel can provide consolation to those who lose a child, but for those who worry constantly about their loved ones, she spoke to genuine feeling without cynicism or crippling irony. Her work offered a fleeting refuge from the most chilling possibility of cases like Samantha Runnion, the civilians who died at the World Trade Center, or the tourists blown up while dancing at a nightclub in Bali—that life's cruelty and pain are ultimately meaningless, that our lovely bones are actually no more than bones.

Super Sincerity

Near the end of the Reagan Era, I once found myself at a film-festival party talking to Norman Mailer, who went on and on about his detestation of yuppie culture. "Do you know the worst thing about it?" he asked, rattling off his words like a Brooklyn bookie. "It places its highest value on *astuteness.*"

Now, Mailer himself was never exactly what you'd call a sucker. By the early 1950s, he and his comrades in that literary troika—Mailer, Vidal, and Capote—had intuited that, in a society dominated by mass media, literary fame was less a matter of writing great books (though that did help) than making oneself a public personality. With no little skill, he began creating advertisements for himself more than forty years before Dave Eggers winkingly declared his own staggering genius. Still, over the years, I've come to think that Mailer got the yuppie ethic pretty much right. If the sixties and early seventies were shot through with sentimental, often dopey ideas of authenticity (in this respect, anyway, hippies and punks were brothers), subsequent decades put a premium on a distinct and extremely narrow idea of being smart—wised-up, pragmatic, self-protective. By the time Clinton took office, our culture had made a fetish of knowingness: which tech stock was hot, which designer was about to break out, which movie is number one at the box office, which Internet site sold the cheapest everything. The flip side of all this knowing has been a loss of courage, a terror of appearing foolish if one championed lost causes, hung out at yesterday's club, or (God help us) admitted to getting teary at Susan Sarandon's cancer in *Stepmom.* At times it seemed that American life, or at least that part of it caught in the media radar, had become a ghastly version of high school in which everyone was supposed to be one of the cool kids. Small wonder that the era's key signature was a free-floating irony that allowed almost anyone to be in on the joke, while remaining outside and beyond and superior to everything else.

For years, such cultivated knowingness felt inescapable. It was there in *Seinfeld*'s frictionless aperçus, David Letterman's cruelty to ordinary people, the Coen Brothers' snickers at almost everything. It inhabited Jeff Koons's meta-Cute sculptures and Jenny Holzer's desiccated truisms, no less banal for adorning museum walls. It stared out from *Vanity Fair* covers, desperate to be the first to announce the impending superstardom of Gretchen Mol (oops!), and from ESPN's *SportsCenter*, where the clever Keith Olbermann–Dan Patrick team convinced a generation of far dumber but equally wiseass sportscasters that their quips were more enjoyable than anything a mere athlete might do. And it prompted the hipster embrace of Don DeLillo, a great Godardian novelist whose every sentence had an ice-sculpture brilliance (all those majestic riffs on car crashes, Lenny Bruce, the CIA) yet only rarely made us feel his characters' warm-blooded aliveness. This worship of "smart" had its analogue in politics, most damagingly among liberals, whose nadir may have been Al Gore, who acted as superior as James Spader but without the joie de vivre.

Long before September 11 supposedly rang the death knell of irony, there were signs that the Age of Smart had begun to crumble of its own brittleness. Beck moved from the multi-culti brio of *Odelay* to the woozy, soul-racked miserabilism of the well-titled *Sea Change*. *American Beauty* started out snide but wound up sad, and Letterman, humanized by heart surgery, was able to get choked up on the air (like his distant precursor Jack Paar) and actually feel kind of good about it. Ingrained cultural habits die hard, and during the Bush years, it's been fascinating to watch brainy artists struggle, not always successfully, to push *beyond smart* without sinking into the mindlessness, anti-intellectualism, or cheap sentimentality that characterizes so much of mass culture. This effort has been especially clear in the work of our interesting younger filmmakers: In a matter of months in late 2002, Wes Anderson's *The Royal Tenenbaums* sought to reach beyond inspired juvenilia to genuine romanticism, Steven Soderberg's *Solaris* staged a gripping tug-of-war between the filmmaker's instinctive chilliness and his desire to show his passionate soul, Alexander Payne's *About Schmidt* found the pathos in the satire of an insurance-selling Everyman, and *Adaptation* staged a wrestling match between screenwriter Charlie Kaufman's solipsistic cleverness and yearning for human empathy, a bout he resolved far more emotionally in his recent film *The Eternal Sunshine of the Spotless Mind*.

Perhaps the most telling example of this onscreen conflict came in *Far from Heaven*, the extravagantly praised postmodern "women's picture" about a suburban housewife, played by Julianne Moore, who falls in love with her black gardener (Dennis Haysbert) after discovering that her husband, Dennis Quaid, is gay. The movie was written and directed by the supremely honorable Todd Haynes, a certified member of the Smart Generation (he studied semiotics at Brown). His filmography ranges from his brilliant debut *Superstar*, which used Barbie dolls to tell the tragic story of the singer Karen Carpenter, to the chilly *Safe*, a hyperabstract picture about a housewife suffering from an unknown disease. At first blush, *Far from Heaven*'s conceit— deliberately mimicking the melodramatic style of fifties director Douglas Sirk—made it sound like the pinnacle of freeze-dried, PoMo intellectualism. Yet ironically, the film's shortcoming was just the opposite. Its simplified picture of the 1950s didn't challenge today's audience. Unlike Sirk, who used overwrought melodrama to shake fifties audiences out of their habitual responses to issues of race and sexuality, Haynes wound up flattering liberal prejudices rather than compelling us to rethink them. His story's pull was emotional not intellectual, personal not political. Its power lay not in its gorgeous period re-creations nor its progressive-minded notions of gender and race—what art film viewer today thinks gays ought to stay in stifling marriages?—but in being such an expertly turned tearjerker, especially in Moore and Haysbert's heartbreaking separation at the railway station. People loved this movie not because it was smart—it actually could have been a lot smarter—but because it made many of us cry. Jorge Luis Borges once said that great art is algebra and fire. Although Haynes hadn't yet learned to bring the two together in harmony, his pointedly postmodern style gave today's hip viewer permission to weep at the movies.

The same kind of old-fashioned emotion was unleashed by Jonathan Franzen's bestselling novel *The Corrections*, whose ambitions were announced in a *Harper's* piece that argued that literary fiction needed to engage the larger society. To that end, Franzen deliberately tried to break free of the highfalutin intellectual carapace that defined his earlier books and tell a traditional saga of a midwestern family. He didn't fully escape, and the novel's weaker sections betrayed his penchant for exhibitionistically spelling out every possible implication (a habit the critic James Wood has dubbed "Franzenism") and erecting skyscrapers of quasijournalistic detail that, for all their snap, carry none of the weight you found in the classic realism of Balzac or even Dreiser. *The Corrections* enjoyed its greatest success performing its most conventional, and, quite possibly, most difficult task: Tracing the tricky emotions of the Lambert family, the book, like Haynes's film, wound up wearing its heart on its well-tailored sleeve—and readers, including me, were left in tears. It was precisely this that led it to be selected by Oprah's Book Club, as close as any author could get to a group hug from the larger society. But vanity crashed into commerce when Franzen half-recoiled from the promo sticker attached to Oprah's embrace. He publicly suggested that the book club's usual selections were cringeworthy in their schmaltziness (you wouldn't catch this would-be lion lying down with Wally Lamb), yet took care not to reject a prize that other writers would kill for. (Winfrey eventually withdrew the offer.) In Franzen's ambivalence about the gift Oprah left under his pillow, you could sense his anxiety that moving beyond smart might somehow sully his literary reputation. As *Reason*'s Charles Paul Freund perceptively noted, the real issue had to do with branding, not literature: Having been published under the tony Farrar, Straus & Giroux imprint, he didn't want to be tossed into the seemingly bottomless well of the déclassé Oprah "O." He got clobbered by those who never tire of calling other people elitists.

While Franzen proved clumsy at negotiating the shoals of of irony and emotion, high culture and low, the opposite was true of White Stripes, a first-rate band whose two members, Jack and Meg White, orchestrated their image with consummate professionalism. From the outset, they showed enormous skills at marketing themselves as a cutting-edge band, always dressing in red and white, cultivating their mystery (was Meg Jack's sister or his . . . wife?), naming an album *De Stijl*, and nabbing MTV Video Awards. Yet as they did all this, they made a point of suggesting that their work was nothing if not sincere. They vaunted their quasi-Luddite sound, boasting on the liner notes of their *Elephant* CD, "No computers were used during the writing, recording, mixing or mastering of this record." More important, they declared their musical devotion to the old blues tradition—covering songs by Robert Johnson, Blind Willie McTell, and Howlin' Wolf—but when they broke free, it was often to do a number by Burt Bacharach or a quirky-innocent tune like their own "We're Going to Be Friends," a song with lyrics so self-consciously cute they sound like something Hello Kitty would sing if she had a mouth.

That could not be said of the songs emerging from rock's emo movement, which finally appeared to get over the hump after years of promising to maybe, just maybe become as big as grunge (the industry desperately needed a trend). Emo gets its name, as you might guess, from "emotion," and that's what you get: Its essence is a raw, almost geeky honesty (ah, those sensitive boys) wedded to the bouncy punk directness of bands like Green Day (ah, those insensitive boys). In late 2003, you couldn't open a music magazine without reading about Thursday, Taking Back Sunday, Saves the Day, the suicide of Elliot Smith, and the potential breakthrough album by Dashboard Confessional, whose singer-songwriter Chris Carrabba was supposed to be the voice of the unironic young: Singing about a kiss, he tells his imaginary lover that "I knew that you meant it, that you meant it, that you meant it." If nothing else, all that *meaning it* made Dashboard Confessional the house band of the new Super Sincerity—one wasn't just sincere, one declared it.

Its philosopher-king is probably Dave Eggers—memoirist, novelist, editor, publisher, impresario, and godfather of the *McSweeney's* empire—whose trademark blend of the earnest and self-consciously cute has made him a literary superstar. He not only flashes his sincerity like a badge ("Thank you for your warmth," says the back cover of *McSweeney's No. 11*) but wears his fears of being insincere as a kind of Tevlar against those who would doubt him, including, of course, himself. His first book, *A Heartbreaking Work of Staggering Genius*, was almost a textbook case of a writer trying to push beyond smart into the real of authentic emotion. It was essentially divided into two very different parts: the first a moving account of how, after his parents died a few months apart when he was in his early twenties, he looked after his kid brother Toph; the second, an exasperating but tortuously funny account of his attempts to be a sincere guy, including his bad-faith attempt to get on MTV's *The Real World* by trying to convince the booker of his good faith. Cluing us in to his strategy (or at least pretending to), he even wrote about his desire to become "well-known for his sorrows, or at least to let his suffering facilitate his becoming well-known, while at the same time not shrinking from the admission of such manipulations of his pain for profit." Although readers over thirty tend to be driven bonkers by the book's labyrinthine self-absorption, this memoir touched something in the youthful mood. Though caught up in meta-media madness, Eggers's writing wanted to be open to experience, to other people, to life; it was generous. Where Jonathan Franzen awkwardly wraps himself in the robes of a Great American Writer, Eggers is more comfortable in his regular-guy T-shirt, Frisbee-flipping his sentences into the distance knowing that someone will catch them. There were plenty of soaring passages in *You Shall Know Our Velocity!*, his bouncy first novel about two American guys, Will and Hand, who zoot blankly from land to land trying to hand out moola and win good karma. Filled with clever riffs—including a classic insight about how free-floating travelers form the modern "Fourth World"—the book aspired to be a globetrotter's *On the Road*. But Will and Hand had none of the early Beats' fierce yearning for transcendence, often sliding into a latter-day Hope-Crosby shtickiness that would have made Kerouac blanch. Eggers's marketing strategy made the publishing world do the same. Demonstrating his No Logo integrity, he eschewed a major corporate house, published the original hardback through *McSweeney's*, and sold it only through independent bookstores. For most readers, the book was impossible to find (I finally bought mine in downtown Des Moines), which may be why Eggers had the paperback brought out by the big shots at Random House.

Whether this implied a lack of sincerity didn't matter. For by then, Eggers had already been freaked out by the inevitable gauntlet of servile and abusive media coverage; he'd already influenced a generation with his books, anthologies, and elaborately designed issues of *McSweeney's* (including CDs or DVDs), whose often retro packaging seems to tap into his generation's bloodstream. He was also the éminence grise of a new literary monthly, *The Believer*, which offered itself as a determinedly optimistic alternative to cheaply nasty ("snarky") book-review politics and small-magazine demolition jobs: "We will focus on writers and books we like," declared its opening manifesto. "We will give people and books the benefit of the doubt." While I'm old enough to roll my eyes at the *McSweeney's* crew's belief that you demonstrate sincerity by announcing it—an odd, bookish echo of Bush's foreign policy statements—I understand how Eggers's insistence on being affirmative would appeal to aspiring writers who dislike the hustling corrosiveness of our literary culture. Anyway, he wasn't merely a writer but something far grander—a writer-entrepreneur. Where those angelheaded hipsters, the Beats, said "Hell, no!" to consumer culture (their private lives were their politics), Eggers asks, "Why not?" then frets about doing it.

I don't say this with disapproval (okay, maybe a little). Like the rest of us, he lives in a society in which shopping has become self-expression and marketing is art's Siamese twin. At this point, who could seriously accuse anyone of "selling out"? A good musician like Moby licenses all seventeen songs from *Play* before it's even released; the fine writer Michael Chabon not only sells *The Amazing Adventures of Kavalier and Clay* to producer Scott Rudin but, in defiance of decades of disillusioned screenwriters, publicly praises this legendary thug's notes on the screenplay. In one of *Babbitt*'s most quoted passages, Lewis's hero gives a speech on culture. "In other countries," he says, "art and literature are left to a lot of shabby bums living in attics and feeding on booze and spaghetti, but in America the successful writer or picture-painter is indistinguishable from any other decent businessman." Back then, this was broad satire; today it's realism. The romantic era of the artist-as-outsider is over, a historical glitch in the long, complicated history of patronage. Today's writers and artists realize that if they can't sell themselves in the marketplace, becoming at least a minor brand, they probably won't survive. (Just look at the number of well-written novels in any bookstore's remaindered bin.) But that doesn't make them any happier about marketing themselves.

"There's something very uncomfortable about the whole thing," says David Foster Wallace, who has the most fruitful mind (and most unruly sense of structure) of his literary generation. "And yet on the other hand, what kind of prima donna says, 'Thank you, major corporation, for your advance, but now you're not allowed to use your marketing tools to try to recoup your investment'? You know, the head just goes around and around and around."

Eggers's head surely must. Canny, charismatic, and devoted to worthy causes (he teaches writing to underprivileged kids), he is, in many ways, the Bill Clinton of contemporary writing. Beyond having enormous personal gifts, he's husband to novelist Vendela Vida, whose ambitious work was often unfairly read through the scrim of his reputation, a personal hero to a great many young writers (it doesn't hurt that he helps them get their work published), a beacon to prominent Friends of Dave such as Zadie Smith, and a Great Satan to those who can't stand him. Barbed words speed through the blogosphere with news of his every move, yet as happens with literary "fame"—which actually means that about 3 percent of the country may know your name, and, if you're a superstar, 0.1 percent of those have read you—the responses he provokes are almost insanely passionate. Lines stretch out the door when he signs his books; the house is packed when he performs on stage with They Might Be Giants. Like him or not, you have to admire Eggers's skill in pulling off a twofer that puts him in the cultural vanguard of Bush World. He has not only managed to make himself a literary brand name, but he's made that brand an icon of anticorporate sincerity.

It Feels So Empty . . .

When the planes hit the World Trade Center, the composer Karlheinz Stockhausen dubbed it "the greatest work of art imaginable for the whole cosmos." You could see why people were furious at him—it was a dumb thing to say—but he did touch on a ghastly truth. Not that killing 3,000 people is an aesthetic act, but the riveting magnitude of the atrocity put today's "transgressive art" in perspective. Faced with such a dreadful expression of hatred for America, it was entirely pre-dictable that Bush World's dominant cultural themes would be tacit-ly, if not explicitly, conservative. Just consider the trends I've been dis-cussing. Shopping is a way of changing your environment or your-self—not of changing the world. Reality TV may democratize televi-sion, but its great topic is still the conquest of riches and fame. Those soft-religion stories invariably wind up preaching acceptance. While Cute is, almost by definition, content-free, the purveyors of Super Sincerity are focused more on personal feelings than on larger social commentary. Small wonder that, after right-wing pressure forced CBS to pulls its inept TV movie on Ronald Reagan, conservatives wrote pieces claiming they'd won the Culture War.

What's obviously missing from the Bush years is any groundswell of cultural rebellion, an absence all the more startling because his presidency cries out for an adversary response. Yes, Michael Moore did become a lefty superstar. Yes, Bush's policies were soundly rebuked by those grizzled World War II veterans Vidal, Mailer, and Vonnegut—no chicken hawks, they—of whom Norman, surprisingly, sounded the calmest. (The angriest, Kurt, called September 11 "a Reichstag fire of our own.") And yes, several entertainment figures spoke out against the war—Janeane Garofalo filling a seat better occupied by Harvard's Stanley Hoffmann—prompting right-wing ideologues to dredge up the hoary specter of "Hanoi Jane Fonda, American Traitor" (as the old bumper sticker had it). Still, we're a long way from the days when Mailer insisted that he would settle for nothing less than a revolution in the consciousness of his time, Bob Dylan and Jimi Hendrix did their best to provide one, and the easy riders and raging bulls of sev-enties Hollywood sought to make radical American epics out of sto-ries about gangsters and country singers.

All this led a friend to insist that the Bush years are a replay of the 1950s, with old-school white dudes in charge, a scarifying sense of for-eign menace, and a clamped-down culture with little tolerance for, let alone interest in, dissent. So it goes, as Vonnegut might say. But such an analogy is actually unfair to the fifties. For while the cliché has it that the Eisenhower Era was conformist and dull, volcanic social changes were bubbling under the seemingly placid, *Father Knows Best* surface. It was the decade when Elvis and Miles Davis broke through, Mort Sahl gave stand-up comedy its teeth, and Hollywood made perhaps the weirdest, darkest, and most subversive studio movies in its history: *Sunset Boulevard, The Big Heat, Kiss Me Deadly, Vertigo, Bigger Than Life, Touch of Evil, House of Bamboo, Written on the Wind*. Next to such witch's brews, the most daring present-day films by our younger directors (*American Splendor, The Royal Tennenbaums, Adaptation, Lost in Translation*) are pretty thin gruel. The most socially radical film of post-9/11 America may well be *Mystic River*, in which Sean Penn's vengeful murder of the wrong man is not only forgiven by his loved ones but becomes associated with a patriotic parade. And it was made by seventy-three-year-old Clint Eastwood, who didn't have to worry about people thinking him a subversive. But that film was an exception. The great movie blockbusters of our day are those Pottering, Hobbiting, Spidermanning mythic narratives of Good and Evil that chase the comet's tail of the video-game boom and whose undeniable pleasures have nothing radical about them. War on Terror anxiety has meshed with a new Hollywood cycle of manly, fifties-worthy imperial epics: *Master and Commander*, the Crusades film *Kingdom of Heaven*, *Tripoli* (about an American who helps topple a corrupt ruler), two different movies about Alexander the Great, a dull post–John Wayne version of *The Alamo*, and, of course, Ed Zwick's brain-dead *The Last Samurai*, in which Tom Cruise's U.S. army officer goes so Japanese that he offers to commit seppuku if he's displeased the emperor. When the first *Matrix* came out in 1999, it dazzled viewers with the witty conceit that our world is actually an illusion concocted by a demonic cyber-intelligence. Four years later, the sequels appeared to have been made by those evil computers—they peddled a chuckleheaded Christ myth that left one admiring the spiritual rigor of *The Lovely Bones* and *Joan of Arcadia*. It seems perfectly appropriate that the Bush Era's most successful "indie" smash was *My Big Fat Greek Wedding*, a sitcommish picture so out of touch with post–LBJ America that Greeks (Greeks!) are considered colorful ethnics with mysterious ways. No matter how old you are, the movie seemed to have been made for your parents.

The same conservatism appears to have muffled the music business, despite exceptions like System of a Down, an Armenian-American metal band that rages against the corporate machine. Hip-hop has retreated from the socially conscious music that hit its peak with Public Enemy and with the exception of OutKast returned to East Coast rap's obsession with booty and money—the transcendent power of bling-bling. As P. Diddy put it back when he was still Puff Daddy, "It's all about the Benjamins." (He's referring to $100 bills, Mr. President.) When Madonna tried to shake things up by kissing Britney Spears and Christina Aguilera on stage, the stunt felt harmless, like Jack Black teaching schoolkids to fight "The Man" in *School of Rock*. "Maybe the concept of edginess doesn't work anymore," fashion designer Anna Sui told *The New York Times*. "You look at Pink with her red hair and punk clothes, and you think she might be punk but then she belts out a torch song. You watch the MTV Video Music Awards, and every single person is saying Coldplay is awesome, but they sound like Michael Bolton to me. You look at Christina Aguilera, and she has all the affectations of somebody who would be a rocker, and then you hear her songs and you think, Is this the Julie London of today?" Although London was actually far cooler than Aguilera could ever be, I get what she's saying.

Aside from the Reality boom, there's a similar retrograde aura to the TV listings. Despite hundreds of channels, most shows are simply spruced-up versions of fifties TV fare: talent contests, game shows, family sitcoms, and crime dramas. NBC's *American Dreams* pretended to offer a serious portrait about how life changed during the 1960s, yet its only real connection to the sixties is the deluge of nostalgic music on its soundtrack (imagine *Forrest Gump*, without the irony). While this was enough to win Emmy Awards, the show paled into nothingness next to the two juggernauts, *C.S.I.* and *Law and Order*. They have dominated the ratings, spawned hugely successful off-shoots, and have a boundless future (and even present) in syndication. On the face of it, they seem radically different. While *Law and Order* is shot through with creator Dick Wolf's love of tabloid America, which is almost a kind of classicism, Jerry Bruckheimer's *C.S.I.* is high-tech and semitopical (racy plots about plushies!). But once you get beneath the surface, both follow a similar formula. Retreating from such character-driven cop shows as *Hill Street Blues* and *NYPD Blue*, the franchises are essentially glitzy updates on Jack Webb's old show, *Dragnet*. They are deliberately, soothingly dull. Although they often deal with sleazy material, especially the *C.S.I.* shows, which are crawling with strippers and weird-sex killers, their whole point is to domesticate anything dangerous. They focus on procedure, play up technical dialogue ("The directionality of the blood tells the story"), feature characters whose off-the-job lives scarcely matter, and paint a reassuring portrait of the social order being preserved, even in fleshpots like Las Vegas. The world may be scary, but these programs show us official competence keeping chaos at bay. Each week on *C.S.I.* you can count on portentous Gil Grissom—played by that enjoyable slab of Danish ham William Petersen—to find the telltale flake of DNA-rich dandruff that will send the cocky murderer straight up the river. TV could hardly get more conservative.

But as with filmmaking during Eisenhower's presidency, television today is not without its trickier undercurrents. While the networks' flagship shows—*C.S.I.* and *American Idol* and *Friends*—champion straight-arrow America, the smaller channels have spawned a swarm of programs challenging their vision. Comedy Central's *The Daily Show* isn't merely the skeptical mirror-image of a so-called "serious" newscast, but its parodic deconstruction—it makes us register the vacuity of correspondents standing self-importantly before a backdrop. For its part, HBO has become the wayward id of network TV, its shows presenting a murkier and more amoral version of existing programs. *Sex and the City* is *Friends* with dirty talk and nudity; *The Wire* is *Law and Order* without either; *K Street* is *The West Wing* without the ideals (or audience). Where the Italian-American family madness on *The Sopranos* lays bare the underbelly of *Everybody Loves Raymond* (oh, those killer matriarchs), *Six Feet Under* plays like a metaphysical riposte to *C.S.I.*: Both shows always begin with a dead body, but where the cop show ties everything up neatly, Alan Ball's drama about a family of morticians suggests that the meaning of everything is always elusive, buried.

The network's whole allure is caught by its brilliantly ambiguous slogan—"It isn't TV. It's HBO."—which both positions it as classy for the elite while also implying that it will give you all the nudity and swearing you can't get on free TV. It has the cachet of PBS, only cool. Such a perfect blend of the high and low makes it catnip for members of the media class who determine the national buzz. HBO's wildness has begun finding echoes on the "nonpremium" channels, which in the second half of 2003 started turning out enjoyably lurid potboilers that were often the closest TV came to social commentary. Just as Fox's *The O.C.* used the old Romeo-and-Juliet story line to paint a class-conscious portrait of the Orange County rich, the network's quickly canceled *Skin* played out the Culture Wars in an admirably sly fashion: It centered on the conflict between a self-righteous Jewish pornography mogul (perfectly played by Ron Silver) and a self-promoting and even more self-righteous Christian D.A., whom the dull viewer might connect with John Ashcroft (and the sharp one with Will Hayes, who was hired in the 1930s to impose a moral code on a Hollywood whose entertainments were thought disreputable by the guardians of social order).

Yet neither of these shows was as delirious as *Playmakers*. This NFL soap opera harked back to such revisionist seventies sports movies as *North Dallas Forty* and *Semi-Tough*, treating professional football as the symptom of national dysfunction. The owner was a rich bastard who treats everyone like chattel. A gay lineman was trying to stay closeted. The coach was a control freak who'd sooner die of prostate cancer than stop coaching. The star rookie was a doper who, contractually obligated to visit a children's hospital as part of the team's PR package, wound up stealing pills from a dying kid—who caught him at it. Even the characters we were supposed to root for were tortured. The veteran running back was busted for domestic violence, while his linebacker pal loathed playing football but lacked the guts to quit. All this was enough to make *Playmakers* the most un-American show on TV— just look what it said about our nation's favorite sport—yet the flabbergasting thing about it was that it appeared on ESPN, which broadcasts NFL games and spends its *SportsCenter* celebrating the heroics of the football players this fictional show was so enthusiastically debunking. Naturally, the NFL got the show canceled. ESPN wasn't just biting the hand that fed it but telling us that its palms taste greasy.

Even *Playmakers*'s assault on America's most popular sport was mild compared to what you found in two comics—one in the daily papers, the other on the Net—that provided the aggressive social commentary missing from novels and films. Drawing on the same surge of cultural energy that created *The Simpsons, South Park,* and the best graphic novels, comic strips became the perfect form for distilling the political and media elite's lies into comprehensible packages. Aaron McGruder's groundbreaking *The Boondocks*, whose young African-American kids engage in a running dialogue with public figures, was so consistently subversive of official opinion that nervous papers took to pulling particular strips or canceling it altogether. For instance, McGruder's Thanksgiving 2001 strip had his hero Huey offering this blessing over the turkey: "We are thankful that *our* leader isn't the spoiled son of a powerful politician from a wealthy oil family who is supported by religious fundamentalists, operates through clandestine organizations, has no respect for the democratic electoral process, bombs innocents and uses war to deny people their civil liberties."

Although this was shocking to see in your morning paper barely two months after September 11, it was mild next to David Rees's Internet samizdat comic strip *Get Your War On* (eventually collected in book form), a belch of fury that was perhaps the most stridently oppositional response to September 11. At a time when anchormen were being somber, Rees was savage. Starting with public-domain clip art of generic office-workers talking on the phone, he created a series of imaginary conversations, larded with hip-hop patois, that turned these expressionless "characters" into readers' outraged surrogates. Rees's work was about *us*—at least the millions of us who, in the aftermath of 9/11, were caught up in fear, confusion, paranoia, and rage. And he expressed these feelings with a black comedy so stunningly mordant, you sometimes gasped as you laughed. Showing perfect pitch for cruelty and cant, he made jokes about Afghans stepping on land mines, Cheney's weird disappearances, Dick Armey's talk of ethnic cleansing, and, of course, death.

Rees continued with his assault long after the war in Iraq, offering the most accurate reflection of how most Americans felt about Bush's halfhearted yet "visionary" plans for outer space:

Although some found Rees's humor heartless, *Get Your War On*'s virtue lay in its hardness, its willingness to express the violent, conflicted, self-hating passions of those who wanted Osama dead but still hated bombing Afghanistan, who opposed American militarism yet still were furious the government couldn't figure out who sent that anthrax. And because it was a *personal* expression of outrage passed for free from e-mail inbox to inbox, Rees was able to maintain his outsider's stance—making us his co-conspirators. Working for neither profit nor fame, he didn't have the slightest qualm about stating with brutal frankness what so many people felt but would not say, at least nowhere near as rudely as we actually felt it. When Bush appointed Henry Kissinger to head the commission investigating the 9/11 attacks, Rees's justice was swift and sure: "Does Bush even know who these motherfuckers are?" a guy says into the phone. "Didn't he get suspicious when he saw Kissinger and John Poindexter licking the blood off each other's hands?" *Get Your War On*'s acid bath helped remove the thick film that came from reading each day's Op-Ed pieties and watching the Bush administration turn the War on Terror to political advantage.

But Magruder's and Rees's head-on responses to America's immediate political reality were anomalous. Most often, the true subversive-
ness of pop culture comes not from radical social commentary but
from sexy song hooks, random bits of sass, explosions of psychic energy
that somehow violate the official version. It works in cockeyed, unruly
ways, which is why traditional leftists often struggle to understand it.
Thomas Frank scoffs at claims that there was something radical about
Madonna's shifting images of sexual identity; for him, she's just another commercial product purveying a bogus form of rebellion. In fact,
she transformed the way millions of young women thought about their
sexuality—and the power of their sexuality—as well as making gay
sensibility familiar to millions of kids who otherwise might not have
had a clue. Was she commercially minded? Yes. Was she corrupt?
Probably, but in this market society what exactly does "corrupt" mean?
Just because pop isn't "pure," that doesn't stop it from changing people's lives; on the contrary, its accessibility helps the process along.
Although it's easy to make fun of Madge now that she's written a children's book, her importance as a star was inseparable from the fact that
she always believed pop is supposed to mean something.

In that sense, anyway, Madonna's most important heir is her fellow
child of Detroit—Eminem, Marshall Mathers, the Real Slim Shady—
whose career never stops wrestling with the difficulty of being an
artistic outsider. From the moment he hit big in early 1999 with *The
Slim Shady LP*—from the atelier of Dr. Dre, a good rapper and great
producer—he was that rarest of creatures, a white rapper so electrifying that even African-Americans thought he was pretty good. His
lyrics brought a new level of personal honesty to the form. Listening
to this CD and its extraordinary follow-up, *The Marshall Mathers LP*,
you learned seemingly everything about him—how he hated his
mom, loved his daughter, wanted to cut up his wife, Kim, felt sympathy and fear for (and of) his fans, boiled over with rage at being raised
poor, white, and humiliated, and fairly glowed with the desire to make
the whole world understand him while insisting we could never really
know him at all. He had a genius for not only putting on masks (each
of his first three CDs' titles calls him by a different name) but for tear-

ing them off, transforming anger, self-pity, and self-loathing into incandescent language. This alone would have been enough to make him America's most galvanizing entertainer, a hip-hop Pied Piper whose visceral allure to white suburban teenagers (he dubbed them "Eric" and "Erica") freaked out the Vice President's wife, which only made Eric and Erica love him that much more. Even as he crossed the lines of race and class, carefully deferring to Dre so that nobody would accuse him of doing an Elvis on black music—he knew that he filled a cultural need for a white rap star—Eminem revealed a startlingly acute awareness of himself as a public figure. When not boasting about his success or mocking his enemies, he was often riffing on what a menace he actually was. Despite that weird Grammys appearance with Elton John, nobody would dare call *him* cute.

Then they started to anyway. It's hard to stay dangerous once people start buying your records in droves. It had always been Eminem's strength that he could use his underclass roots and miserable past as a source of power and authority. But as he grew more popular, his rebel status grew harder to maintain. And he knew it. His CD *The Eminem Show* was a hyperbolic attempt to figure out how to stay an outlaw in a culture intent on lionizing him. This was probably clearest in the brilliant video for "Without Me," which cast him as a superhero saving a young boy from committing a crime—namely, playing an Eminem CD with a "Parental Guidance" sticker on it. A hilarious, densely imagined provocation, this four-minute burst of energy found him electrocuting Dick Cheney, dancing around as Osama bin Laden, mocking everything from Moby's music to *Survivor*, and vaingloriously telling his listeners that they depend on him "because it feels so empty without me." Yet far from making him one of America's Most Wanted, this only made Americans want more of him.

2002 belonged to Eminem. He had the year's best video and won raves for his autobiographical movie *8 Mile*, whose closing anthem ("Lose Yourself") would win the Oscar for Best Original Song, a painfully square accolade that Bob Dylan only nabbed forty years into his career. Less happily, Eminem was embraced by the graying mainstream media, which obviously *did* feel empty without him. *The New*

York Observer ran a dweeby article headlined GUESS WHO THINKS EMINEM'S A GENIUS? MIDDLE-AGED ME. Andrew Sarris compared him to James Dean, Frank Rich to Elvis (a comparison Eminem himself had made much earlier), and Maureen Dowd wrote a smart, uproarious *New York Times* column about how her women friends gleefully blasted his songs as they drove. (I still like to imagine Maureen's pals rapping about "bitches on my dick.") None of this did his street cred any good, especially once he began playing the elder statesman at the MTV Awards, graciously clapping for those who beat him instead of punching the nearest stranger. Flush with his acting success in *8 Mile,* he tried to stop the *Girls Gone Wild* sex tape he made from hitting the streets. By the time *The New York Review of Books* ran a 5,000-word appreciation in its fortieth-anniversary issue, complete with praise for Shady's verbal dexterity from none other than Nobel Prize–winning poet Seamus Heaney—who has remained scandalously mute about the genius of Snoop Doggy Dogg—Eminem's radicalism had been swallowed by the big box. Even when he rapped about killing the President, the Secret Service just yawned. Marshall was too rich to think about doing anything like that. He'd become Exhibit Number One of how hard it's become to be a rebellious artistic outsider in today's America. His problem was not that the government was trying to ban his CDs but that the The Man was playing them as he drove to the office.

Working Class Hero™

On Oscar night, 2003, Eminem didn't turn up at the ceremony to collect his hardware—he knew it wouldn't be cool. The troublemaker who did show was Michael Moore, whose *Bowling for Columbine* had been named Best Documentary. Joined on the stage by the other nominees for best nonfiction film, Moore startled the crowd by saying, "We like nonfiction and we live in fictitious times. We live in the time where we have fictitious election results that elects a fictitious president. We live in a time where we have a man sending us to war for fictitious reasons. Whether it's the fiction [*sic*] of duct tape or fiction of orange alerts, we are against this war, Mr. Bush. Shame on you, Mr. Bush, shame on you. And anytime you got the Pope and the Dixie Chicks against you, your time is up." Although Hollywood is notorious for being liberal, these words were greeted by far louder boos than applause. After all, it's one thing to be boldly antiwar when you are on *The Daily Show* or speaking at a Bay Area demo, but no star is about to cause a ruckus by tossing a Molotov on the film industry's big night. Even Susan Sarandon did little more than flash a timid peace sign. The sole exception was Moore, who used his appearance on the world's biggest showcase, beamed live to more than a billion people worldwide, to say exactly what he wanted to say. Of course, assailing the war couldn't hurt *him*. That's why canny old pros like Jack Nicholson and Harrison Ford looked on with such bemusement. They recognized a performer milking his money role. In attacking the President on live TV before the whole world, Moore was engaged in a classic piece of Bush World branding. He was marketing himself as our era's leading provocateur.

Like all good populists and most bad ones, Moore thrives during periods of fear, anger, and resentment. He first made his name in the late 1980s with *Roger & Me*, a documentary about his attempts to get General Motors CEO Roger Smith to visit Flint, Michigan, to see the devastation caused by his business decisions. Following on the heels of *Roseanne*, Moore provided a supersized blue-collar response to Reaganism, whose Morning in America couldn't disguise the Twilight of the American Working Class. The most successful documentary in history (until it was surpassed by *Bowling for Columbine*), the movie established Moore's jokey, confrontational, media-guerrilla style, which often plays like a cross between *60 Minutes* and *Punk'd*. Over the next decade, Moore parlayed *Roger & Me*'s success into a left-wing cottage industry, writing a bestselling book, *Downsize This!*, creating short-lived but acclaimed television shows (*TV Nation, The Awful Truth*), and directing two movies, the laugh-free comedy *Canadian Bacon* and a second documentary, *The Big One*, a book-tour chronicle in which Moore's ostensible concern for working people got swamped by his camera-hogging narcissism. (Although he does a lot of aw-shucksing, he rivals Bill O'Reilly in his capacity for self-promotion.) While this multimedia productivity kept Moore in the public eye and made him rich, his work didn't resonate in the nineties. It's never easy for the left to attack a Democratic president, especially one who's following twelve years of Republican rule, and Bill Clinton was also blessed by an economic boom. Amid seeming peace and prosperity, Moore's left-wing satire seemed beside the point—it was right-wing cut-ups like Rush Limbaugh who were really going to town.

That instantly flipped with the "fiction" of George W. Bush's election. Given a worthy target, Moore's career took off: He didn't merely jump on the Bush-bashing bandwagon, he often appeared to be its Clydesdale. Indeed, his ballcap, gibbous belly, and working-class shtick turned him into an international icon—perhaps the left's first new one since Che Guevara. His book *Stupid White Men* sold 4 million copies; the follow-up, *Dude, Where's My Country?*, became the #1 bestseller. His one-man show in London played to huge crowds and critical raves—the Brits find him the second coming of Mark Twain. (I eagerly await his *Huckleberry Finn.*) By every external standard, *Bowling for Columbine* became the most successful documentary of all time. It broke all box-office records, nabbed the Oscar, and won a huge award at the Cannes Film Festival—Europeans adore anything that shows Americans to be buffoonish barbarians.

Moore's huge success could hardly be more fitting, for his rebellion makes him an almost perfect emanation of Bush's America. His style brings together many of our big-box culture's leading leitmotifs—tabloid news, Reality TV, obsessive branding, self-proclaimed sincerity—and weds them to a political vision every bit as reductively binary as that of President Bush. Moore is another Us vs. Them guy, although in his case, "They" are the rich, politically connected elite who run "the corporation known as the United States of America," while "We" are ordinary working people who have been systematically robbed, cheated, and lied to by those in power. This vision of life dovetails perfectly with his carefully crafted image as a shambolic, blue-collar lazybones, brainy but not a sellout, who's aghast at what's being done to the little guy. It's always been part of his allure that, in a day when most media people appear to be androids manufactured in an industrial park in Stepford, he flaunts the tokens of down-home authenticity, drooping Kmart jeans, a flat midwestern voice, a body that's a stranger to gyms—a few months on Atkins could kill his career. One shouldn't be shocked that, off camera, Moore lives the life of a media superstar—being chauffered around by his publisher, owning a nice apartment on the Upper West Side (not in Flint), and keeping the relentless schedule of a hard-driving CEO. For the Michael Moore that the world sees is a public persona every bit as consciously invented as Twain's or Pee-wee Herman's. "Michael Moore" comes complete with a creation myth, which, as he tells it, is also a story of the Fall. Moore grew up in Flint during the fifties and sixties, back when the city was something of a working-class paradise (his dad made spark plugs for GM), with secure jobs, good benefits, home ownership, and company loyalty. Over the next decades, he watched this Eden destroyed by corporate heads who shut down factories and laid workers off, by weak union leaders who compromised rather than fought, and by complicit politicians who chased pipe dreams—like transforming Flint into a tourist destination—instead of defending the blue-collar people who had built the city.

This homespun version of Paradise Lost has obviously filled Moore with an abiding sense of rage. But like Twain, he has always been sharp enough to know that Americans prefer their anger softened with laughter. Of course, humor comes in different flavors, and he knows enough to aim his satire at many different tastes. Some of his jokes are broad as a Texas barn, as when he makes fun of Miss Michigan or calls a book chapter "Woo Hoo! I Got Me a Tax Cut!" Others are slyer. There's a nifty bit in *The Big One* when Moore visits a Milwaukee auto parts manufacturer that's just relocated its factories south of the border. He brings with him an enormous check for 85¢ that he wants to give the company's president—to pay the first hour's wage for a Mexican worker. Moore has a world-class adman's knack for the catchy idea, and one can only admire the pop-culture brio of titles like *Stupid White Men, Bowling for Columbine,* or *Fahrenheit 9/11,* his agitprop documentary about Bush that became a sensation at the 2004 Cannes Film Festival. The last title contains an allusion to Ray Bradbury and

François Truffaut that will probably escape many Americans, and it reminds us that, for all his workingman iconography, Moore knows how to play the hipster game. He often comes off as something of a lefty David Letterman—one whose core audience is the educated elite, not the folks working in factories, restaurants, or at Wal-Mart. And it shows. One unpleasant feature of his work has always been that, in his eagerness for a crowd-pleasing laugh, he often plays to the worst instincts of his audience, mocking those he's supposed to be defending. As Pauline Kael wrote of *Roger & Me*, Moore uses "leftism as a superior attitude. Members of the audience can laugh at ordinary working people and still feel that they're taking a politically correct position."

Moore's politics have inevitably made him a target of the right, which delights in exposing his personal hypocrisy, be it that Manhattan apartment or accusations that this champion of the working class exploits his own employees. Just as inevitably, his work has been greeted by the left with mixed feelings. *Salon* attacked him for his routine factual inaccuracies, a weakness of his work since *Roger & Me*. For instance, Moore's suggestion that the Columbine killers went to a bowling class on the morning of the murders, which gave that movie its title, is flatly untrue. His response to such complaints is positively O'Reillyesque. Like the great Bill, he believes that all criticism is *personal;* he reacts by going on the attack, claiming that those who fault him are cowardly, dishonest, or in the corporate pocket.

Facts aside, *Dissent* fretted that Moore's style marked the triumph of entertainment over serious left-wing politics. When *Bowling for Columbine* came out in the fall of 2002, I myself gave the film a harsh review, partly because it was clumsily made, but mainly for things I thought low: its cheap shots at dopey militiamen and gaga Charlton Heston, its attacks on TV sensationalism even as Moore used the same techniques, and above all, its slipshod political thinking. There is no defending the montage sequence in which he played Louis Armstrong's "What a Wonderful World" over footage of countries where the U.S. has made war or toppled governments—Iran, Guatemala, Nicaragua, Afghanistan, etc.—and then ended with shots of the planes hitting the World Trade Center. What stank about this scene was neither its suggestion that much U.S. foreign policy has been reprehensible (it obviously has been) nor that such behavior is part of the context that triggered anti-American terrorism (ditto). It was that Moore had engaged in a kind of glib historical leveling that I associate with the right. Watching it in a left-wing film, I suddenly grasped how irked and embarrassed countless African-Americans must be when Al Sharpton is both presumed and assumed to represent their point of view.

If the right is unnervingly tolerant of its loose cannons—you don't find conservative intellectuals going after Rush Limbaugh—it's long been a weakness of the left that its members, sanctimonious about ideological purity, tend to turn on one another like spiders in a jar. Looking back, I realize that I made the same mistake about *Bowling for Columbine*. I constantly meet brainy lefties who loved the movie, and when I grumble about the Louis Armstrong montage or the cruelty to Ben Hur, they instantly agree that these are cheap tricks and wish Moore didn't employ them. But then they go on to say that they could overlook these obvious flaws because they admire what Moore was trying to do. In the very middle of the quiescent Bush years, even as the Republicans were winning the midterm elections and the War on Terror seemed to overshadow everything, here was a film that tackled all sorts of important issues that our culture was ignoring. It raised questions about the connection between violence at home and violence abroad, had Marilyn Manson explaining how the media instills consumerism and fear, and even offered some hope in the sequence when Moore took two Columbine survivors to Kmart and actually got the chain to stop selling ammo—a victory for the good guys. As for Moore's cheap tricks, that was just part of the price of the ticket.

For all his skill at making pop culture, Moore's recent prominence says less about him than about the slow degeneration of the left, especially the wing that is more liberal, or even radical, than today's Democratic Party. A hundred years ago, the left took its strength from offering a muscular blend of theory and action. American radicals—and this included genuine proletarians—read Marx and Engels to understand the workings of class struggle, the ironclad laws of history.

It was considered essential to the left that its action would be ground-ed in a coherent social analysis based on the study of history. Over the course of the decades, that faith in theory was lost, and by the 1960s, the New Left was putting the premium on action. I remember how my fellow students sneered at Old Left professors for being all talk—we were supposed to take to the streets.

Since the fall of communism and the rise of centrist Democrats, even the faith in action has largely disappeared. The remnant of the left is largely defined by patterns of consumption—which magazines we read and which movies we see—or by newfangled ideas of organ-izing—such as Howard Dean's Internet-grassroots campaign. What passes for the serious left isn't a set of shared ideas or values attached to a living social movement. It's an *audience* brought together by big-name freelance "radicals"—Moore, Noam Chomsky, Ralph Nader, Arianna Huffington, Jim Hightower, and showbiz figures like Sarandon or Martin Sheen. What these folks have in common isn't a vision of the world—it's fame. The most popular of the bunch, Moore doesn't pretend to offer a serious analysis. Read any few pages of *Stupid White Men* or *Dude, Where's My Country?* and you quickly grasp that, as a social thinker, he's a very clever comedian. And he has shrewdly tapped into a yearning for political change that has recently had very few outlets. For a great many viewers, applauding at the end of *Bowling for Columbine* at the plex is as activist as politics gets.

Because Moore specializes in the comedy of outrage, I've often heard him described as the left-wing alter ego of right-wing bomb-thrower Ann Coulter. Yet such "moral equivalence" (to borrow that beloved con-servative term) is more than a little unfair. Where he often comes up with genuinely funny satirical thrusts, her idea of a joke is to fire off a sense-less, sub–Don Rickles insult, such as calling Katie Couric "the affable Eva Braun of morning TV." This isn't just unfunny and ideologically inaccu-rate—Ann, baby, *you're* Eva Braun; Katie's Madame Mao—it's part of the right's infuriating habit of linking the left to Hitler with phrases like "feminazis" or "stormtroopers of P.C." Where Moore idealizes a post-WWII America that offered working people more prosperity than at any point in human history, she looks at that same period with lovestruck eyes for—Joe McCarthy. Where he has staked out new terrain for the left, winning over young people by not conforming to the stereotype of the gray and graying radical, she has simply followed in the wake of Rush Limbaugh and the media's countless other Id Conservatives, the ideological shock troops who keep pushing the acceptable boundaries of conservative thinking ever farther to the right. While such antics are useful to the Republican elite (her work is so virulent she makes Tom DeLay look like a centrist), they also make her Joe Pesci in a Martin Scorsese gangster movie—useful for roughing up the other side, until he becomes such a loose cannon that his cronies have to whack him.*

The left has no need to cut Moore loose, whose work offers no call to violence or explosion of anger. On the contrary, he performed two valuable services. He put class politics back on the table and provided an antidote to what has so long bedeviled the left: its tendency to think and act like a humorless elite still feeding on memories of the sixties. He's done what the Democrats and *The Nation* have signally failed to do—put left-wing ideas in popular form. For all his shortcomings, no cultural figure has done so much to turn people against George W. Bush and his cronies. *Fahrenheit 9/11* is an infinitely more effective anti-Bush commercial than anything dreamed up by the Kerry campaign. Moore's persona is a useful riposte to the Populist Social Darwinism of the right, for unlike the President or Rupert Murdoch, his isn't the faux populism of the well-born. It's something far weirder and more compelling. A working-class child of what is now the Rust Belt, Michael Moore has made a fortune by donning a ballcap and playing the role of the blue-collar hero for millions eager to find somebody who's willing to stand up—even at the Oscars—and declare his opposition. I don't know the man personally, but Moore must surely marvel at the sweet irony that, thanks to a president he thoroughly detests, his share of the Ownership Society keeps getting bigger.

*This began happening to Coulter with the publication of her McCarthy-adoring *Treason*, which was so extreme in its rhetoric—"Everyone says liberals love America, too. No, they don't"—that even conservatives like Bill O'Reilly and the *The Wall Street Journal*'s Dorothy Rabinowitz took care to distance themselves from its ravings. Republicans know that it's amateurish politics to claim, as does Coulter, that Democrats like Al Gore are traitors. The professional move is to insinuate it.

CHAPTER 7

Postcards from the Wedge

Private faces in public places
Are wiser and nicer
Than public faces in private places
—W. H. AUDEN

While Democrats are notorious for raucous political conventions that shipwreck party unity—who will forget red-faced Mayor Daley calling Senator Abraham Ribicoff a "kike" in 1968 Chicago?—Republicans have become famous for putting on a good public face. The glaring exception was the 1992 convention in Houston. Even as the party was renominating President George H. W. Bush, a thin-lipped caricature of WASP blandness, a group of rollicking upstarts turned the convention's sound-bite portion into a rightwing Walpurgisnacht with Pat Buchanan throwing down lightning bolts from atop Bald Mountain. "A religious and culture war" was under way, Buchanan declaimed in a famously lethal line, "a struggle for the soul of America." But most Americans weren't keen on spiritual battle. They'd just won the Cold War and found such apocalyptic thinking more than a little scary; they wanted a breather from Armageddon. Were these ranters the soul of the Republican Party? Poor, dull George found himself in the most ironic of positions. He'd spent his career in a party that wielded wedge issues like Paul Bunyan's ax, but for once, the wedge was cutting him off at the knees. The public associated Bush with the very reactionary fanatics who were unhappiest with his presidency. Not surprisingly, Bush got creamed.

The lessons of that humiliating defeat were not lost on his son, the party leaders, or even the fruitcake right, all of whom realized that, in a nation that could still embrace Bill Clinton after the Monica scandal, the smart move was to come across inclusive. You didn't actually have to be that way, thank Heaven, but a well-run Republican Convention should resemble a Democratic Convention, only *orderly*—like a Hollywood remake of some crazy foreign film. That's precisely what the party offered in 2000 when it nominated George W. Bush in Philadelphia. Each time you turned on the TV, you were greeted with a jamboree of tolerance. The Republicans gave you women praising diversity. They gave you openly gay Arizona congressman Jim Kolbe, who got to talk for only three minutes, but no matter. Although his appearance was piddling by enlightened standards, for the GOP it was groundbreaking—in '92 you saw placards saying GOD HATES FAGS. Most indelibly, they gave you an endless parade of African-Americans. There were so many black faces on stage and so many white ones in the audience that skeptics compared the scene to an NBA game or a minstrel show. That only 4 percent of the delegates were black was not exactly a shock. The Republicans had long since traded away the African-American loyalty they had enjoyed in the wake of the Civil War, becoming a party that spent half a century wooing white voters with tacit racism—from Goldwater's defense of states' rights and Nixon's "southern strategy" to Reagan beginning his 1980 campaign at the Neshoba County Fair in Philadelphia, Missisippi, where three white civil rights workers had been famously murdered only sixteen years earlier. One wondered: Wasn't that 4 percent haunted by Willie Horton, trotted out as a bogeyman by Bush I to destroy Michael Dukakis? To be fair, not all the Republican talk about tolerance was palaver. Many neocons, for instance, are embarrassed by the party's history of race-baiting, while libertarians are aghast at laws that would outlaw anyone's private sexual conduct. The tolerance of homosexuality is personal to Dick Cheney, whose daughter, Mary, is openly lesbian—to the unconcealed horror of her uptight mother, Lynne, who still thinks of this as a shameful family secret long after the whole world has been let in on the news.

Even as the economic raison d'être of a Bush presidency required double-dealing—it had to feign populism as it geared up to help the upper class—the campaign also faced the tricky task of playing it both ways on social questions. It labored to convince swing voters that Bush was openminded even as he nudged and winked and studded his speeches with biblical language to assure the hard right that, of course, he really wasn't. Believing that his father had lost reelection because he'd been insufficiently attentive to the Christian right, Bush was careful not to repeat the mistake. He offered them the vision of an earlier, better America before Bill and Hillary, before Stonewall, before Women's Lib and the Great Society—a land in which God-fearing Republican businessmen would practice the old-fashioned white paternalism. Once elected, this is precisely what his administration set about doing, although the President doesn't want to keep minorities down. He just wants to keep them quiet. Still, he went after programs such as affirmative action and Head Start that are associated with African-Americans. He whittled away at abortion rights rather than attacking them head-on (a surefire political loser). And he made a big deal of opposing gay marriage.

No doubt the religious right wishes that Bush had been even more aggressive—Close down drag shows! No condoms for minors! Put the Ten Commandments on the $10 bill!—but they have been reasonably satisfied with his performance. Even if the President can't roll back the clock, the faithful count on his palefaces to hold the fort against what they see as modernity's hypermodern redskins (to use a cultural opposition made famous in a 1938 essay by Philip Rahv). They want him to keep them safe from abortion-loving feminists, homosexuals who proselytize for their immoral lifestyle, African-Americans who keep demanding special treatment. There's only one problem. The redskins have already begun entering the fort from every possible direction. While a few may have scaled the walls firing arrows, most knocked on the door politely, emulated palefaces, or spent so much time appearing on TV they came to be thought of as friends. And they've come to change what's going on inside the fort's walls, for it turned out that a lot of palefaces wanted to be redskins all along. Although Bush World is an era of political retrenchment, that doesn't mean the real world isn't evolving, even if this change is sometimes painfully slow. With each passing year, it gets harder to tell the palefaces from the redskins in America's big-box culture that permits personal identity to be more fluid than at any time in human history.

Guess Who's Still Coming to Dinner

In the middle of the Lewinsky scandal, Toni Morrison put forth her widely quoted opinion that Bill Clinton was our first black president. While the stereotypes she employed were more than a little unflattering to African-American men—she had him being "metaphorically seized and body searched" on account of his "unpoliced sexuality"—the analogy contained a kernel of truth that the President himself eagerly embraced, happy to be wrapped in white negritude. More than any of his predecessors, Clinton felt a kinship with African-Americans. Naturally, this didn't stop him from turning racial prejudice to personal advantage during the 1992 campaign, executing the retarded black man Ricky Ray Rector, or publicly smacking down the irrelevant rapper Sister Souljah, but it did mean that he always gave his finest, most passionate speeches in black churches. Once he'd left office, he moved to an office in Harlem. Whether he deserves the credit or not, a National Urban League study showed that, during Clinton's last year in office, the poverty rate among African-Americans had reached an all-time low.

The ascent of the Bush adminstration officially marked the Return of the White Men, although the President and his team are not nearly as stupid as Michael Moore's book urges us to think. When it comes to the painful enigma of race in America, they're extremely cunning. They don't want to confront the problem—which might become unpleasant—they just want to nullify it as an issue. Bush spent his 2000 campaign trying to do just that. Although he and Karl Rove knew they didn't have a prayer of winning over black voters, they knocked themselves out suggesting that Bush was minority-friendly, lest he seem like a bigot to all those softhearted soccer moms. When he announced his candidacy, two of the key people at his side were black, Condoleezza Rice and flashy J. C. Watts, the only black Republican in Congress, who would later reassure party faithful that they needn't worry about Bush being dumb with the quintessentially Republican line "You can *buy* clever."* This was just the beginning. Beating the compassionate conservative drum, Bush constantly visited minority schools and assailed "the soft bigotry of low expectations." Meanwhile, his campaign staff perfected the soft bigotry of high expectations: They took special care to stage photo ops in which Bush was surrounded by people of color. (Predictably, Al Gore's consultants urged him to keep black faces out of his campaign imagery.) This didn't mean that Bush felt any connection to the minority groups his staff was sticking in his ads. Newt Gingrich once said of GOP congressman Jack Kemp, a former NFL quarterback, that he had "showered with more blacks than most Republicans have shaken hands with." As owner of the Texas Rangers, Bush obviously didn't shower with his team, but he did shake a lot of black hands. Still, this didn't save him, as Frank Bruni reported, from embarrassing white-guy behavior. Candidate Bush not only confused two black reporters who looked nothing alike, but asked one of them if he was listening to rap on his Walkman. The answer: John Coltrane.

I've never heard anyone claim that Bush is himself a racist, but there can be an abyss between personal feelings and political acts. Although it was said that Ronald Reagan didn't have a bigoted bone in his body, that didn't stop him from enacting policies that made life much harder for African-Americans. The same disjunction is true of Bush, whose willingness to make race a wedge issue became blatant during his primary campaign. Desperate for a win in South Carolina, he purposely spoke at the vile Bob Jones University while Rove's campaign orcs did a smear job on John McCain, promoting rumors that the senator's adopted Bangladeshi daughter, Bridget, was actually his

---

*But you can't buy everything. In 1995, Watts wrote an essay predicting that by 2002 there would be more black Republicans in Congress than white Democrats. Seven years later, the frustrated Watts quit his own House seat, reducing the number of black congressional Republicans to zero.

illegitimate child with a black woman.* The strategy worked with South Carolina's Caucasian voters—white men are Bush's solid base—but had a chillingly familiar ring to African-Americans, who showed their feelings in the November general election. In Bush's home state of Texas, where blacks remembered both Dubya's record as governor and his father's vote against the 1964 Civil Rights Act, they went against him to the tune of 95 percent.

Even after his election, Bush continued to play it both ways. As usual, the Republicans were shrewd about symbolism. In his two gaudiest appointments, he named Colin Powell Secretary of State, making him the highest-ranking African-American in American history, and Condoleezza Rice his National Security Advisor, the first African-American woman to hold such a high post. In one of his most trumpeted educational achievements, he hooked up with Ted Kennedy on the No Child Left Behind plan, a system of national standards and federal rewards designed to help students in bad schools. Off the front pages, however, his record was, shall we say, checkered. He cut back Head Start, betrayed Kennedy by giving No Child Left Behind only two-thirds of the promised funding, made John Ashcroft Attorney General despite his connection to white supremacist groups, and nominated people with atrocious civil rights records for important federal judgeships. In line with a trademark Republican tactic in the post–Clarence Thomas era, some of his most egregious selections were African-American: Bush proposed to fill an opening in the District of Columbia's pivotal U.S. Court of Appeals with Janice Rogers Brown, a California Supreme Court Justice who, according to *The Los Angeles Times*, has dubbed the New Deal "the triumph of socialist revolution" and isn't sure the Bill of Rights applies to the states.

---

*The racist right is especially fond of charging that its enemies have fathered illegitimate children with black women—the same accusation was leveled against Bill Clinton. In fact, the most prominent modern politician of whom this charge was true was the hypocritical Dixiecrat Strom Thurmond, whose seventy-eight-year-old daughter, Essie Mae Washington Williams, went public in December 2003, saying, "There are many stories like Sally Hemings's and mine." The real slick willies belong to the conservatives.

Through it all, Bush clearly wished that the whole race issue would just go away without anyone getting too angry. Placating the right, the federal government sued the University of Michigan over its affirmative-action program—even though both Powell and Rice are both living proof of what such programs can do. (The two broke Republican ranks by making clear their support for racial preferences.) But when the Supreme Court offered a mixed decision, allowing race to be a factor in admissions, Bush declared himself satisfied— even though his own Justice Department had argued for a different result. He knew that a strong anti–affirmative action decision might prove political dynamite, and anyway, addressing racial questions can only cause a politician trouble. That's why he and other party big shots so quickly scuttled Mississippi Senator Trent Lott after he'd been caught singing the praises of the 1948 Dixiecrat candidacy of closet miscegenator Strom Thurmond. Nobody in the GOP was surprised by Lott's bigotry, but when the incoming Senate Majority Leader began spouting such things in public, he gave the Republicans' game away— and that *was* offensive. Although Lott tried to save his skin by suddenly spouting equal-opportunity rhetoric, Republicans didn't want its Senate Majority Leader making like Martin Luther King. He was soon replaced as leader by creepy-crawly Dr. Bill Frist, who could be counted on to say all the right things about race, though other character questions were raised by his med-school habit of adopting cats from rescue shelters and then dissecting them.*

The quick dispatch of Lott was designed to take talk of conservative racism off the table. The trouble, of course, is that race remains an enduring cultural wound that, despite all the attempts to suppress it,

---

*Replacing Lott gave Frist a free ride. As he was pushing through the Medicare bill with all those provisions helping corporations, few people knew that Frist's father and older brother had founded HCA/Columbia, the largest chain of for-profit hospitals in America, a company notorious for overcharging the government so much on medical care that it was fined nearly a billion dollars. The Senator himself has an estimated $26 million stake in HCA, but because it's in a blind trust, he's offended by suggestions that this might in any way influence his desire to open up Medicare to private health plans.

keeps bleeding into our national consciousness, even in domains that feel safe. That was the lesson of the 2003 scandal surrounding Rush Limbaugh's claim on ESPN that slumping Philadelphia Eagles quarterback Donovan McNabb had been "overrated" because "the media has been very desirous that a black quarterback can do well." Although it was widely agreed that this was a dumb thing to say—as the rest of McNabb's Pro Bowl season confirmed—the talk shows were abuzz with those wondering whether Rush's comment was actually bigoted or whether African-Americans were being hypersensitive (here came the stinger) as usual. On ESPN's breezy Sunday-morning show *The Sports Reporters*, *The Miami Herald*'s wonderfully named Dan LeBatard asked someone to "explain where the racism is" in Limbaugh's statement. In theory, it should be no more inherently racist to call a black quarterback overrated than a white one, even if, like McNabb, he goes to the Pro Bowl every year; nor is it necessarily racist to suggest that some media folk want black QBs to do well. But as Watergate-fanatic-turned-radio-host G. Gordon Liddy told Ted Koppel, the startling thing about Limbaugh's controversial statement was that it felt so dated. After all, this is a league with tremendous black quarterbacks like Michael Vick and Steve McNair and long-standing black mediocrities such as Kordell Stewart and Tony Banks.

But if Limbaugh's commentary was passé, it had sharp teeth. For we still live in an impure world of racial code words and innuendoes—context is all. Had the assessment of McNabb come from, say, Jim Rome, a white sports-talk host often knocked for being soft on black athletes and callers, fans might have argued the claim on its merits. But they came from Limbaugh, who has sometimes used black dialect ("ax" for "ask") when discussing black leaders and has made his name by being deliberately outrageous: "The NAACP should have riot rehearsal," he once cracked. "They should get a liquor store and practice robberies." Knowing this, one had to ask why he chose to bring up race in the first place. After all, conservatives like Limbaugh always claim to be in favor of a totally color-blind society; they support laws that would remove all racial information from state-government forms. So why focus on McNabb's skin color on a Sunday pre-game show? Or why not mention the overrated defensive back Jason Schorn and say he got all those endorsement deals because he's white? The reason is simple. It fit Limbaugh's agenda to suggest that "liberals"— that is, the media and the government—keep bending over backward to give African-Americans special treatment. (This will come as news to most black Americans, who still have a far higher level of poverty than the rest of the country.) While big-time public figures no longer claim that blacks are inferior, they can still nab a huge audience by pretending to talk about "the media" when they're actually stirring up underlying racial resentments—which is precisely what Limbaugh was doing in the McNabb case. Like many of those who rushed to say that the Jayson Blair scandal was actually about *The New York Times* favoring a reporter simply because he was black, he was practicing a kind of second-degree racism—on the carom, if you will. And when he was called on it—not by his ESPN colleagues, alas—he beat a retreat to the bully's pulpit of his radio show, where he could insist that widespread revulsion at his words proved they were true (what reasoning!), and where, if anyone disagreed, he could just cut them off. I would have loved to see an on-air confrontation between Limbaugh and McNabb, but nobody wanted that—not Rush, not ESPN, which hired him precisely because he's a hot-button figure, not even the National Football League, 70 percent of whose players are black. Like the President, those in charge of mass culture hark back to the bottled-up fifties, preferring to gloss over our country's racial problems. It wasn't for nothing that Hollywood's big Civil War romance *Cold Mountain* had so few black faces, ducking the troublesome fact that its southern lovers were, well, on the side of slaveowners.

Although it would be pretty to think that old-school bigotry is found only among right-wing talk-show hosts and benighted southerners—"I don't think we should lynch him," said Alabama Senator Richard Shelby of Trent Lott with exquisite obliviousness—Bush World has seen our official culture implicitly return to shopworn notions of the Good Negro. Naturally, the administration flaunts straitlaced Colin Powell and Condi Rice, but they are hardly the only

ones. Powell himself has two highly visible heirs: his actual son
Michael, the FCC Commissioner, and Brigadier General Vincent
Brooks, who conducted the Iraq war press conferences with the same
smooth self-containment that made Powell a star in the first Gulf War.
You even found similar figures being idolized by the showbiz left. For
all its busting of fifties stereotypes, Todd Haynes's *Far from Heaven*
served up the kind of fantastically noble black gardener that had
African-American audiences chortling five decades ago. He was played
by Dennis Haysbert, who brought a similar, uh, nobility to *24*'s
President David Palmer. Haysbert is a fine, deeply centered actor, but
you had to wonder what retrograde fantasy liberals were buying in
these celebrations of his superhuman decency and self-control. This
same fantasy was also found in the sports world, which spent Tyrone
Willingham's first year as Notre Dame football coach praising the way
he gave the Domers "dignity." As code words go, this ranked a step
above "articulate" and miles beyond "athleticism." Still, it hinted at the
decorum that white America expects of its African-American coaches,
especially at major white colleges. No black could hope to emulate
Bobby Knight's tempestuous run at the University of Indiana, when
he spent decades flinging chairs, abusing players, cursing referees,
roughing up opposing fans, and telling reporters to kiss his ass.
African-American coaches must be sober, self-controlled, and most
important, careful not to make fans, alumni, media folks, or university officials feel uncomfortable about race.

The most spectacular proof of this came in the winter of 2002,
when University of Arkansas basketball coach Nolan Richardson provided one of the Bush Era's most spectacular meltdowns. The lone
black coach at Fayetteville, Richardson had been one of the sport's
biggest names, having a .700 win-loss percentage, going to the NCAA
tournament thirteen times, and capturing the national title in 1994.
But during the 2001–2002 season, the team was playing badly. Despite
his long-term success, his coaching came under attack in and out of
the media, prompting talk that he should be fired. Richardson is no
smoothie like Willingham or the University of Kentucky's Tubby
Smith, and at a press conference defending his coaching, he suddenly

raised a subject that's taboo, especially in the state of Arkansas: "My great-great-grandfather came over on the ship. Not Nolan Richardson. I did not come over on that ship. So I expect to be treated a little bit different. Because I know for a fact that I do not play on the same level as the other coaches around this school play on. I know that. You know it. And people of my color know that. I haven't hit anyone. I haven't thrown any chairs. I haven't even asked the media to look upstairs and kiss my whatever. I haven't done any of that. I just want you to do your job and let me do my job. When I look across the people in this room, I see no one who looks like me, talks like me, or acts like me. Why don't you or the editors recruit like I am recruiting?"

Four days later, Richardson was bought out of his contract and let go. His words were widely thought to lack "dignity."

The Colin and Condi Show

Whites often accuse African-Americans of playing "the race card," but there are a great many cards in that particular deck and they can be played by people of all hues. A favorite card trick is to use high-profile blacks as alibis or beards to mask the underlying reality of power. Hollywood hailed it as a breakthrough when Denzel Washington and Halle Berry won Academy Awards on the same night in 2002—A CHANGE HAS COME, trumpeted *The Los Angeles Times*—momentarily disguising the fact that, for all its supposed liberalism, the film industry gives black people almost no clout. The same dynamic emerged in the Bush administration. Even as it displayed little interest in helping black America, its inner circle boasted two well-known African-American faces, Colin Powell and Condoleezza Rice, whose inclusion was designed to appeal across the political spectrum. Liberals are always happy to see blacks get jobs in any government and secretly hoped that Colin and Condi would be less doctrinaire than Bush and Cheney. Conservatives could point to them as an object lesson: If blacks just apply themselves, they can do as well as whites. Of course, symbolism isn't everything. One night on the sitcom *Whoopi*, Whoopi Goldberg's character, Mavis, was grumbling about Bush's policies to her uptight Republican brother, Courtney, who replied, "What about Colin and Condoleezza?"

"That's *two* hired," she snapped back. "What happened to the other 37 million of us?"

Although it would be wrong to suggest that Powell and Rice achieved their present stature purely through tokenism, it's impossible to discuss their careers without bringing up race—Bush didn't appoint them while wearing a blindfold. It took some political courage to give two African-Americans such important national-security posts; one of Al Gore's advisors told *Salon* that, had he won, his man would probably not have dared do the same thing. Of course, rather like Nixon making overtures to China, it's easier for Republicans to give power to African-Americans because they don't have to face the mudslinging of—Republicans. In fact, the real sustained courage has been shown by Powell and Rice, two smart, complex, driven individuals who have made their way in a white man's world hedged in by clichés and restrictions. These are not mediocrities like Clarence Thomas, a beneficiary of the very race preferences he would deny others. Judged by the distance they've traveled, good soldier Colin and Bach-playing Condi are the administration's two most impressive members—genuine Horatio Alger stories in an administration that specializes in fake populism. Where their privileged-son boss coasted into the White House, they fought their way up in a society where, as Rice has said, blacks had to be "twice as good" to achieve the same rewards as whites. Twice as self-disciplined, too: Just as Nolan Richardson couldn't get away with pulling a Bobby Knight, so no African-American cabinet member could mouth off at press conferences like Donald Rumsfeld (or Newt Gingrich, who spent 2003 angling to be Powell's replacement). Powell and Rice know this in their bones. Although they have spent their entire lives trying to confound racial categories, they understand that in modern America it is their fate—an exhausting one, I would think— to endure the Jackie Robinson Syndrome. They are judged not only as individuals but as racial icons. They have to uplift their race. Men like George Bush don't even need to uplift themselves.

As a former four-star general, strategist-cum-emcee of Operation

Desert Storm, and author of a bestselling autobiography, *My American Journey*, Secretary of State Powell is by far the better-known and more popular of the two, an enormously reassuring man who preceded Oprah as America's most trusted public figure. In the years after Gulf War I, he filled our culture's need both for a military hero (General Schwarzkopf was, to borrow a joke from *Catch-22*, too much a *Scheisskopf*) and for an African-American leader who wasn't always bringing up bad news. Whether talking about the war or his wife Alma's clinical depression, he came off as a grown-up in a world of childish politicians. This allowed him to become the first national political figure whose allure seemed to transcend his blackness. Whites liked being able to like him. Had he run against Al Gore or George Bush in the 2000 election, he may well have been elected, which is why he was able to pick his job in the Bush administration. Landing him was a feather in Dubya's cap—it boosted people's confidence at home and abroad—and became another groundbreaking role for Powell, who takes pride in having been the first African-American to occupy so many high offices. He was doubly happy to take this plum position because, as Bob Woodward has reported, he felt (mistakenly) that it would put him in a position to soften Bush's policies. Still, he is, on most matters, a moderate, not a liberal; he disputed any connection between discrimination against gays in the military and earlier discrimination against blacks. As the Clinton administration learned when he opposed their plans for intervening in both Sarajevo and Kosovo, Powell's memory of America's failure in Vietnam has made him, on military questions, profoundly conservative. He has spent years advising against U.S. intervention and insisting on the use of "overwhelming force" should American troops be deployed.

Before September 11, Powell's instinctive caution made him something of a wallflower in a Bush administration notorious for a foreign policy about as delicate as a Pamplona bull run. *Time* put him on the cover with the headline, WHERE HAVE YOU GONE, COLIN POWELL?, and he himself used to joke that he'd been put in the refrigerator. Even after the U.S. began bombing Afghanistan, public attention was focused on Rumsfeld, not the Secretary of State, who, behind the scenes, kept insisting that the War on Terror needed to be a multilateral effort. In *Bush at War*, we learn that after the terror attacks, Powell tried to slow down those eager to go after Iraq. Terming Cheney's acolytes "the Gestapo," he rolled his eyes about Rummy and Wolfowitz, asking then–Chairman of the Joint Chiefs of Staff Richard Shelton, "Can't you get these guys back in the box?"

It was Powell himself who would wind up getting boxed. But he was still needed. He'd proved during the first Gulf War that he was one of this country's most persuasive talkers—he earned big money giving motivational speeches after he retired from the military—and while Rumsfeld was busy becoming a sex symbol by bullying reporters in press conferences, Powell was busy explaining U.S. policy to the world. At one point he even turned up on MTV's *Be Heard: A Global Discussion with Colin Powell*, where a Norwegian girl beamingly asked how he felt about representing a country perceived as the Satan of world politics. Leaning back slightly in his dark suit, his military bearing a little softer than usual, he replied that he rejected her premise. He explained how the U.S. has fought for freedom all over the globe, how after World War II it didn't claim Japan or Germany but helped those countries build themselves back up. "The only land we ever asked for," he said, "was enough land to bury our dead." Boy, was the man good.

As he cruised through tougher-than-usual questions about AIDS and Israel, al-Qaeda and condoms—freaking out the nitwit right by endorsing their use—I could only admire his fabled steadiness. Faced with a world increasingly skeptical about the War on Terror, he'd become the Bush team's best and most plausible mouthpiece, not least because he's black. He was trusted by the American public—you didn't think he'd blow up the world to stop an "axis of evil" from doing the same thing—and by a Republican administration to whom he'd proven as loyal a company man as Tiger Woods to Nike. A classic bootstrapper, he exuded competence, decency, discretion. And he provided racial cover for an administration not exactly renowned for caring about people of color. Can you picture Dick Cheney trying to convince MTV viewers in Cairo, Jakarta, Islamabad, or the Bronx that the U.S. government has their best interests at heart?

Then again, Cheney and the Pentagon were calling the shots for Bush. Powell rode on their backs like a rhinoceros bird, whispering words about running too fast on dangerous ground. As John Newhouse notes in his book *Imperial America*, "Not since William Rogers, who served in the first Nixon administration"—under Henry Kissinger, you might say—"has a secretary of state been rolled over as often—or as routinely—as Powell." Such impotence must have been deeply frustrating, and one can only guess at the rage beneath that placid surface as he and the State Department were dissed at every turn by a bellicose administration that thinks diplomats weak, even cowardly. One of the memorable passages of *My American Journey* expresses his fury at the "anti-democratic disgrace" of the way America's leaders supplied manpower for the Vietnam War: "I can never forgive a leadership that said, in effect: These young men—poorer, less educated, less privilged—are expendable (someone described them as 'economic cannon fodder'), but the rest are too good to risk. I am angry that so many of the sons of the powerful and well placed and so many professional athletes (who were probably healthier than any of us) managed to wangle slots in Reserve and National Guard units." Publically, of course, he supported his president. When a senator publicly asked him about Dubya's inglorious stint in the National Guard, he snapped, "Don't go there."* I'd love to learn how Powell really felt about being ordered around, or called timid, by the arrogantly clucking collection of chicken hawks who have set the Bush years' foreign policy.

*Powell is no softy, as he shows in this rumination on the My Lai massacre in Vietnam: "I recall a phrase we used in the field, MAM, for military-age male. If a helo spotted a peasant in black pajamas who looked remotely suspicious, a possible MAM, the pilot would circle and fire in front of him. If he moved, his movement was judged evidence of hostile intent, and the next burst was not in front, but at him. Brutal? Maybe so. But an able batallion commander with whom I had served at Gelnhausen, Lieutenant Colonel Walter Pritchard, was killed by enemy sniper fire while observing MAMs from a helicopter. And Pritchard was only one of many. The kill-or-be-killed nature of combat tends to dull fine perceptions of right and wrong."

He swallowed his rage toward the Cheneyites. One of Powell's Rules is "Get mad, and get over it," an axiom that served him well on his triumphant arc from the son of Jamaican immigrant garment district workers in the Bronx, through the ROTC program at CCNY (no West Pointer, Colin), and up to the highest reaches of government. He had become a career soldier because in the late fifties (as today) the U.S. military was our most egalitarian institution; unlike pro sports or showbiz, escape routes that lure many young African-Americans, successful soldiering doesn't require extraordinary gifts, only extraordinary self-command. Powell would not have risen so high without a nuts-and-bolts mind—he loves working on cars—and a taste for authority that made him, as he puts it, "a soldier schooled in obedience." Part of that schooling was learning how to protect the people and institutions he was serving, whether overlooking allegations of massacre in Vietnam, playing along with Iran-Contra while doing nothing illegal himself, or, as Secretary of State, promoting an Iraq war he didn't believe in. It was this quality that led Harry Belafonte to assail his "house slave" mentality, a nasty shot that stung all the more because Powell surely felt it as the lowest of blows.

As a military man who has eluded being typecast as an ordinary politician, Powell has often been compared to Dwight Eisenhower. But he's probably closer to the elder George Bush, especially in his style of self-promotion. Although short on the vision thing, he's great at the networking thing—having mentors, making contacts, sending thoughtful notes, building up connections. He has enormous skill at manipulating the bureaucracy (where Rummy punches like Tyson, Colin has mastered Ali's rope-a-dope) and boosting his public image. As Woodward could attest, he's gifted at working the press—off the record, of course—and knows how to tell his story in a way that forgives his own trespasses, plays up his achievements, and makes him seem a modest, charming, down-to-earth fellow. Never one to go to the wall for any idea, he plays both sides of nearly every street—being both for and against war in Iraq, convincing both liberals and conservatives he's actually one of their own. Naturally, he was run over by Rummy and Cheney. Once he leaves the administration, it will be fascinating to see how he spins his time as Secretary of State, when he became renowned for two things: watching his rivals make the big decisions, including their inept ones about how to rebuild Iraq, and giving firm (but insincere) speeches to the U.N. about WMD. When it came time to negotiate Iraqi debt relief, the President sent former Secretary of State James Baker III, which Powell had to find humiliating. So humiliating that in early 2004, he turned up seemingly everywhere—talking on *Nightline*, writing in *Foreign Affairs*—to make the point that there's more to U.S. foreign policy (and his work as Secretary of State) than what one sees in the War on Terror. And to be fair, old State Department observers such as Newhouse say that he actually raised morale at the State Department by fighting harder for its prerogatives than anyone in two decades.

In the end, Powell may well be remembered less for what he accomplished than how he presented himself. Whether giving Gulf War briefings or talking to the planet's teens, he has mastered the art of addressing the public with a cool, TV-friendly eloquence (he talks rather than orates) that is strikingly race-neutral. Not for him the rolling biblical sentences of Dr. King or Barbara Jordan; not for him the snake-oil patter of J. C. Watts or Al Sharpton, in or out of his velour tracksuit. Powell's stolid calm offered the world the embodiment of an imaginary Bush administration far more sensible and humane than the real one. Each time I see him speak, I remember covering the 1988 and 1992 Democratic conventions when Jesse Jackson was trotted out to articulate the dreams and aspirations of a party about to betray them. As Jesse spoke, the crowd would whoop and weep and applaud—he had Atlanta's Omni swooning—and then once the euphoria died down, the convention would go about its business of nominating bloodless Michael Dukakis or DLC hero Bill Clinton. Jackson's power lived and died with his words. The party wanted his passion and biblical cadenzas, not him. (Lately, nobody takes black presidential candidates seriously, be it Al Sharpton dominating the Democratic debates with his quick wit or ultraconservative Alan Keyes flashing his loony smile and batting his flirtatious eyelashes as he brilliantly preaches Taliban-style policies for the Republican Party.)

Although black politicians' eloquence clearly appeals to a white America whose own politicians display all the passion of a limp Freedom Fry, it carries far less authority than its persuasiveness might lead you to think. Aside from Martin Luther King, who could mobilize millions as a power base, or Muhammad Ali, who casually radicalized a generation with his patter, the African-Americans who've gained national clout are those skillful at working behind closed doors, men like the late Commerce Secretary Ron Brown and silky presidential confidant (and corporate-board denizen) Vernon Jordan, who could have taught Ralph Ellison the financial upside of being an "invisible man." Like them, Powell is a master of whispers and will doubtless leave office hugely admired—one awaits his memoir dissociating himself from every mistake in Iraq. Yet it's one of the crushing ironies of his career that, at the peak of his official power as Secretary of State, he would have wielded his most influence had he chosen to resign and passed public judgment on ventures like the war in Iraq. Having spent a career working himself to an exalted position, he discovered he had no real authority, not even prime access to the President's ear. As cruel as it may be to say, he has reaped what his caution sowed. For Colin Powell is a man who might have been president—an epoch-making president—but, given an opening, chose against pursuing greatness.

For all Powell's gifts, he wound up being outpaced by another deft behind-the-scenes player, Condi Rice, who entered the administration with a far smaller reputation than the Secretary of State but emerged as the more original, and loyal, figure—the genuine good soldier. The forty-nine-year-old Rice is something new in our national life, an African-American woman at the epicenter of power who breaks all the familiar molds, starting with her unusual name: Condoleezza was her mother's riff on the Italian musical term *con dolcezza*—"with sweetness." But watching her in action, one is struck less by sweetness than rigid self-control. She has superb posture (ballet training) and wears nicely tailored clothes with vivid earrings. Defending President Bush on *Meet the Press* or *Charlie Rose*, she answers questions with a smile so tight you wonder what she's really thinking; even more than the preternaturally calm Powell, she radiates sublimation. Many liberals are shocked that a black woman could be a staunch Republican, yet her affiliation is not altogether baffling. It expresses both her buttoned-down temperament and family history. When she was a child, the Democrats who ran Jim Crow Alabama wouldn't let her father register to vote. Although she's more liberal on social issues than much of the Bush administration, she's very much in line with the Republicans' corporate agenda—hence that Chevron tanker named *The Condoleezza Rice.*

Rice's life has been a remarkable act of self-creation. The daughter of a Presbyterian minister, she was born in segregated Birmingham, Alabama, a city known for racist violence: Condi was friends with one of the four girls killed in its infamous 1963 Sunday-school bombing. She was brought up in a well-educated, middle-class family that preached cultivation and achievement, training her to hurdle social barriers—Condi became the first black to attend classes at Birmingham Southern Conservatory of Music. An academic whiz kid, she graduated from high school at sixteen, took her B.A. at nineteen, and, after earning her Ph.D. in international studies (under Madeleine Albright's father), wound up at Stanford University, where she eventually became its youngest-ever provost. Like Powell, she possesses enormous self-discipline, but, unlike him, she followed a daringly unconventional path. She was a competitive figure skater, plays classical piano—she's practically an inverse Slim Shady—and, having coauthored two books on the subject, is known for her expertise on Russia and the former Soviet Union. Having ventured along such an unlikely road, she would understand perfectly the impulses that activate the opera-singing brother in Richard Powers's *The Time of Our Singing,* a "colored" character who tries (futilely, it turns out) to create a personal destiny free of the socially imposed strictures of race. Rather like Virginia Postrel, Rice thinks that "being oneself" can be the result of choice, insisting in a radical 1999 speech, "We need a more inclusive notion of culture and identity—one that does not make culture a barrier, where the price of admission is origin and blood. I am one who believes that cultures can be adopted."

Rice's knowledge of foreign affairs got her into the administration of Bush I, where, as a protégé of National Security Advisor Brent Scowcroft, she became known for being realistic but firm, drawn (like so many conservatives) to a worship of clarity. "Doubt, ambiguity and caution are just not part of the picture," observed Nicholas Lemann in *The New Yorker*, noting that Rice "believes in belief as an all-conquering force." If her hard-line centrism made her the ideal National Security Advisor to juggle the competing mega-egos of Rummy, Powell, and Cheney, so did her private blend of gentility and sharpness, not unlike Barbara Bush's. Her manner must have proved comforting for a badly-informed commander-in-chief surrounded by alpha males who threatened to diminish his own glory, especially once his maternal communications guru, Karen Hughes, left the White House. Discreet, sports-mad, and as obsessed with working out as the President himself, Rice often weekends with the Bush family at Camp David, her manner helping this well-known momma's boy relax: "I can be totally unscripted or unrehearsed with Condi." Their personal connection has led to speculation that she is less a true foreign policy advisor than a presidential nursemaid (an insinuation that plays invidiously on the cliché of the "mammy"). This notion has been reinforced by her positive response to pre-9/11 intel, her inability to control the bickering between the State Department and Defense, and by reports that Cheney goes over her head whenever he wants to push a policy on the President. Bush's own words sometimes encourage the same impression. He once said that Rice's job is to bear the brunt of his fiery temper and keep him calm: "She's a very thorough person, constantly mother-henning me."

Such statements have led some people to doubt her real power. During the "yellowcake uranium" flap, it was casually bruited by insiders that, to protect Cheney's rear end, Rice might have to take the fall for those mistaken words in Bush's State of the Union speech. (No fool, she was busy pinning blame on the CIA. You could tell because she said, "I'm not blaming anyone here.") But Rice's fall was never in the cards, for her importance to the President goes well beyond the personal. As the sole high-profile woman in the administration, and African-American to boot, she's a perfect twofer, the ideal riposte to those who charge that Bush is running an old boys' club. Rice has said often she intends to leave office in 2004, and in an attempt to prove that the right is a big tent, her name was often put forward as a potential vice presidential nominee or Republican candidate for governor of California should Arnold grow weary of the splendors of Sacramento. In fact, the old boys would never really back her—no matter how many bullets she takes for Dubya.

Perhaps because the precise nature of her influence remains so elusive, many people, especially in the media, don't always take her altogether seriously. The editors of a favorable December 16, 2002, *Newsweek* cover story found so little to say about our National Security Advisor that they virtually turned her into the Condoleezza Rice Barbie, including a sidebar on her favorite accessories—Ferragamo pumps, Yves Saint Laurent No. 10 red lipstick, copies of *Vogue*, and Scott Turow novels. Rather than rashly accusing the magazine of sexism, I have been eagerly awaiting future sidebars on male officials that might tell me about Dick Cheney's fondness for Calvin Klein wifebeaters, Rummy's candy bowl filled with Viagra (for press conference use only), or John Ashcroft's Special Edition DVDs of *The Omega Code* and *Jonah: A Veggie Tales Movie.* Alas, they never seem to materialize. Erudite, elegant, politically calculating, Rice fits none of the clichés of African-American womanhood, stereotypes that remind us just how limited mainstream culture's concepts of black women actually are. Possessed of a manner no less distant for seeming affable, she exudes no sass (current version: Queen Latifah), no effusive warmth (Oprah Winfrey, who taught Bill Clinton a lot about feeling other people's pain), and no sex (Lil' Kim). You feel that if Condi ever tried to relax, her brain would go off like a car alarm.

There's no other woman quite like Rice in American public life. The private Condi remains so enigmatic that the satirical comic *The Boondocks* devoted several strips to its young heroes' scheme to find her a boyfriend: "Maybe if there was a man in the world who Condoleezza truly loved," Caesar says to Huey, "she wouldn't be so hellbent to destroy it." They call the White House to find out about her love life and are startled by what they hear.

Although *The Washington Post* pulled these strips because they were "personal"—fueling, it was whispered, unfounded rumors that the unmarried Rice is a lesbian—they underscored the fact that she is the most officially powerful black woman in our nation's history yet nobody quite knows what to make of her. We may not learn much more until she leaves this White House and (if it ever happens) throws her hat into the political arena. Then we'll finally discover if she's as straitlaced and as right-wing as she now appears. I won't be surprised if we never find out, for even more than Powell, Rice seems loath to expose herself to the prying and rigors of political campaigning—she was even touchy about testifying before the 9/11 Commission. Her whole life suggests a self-control that would be violated by the public openness of electoral politics.

It wasn't always so. When she was sixteen, she attended a class at the University of Denver in which a professor talked approvingly of William Shockley's theory of "dysgenics," which held that human evolution was heading backward because people with lower IQs (meaning black people) were reproducing faster than whites. Rice sprang from her seat and told the professor, "I'm the one who speaks French. I'm the one who plays Beethoven. I'm better at your culture than you are." One has been waiting for some moment nearly so grand during her time in the White House. Which is why, of all the key figures in the Bush administration, she remains the great mystery—and perhaps the great tragedy. One imagines her at the piano playing quietly, loyal to the culture she's adopted, whatever that may be.

Although most people I know, white and black, are unhappy with Powell and Rice for being so dull and dutiful—it's easy to have foolish fantasies that African-Americans, even Republican ones, might behave differently in power—these qualities make them the perfect expression of the Bush administration's idea of racial inclusiveness. Seeing Colin or Condi in action, I'm reminded of how I used to watch Sidney Poitier films and be flabbergasted that it was his destiny to have a career limited by the white culture's desperate need for an African-American actor who would wipe away the black man's mythic aura of threat and replace it with something safer and more palatable. He domesticated the African-American actor for white audiences— Denzel Washington and Morgan Freeman stand on his broad shoulders. In trying to describe Poitier's character in *Guess Who's Coming to Dinner*, James Baldwin called him a man for whom "the word 'prodigy' is simply ridiculously inadequate." The same might be said of Powell and Rice, but their other, considerable achievements will inevitably be overshadowed by the necessary symbolic feat of making it become acceptable for African-Americans to occupy the most delicate positions in the land. They are milestones in our nation's slow movement toward social justice.

The Matrix Evolutions

Out in the world, things do keep changing. It's now been years since Charles Barkley made his famous joke about how weird it is when the best rapper is white and the best golfer is black. These days, tired old conceptions of race are melting before our very eyes. Turn on the U.S. Open and the flamboyantly joyous Serena Williams doesn't simply dominate, she wears sexy skin-hugging catgirl outfits (like an Anna Kournikova who can play), talks freely of spending her dough, and never attempts to curry favor. Walk through a midwestern shopping mall and you'll see some thirteen-year-old wigga, pants riding low, calling his friend "dawg" and engaging in the elaborate street handshake of a latter-day White Negro. Switch to MTV and Outkast is doing an inside-out Beatles video for "Hey Ya!" Pick up Colson Whitehead's *John Henry Days* and you'll find a novel that wittily explores black authenticity in a fictional form indebted to Thomas Pynchon and Don DeLillo. Pop into Sofia Coppola's *Lost in Translation* and you'll see an American movie about Tokyo that takes more from Hong Kong's Wong Kar-Wai than from anyone in the seventies Hollywood generation her father was the leader of. Open *The New York Times* and you'll read how marketers are looking for "ethnically ambiguous" models, both for their look and their tacit, buying-breaks-all-barriers message. (Of course, even more cringe-worthy versions of this idea can still be found, as in the ghastly hit comedy *Bringing Down the House*, where Steve Martin's uptight WASP lawyer becomes loose and authentic after hooking up with an escaped convict, played by Queen Latifah.)

Nothing displays this racial and cultural crazy-quilt more profoundly than the *Matrix* trilogy—the most zeitgeisty pictures of the last decade. Its creators, the Wachowski brothers, have clearly been on a massive cultural shopping spree. An exuberant mulch of cyberpunk, kung fu movies, video games, comic books, hip-hop, Philip K. Dick novels, groovy trench coats, and operatic Hong Kong violence, these movies give us John Woo by way of Sergio Leone by way of Akira Kurosawa by way of Dashiell Hammett. The sinister figures are all white men in black suits, while aside from the hero Neo's love interest—a weathered butch chick with a mean leg-kick—the heroes are all black, Asian, or racially mixed. (Mr. Limbaugh, Ms. Coulter, start your engines.) The Wachowskis have nothing remotely intelligent to say about race, but in classic pop-culture terms this hardly matters. The trilogy's proud racial swirl underscores a huge shift in our cultural mythos. Trained on the fluid identities of video games, the Internet, and anime, today's mass audience—including white American teenagers—thinks that true cool is not black, white, or Asian. It's a hybrid of racial styles.

Of course, the fight for civil rights is a slow, messy thing, and only a dope would think that everyday racism has been overcome by media images. But pop culture is the closest thing Americans have to a common culture, and these media images *are* inexorably transforming the national psyche. This doesn't mean that we are near to having racial equality (although African-American life is freer and more prosperous than it has ever been). Nor does it mean that today's young white hip-hop fan wants to *be* black any more than Condi Rice wants to be white just because she plays Mozart, Yao Ming wants to be black because he plays in the NBA, or DMX wants to be Chinese because he's starred in kung fu movies with Jet Li. It doesn't even mean that white teenagers are suddenly going to buy R. Kelly CDs and blacks will line up for tickets to a Dave Matthews concert. But what it does mean is that racial and cultural styles have becomes far more fluid than they were even twenty years ago. If we can't select our skin color, we *can* decide on our own taste. Fueled by the market—which codifies styles and turns them into commodities available to anyone with money—identity becomes ever more a matter of choice. The combined effect of all these choices is to diminish the role of color as a fundamental marker of personal identity.

Early in *The Time of Our Singing*, a Jewish father tells his half-black son, "Race is only real if you freeze time." That is, race is a kind of fiction—powerful, yes; volatile, to be sure—but no more absolute for that. What we think of as black, white, Latino, or Asian seems solid only if we pretend that life does not go on and that things do not change, merge, blend into one another. That pretense remains strong in our political life, which seems trapped in a deep freeze. Meanwhile, in the popular culture that most Americans think of as more authentic than anything in our party politics, there's an obvious yearning to push beyond old categories and find newer, more personal methods of self-definition that encourage freeing the soul rather than straitjacketing it. James Baldwin offered a beautiful version of this idea in "The Devil Finds Work," his great essay about race in the movies: "Identity would seem to be the garment with which one covers the nakedness of the self, in which case, it is best that the garment be loose, a little like the robes of the desert, through which robes one's nakedness can always be felt, and sometimes, discerned. The trust in one's nakedness is all that gives one the power to change one's robes."

In writing these moving words, Baldwin wasn't referring only to race.

Gaysplosion, 2003

During his 2000 vice presidential debate with the dreary moralist Joe Lieberman, Dick Cheney was asked if gay and lesbian couples should have the same constitutional rights as heterosexual couples. No doubt because he has a lesbian daughter, Mary (who once worked as Coors's liaison to the gay community), Cheney replied, "People should be free to enter into any kind of relationship they want to enter into." As for gay marriage, he said, that should be left up to the individual states.

His answer suggested that, while a Bush administration would undoubtedly be less gay-friendly than its pseudo-friendly Democratic predecessor, their campaign felt confident enough in the Christian right's support that—even though Gary Bauer had famously compared gay marriage to terrorism in that year's Republican primaries—it didn't plan to make hay by attacking homosexuality. For the first two years of Bush's term this largely proved true. Granted, the President and his team made reassuring noises to the right that they didn't endorse "the homosexual lifestyle" (as if gay people cruised Des Moines at night terrorizing the locals while humming "YMCA"). Granted, the administration's education bill did contain a small, deliberately confusing provision that threatens to withhold funds from schools that won't let groups that discriminate against gays use their facilities. And granted, Bush praised Senator Rick Santorum for being "inclusive" after he had compared homosexuality to incest, polygamy, adultery, and "man on dog" action.* Yet in the main, the administration treated gay issues rather as it treated questions of race—it tried not to notice them. Gays and lesbians largely reciprocated, partly because their community had lost its activist edge and partly because they saw nothing good coming from dealing with Bush and his cohort.

But as Aunt Rose says in one of Grace Paley's stories, "Change is a fact of God, from which no one is immune." Despite the administration's attempts to keep gay issues on the back burner, they kept turning up in the unlikeliest places—like sports radio. If homosexuality

---

*The President's defense of Santorum, so different from his eagerness to deep-six Lott, suggests that open homophobia is more socially acceptable, at least among Republicans, than is open racism. Me, I kept wondering why nobody noticed that Santorum's use of the "man on child" and "man on dog" terminology suggests some acquaintance with the world of "adult" entertainment. Do *you* use these idioms? I don't. But pornographers do.

threatens anything more than traditional religion, it's the American ideal of masculinity. I've never heard so many nervous giggles and too-hearty guffaws than during that week in May 2002 when a *Details* article led to a volley of rumors that New York Mets catcher Mike Piazza was gay: ESPN Radio's normally suave Dan Patrick broke for a commercial saying, "Don't read *Details* magazine"—a quip that had his flunkies rupturing themselves with laughter. To my surprise, I found myself longing for the late Howard Cosell. Instead of sniggering or telling us that America just isn't ready for gay ballplayers, the old egomaniac would have insisted that it *should be*. I could just hear him championing anyone with the courage to do for gay athletes what was done for black Americans by "the great *Jackie Roosevelt Robinson* of the erstwhile *Brooklyn Dah*-juz."

Still, such moments proved ephemeral until the second half of 2003, when America suddenly hit a gay-lib trifecta. In late June, the U.S. Supreme Court overruled the Texas state law against sodomy in the case of *Lawrence* vs. *Texas*. In early August, the New Hampshire–based Reverend Gene Robinson was named the first openly gay bishop in the Episcopal Church's history, prompting talk of an international schism. By mid-November, when the Massachusetts Supreme Court ordered the legislature to rewrite the state's marriage laws to include gay couples, the changes had been coming so rapidly that everybody was slightly unnerved—even gays, who applauded their new rights but feared that same-sex marriage, itself a vexed question in that community, might become the fuse that would ignite a nasty political backlash. It had, after all, happened before. When in 1993 the Hawaii Supreme Court suggested that gays and lesbians had a right to marry in the state, this prompted an outcry that led thirty-four states to pass laws saying they would not recognize same-sex marriage. Just to be safe, the U.S. Congress then passed the Defense of Marriage Act—signed by William Jefferson Clinton—which declared those state laws constitutional.

Predictably, the courts' expansion of gay rights met with hysteria by those on the right, who like their outrage spiked with opportunism. Matthew D. Staver, who runs the right-wing Liberty Council, told *The*

New York Times Magazine that the Supreme Court decision would "awaken the sleeping giant" of conservative Americans and get them involved once again in the culture wars. Although these words were odd—we're to think the right has been *dozing*?—Staver sounded sober next to the Supreme Court's panting Antonin Scalia. The Justice may well be as charming as Hugh Grant in private, but put him on the bench, and he's like Goofy behind the steering wheel—smoke pours from his ears. His dissent in *Lawrence* vs. *Texas* claimed that the court "had taken sides in the culture war," seemingly oblivious that by dishing up the conservative term "culture war" he showed that he'd taken sides, too. After sneering at those who "coo" over gay rights, he accused the court of having "largely signed on to the so-called homosexual agenda." Scalia was not wrong to recognize that such an agenda exists—gay activists do actively seek to assure that gays and lesbians have the same rights and freedoms as everyone else. But from the Justice's tone, you might have thought that he was talking about some fiendish attempt by Barney Frank, Tony Kushner, and Andrew Sullivan to get into his robes.

Not everyone on the right was as overwrought. The libertarian magazine *Reason* ran articles supporting gay marriage on the grounds of individual freedom. Some more traditional conservatives and neocons also supported this right—not in the name of freedom (which they fear) but of morality. In *The New York Times*, David Brooks began a column with one of the weirdest things I've ever seen in that newspaper: "Anybody who has several sexual partners in a year," he wrote, "is committing spiritual suicide. He or she is ripping the veil from all that is private and delicate in oneself, and pulverizing it in an assembly line of selfish sensations. But marriage is the opposite." Reading such words, I couldn't decide whether Brooks really hates sex that much or whether he was merely establishing his anti-erotic bona fides so that his conservative readers would follow him to the next step: He argued that gay marriage is good because it leads gays to moral commitment and (this Brooks left implicit) puts monogamy in the place of the "promiscuity" that too many on the right associate with homosexual life. In a way, this echoed the argument made by Bishop Robinson, who noted that, at present, the church and the state are perfectly prepared to honor the marriage of a drunken couple who (like Britney Spears and her pal) impulsively wed on the Las Vegas Strip but disdain his own thirteen-year commitment to his partner, Mark Andrew.

Naturally, such sober arguments did little to sway conservative politicians. Always looking for an electoral edge—or is that wedge?—the Republicans leaped on the issue of gay marriage. Knowing that a majority of Americans oppose it, cat-dissecting Senate Majority Leader Bill Frist came out for a constitutional amendment calling for its ban, and President Bush—after making gestures toward remaining tolerantly neutral—told Diane Sawyer that "if necessary" he would "support a constitutional amendment which would honor marriage between a man and a woman, codify that." The necessity here was, of course, political—if the election proved close, Bush would fling down the gay card. In fact, I expected him to do precisely that shortly after the Democratic convention in Sodom-on-Charles. But his timetable got skewed when San Francisco began issuing same-sex marriage licenses on the orders of its newly elected mayor, Gavin Newsom, a dapper, straight, married Catholic whose canny political maneuver let him surpass English soccer star David Beckham as the world's top-ranking metrosexual.

San Francisco's photogenically joyous weddings were a tipping point. Facing angry pressure from its right-wing Christian base, which he'd been placating with empty biblical phrases for most of his term, Bush endorsed the amendment in February. But not happily. Even as his mouth pronounced heterosexual marriage the linchpin of civilization, his body seemed to be slinking out of the room. For a second, I almost felt bad for him. By all accounts Bush is not personally homophobic—he's even appointed gay aides to the White House staff. But after San Francisco, he was forced to twist himself into an ideological pretzel. He had to signal the Christian right that he condemns homosexuality, at the same time reassuring swing voters that he's actually tolerant, all while hiding the fact that he doesn't give a damn about the issue—warrior CEOs have bigger fish to fry. His bad faith is revealing. In backing the amendment and violating his professed states'-rights principles—"So at last it is official," wrote *The Economist,* "George Bush is in favour of unequal rights, big-government intrusiveness and federal power"—he again revealed that he will do whatever it takes to win the election, even if he's ashamed of, or opposed to, what that might be.

Like the Pledge of Allegiance ruckus raised by his father to suggest that Greek-named Michael Dukakis wasn't a real American, so the attack on gay marriage is a symbolic issue fat with political advantage. Even as it pleases the party's conservative base and lures moderates who agree with the Republican position, it puts Bush's opponents on the spot. You can understand why so many liberals—from the openly gay Congressman Frank to TalkingPointsMemo's Josh Marshall—wish the same-sex marriage battle would simply disappear as fast as the next Angelina Jolie picture. From the moment the country saw those shots of kissing male newlyweds, John Kerry had to do some fancy footwork. Mirroring Bush's own flip-flop, the Massachusetts senator was suddenly a born-again champion of states' rights. Although Democrats ought to support gay marriage, none of the party's leading lights will take such a position, because they see it not as a question of principle but a political trap: They can either support gay marriage, a surefire electoral loser, or disavow it, thereby disappointing the gays who are a key part of their base (although Kerry's vote against the Defense of Marriage Act should help him). In either case, they will still be assailed for supporting same-sex civil unions, which Karl Rove's minions will surely treat as the slippery slope to gay couples being showered with arborio rice on the steps of the National Cathedral.

Although gay rights is undoubtedly a usefully divisive issue for Republicans, as segregation once was for Democrats, it's worth pointing out that Bush and his party are both morally and historically on the wrong side. When the decisions came down in Texas and Massachusetts, I could only bow my head in respect for the courts and, more important, for the men and women who filed these suits. Challenging an antisodomy law in *Texas?* That's brave. They had the courage to fight for our constitutional rights—and all of them are all of ours—in an era when the right is hell-bent on limiting them. It speaks volumes about today's conservatives, especially the religious branch, that their proposed amendment banning gay marriage would be the first one ever to explicitly *diminish* the constitutional rights of any group of individuals. Which is to say, it is un-American.

It's also a red herring. Conservatives insist that same-sex marriages threaten the traditional sanctity of the male-female bond, but if there's a "crisis" in marriage, it has nothing whatsoever to do with gays and everything to do with a far vaster change: Traditional husband-wife unions no longer mean what they did even fifty years ago. As our astronomical divorce rate makes clear, modern life has radically transformed the nature of the heterosexual couple. Keeping gays from getting married won't alter *any* of this. Anyway, it's a lost cause. What really inspires the right's panic about gay rights is surely its frustrated awareness that open gay life is here to stay. In the thirty-five years since Stonewall, gay Americans have made breathtaking strides; our national attitudes toward homosexuality have changed more profoundly than Western attitudes had in the previous thousand years. Back in 1991 (according to *The New York Times*), 71 percent of people said gay sex was always wrong; eleven years later, that number had dropped to 53 percent, with a full third of Americans saying it wasn't wrong at all. And though a large majority of Americans still oppose gay marriage, 49 percent are in favor of civil unions. Such attitudes are being ratified in the workplace, where nine of the ten largest Fortune 500 companies—including Wal-Mart, hardly the guiding star of the liberal elite—have adopted antidiscrimination rules about gay employees.

Statistics may actually say less about how things have changed than the increasingly evident mainstreaming of gay culture. As more and more gays and lesbians come out, more and more straights suddenly realize they know and like someone who is gay or lesbian. When *The New York Times* asked if she and Dubya have gay friends, Laura Bush unhesitatingly replied, "Sure, of course. Everyone does." Even if they don't know them personally, Americans have grown used to seeing sympathetic gay characters on sitcoms (*Will and Grace*), daily talk shows starring Rosie and Ellen, Isaac Mizrahi selling clothes at Target, Showtime's *The L Word* (with its garrulous lesbians), or on Reality TV from *Boy Meets Boy* to *The Amazing Race 4*: When the gay couple Chip and Reichen won that last show's globe-trotting challenge, an emotional Chip declared, "We're Americans. We're teammates and we just happen to be gay." Such programs—part of what *Vanity Fair* called "TV's Gay Heatwave"—were not aimed at the coastal elite.

Oddly enough, the one gay program that *was*, HBO's six-hour adaptation of Kushner's *Angels in America*, made very little noise for its $60 million. (The whole run of *Tales of the City* couldn't have cost nearly that much.) Although pundits like Frank Rich expected the production to prove incendiary, the right barely noticed its progay stance and Reagan-bashing. Betraying their touchingly old-fashioned faith in the centrality of the broadcast networks—especially the demonic-liberal CBS—conservative culture warriors were far more exercised by that bad Ronald Reagan bio-film than anything Kushner and Mike Nichols had to offer. And in a way this was fitting, for *Angels in America* hit TV screens wreathed with claims of magnificence it couldn't deliver—sometimes being good just doesn't seem enough. Although I admire Kushner's visionary excess and desire to confront the seeming apocalypse of AIDS with an intimate spectacle that embraced everything—religious transcendence, casual sodomy in the park, Roy Cohn explaining why he's not a homosexual—I spent too much of the running time thinking all the wrong things. Why did a TV movie so expensive have such Ed Wood special effects? Why was Meryl Streep playing a rabbi? Why didn't Kushner's angels see a bit more of America?

Of course, to see the nationwide mainstreaming of gay culture, you need only look at all the straight young men with earrings, buff physiques, and other displays of "manscaping" that you never would have found two decades ago. Even as the right was quietly going after homosexuality, the culture was loudly, if briefly, embracing its style. The cultural flagship for this was, naturally, *Queer Eye for the Straight Guy*, which became a sensation not only because the quipping, sweet-natured Fab Five played everything bouncy but because they offered straight men a valuable service: They taught them how to look, and shop, in a consumer culture devoted to the surface of things. In the process, they offered the most innocuous possible version of gayness—one that made straight men better able to please their girl-friends—and part of the show's fun was seeing the heartfelt gratitude of both the guys and gals when a mossy pit turned into a clean bath-tub or baggy-ass jeans were replaced with well-tailored trousers. Such charm did exact a cost, however: Gay life was neutered. Although the hideously dressed fashion advisor Carson Kressley did flirt, the closest the Fab Five ever came to real sexuality was when they found a "snug-ger fit" condom in a guy's medicine cabinet, and Kressley said to him, "Oh, honey, so *sad* for you." If only they'd axed the boring culture guy and brought on somebody who could teach their clients how to be good in bed—the girlfriends would have been even more grateful.

The sexlessness of pop culture's conception of gayness was bril-liantly spoofed in one of the *The Daily Show*'s best-ever bits, Stephen Colbert's analysis of what he called 2003's "Gaysplosion." After explaining the fad ("Remember the Latin Music Explosion? It's just like that—but with sodomy"), he told Jon Stewart that he himself had become gay.

"You're *gay*?" asked Stewart, incredulous.

"Yep."

"You've had sex with men?"

"What? What are you talking about? I've seen those shows—*Queer Eye, Will and Grace.* There's no sex. Sex? How do they even *do* that? It makes no sense."

"Then how are you gay?"

"It's about being an *outsider.* Charming, helpful, catty—but *harm-less.* It's about showing straight people how to loosen up—you know, like the way black people taught us to dance."

Indeed, rather like Colin and Condi in the White House, the Fab Five became an almost perfect emblem of Bush World, for they offered the soothing, domesticated version of a subculture that main-stream America has been raised to find frightening or immoral. And like Colin and Condi, they serve a worthy goal: They are helping to open up our culture. America, they're putting their queer shoulders to the wheel. But in the process, they mask the extent to which there still is enormous homophobia even in the media—in a movie like *Bad*

Boys 2, every other word seemed to be "faggot." And they offer a vision of gay life that, for all its charm and consumerist "buysexuality" (as *New York*'s Simon Dumenco dubbed it), has been stripped of all the emotional depth, gender-twisting, and rebel audacity refined through thousands of years of being outsiders. You'll find no hint of the angry passion of Tony Kushner, the subversive activism that fired ACT UP, the wrenching losses of the AIDS epidemic, the hyperrefined aestheticism of Wilde or tawdry glamour of Liberace, the proud hedonism that saw sexual pleasure, freely shared and enjoyed, as a worthy human activity in and of itself. (For sex, you had to watch *The L Word*.) Instead, we get these five friendly gay men teaching some poor chump to trim his nose hair. Small wonder that their act grew thin fast. It wasn't *about* anything. You'd never know from watching *Queer Eye* or *Will and Grace* that many gay men dress badly, have messy apartments, and can't cook.

In such a cultural moment, it was perhaps fitting that gay and lesbian America's most beautifully giddy display of social rebellion should have turned out to be the profoundly conservative act of getting married. Such domesticity helps explain why so many gays who fight for the right to same-sex marriage don't like the idea of it any more than Justice Scalia, albeit for opposite reasons. They fear it may cheat gay life of its specialness, its splendor.

"The privilege of being gay," John Waters cheerfully told *Fresh Air*, "was that you didn't have to get married or have kids. Now Provincetown will be the new Niagara Falls, and gays have more babies than Catholics."

And to think the right finds this too *radical*.

The Devil Is a Woman

In *The Progress Paradox: How Life Gets Better While People Feel Worse*, Gregg Easterbrook notes that the movement toward real equality for women keeps showing encouraging gains. Having shrunk by 16 percent in the last two decades, the gap between men's and women's wages is the smallest in history. In 1995, 8 percent of the managers of

Fortune 500 companies were female; seven years later, the figure was 16 percent, with an ever-larger pool to choose from. While this change is far slower than we should desire, such progress still more than overcomes the ideological weight of the occasional antifeminist trend-piece in *The New York Times Magazine* about how a few upper-middle-class women are choosing to "opt out" of careers and go back to traditional wifely roles. So what if women can't have it all? That doesn't mean they want what they used to have, which is why our *ideas* of women are being pushed forward by what we see every day: Nancy Pelosi is now House Minority Leader, LPGA queen Annika Sorenstam feels free to compete with male golfers, and chopsocky chicks are now killing Bill and anybody else who messes with them.

The one place where women's rights are not advancing is in the Bush administration, which talks a great feminist game when it comes to women in Kandahar, but can barely be bothered to mention the subject in the United States. The White House is about as female-friendly as the Augusta National Golf Club. The President did dutifully drop some women in his cabinet (as ever, he knows his PR), but aside from Condi Rice, none has any significant power even in her own bailiwick. As Molly Ivins and Lou Dubose joked in *Bushwhacked*, "[T]ry to write a book about the influence labor secretary Elaine Chao has had on labor policy, or [now departed] EPA director Christine Todd Whitman on environmental policy." The administration's one big statement on women's issues came when Bush signed the bill banning so-called partial-birth abortions, a calculated sop to the Christian right that will let him avoid having to try to outlaw abortion altogether—one of the few wedge issues that can actually take down a Republican. (In his illuminating book *Bearing Right: How the Conservatives Won the Abortion War*, William Saletan notes Bush's skillful tiptoeing act, calling him "the perfect synthesis" of nineties social attitudes: "He was pro-life and pro-choice.") If anyone symbolizes the administration's old-school ideas of womanhood, it is Laura Bush, who has downscaled the First Lady position back into being a wife, a helpmeet, a lesser half. Although she's likable, her most enduring image is that polite grimace at Jacques Chirac's weasel-kiss gallantry. Put simply, Laura is less memorable for who she is, a thoroughly nice woman with nothing much to say, than for who she is not—Hillary Clinton, who wanders through Bush World like a feminist wraith.

It's only fitting that the recessive Laura should position herself as the anti-Hillary, for the junior senator from New York is herself a wedge issue, the living embodiment of the women's movement that the administration wants to ignore. This makes her the dominant female politician in the United States, a landmark towering over Rice, Pelosi, or fleeting Democratic presidential hopeful Carol Moseley Braun; these days, she matters far more than Al Gore or even her husband, who weekly grows smaller in history's rearview mirror. She is by far the most popular politician in the Democratic Party, and she knows it: When she hosted Iowa's Jefferson-Jackson Dinner in the autumn of 2003, overshadowing all the party's would-be nominees, she was getting her own cards in order for a 2008 run, using her drawing power to give the party a boost during a contentious campaign while also reminding everyone that the others sit in her shadow. Such is her impact that the race for the 2004 nomination was often seen through the scrim of her ambitions. Some pundits claimed that Wesley Clark was her stalking horse; others insisted that she secretly hoped the Democrats would go for Howard Dean, a nominee certain to be trounced, leaving the White House free for her four years hence; not a few thought that she was simply waiting, like a shark, for the Bush presidency to start bleeding. It was part of her myth that, should she have wanted it, the nomination would have been hers for the asking. She was, in Chris Matthews's words, "The Lady in Waiting, Madam Hillary."

Hillary comes to us buried beneath Pompeii-worthy layers of mythology—the real her is not easy to recognize. During the notorious 1992 Republican convention, even before she entered the White House, the right was already demonizing her, claiming (falsely, of course) that she'd once written a paper saying that children ought to be allowed to sue their parents for being asked to mow the lawn. If Bill Clinton was portrayed as the avatar of sixties amorality, Hillary was cast as that decade's ballbusting anima who had to be stopped in her tracks. When she was caustic, she was called "unfeminine"; when she was "feminine," she was accused of cynically faking it. No woman this side of Madonna has taken more grief for trying out different looks— each new hairdo was taken as further proof that she had no authentic inner core. Depending on the day and the observer, Hillary has been viewed as a self-promoter, a First Lady Macbeth, a sadly betrayed wife and perhaps an enabler, a latter-day Rosa Luxemburg, a victim of the right, a know-it-all who torpedoed national health care, a doting mother, a "bitch" (that from Newt Gingrich's mom), an internationally known champion of feminist causes, and an opportunistic hustler— snatching her Senate seat from honest-to-God New Yorkers. As Garry Wills made clear in a thoughtful, touching piece in *The New York Review of Books*, Clinton has been the flashpoint for all the hopes, fears, and hatreds inspired by the Women's Liberation Movement. With or without the "Rodham" standing defiantly in the middle of her name, she is at once herself—and more than herself.

One of the biggest surprises of the Bush years was the popular fascination that greeted the publication of her book *Living History*, which sold 1.7 million hardback copies and more than earned back its enormous $8 million advance. *Time* excerpted it, thousands queued to buy it, and ABC even got a ratings bonanza out of a Sunday night interview with Barbara Walters, "Hillary Clinton's Journey: Public, Private, Personal." While the show helped viewers fondly recall those heady days when the Oval Office became the Oral Office, it also let Clinton play her assigned role in a modern American ritual. She shared her pain with millions to hawk her book and clear the air for her later campaigns—nobody could say she hadn't put in hard time talking about Monica. Doing this must have been weird, for Lewinsky was both the source of her deepest personal humiliation and, for this very reason, her source of redemption. Hillary is smart enough to know that nothing boosted her image more than her exemplary behavior during the adultery/impeachment hullabaloo. It humanized her and underscored her loyalty: She, who'd once dismissively said she wasn't Tammy "Stand by Your Man" Wynette, had stood by her straying man despite personal pain and public embarrassment. Near the end of the hourlong interview, which raised countless unasked questions—why would a woman who terms herself "very private" choose to write a multimillion-dollar memoir and then promote it on TV?—Walters posed the one she thought all of America wanted answered. Why *had* Hillary stood by her man?

The answer revealed Hillary in all her politicized splendor. After carefully explaining that Bill was her husband and that only she and Chelsea were entitled to judge his private behavior—the obligatory "personal" stuff—she got back on message: "He was also my president and I thought he'd done a great job." Never let it be said that this woman doesn't keep her eye on the ball. Although she's smart and uncommonly verbal, she goes through her talking points as robotically as George W. Bush. *Living History* is almost violently dull because of its near-total impersonality once Hillary hits adult life. She doesn't just write in the stillborn jargon of the cautious politician, she systematically suppresses all the sarcasm, profanity, and guffawing wit that her friends say she shows in private. She seems not to grasp that, for many of us, her rants and gaffes are her finest moments.

One does understand her caution. Although *Living History*'s high sales confirmed her popularity, she's an even more polarizing figure than President Bush because she feels no qualms about poaching in the traditional male preserve of national politics. She's the leading edge of that first generation of women for whom becoming president is more than a daydream, and living in the White House clearly increased her sense of possibility. Rather like Bobby Kennedy after his brother's assassination, she has the bearing of one whose destiny is to seek the presidency. (She even followed Bobby's carpetbagging move to New York.) While Hillary's edge puts millions of voters off, that's no certain barrier to electoral success. As Margaret Thatcher demonstrated, steeliness may help a woman achieve power, although it must be said that Dame Maggie had far sturdier and bolder ideological principles. Like her husband, Hillary has ideals that tend to sway like an anemone. One of the most telling moments in the congressional debate on the Iraq War Resolution was hearing her lucidly lay out all the reasons why one should vote No—then watching her vote Yes. A calculated move. She knows the only way a woman Democrat has a prayer of becoming president is if the world sees her hawk's talons. That's why she went to Afghanistan and Iraq, declared the capture of Saddam "terrific," and sought a seat on the Senate Armed Services Committee, although she would sooner have a fling with Dick Cheney than admit to any such motives. As Elizabeth Kolbert pointed out in a perceptive *New Yorker* profile, Clinton is not one who admits to any kind of personal ambition—she's always working, we're to believe, for the universal good. It has always been one of the most unattractive features of the Clintons that they tend to forgive their own sins because they feel sure that, in the end, they are justified by all the good they are doing. Hillary may have this disease even more than her husband. A guy who likes a good time, Bill doesn't sanctimoniously lecture us about materialism on his way to an eight-million-buck payday. Hillary does, giving off a sour whiff of the Social Services bureaucrat who always knows what's best for everybody.

If her politics are disappointing to those who would make her a feminist icon, her ambitions are sweet agony for the right, which has spent a dozen years vilifying her not for what she actually is—a pragmatic, mainstream Democrat who's all about winning office—but for being the sort of dangerous radical who wants to turn abortion and lesbianism into sacraments. Sure, she backed NAFTA, welfare reform, and war in Iraq. No matter. Conservatives still need to believe that, in some secret Soviet soul that she's hiding from the public, she's channeling the politics of mid-sixties Berkeley. In the loopy intensity of such a fantasy, one feels a hysterical reaction against the very image of womanhood she represents—brainy, self-assured, challenging in its presumption of equality. Writing about that interview with Walters, *Washington Post* TV critic Tom Shales called Clinton "chillingly chilly" and suggested that "she may have emotions like ordinary people" but is "scarily proficient at suppressing them." Much of the hostility toward Hillary has nothing to do with her values or her work or even her power. It has to do with her style, which in its way is as controlled as Condi Rice's or Martha Stewart's. ("Martha is a friend of mine," she said when Stewart first got in legal trouble, "and I'm very sorry for what she's going through now. . . . I think there's more at work than meets the eye.") Hillary is reckoned cold, hard, brittle—unfeminine—in a culture that still prefers even its ass-kicking babes to be likable. We want Jennifer Garner to weep copiously in every episode of *Alias*, *Kill Bill*'s Uma Thurman to be a lioness defending the life of her daughter, and Charlie's Angels to be silly, sexy girls. We want the tireless hugging of Oprah, who wears her inner life and battered history like a tiara.

Hillary does none of this, which is all the more noticeable because she's married to a man famous for his open-armed charm. Where he's personal, she's impersonal; where he feeds on inspiration, she thrives on perspiration. Their differences meant that she joined Yoko Ono, Imelda Marcos, and Nancy Reagan in the line of supposed devil-women who so often take the heat that their more-powerful husbands actually deserve—to this day, Bill Clinton's admirers blame his bad decisions on her. The last First Lady to get such grief was Reagan, who was mocked for her coldness, taste for free clothes, and addiction to the paranormal. (It later emerged that on many issues, like abortion, she offered far wiser counsel than the ideologues and hatchetmen who worked for her husband.) Hillary, detractors said, was too headstrong, too ideological. Perhaps this is true, but one wonders exactly how it came to pass that a president could be bullied in this way—especially by a woman who adores him. For when it comes to her marriage, Hillary clearly thinks with her heart. When it comes to the outside world, however, she's precisely the opposite—especially in her political life, where she admirably goes about doing exactly what needs to be done every single day. Traumatized by her experience of the media during his presidential period, she views reporters with open mistrust and takes no delight in baring her private self for the public. While these qualities are generally admired in a man—think of all the plaudits for Bush's "discipline," Rumsfeld's "tough-mindedness," Cheney's "laconic" Wyoming style—they are thought to make a woman *controlling*.

Of course, what finally matters is who's controlling whom, and to what end. At the moment control rests in the hands of a president, a party, and an ideology uninterested in, and often hostile to, the aspirations of millions of people—black and white, straight and gay, male and female—who believe that America should be a land where people are free to make and remake themselves, to don whatever robes of identity they choose. In the acclaimed speech the young Hillary Rodham gave at Wellesley on her graduation day in 1969—where she openly disagreed with the official graduation speaker, Senator Edward Brooke—she summoned up some of the idealism of that generation by saying, "Every protest, every dissent, whether it's an individual academic paper or Founder's parking lot demonstration, is unabashedly an attempt to forge an identity in this particular age."

Approvingly quoting these lines at the end of his essay, Wills adds, "For some, that is still a frightening prospect." The Bush administration is among that number and Hillary Clinton is adamantly not. Which is why I wish that the stars could be so aligned that Hillary would run against George W. Bush. It's the natural payoff to two presidencies built on opposition. Set these two polarizing figures battling over the future of America, and if the magnetic charge doesn't cause power lines to explode all over Bush World, it might just spark something new. At the very least, watching those two go head-to-head would make *Celebrity Boxing* look like nothing.

Escape from Bush World

Nobody has ever lived without daydreams.

—ERNST BLOCH

In *The Natural: The Misunderstood Presidency of Bill Clinton,* Joe Klein tells the story of Newt Gingrich, then Speaker of the House, listening to a pre-Monica State of the Union speech. As Bill Clinton effortlessly dominates the chamber, Newt finds himself thinking, "We're dead. There's no way we're going to beat this guy."

Tens of millions of Americans have the same dreadful feeling about George W. Bush, albeit with one slight difference. They think they actually *did* beat him in the 2000 election—and he still wound up becoming president. Ever since, he's seemingly been favored by some capricious god. Just when his class-war policies made him look like a one-term wonder, September 11 turned him into a wartime leader; just when the Iraq adventure's popularity was in a $87 billion free fall, Coalition forces caught Saddam Hussein; just when he looked to be saddled with a calamitous economic record, the GDP's growth rate took a leap that made the turnaround appear far more dramatic than it actually was for ordinary citizens. Could capturing Osama be far behind?

As if that weren't enough, the ADD-stricken media have given him the easy ride any president would covet. Not only did they dutifully broadcast his photo ops and play along with scripted press conferences, they quickly lost interest in scandals such as the White House's vengeful outing of CIA operative Valerie Plame. Even when Enron became an international watchword for corporate crookedness, Bush's close (and denied) personal ties to its head, Kenneth Lay, received vastly less coverage than had Hillary Clinton's $100,000 stock market killing. If you wonder why so many people wrote books calling Bush a liar, it's partly because big media, especially television, proved so lax about scrutinizing the Orwellian abyss between the administration's rhetoric ("Healthy Forest Initiative") and what it was actually doing—letting big timber companies (read: contributors) harvest old-growth trees in national forests. When an obviously campaigning Bush visited a black New Orleans church in early 2004 to resurrect long-dead talk about "faith-based initiatives," his speech prompted one comically named CNN anchor, a sheep in Wolf's clothing, to bleat that these were programs the President "cares deeply about." By that point, even Dubya's supporters had long since conceded that he didn't give a damn about them.

It is easy to make the case that Bush has done a bad job, even if you consider his supposed achievements. True, he ousted the Taliban, but after September 11, any president would have done that—and worked harder to rebuild Afghanistan. True, he toppled Saddam, but any president could have done that—though most wouldn't have—and done so without misleading the public about the reasons, alienating the world with his arrogance, and fouling up the reconstruction through slipshod planning. True, the economy recorded hopeful-sounding growth at the end of 2003, but any president could wring a couple of good turn-around quarters from a trillion-dollar tax cut—and most wouldn't have given billions in tax relief to those who ship jobs to Bangalore and Chihuahua while dinky-tax-break American workers go unemployed.

Any president would have enjoyed deep public support after the terror attacks. But who else would have used his newfound authority to tear apart national unity, ram through Darwinian policies that widened the divide between Winners and Losers, and play the Disquieting American so rudely that he would offend even sympathetic allies? One job of a president is to pull Americans together, a task all the more important when mass culture is one gigantic centrifuge that sends us flying in all directions. Instead, Bush has made ours a nastier, angrier, more fragmented society, and done so with an inviolate self-righteousness. As Norman Mailer put it one night on *Charlie Rose*: "He's never sorry for what he's done."

Such a record might leave you baffled about why his approval ratings still hover around 50 percent. I often am. Yet, if you view things unemotionally, the reasons aren't altogether mysterious. For starters, Bush plays to his strengths. Once it was pushed in his face, he saw the true danger of Islamic fascism, and, far more surely than any of his Democrat rivals, grasped that the American psyche would be dominated by the desire for protection—the terror attacks colonized our unconscious. The nation wanted action, and Bush gave it to them, declaring a War on Terror, announcing a doctrine of preemption, and swatting aside two undeniably malignant regimes. He showed the same willingness to act aggressively in domestic affairs, pushing through two huge tax cuts, a Medicare plan and an education-reform package, and then proposed a sweeping policy of immigration reform that preempted (that word again) two better bipartisan proposals already in Congress that he hadn't bothered to fight for. You can argue that his polices are wrong: They are. You can argue that they blatantly serve the corporate agenda: They do. You can argue that he presented them dishonestly: He did. You can argue that they prove he is not really a conservative, uses incumbency to buy votes, and keeps copying Clinton's sly habit of filching the other party's winning issues.

But no matter how you argue it, there's no denying that Bush has gotten things done. He's made a far bigger mark than either his father or Bill Clinton. Like Ronald Reagan before him, he has given America guns and butter—and asked for no sacrifice in return. Maxing out the country's credit cards, he has run up record-smashing deficits whose real effect won't be felt until long after his reelection campaign. They are strewn across our future like land mines. The majority of Americans have gone along, for as Clinton observed, "When people feel uncertain, they'd rather have someone strong and wrong than weak and right." Especially when the landmines haven't yet started to explode. Bush's record has been wretched on most issues, yet the country is not a crumbling disaster area. For most of us, the United States remains a glorious place to live— our big-box culture delivers the goods.

Beyond this, Bush is an extremely canny politician (canny enough to hire Karl Rove, anyway) who is adroit at wearing different public faces to suit changing occasions. He was the wise CEO when pushing his unsound fiscal policy, the "compassionate conservative" when adding to Medicare, Prince Hal when warning us about all the WMDs in Iraq. He even played Dubya the Dope whenever necessary. His handlers had spent years insisting that Bush was on top of everything in his domain, but during the "yellowcake" fracas and the Valerie Plame scandal, all that changed. Questioned about these things, the President acted as if he wasn't really sure what was going on in his own White House: He's always just as dumb as he needs to be.

"Cynicism leaves no monuments," he told Ohio State University grads in 2002, but failed to add that it *does* run political campaigns. Having lost the popular vote the first time around, he and Rove know electoral college arithmetic the way John Ashcroft knows his *Osmonds' Songbook*. That's why, in the run-up to the 2004 election, the President belatedly began showing some interest in what was going on in the country. Suddenly the man got *active*, pandering to his base and swing voters. Placating the Christian right, he proposed a $1.5 billion program to promote marriage, which was like carrying coals to Las Vegas. Wooing Latinos, he came up with that immigration plan.* Proving his concern for consumers, the feds clamped down on Ephedra and started pretending to care about mad cow disease. To show his commitment to racial equality, he stopped in Atlanta on his way to a $2,000-a-plate fundraiser and placed a wreath in honor of the seventy-fifth anniversary of Martin Luther King's birth; to show his commitment to the racist right, he far more quietly used the Senate recess to appoint dodgy Charles Pickering Sr. to a federal judgeship, infuriating black Americans. It's good to be king.

Because his father was chided for lacking the vision thing, he sought to wrap himself in Big Ideas, including outer-space travel, which presidents often trot out in hopes of getting a JFK-style PR boost from its

---

*Although many conservatives were furious at this proposal (which will never get through the Congress), the White House knew the right had nobody else to vote for. The potential beneficiary here was, as usual, Bush's corporate base, which adores the idea of a huge pool of cheap, easily controlled labor. You could just see the owners of Denny's and Holiday Inn high-fiving.

rocketry. When he announced his desire for missions to the moon and Mars (an unpopular idea he quickly stopped mentioning), Bush could hardly have been a less persuasive visionary. He referred to NASA astronauts as "space entrepreneurs"—the latter word being, it seems, his highest accolade. He offered cost estimates that an expert described as "nonsense, if not outright dishonesty," and, in praising American boldness, declared that "the desire to explore and understand is part of our character." This from a notoriously incurious man who hates leaving home, especially without his own pillow.

Watching Bush do all this—while also fattening up his $200 million war chest—made it easier than ever to dislike him personally. Like Margaret Thatcher during her heyday, he is a whetstone against which untold millions sharpen their rage and alienation. Yet it's foolish to fixate purely on the man himself. If George W. Bush vanished tomorrow, beamed up by aliens or felled by a killer pretzel, everything genuinely awful about his presidency would still be in place. Oil entrepreneur Dick Cheney would be president. (Just typing these words makes my blood run cold.) Pest-control entrepreneur Tom DeLay would still be running the House. Medical entrepreneur Dr. Bill Frist would still be running the Senate, where sensible conservatives like Nebraska's Chuck Hagel currently enjoy less favor than morality entrepreneur Rick Santorum. The Republican Party would still be in the thrall of corporations and born-again right-wingers. Fox News would still be unbalanced, Winners still lording it over Losers, and our foreign policy militarists would still be thinking that "empire" is not such an unpleasant word after all. Put simply, Bush World is not simply the emanation of one sore winner. It's a collection of ideas, values, symbols, and policies that should be opposed and defeated. While hating Bush and his right-wing cronies does fuel a sense of opposition, personalizing the anger is bad politics. "Their job is to beat us," insists Clinton. "Our job is to beat them. If they come at us with a deal we think is a scam, we ought to be smart enough to expose it. So I'm not mad at them. That's their job."

But our job goes beyond just defeating Bush in 2004. After all, Clinton unseated his father in 1992, and a decade later, the right wing had more power than ever. That's why we must reverse the great historical flip-flop in our political iconography. Forty years ago, the left represented the future—it crackled with pleasurable possibility—while the right symbolized the repressive past. Change means movement, said the great organizer Saul Alinsky, and during the sixties, the political counterculture had the fire to get things moving. Although many of its grandest ideas never bore fruit—they were blighted by naïveté, Vietnam, and the triumph of political hacks—America is a better place for the Civil Rights Movement, the War on Poverty, Women's Liberation, Gay Liberation, the Peace Movement, and all the new expressive freedoms, from more honest speech to sexual liberation.

But this victory planted the seeds of defeat. As the sixties' changes became incorporated into the larger society, the left entered a period of intellectual stagnation, complacency, and corruption. Many of its best minds were drawn into the universities, where, caught in the jargon-laden briar patch of academic prose, they cut themselves off from the larger society. Counterculture publications, from *Rolling Stone* to the average "alternative" newspaper, grew more concerned with profits than causes, becoming object lessons in the mainstream's power to co-opt outsiders. And old-fashioned liberals, who'd been mocked for their timidity during the sixties, lost their confidence. Although various individual constituencies flourished—or at least established strong lobbying groups—the left as a whole did not. The hard left guttered, then all but vanished, especially after communism's fall; freaked out by McGovern's crushing loss in 1972, the Democrats refashioned themselves as a centrist, corporate party perched atop a dwindling base of support. Pop culture once fueled the passion for progressive causes, but as Danny Goldberg argues in *Dispatches from the Culture Wars: How the Left Lost Teen Spirit*, the left grew hopelessly out of touch with the young. It fell prey to a prissy liberal moralism that reached its nadir in the 2000 presidential campaign, when candidates Gore and Lieberman threatened the film, movie, and video-game industries with legal action if they didn't clean up their acts.

Today, it's the right that offers freedom, fun, and authenticity. Four decades after Goldwater's debacle against LBJ, it doesn't merely control the federal government but offers a vision of America as sleekly High Concept as *Pirates of the Caribbean*. Skillful at marketing the past as the future, it stands for lower taxes, freedom from government interference (except in your personal life), private ownership of almost everything, and a military so powerful that we can crush any continent that defies us. The sixties have been stood on their head: Even as the Bush administration spends and spends, insisting that Americans can have it all (why, buying that SUV is good for the country), lefties are stuck playing the nattering scold. They talk of rolling back tax cuts and fret over the deficit. (One bitter irony of Clinton balancing the budget is that it left Bush free to prosper by busting it.) The transformation may be even more striking in foreign policy. In the wake of September 11, the right claims it wants to free oppressed people, while the left is too often caught saying that it's a mistake to oust a monster like Saddam. Who would have believed that possible in 1968?

Not everyone on the right agrees on every single issue (libertarians and the Christian right have radically different attitudes toward drugs and homosexuality), nor have the Republicans practiced the same conservatism when in power as they preached when they were out of it. Far from shrinking the government, the Bush administration has done more to increase it than any president since LBJ. No matter. Consistency is for amateurs. The bottom line is that conservatives have become far better than liberals at saying, "We're right." Who was the last Democrat who could say this with absolute conviction: Barbara Jordan? Claiming to defend the idea of right and wrong, conservatism has given us William Bennett's *Book of Virtues*, Christian book-censors (catch *that*, Holden Caulfield), and politicians who assailed the private immorality of unwed mothers, poor drug addicts, and the philandering Clinton. Although these claims to virtue were hypocritical— conservatives didn't go crazy over Newt's infidelity, Rush's addiction to illegal drugs, or Bennett's gambling jones—they tapped into Americans' deep belief in personal responsibility, making it seem that the squishy left always blamed everything from street crime to unwanted children on society as a whole. Focusing on personal morality, they effectively hijacked and privatized "character," which allowed them to ignore incomparably larger issues of public morality—for example, CEOs who protect their own stock options while letting pension plans collapse for thousands of workers. And the left did not make them pay for this. It failed to create its own book of virtues that includes compassion for the poor, fairness to workers, honesty toward the public. Who cares if Dubya only has sex with Laura if he's in bed with every CEO in the country?

Although the right officially believes in "traditional" American values, it's no more sentimental about the past than an L.A. real-estate baron. It actually wants radical change—appointing judges who will overturn liberal decisions, redrawing congressional districts to ensure Republican victories, seeking to change long-standing Senate rules so that the Democratic minority has fewer ways of slowing legislation, appointing K Street lobbyists with conservative credentials, and of course pushing untrammeled capitalism, the most revolutionary force on the planet. Meanwhile, the left has been downright Proustian, hoping to recapture a past that is forever gone. You saw this on the hard left, where too many progressives kept trying to paint a Hitler mustache on Bush or inflate cheap attacks on the Dixie Chicks into a new McCarthyism; one sensed a perverse nostalgia for the bad old days when the left held the moral high ground. You saw the same thing in the Democratic Party faithful, who kept refighting the 2000 election—Hey, folks, it's over, and we lost—and even now remains bewitched by a Clinton presidency that looks increasingly irrelevant, more an interregnum than an accession to power. The most talented Democratic politician in half a century, he didn't merely blow his second term by getting a blow job, he left (aside from his wife) no enduring legacy in the White House, Congress, or Democratic Party. To be fair, Clinton Nostalgia is not wholly inexplicable, for he was a larger-than-life character (and marvelous performer) who grasped the importance of presenting himself as a fresh kind of Democrat, steering a third way between traditional liberalism and Reaganite reaction. He was canny enough to know that, in an easily bored media culture where myths can become threadbare in a few months, a politician must obey Ezra Pound's injunction to "make it new." Think of all those different George Bushes.

During the seemingly endless Democratic campaign, when even the C-SPAN cameras seemed to be yawning, I kept being struck by the way honest, doomed Richard Gephardt talked about the New Deal as if most voters had been around to hear Roosevelt's Fireside Chats. Sure, those programs are important, but they now feel as old as the Civil War; after all, a forty-year-old didn't vote for the first time until Reagan faced Mondale in 1984, more than half a century after FDR's first election. But Gephardt wasn't the only one with one foot in a time capsule. The value of newness was lost on all the Democratic candidates except Vermont's Howard Dean, the onetime wrestler (Jon Stewart dubbed him "Garp") who became the first candidate to lambaste Bush's policies head-on and attack his fellow Democrats for capitulation. Dean escaped the axiom underscored by the debate over invading Iraq: *Republicans lie, Democrats weasel.* Where Bush told the public things that simply weren't true to justify a war he wanted to fight, most Democrats adopted "nuanced" positions that looked (and still look) evasive. Kerry voted *for* the war resolution, then suggested he'd been duped; he was prone to saying things like "I actually did vote for the $87 billion before I voted against it." Although Dean's tough-guy antiwar stance propelled him to the head of the pack, what made his campaign fascinating was the way he put it together. By now, everybody knows how he raised funds on the Internet (an heir of McGovern's pioneering direct-mail solicitations) and used the web's connectivity to create a new kind of community. Supporters felt part of a grassroots movement that they could join with a mouse click. They could read that day's campaign materials without the media "filter" (as politicians now call people like me), share their thoughts online, and send money—millions!—when their candidate needed an infusion. Most important, perhaps, they learned how to hook up with like-minded people. Following his *Yearrgggh* concession speech after the Iowa caucuses, they could even write Dean to remind him, as one did, that he had to be careful about his antics because "appearances count." Dean insisted that his candidacy was about empowering other people—*Time*'s Joe Klein said that he had "the most powerful 'you' in American politics"—and his campaign's meet-ups energized supporters by helping them escape their sense of isolation. His presidential run became the political equivalent of a flashmob. And it led to another: Fleeing Dean, Democratic voters suddenly embraced Kerry, a plausible if uninspiring candidate who, in a matter of six weeks, went from being a dead dog to the party's Rin Tin Tin.

Dean tapped into some of the same communal energy as Moveon.org, the web-based liberal group that raised money, let its members vote on the group's direction, and even staged a huge contest in which 3,000 different people and groups created their own anti-Bush commercial. (CBS refused to air the winner during the Super Bowl, evidently hoping to keep Janet Jackson, breweries, and the makers of Levitra unsullied by politics.) Far more than Dean's actual policies, which showed him to be a snappish centrist disguised as a bellowing reformer, his groundbreaking use of new technology did something the Democrats hadn't done in eons. Using the Internet, it tapped into the great pop-culture form of the moment. Dean's kids felt they were part of a cause whose best days were ahead rather than already gone. Small wonder Al Gore rushed to give him a kiss-of-death endorsement. An eternal wannabe, the now-braying Al obviously fantasized about making that same kind of rolled-up-sleeves presidential run. (Only the tone-deaf Gore would have tried to run against special interests as a sitting vice president who'd been in office for eight years.) He would have been wiser to study earnest but sharp John Edwards, something of a Tarheel Tony Blair, whose stirring "two Americas" speech brought to life the populism that had been stillborn in Gore's 2000 campaign. Better than anyone, Edwards made it clear that Bush's great weakness was the public sense that he was in the pocket of the powerful. It was a shame he lacked the killer instinct—or even a second speech.

A large field of presidential hopefuls often shrinks each of them, and watching the large 2004 crop, I forced myself to think back to 1992, when Bill Clinton sometimes seemed no more impressive than Paul Tsongas. Yet even knowing this, I sometimes fantasized about the ideal Frankenstein candidate one could stitch together from the contenders. He would have the passion of Dean, the good looks and trial-lawyer eloquence of Edwards, the physical stature and gravitas of Kerry, the brains and record of Wesley Clark, and the left-wing dreams of Kucinich—topped off by the sharp wit, and incomparable hairdo, of Al Sharpton. But such daydreams all too easily turned into nightmares: I kept picturing Kerry's yard-long face atop Dean's ham of a neck, framed by Kucinich's hairline and Wesley Clark's sweaters, and talking about Tawana Brawley with all the moral smugness of Joe Lieberman. The scariest thing was, I thought even this second jerry-built Democrat would be a better president than George W. Bush. And I surely wouldn't have been the only one.

By late 2002, the President had enraged enough people that he actually did something that seemed almost impossible: He gave the left a jump start. 2003 became The Year of Living Angrily. Simply hating Bush could pass as a political program, which turned the Democratic debates themselves into a Bush-bashing chorale. The first time the stolid Gephardt called Dubya "a miserable failure," both he and the audience got so keyed up that he kept repeating the phrase over and over. But all that changed in the Iowa caucuses, when anger was not enough. Suddenly, 2004 had become The Year of Beating Bush. After years of sneering at the Democratic Party, even Michael Moore got into the act. Not caring that he savaged the Kosovo bombing in *Bowling for Columbine*, he turned his ballcap into a placard for Wesley Clark, who led the NATO operations that did the bombing, claiming that the general would be the strongest nominee in the fifteen swing states that would decide the election. You knew the Bush-bashers were playing for keeps when a professional rabble-rouser like Moore was urging his fellow lefties to be practical and vote for the guy with the stars. Democratic voters began talking obsessively about their candidates' "electability"—the same term Republicans had used in discussing Bush four years earlier. This concept is much beloved by the mainstream media because it puts a premium on politics as a horse race (exciting), not a battle of ideas (dull). It proved especially alluring to the Dean-loathing punditry, who could now, without fear of seeming biased, kick him for the impolitic statements that supposedly made him unelectable—even when those supposed "gaffes" told the truth. This was all to the benefit of Kerry, whose ponderousness ("The Comeback Kerry"?) could suddenly be read as "stature." Although I didn't know anybody who thought him a great candidate, he was good enough. *The Nation*'s William Greider compared his liberalism to that of the editorial board of *The New York Times:* so establishment it will make you crazy, but still better than *The Weekly Standard*. And Bush-haters were prepared to accept that. Talking to people in the weeks after Kerry wrapped up the nomination, you could feel them wanting to believe he would win in November—like kids clapping their hands to save Tinkerbell.

The Wake-up Call

I began this book by saying that, in the 2000 election, I made the worst political mistake of my life. In fact, I made two mistakes. The first had to do with the candidates. Although Al Gore was no better than I imagined, George W. Bush was much, much worse than I feared. But my second, far more serious mistake was complacency, the vice that we snobs on the left often impute to Republican suburbanites barbecuing on their patios in satellite cities with ten Starbucks and no good bookstores. Writing in *Slate*, Michael Kinsley noted that most Americans have become blasé about the liberty that millions of illegal immigrants risk everything to enjoy. "After 230 years," he pointedly observed, "we don't need to love freedom in order to have it." Bored by a presidential campaign that featured no one I admired, I had sat back and assumed that somehow everything would work out fine without any effort from me. I had forgotten that our democracy is a state of grace that must be earned over and over, not the air that we can breathe without giving it a thought. Nor can we count on our liberties being defended by leaders of any stripe. As the great socialist Eugene V. Debs famously declared, "I would not lead you into the promised land if I could, because if I could lead you in, someone else would lead you out."

George W. Bush is doing just that to millions of Americans, and to stop him, one must fight—even when it's hard or boring. This fight means getting news from places other than the TV, which, in its marriage of triviality and power worship, tells one almost nothing about what's really going on in the world. It means paying constant attention to the White House's machinations, for more than any president in our lifetimes, Bush doesn't merely feed on the public's lack of attention but wields secrecy like a weapon. It means ponying up money to Kerry and other candidates who oppose the President and his Republican cronies whose corporate ties have left them flush with cash to bombard the country with their own propaganda. And it means, if necessary, carrying the battle to the streets, which is where most of our freedoms were won in the first place. Although the Bush administration works hard to create a pacifying sense of powerlessness (think of Dubya's lordly disdain about the antiwar demonstrations), it remains fearful of popular opinion: It hasn't forgotten that the majority of voters chose against him last time. When the shockingly un-American provisions of Patriot Act II were leaked to the wider world, the instant outcry helped stop its careless passage—even Bill O'Reilly stood on the side of the angels. Once the public heard about Operation TIPS, which would have turned informing into a national ethic, the revulsion was so powerful that Congress wound up explicitly banning it. After the media belatedly began covering the FCC's decision permitting big corporations to own an even higher percentage of media outlets, the reaction was so negative that the Senate Commerce Committee actually found the gumption to roll it back (though, typically, the White House still hopes to push it through under the public radar).

Such triumphs may not sound big and glamorous, but that's how freedom is gained and maintained—slowly, painfully, against the wishes of those in power, however benevolent they may think themselves (and Bush does think himself a creature of Good, following God's master plan). As Woodrow Wilson put it during the 1912 election campaign, "Liberty has never come from the government. Liberty has always come from the subjects of government. The history of liberty is the history of resistance." He was absolutely right, which is why in an election year, it's worth remembering that the freedoms and pleasures we enjoy weren't sent down from heaven or plucked off a tree. They were born of centuries of struggle by untold millions who fought and bled and died to assure that the government can't just walk into our bedrooms or read our mail, to protect ordinary people from being overrun by massive corporations, to win a safety net against the often-cruel workings of the market, to stop businessmen from compelling employees to work more than forty hours a week without extra compensation, to make us free to criticize our government without having our patriotism impugned, and to make sure that our leaders are answerable to the people when they choose to send our soldiers into war. In one way or another, George W. Bush has tried to taint the fruit of all those struggles. Although he probably doesn't think so, he stands for the power of the privileged few against the needs of the many.

It is too late in our history to expect miracles from any leader, but we can daydream of a president whose best moments offer us a glimpse of utopia. John F. Kennedy was in many ways a disappointment, shaky about Vietnam and timid on civil rights. Yet even when he was being petty or self-promoting, he had a gift for making the world shimmer with possibility. When he declared his intention to land a man on the moon by the end of the 1960s, he wasn't motivated (as some thought) by starstruck idealism but by a desire to triumph in the battle of ideas that was the Cold War. He wanted a dazzling *coup de théâtre* to show the world that the United States, not the Soviet Union, was the future—the real source of hope and progress. He believed that if America was great the whole world would follow it, and he had the charisma to make that idea seem inviting, not threatening, to people all over the globe. An almost opposite alchemy is at work in President Bush, who, like JFK, adores bold strokes but diminishes everything he touches. He creates enormous tax cuts that leave most citizens poorer. He angers the world by invading foreign lands and then, as an improvised afterthought, tries to claim that he had waged war out of an idealistic love of freedom. Even when he proposes a voyage to Mars or a program to stop AIDS in Africa, such initiatives seem dinky and grudging—a sop to swing voters or a campaign stratagem—rather than an optimistic step forward.

Each time I hear him speak, I wonder if he will say something that, even briefly, will make me believe that he is creating a future to which I would want to belong. And each time I wind up feeling as empty as I did during his 2004 State of the Union address: He spent the opening minutes high-fiving himself for his administration's achievements, but spared not a moment to offer an olive branch to his opponents, take note of the millions of unemployed, or to acknowledge that the star of the 2003 address—Saddam's weapons of mass destruction—hadn't materialized. To do that would be to admit fallibility, and this he cannot do. Instead, he offered a stark vision of life that possesses (it must be admitted) enormous visceral power:

We know that you are frightened of terrorists—we will kill them.

We know you want money—we will cut taxes.

We know you worry that American life has lost its moral center—we will restore traditional values by promoting abstinence not contraception, banning gay marriage, and supporting drug tests in our schools.

Even as the President trumpeted his "bold" new initiatives, which his tax cuts mean the country cannot possibly afford, he remained very much a man of the past. Try though he may, George W. Bush never reaches beyond the given to imagine tomorrow. For all his flaws, his predecessor, Bill Clinton, did. He exuded optimism; he made people think that the future was boundless and exciting. For all his apparent triumphs, Bush does not; indeed, the great horror of his vision of America is that it's so very, very small. And if there is any virtue to be found in his presidency, it's that—by its naked dishonesty, disquieting militarism, and sheer extremity of its devotion to the Winners—he has given millions of us (to use one of his own favorite terms) a wake-up call. After all these years of watching the right ascend almost unchallenged, George W. Bush has provided a useful reminder that we can no longer sit idly, caught up in the private pleasures of our big-box culture, expecting virtue to triumph magically and our government to automatically do the right thing. To escape Bush World, we cannot hide or flee. We must create the world *we* want.

Acknowledgments

I must first thank Laurie Ochoa, editor of *L.A. Weekly*, for whom it's been my great pleasure to work. After giving me the freedom to write a column, "On," that became the springboard for this book, she then edited my words with great skill and unflappable grace, even as piece after piece came in too long. Without her, *Sore Winners* would not exist. And without the assistance of my colleagues at the *Weekly*, it would be a far feebler piece of work. They have given me ideas, pruned my linguistic thickets, corrected my errant "facts," and e-mailed me stories I would otherwise have missed. I am in their debt.

Although *Sore Winners* is very much a book of the present, it could not have been written without the help of friends, mentors, and loved ones who have shaped my thinking over many years: Craig Lambert, Christian Koch, Michael Levenson, Michael Ventura, Virginia Gapp Powers, and Jane Alcala. I could not have survived as a writer without the help of Joel E. Siegel, whose recent death still stuns me; Charles Paul Freund, who ran my first piece; Jay Levin, who hired me to write about movies in Los Angeles; David Denby, who saved my career; Terry Gross and Phyllis Myers, who delighted my mother by broadcasting her son's voice on NPR stations all over my home state of Iowa. At *Vogue*, I was treated splendidly by Shelley Wanger, Laurie Jones, Richard David Story and, of course, Anna Wintour: She offered me as close to regal treatment as any film critic could hope to receive. Thanks, too, to Ruth Reichl and William Sertl, who, among many other fine things, made me *Gourmet's* "Southeast Asia Correspondent"—the world's coolest business card.

In an act of restitution, I must note my indebtedness to George Gund. In 1989, he gave me a travel grant to write a book on international cinema. That book never materialized, partly owing to the comedy of history. I did my research during the days of Tiananmen Square and the collapse of communism; I spent much of the year flying off to interviews in places like Moscow and Warsaw only to be stood up by famous filmmakers who, exulting in their newfound freedom, had left the country without bothering to inform me. While this was hell on the film book, it transformed my perceptions of politics and culture. I would like to think that Mr. Gund's largesse has finally borne fruit on these pages.

Among writers, it's almost a moral obligation to rant about the snakes and weasels in publishing. Yet here, too, I could not have been more fortunate. My agent, Bonnie Nadell, isn't merely smart and efficient, she makes business a pleasure. My editor, Gerry Howard, is that most oxymoronic of paragons—a cultural omnivore with good taste. (I'm grateful that he has made an exception in my case.) His assistant, Rakesh Satyal, calmly handled everything from my typos to my dimmest queries. I can't fail to mention that Doubleday's editor in chief, Bill Thomas, was once a student of mine at Georgetown—unlike our president, he *did* the assigned reading—and it both delights and humbles me to realize that he now, in a sense, grades my work.

I am also humbled to have friends who, month after month, did that most foolhardy of good-hearted things: They not only asked what I was working on but, unlike jesting Pilate, stayed around to listen to my long, self-absorbed, still-unformed maunderings. Not a day passed that I didn't filch a smart idea or good joke from Jonathan Gold, Michael Jackson, Kit Rachlis, Steve Erickson, Arion Berger, Vikram Jayanti, Manohla Dargis, or my beloved sister, Rebecca Powers, a good-hearted Fury who is more honest and principled than I could ever hope to be.

Heading to the finish line, I must single out the two people who put up with the most in the genesis of *Sore Winners*. Tom Carson didn't merely spend hours talking me through various stages of this book, but when I completed the manuscript, he went over every line, expurgating many duff jokes and forcing me to think harder about the mysteries of Martha Stewart. While none of this book's vices are his doing, many of its virtues are; indeed, if I myself could read any writer on Bush World, it would be Tom. Finally, I must try to find words to thank my wife, Sandi Tan, who endured months of listening to me tap on computer keys, mutter unhappily, and then tap some more. Through it all, she was my goad, inspiration, brainstormer, therapist, lodestar, lab rat, and, above all, my love.

A Select Bibliography

Sore Winners is a work of pop mythology, and in keeping with that spirit, I have tried not to weigh the book down with apparatus. Virtually everything I write about, be it the special bridge built in Aqaba or Michael Moore's backstory, has already been well-documented in the popular media. When I have been particularly struck by a little-known fact or an interpretation, I have tried to incorporate the source into the text itself. But as anyone who's ever written journalism knows, there are often ideas in the air that seem to have been authored by everyone and no one. Two years ago, who would have predicted that, by the fall of 2003, seemingly half of America would be publishing an anti-Bush book?

William Butler Yeats told the story of going to a political meeting and sitting silently in the back of the room. When the proceedings ended, he realized that every single thing he'd wanted to say had eventually been said by someone else. I often had the same feeling while writing this book. Every time I turned around, someone else seemed to be offering annoyingly intelligent thoughts about Bush's use of religious code words, dissecting *American Idol* and *Harry Potter,* or describing the bucking-bronco rides of Colin and Rummy. It's part of big-box America that we have platoons of brainy critics, and you have to go a long way to dream up a cultural idea that hasn't already been at least fingered by such whizzes as *Vanity Fair*'s James Wolcott, *Time*'s James Poniewozik, *The New York Times*'s Frank Rich, *GQ*'s Tom Carson, *The New Republic*'s James Wood, *The Village Voice*'s J. Hoberman, *Reason*'s Charles Paul Freund, or *The Los Angeles Times*'s Manohla Dargis. The same is true of our political commentators and reporters. Even those I have criticized often told me valuable things I hadn't seen elsewhere. I criticize Frank Bruni's political coverage in *Ambling into History*, but I was often indebted to his sharp eye for character detail—Dubya's pillow, for instance.

Given the surfeit of material, what follows is a highly select list of sources for *Sore Winners*. Before presenting them, I do want to note two things. The section heading "Reality TV Isn't Reality (But Then

Again, What Is?)" is my admiring nod to the late Marvin Mudrick. The crack about Rousseau's *Confessions* was made by Stanford University's late, great Ian Watt, he of the lacerating grin, who also introduced me to Voltaire's marvelous remark that begins the final paragraph of Chapter 2. Beats me where he got it.

Alterman, Eric. *What Liberal Media? The Truth about Bias and the News.* New York: Basic Books, 2003.

Auletta, Ken. "Vox Fox: How Roger Ailes and Fox News are changing cable news." *The New Yorker* (May 16, 2003).

Bellow, Adam. *In Praise of Nepotism: A Natural History.* New York: Doubleday, 2003.

Berman, Paul. *Terror and Liberalism.* New York: W.W. Norton, 2003.

Blumenthal, Sidney. *The Permanent Campaign.* New York: Simon & Schuster, 1980.

Bozza, Anthony. *Whatever You Say I Am: The Life and Times of Eminem.* New York: Crown Publishers, 2003.

Brill, Steven. *After: How America Confronted the September 12 Era.* New York: Simon & Schuster, 2002.

Brookheiser, Richard. "The Mind of George W. Bush." *The Atlantic Monthly* (April, 2003).

Brooks, David. *Bobos in Paradise: The New Upper Class and How They Got There.* New York: Simon & Schuster, 2000.

Bruni, Frank. *Ambling into History: The Unlikely Odyssey of George W. Bush.* New York: HarperCollins, 2002.

Bush, George W. *A Charge to Keep: My Journey to the White House.* New York: Perennial, 1999.

Cockburn, Alexander. "Judy Miller's War." *CounterPunch* (June 16–30, 2003).

Conason, Joe. *Big Lies: The Right-Wing Propaganda Machine and How It Distorts the Truth.* New York: St. Martin's, 2003.

Corn, David. *The Lies of George W. Bush: Mastering the Politics of Deception.* New York: Crown Publishers, 2003.

Coulter, Ann. *Slander: Liberal Lies about the American Right.* New York: Crown Publishers, 2002.

———. *Treason: Liberal Treachery from the Cold War to the War on Terrorism.* New York: Crown Forum, 2003.

Decter, Midge. *Rumsfeld: A Personal Portrait.* New York: ReganBooks, 2003.

Dower, John W. *Embracing Defeat: Japan in the Wake of World War II.* New York: The New Press, 1999.

Easterbrook, Gregg. *The Progress Paradox: How Life Gets Better While People Feel Worse*. New York: Random House, 2003.

Eggers, Dave. *A Heartbreaking Work of Staggering Genius*. New York: Simon & Schuster, 2000.

———. *You Shall Know Our Velocity*. Brooklyn: McSweeney's Books, 2002.

Erickson, Steve. "George Bush and the Treacherous Country." *L.A. Weekly* (February 13–19, 2004).

Fallows, James. "The Age of Murdoch." *The Atlantic Monthly* (September 2003).

Felix, Antonia. *Condi: The Condoleezza Rice Story*. New York: Newmarket Press, 2002.

Fineman, Howard. "Bush and God." *Newsweek* (March 10, 2003).

Frank, Thomas. "Get Rich or Get Out." *Harper's* (June 2003).

Frank, Thomas, and Matt Weiland, eds. *Commodify Your Dissent: The Business of Culture in the New Gilded Age*. New York: W.W. Norton, 1997.

Franken, Al. *Lies and the Lying Liars Who Tell Them: A Fair and Balanced Look at the Right*. New York: Dutton, 2003.

Franzen, Jonathan. *The Corrections*. New York: Farrar Straus & Giroux, 2001.

Gabler, Neal. *Life: the Movie, How Entertainment Conquered Reality*. New York: Alfred A. Knopf, 1998.

Goldberg, Bernard. *Bias: A CBS Insider Exposes How the Media Distort the News*. Washington, D.C.: Regnery Publishing, 2002.

Hart, Peter, and Fairness and Accuracy in Reporting. *The Oh Really? Factor: Unspinning Fox News Channel's Bill O'Reilly*. New York: Seven Stories Press, 2003.

Hatfield, J.H. *Fortunate Son: George W. Bush and the Making of an American President*. New York: Soft Skull Press, 2001.

Hine, Thomas. *I Want That! How We All Became Shoppers*. New York: HarperCollins, 2002.

Hitchens, Christopher. *A Long Short War: The Postponed Liberation of Iraq*. New York: Plume, 2003.

Hofstadter, Richard. *Social Darwinism in American Thought*. Boston: Beacon Press, 1944.

Ivins, Molly, and Lou Dubose. *Bushwhacked: Life in George W. Bush's America*. New York: Random House, 2003.

———. *Shrub: The Short but Happy Political Life of George W. Bush*. New York: Random House, 2000.

Kagan, Robert. *Of Paradise and Power: America and Europe in the New World Order*. New York: Alfred A. Knopf, 2003.

Kagan, Robert, and William Kristol, eds. *Present Dangers: Crisis and*

Opportunity in American Foreign and Defense Policy. San Francisco: Encounter Books, 2000.

Kaplan, Robert D. *Warrior Politics: Why Leadership Demands a Pagan Ethos*. New York: Random House, 2002.

Karp, Walter. *The Politics of War: The Story of Two Wars Which Altered Forever the Political Life of the American Republic (1890–1920)*. New York: HarperCollins, 1979.

Katovsky, Bill and Timothy Carlson. *Embedded: The Media at War in Iraq*. Guilford, CT: The Lyons Press, 2003.

Klein, Joe. *The Natural: The Misunderstood Presidency of Bill Clinton*. New York: Doubleday, 2002.

Krames, Jeffrey A. *The Rumsfeld Way: Leadership Wisdom of a Battle-Hardened Maverick*. New York: McGraw-Hill, 2002.

Kristol, Irving. *Neo-Conservatism: The Autobiography of an Idea*. New York: Free Press, 1995.

Krugman, Paul. *The Accidental Theorist and Other Dispatches from the Dismal Science*. New York: W.W. Norton, 1998.

———. *The Great Unraveling: Losing Our Way in the New Century*. New York: W.W. Norton, 2003.

Lexington. "Red George." *The Economist* (July 3, 2003).

Lind, Michael. *Made in Texas: George W. Bush and the Southern Takeover of American Politics*. New York: Basic Books, 2003.

McLaughlin, Emma, and Nicola Kraus. *The Nanny Diaries*. New York: St. Martin's, 2002.

Miller, Mark Crispin. *The Bush Dyslexicon: Observations on a National Disorder*. New York: W.W. Norton, 2002.

Mills, C. Wright. *The Power Elite*. New York: Oxford University Press, 1956.

Moore, James, and Wayne Slater. *Bush's Brain: How Karl Rove Made George W. Bush Presidential*. Hoboken: John Wiley & Sons, 2003.

Moore, Michael. *Dude, Where's My Country?* New York: Warner Books, 2003.

———. *Stupid White Men . . . and Other Sorry Excuses for the State of the Nation!* New York: ReganBooks, 2001.

Newhouse, John. *Imperial America: The Bush Assault on World Order*. New York: Alfred A. Knopf, 2003.

O'Reilly, Bill. *The No Spin Zone: Confrontations with the Powerful and Famous in America*. New York: Broadway Books, 2001.

———. *The O'Reilly Factor: The Good, the Bad, and the Completely Ridiculous in American Life*. New York: Broadway Books, 2000.

———. *Who's Looking Out for You?* New York: Broadway Books, 2003.

Packer, George. "War After the War: What Washington Doesn't See in Iraq." *The New Yorker* (November 24, 2003).

Pilger, John. *The New Rulers of the World.* London: Verso, 2002.

Pollack, Kenneth M. *The Threatening Storm: The Case for Invading Iraq.* New York: Random House, 2002.

Postrel, Virginia. *The Substance of Style.* New York: HarperCollins Publishers, 2003.

Powell, Colin, with Joseph E. Persico. *My American Journey.* New York: Random House, 1995.

Priest, Dana. *The Mission: Waging War and Keeping Peace with America's Military.* New York: W.W. Norton, 2003.

Rieff, David. "Blueprint for a Mess." *The New York Times Magazine* (November 2, 2003).

Rumsfeld, Donald. *Pieces of Intelligence: The Existential Poetry of Donald Rumsfeld.* Edited and compiled by Hart Seely. New York: Free Press, 2002.

Saletan, William. *Bearing Right: How Conservatives Won the Abortion War.* Berkeley: University of California Press, 2003.

Sciolino, Elaine. "Laura Bush Sees Everything In Its Place, Including Herself." *The New York Times* (January 15, 2001).

Seabrook, John. *Nobrow: The Culture of Marketing, The Marketing of Culture.* New York: Random House, 2000.

Shafer, Jack. "Follow That Story: Deep Miller." *Slate* (April 23, 2003).

———. "Reassessing Miller." *Slate* (May 29, 2003).

Suskind, Ron. "Why Are These Men Laughing?" *Esquire* (January 2003).

Tapper, Jake. *Down & Dirty: The Plot to Steal the Presidency.* New York: Little, Brown, 2001.

Thomas, Evan. "The Quiet Power of Condoleezza Rice." *Newsweek* (December 16, 2002).

Twitchell, James B. *Living It Up: Our Love Affair with Luxury.* New York: Columbia University Press, 2002.

Weisberger, Lauren. *The Devil Wears Prada.* New York: Doubleday, 2003.

Willis, Ellen. *Don't Think, Smile! Notes on a Decade of Denial.* Boston: Beacon Press, 1999.

Woodward, Bob. *Bush at War.* New York: Simon & Schuster, 2002.

Index

Lott, Trent, 83, 163, 196, 260, 305, 305n., 307, 324n.
Louis, Joe, 100
Lovely Bones, The (Sebold), 262, 268, 271–72, 282
Lowry, Rich, 45
Lynch, Jessica, 137–39, 148, 167, 235, 270

Madonna, 252, 283, 288
Mahdi, The, 63, 63n.
Maher, Bill, 84
Mailer, Norman, 9, 17, 272–73, 281, 342
Makyia, Kanan, 120
Mann, James, 129
Manthey, Jerri, 260, 261
Marcuse, Herbert, 250, 251
Marshall, Josh, 196
Martin, Steve, 167
Martinez, Melquiades R., 249
Matalin, Mary, 260
Matrix trilogy, 47, 48, 167, 282, 322–23
Matthews, Chris, 45, 182, 206n., 210n., 247
McCain, John, 22, 26, 28, 105, 303–4, 304n.
McClintock, Tom, 183
McConnell, Mitch, 162
McDermott, Jim, 121
McGinnis, Joe, 12, 203
McGovern, George, 114, 346, 349
McGruder, Aaron, 214–15, 286, 288
McKinley, William, 126
McLaughlin, John, 238
McNabb, Donovan, 306–7
McNamara, Robert, 130
Media: alternative, 193, 346; American divisiveness and, 7, 246–47; bias wars, 197–200; Bush and, 27–28, 44–45, 51–58, 105, 341; centralization of, 194; Clinton and, 27, 51, 54, 55–56, 204; conservative, 55, 89, 191, 193, 197–98, 207–13, 216, 217, 219; embedded status, 231–41, 260; entertainment vs., 195; Gore and, 27, 51; hype and "Ministry of Fear," 61; liberal

and left, 51, 53–54, 191, 196–97, 198, 199–200, 213–41, 307; P.C. approach, 236; radio, conservative, 209; Rumsfeld and, 128–29; Schwarzenegger campaign, 185–86; September 11, 2001, and, 61, 67–76, 222; Washington press corps, 189–91
Milbank, Dana, 190
Miller, Dennis, 158
Miller, John, 65
Miller, Judith, 223–24, 225, 239, 243
Miller, Mark Crispin, 24
Mission, The (Priest), 114
Mitchell, Andrea, 237
Mondale, Walter, 50
Moore, Michael, 9, 53, 118, 216, 281, 290–97, 302, 351
Moran, Terry, 190–91
Morris, Edmund, 113
Morris, Erroll, 130
Morrison, Toni, 302
Moyers, Bill, 51
MSNBC, 70, 179, 201, 205–6, 206n.
MTV, 154, 245; *Punk'd*, 174; *The Real World*, 278; *Rich Girls*, 174
Murdoch, Rupert, 69, 103, 151, 156, 200–202
Musil, Robert, 42
Myers, Richard, 115
Mystic River (film), 282

Nader, Ralph, 1, 2
Nation, The, 53, 57n., 83, 215–16, 217–21, 223, 228, 297; Nation Books, 57n., 216
National Review, The, 55, 119
Natsios, Andrew, 125
Natural, The (Klein), 341
Navasky, Victor, 57n.
NBC, 194, 205, 236, 237, 269, 270; *American Dreams*, 283; *Dateline*, 176; *Friends*, 244, 258, 284
Neocons (neo-conservatives), 8, 76, 77, 103–9, 104n., 116, 133, 137, 142, 161, 214; bankrupting government and, 40, 56

About the Author

John Powers is Deputy Editor of *L.A. Weekly,* where he writes a weekly media/culture column called "On." He is also critic-at-large for NPR's *Fresh Air,* for whom he's been doing commentaries since 1996. He was the film critic at *Vogue* for six years and an international correspondent for *Gourmet.*

Powers holds a Ph.D. from Stanford University and has taught at Georgetown University. His journalism has appeared in *The Washington Post, The Los Angeles Times, Rolling Stone, Harper's, The Nation,* and other publications. He lives in Pasadena, California, with his wife, filmmaker Sandi Tan.